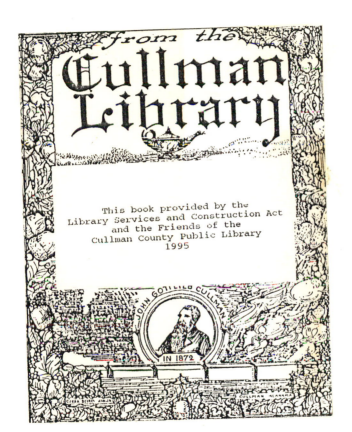

ISABEL ARCHER

Major Literary Characters

THE ANCIENT WORLD THROUGH THE SEVENTEENTH CENTURY

ACHILLES
Homer, *Iliad*

CALIBAN
William Shakespeare, *The Tempest*
Robert Browning, *Caliban upon Setebos*

CLEOPATRA
William Shakespeare, *Antony and Cleopatra*
John Dryden, *All for Love*
George Bernard Shaw, *Caesar and Cleopatra*

DON QUIXOTE
Miguel de Cervantes, *Don Quixote*
Franz Kafka, *Parables*

FALSTAFF
William Shakespeare, *Henry IV, Part I, Henry IV, Part II, The Merry Wives of Windsor*

FAUST
Christopher Marlowe, *Doctor Faustus*
Johann Wolfgang von Goethe, *Faust*
Thomas Mann, *Doctor Faustus*

HAMLET
William Shakespeare, *Hamlet*

IAGO
William Shakespeare, *Othello*

JULIUS CAESAR
William Shakespeare, *Julius Caesar*
George Bernard Shaw, *Caesar and Cleopatra*

KING LEAR
William Shakespeare, *King Lear*

MACBETH
William Shakespeare, *Macbeth*

ODYSSEUS/ULYSSES
Homer, *Odyssey*
James Joyce, *Ulysses*

OEDIPUS
Sophocles, *Oedipus Rex, Oedipus at Colonus*

OTHELLO
William Shakespeare, *Othello*

ROSALIND
William Shakespeare, *As You Like It*

SANCHO PANZA
Miguel de Cervantes, *Don Quixote*
Franz Kafka, *Parables*

SATAN
The Book of Job
John Milton, *Paradise Lost*

SHYLOCK
William Shakespeare, *The Merchant of Venice*

THE WIFE OF BATH
Geoffrey Chaucer, *The Canterbury Tales*

THE EIGHTEENTH AND NINETEENTH CENTURIES

AHAB
Herman Melville, *Moby-Dick*

ISABEL ARCHER
Henry James, *Portrait of a Lady*

EMMA BOVARY
Gustave Flaubert, *Madame Bovary*

DOROTHEA BROOKE
George Eliot, *Middlemarch*

CHELSEA HOUSE PUBLISHERS

Major Literary Characters

DAVID COPPERFIELD
Charles Dickens, *David Copperfield*

ROBINSON CRUSOE
Daniel Defoe, *Robinson Crusoe*

DON JUAN
Molière, *Don Juan*
Lord Byron, *Don Juan*

HUCK FINN
Mark Twain, *The Adventures of
    Tom Sawyer, Adventures of
    Huckleberry Finn*

CLARISSA HARLOWE
Samuel Richardson, *Clarissa*

HEATHCLIFF
Emily Brontë, *Wuthering Heights*

ANNA KARENINA
Leo Tolstoy, *Anna Karenina*

MR. PICKWICK
Charles Dickens, *The Pickwick Papers*

HESTER PRYNNE
Nathaniel Hawthorne, *The Scarlet Letter*

BECKY SHARP
William Makepeace Thackeray, *Vanity Fair*

LAMBERT STRETHER
Henry James, *The Ambassadors*

EUSTACIA VYE
Thomas Hardy, *The Return of the Native*

TWENTIETH CENTURY

ÁNTONIA
Willa Cather, *My Ántonia*

BRETT ASHLEY
Ernest Hemingway, *The Sun Also Rises*

HANS CASTORP
Thomas Mann, *The Magic Mountain*

HOLDEN CAULFIELD
J. D. Salinger, *The Catcher in the Rye*

CADDY COMPSON
William Faulkner, *The Sound and the Fury*

JANIE CRAWFORD
Zora Neale Hurston, *Their Eyes Were
    Watching God*

CLARISSA DALLOWAY
Virginia Woolf, *Mrs. Dalloway*

DILSEY
William Faulkner, *The Sound and the Fury*

GATSBY
F. Scott Fitzgerald, *The Great Gatsby*

HERZOG
Saul Bellow, *Herzog*

JOAN OF ARC
William Shakespeare, *Henry VI*
George Bernard Shaw, *Saint Joan*

LOLITA
Vladimir Nabokov, *Lolita*

WILLY LOMAN
Arthur Miller, *Death of a Salesman*

MARLOW
Joseph Conrad, *Lord Jim, Heart of
    Darkness, Youth, Chance*

PORTNOY
Philip Roth, *Portnoy's Complaint*

BIGGER THOMAS
Richard Wright, *Native Son*

CHELSEA HOUSE PUBLISHERS

Major Literary Characters

ISABEL ARCHER

Edited and with an introduction by
HAROLD BLOOM

CHELSEA HOUSE PUBLISHERS
New York ◊ Philadelphia

Jacket illustration: Woman in a Fur Hat (c. 1915) by Gretchen Rogers
(Gift of Miss Anne Winslow; Courtesy of the Museum of Fine Arts, Boston).

Chelsea House Publishers

Editor-in-Chief   Remmel T. Nunn
Managing Editor   Karyn Gullen Browne
Picture Editor   Adrian G. Allen
Art Director   Maria Epes
Manufacturing Director   Gerald Levine

Major Literary Characters

Senior Editor   S. T. Joshi
Associate Editor   Richard Fumosa
Designer   Maria Epes

Staff for ISABEL ARCHER

Picture Researcher   Ellen Barrett
Assistant Art Director   Howard Brotman
Production Manager   Joseph Romano
Production Coordinator   Marie Claire Cebrián

Printed and bound in the United States of America

First Printing

1   3   5   7   9   8   6   4   2

Library of Congress Cataloging-in-Publication Data

Isabel Archer / edited and with an introduction by Harold Bloom.
p.   cm.—(Major literary characters)
Includes bibliographical references and index.
ISBN 0-7910-0934-3.—ISBN 0-7910-0989-0 (pbk.)
1. James, Henry, 1843–1916. Portrait of a lady.   2. James, Henry, 1843–1916—
Characters—Isabel Archer.   3. Archer, Isabel (Fictitious character)
I. Bloom, Harold.   II. Series.
PS2116.P63I74   1992
813'.4—dc20
91-26317
CIP

CONTENTS

THE ANALYSIS OF CHARACTER   ix

EDITOR'S NOTE   xv

INTRODUCTION   1
Harold Bloom

CRITICAL EXTRACTS
Henry James 5   Horace E. Scudder 8   Margaret Oliphant 10
Henry James 15   Cornelia Pulsifer Kelley 19   Yvor Winters 23
Edward Sackville West 24   Graham Greene 28   F. R. Leavis 32
Richard Chase 37   William H. Gass 41   Richard Poirier 45
Leon Edel 51   Dorothea Krook 57   Laurence Bedwell Holland 60
Manfred Mackenzie 64   Lisa Appignanesi 72   Ronald Wallace 76
Peter Jones 80

CRITICAL ESSAYS

THE FEARFUL SELF   91
Tony Tanner

MARRIAGE AND THE NEW WOMAN
IN *THE PORTRAIT OF A LADY*   104
Annette Niemtzow

REVISION AND THEMATIC CHANGE
IN *THE PORTRAIT OF A LADY*   119
Nina Baym

TRANSCENDENTAL IDEALISM AND TRAGIC REALISM IN
THE PORTRAIT OF A LADY   131
Zephyra Porat

JAMES, PATER, AND THE DREAMING
OF AESTHETICISM   152
Jonathan Freedman

THE DELICATE ORGANISMS AND THEORETIC TRICKS
OF HENRY JAMES   164
Stephanie A. Smith

THE FEMININE ORPHAN AND THE
EMERGENT MASTER   181
William Veeder

CONTRIBUTORS   203

BIBLIOGRAPHY   205

ACKNOWLEDGMENTS   211

INDEX   213

THE ANALYSIS OF CHARACTER

Harold Bloom

"Character," according to our dictionaries, still has as a primary meaning a graphic symbol, such as a letter of the alphabet. This meaning reflects the word's apparent origin in the ancient Greek *charactēr*, a sharp stylus. *Charactēr* also meant the mark of the stylus' incisions. Recent fashions in literary criticism have reduced "character" in literature to a matter of marks upon a page. But our word "character" also has a very different meaning, matching that of the ancient Greek *ēthos*, "habitual way of life." Shall we say then that literary character is an imitation of human character, or is it just a grouping of marks? The issue is between a critic like Dr. Samuel Johnson, for whom words were as much like people as like things, and a critic like the late Roland Barthes, who told us that "the fact can only exist linguistically, as a term of discourse." Who is closer to our experience of reading literature, Johnson or Barthes? What difference does it make, if we side with one critic rather than the other?

Barthes is famous, like Foucault and other recent French theorists, for having added to Nietzsche's proclamation of the death of God a subsidiary demise, that of the literary author. If there are no authors, then there are no fictional personages, presumably because literature does not refer to a world outside language. Words indeed necessarily refer to other words in the first place, but the impact of words ultimately is drawn from a universe of fact. Stories, poems, and plays are recognizable as such because they are human utterances within traditions of utterances, and traditions, by achieving authority, become a kind of fact, or at least the sense of a fact. Our sense that literary characters, within the context of a fictive cosmos, indeed are fictional personages is also a kind of fact. The meaning and value of every character in a successful work of literary representation depend upon our ideas of persons in the factual reality of our lives.

Literary character is always an invention, and inventions generally are indebted to prior inventions. Shakespeare is the inventor of literary character as we know it; he reformed the universal human expectations for the verbal imitation of personality, and the reformation appears now to be permanent and uncannily inevitable. Remarkable as the Bible and Homer are at representing personages, their characters are relatively unchanging. They age within their stories, but their habitual modes of being do not develop. Jacob and Achilles unfold before us, but without metamorphoses. Lear and Macbeth, Hamlet and Othello severely modify themselves not only by their actions, but by their utterances, and most of all through *overhearing themselves,* whether they speak to themselves or to others. Pondering what they themselves have said, they will to change, and actually do change, sometimes extravagantly yet always persuasively. Or else they suffer change, without willing it, but in reaction not so much to their language as to their relation to that language.

I do not think it useful to say that Shakespeare successfully imitated elements in our characters. Rather, it could be argued that he compelled aspects of character to appear that previously were concealed, or not available to representation. This is not to say that Shakespeare is God, but to remind us that language is not God either. The mimesis of character in Shakespeare's dramas now seems to us normative, and indeed became the accepted mode almost immediately, as Ben Jonson shrewdly and somewhat grudgingly implied. And yet, Shakespearean representation has surprisingly little in common with the imitation of reality in Jonson or in Christopher Marlowe. The origins of Shakespeare's originality in the portrayal of men and women are to be found in the *Canterbury Tales* of Geoffrey Chaucer, insofar as they can be located anywhere before Shakespeare himself. Chaucer's savage and superb Pardoner overhears his own tale-telling, as well as his mocking rehearsal of his own spiel, and through this overhearing he is emboldened to forget himself, and enthusiastically urges all his fellow-pilgrims to come forward to be fleeced by him. His self-awareness, and apocalyptically rancid sense of spiritual fall, are preludes to the even grander abysses of the perverted will in Iago and in Edmund. What might be called the character trait of a negative charisma may be Chaucer's invention, but came to its perfection in Shakespearean mimesis.

The analysis of character is as much Shakespeare's invention as the representation of character is, since Iago and Edmund are adepts at analyzing both themselves and their victims. Hamlet, whose overwhelming charisma has many negative components, is certainly the most comprehensive of all literary characters, and so necessarily prophesies the labyrinthine complexities of the will in Iago and Edmund. Charisma, according to Max Weber, its first codifier, is primarily a natural endowment, and implies a primordial and idiosyncratic power over nature, and so finally over death. Hamlet's uncanniness is at its most suggestive in the scene of his long dying, where the audience, through the mediation of Horatio, itself is compelled to meditate upon suicide, if only because outliving the prince of Denmark scarcely seems an option.

Shakespearean representation has usurped not only our sense of literary character, but our sense of ourselves as characters, with Hamlet playing the part of the largest of these usurpations. Insofar as we have an idea of human disinterestedness, we tend to derive it from the Hamlet of Act V, whose quietism has about it a ghostly authority. Oscar Wilde, in his profound and profoundly witty dialogue, "The Decay of Lying," expressed a permanent insight when he insisted that art shaped every era, far more than any age formed art. Life imitates art, we imitate Shakespeare, because without Shakespeare we would perish for lack of images. Wilde's grandest audacity demystifies Shakespearean mimesis with a Shakespearean vivaciousness: "This unfortunate aphorism about art holding the mirror up to Nature is deliberately said by Hamlet in order to convince the bystanders of his absolute insanity in all art-matters." Of *Hamlet*'s influence upon the ages Wilde remarked that: "The world has grown sad because a puppet was once melancholy." "Puppet" is Wilde's own deconstruction, a brilliant reminder that Shakespeare's artistry of illusion has so mastered reality as to have changed reality, evidently forever.

The analysis of character, as a critical pursuit, seems to me as much a Shakespearean invention as literary character was, since much of what we know about how to analyze character necessarily follows Shakespearean procedures. His hero-villains, from Richard III through Iago, Edmund, and Macbeth, are shrewd and endless questers into their own self-motivations. If we could bear to see Hamlet, in his unwearied negations, as another hero-villain, then we would judge him the supreme analyst of the darker recalcitrances in the selfhood. Freud followed the pre-Socratic Empedocles, in arguing that character is fate, a frightening doctrine that maintains the fear that there are no accidents, that overdetermination rules us all of our lives. Hamlet assumes the same, yet adds to this argument the terrible passivity he manifests in Act V. Throughout Shakespeare's tragedies, the most interesting personages seem doom-eager, reminding us again that a Shakespearean reading of Freud would be more illuminating than a Freudian exegesis of Shakespeare. We learn more when we discover Hamlet in the Freudian Death Drive, than when we read *Beyond the Pleasure Principle* into *Hamlet*.

In Shakespearean comedy, character achieves its true literary apotheosis, which is the representation of the inner freedom that can be created by great wit alone. Rosalind and Falstaff, perhaps alone among Shakespeare's personages, match Hamlet in wit, though hardly in the metaphysics of consciousness. Whether in the comic or the modern mode, Shakespeare has set the standard of measurement in the balance between character and passion.

In Shakespeare the self is more dramatized than theatricalized, which is why a Shakespearean reading of Freud works out so well. Character-formation after the passing of the Oedipal stage takes the place of fetishistic fragmentings of the self. Critics who now call literary character into question, and who proclaim also the death of the author, invariably also regard all notions, literary and human, of a stable character as being mere reductions of deeper pre-Oedipal desires. It

becomes clear that the fortunes of literary character rise and fall with the prestige of normative conceptions of the ego. Shakespeare's Iago, who wars against
being, may be the first deconstructionist of the self, with his proclamation of "I
am not what I am." This constitutes the necessary prologue to any view that
would regard a fixed ego as a virtual abnormality. But deconstructions of the self
are no more modern than Modernism is. Like literary modernism, the
decentered ego came out of the Hellenistic culture of ancient Alexandria. The
Gnostic heretics believed that the psyche, like the body, was a fallen entity,
mechanically fashioned by the Demiurge or false creator. They held however
that each of us possessed also a spark or pneuma, which was a fragment of
the original Abyss or true, alien God. The soul or psyche within every one of
us was thus at war with the self or pneuma, and only that sparklike self could be
saved.

Shakespeare, following after Chaucer in this respect, was the first and remains
still the greatest master of representing character both as a stable soul and a
wavering self. There is a substance that endures in Shakespeare's figures, and there
is also a quicksilver rendition of the unsettling sparks. Racine and Tolstoy, Balzac and
Dickens, follow in Shakespeare's wake by giving us some sense of pre-Oedipal
sparks or drives, and considerably more sense of post-Oedipal character and
personality, stabilizations or sublimations of the fetish-seeking drives. Critics like Leo
Bersani and René Girard argue eloquently against our taking this mimesis as the only
proper work of literature. I would suggest that strong fictions of the self, from the
Bible through Samuel Beckett, necessarily participate in both modes, the sublima-
tion of desire, and the persistence of a primordial desire. The mystery of Hamlet
or of Lear is intimately invested in the tangled mixture of the two modes of
representation.

Psychic mobility is proposed by Bersani as the ideal to which deconstructions
of the literary self may yet guide us. The ideal has its pathos, but the realities of
literary representation seem to me very different, perhaps destructively so. When
a novelist like D. H. Lawrence sought to reduce his characters to Eros and the
Death Drive, he still had to persuade us of his authority at mimesis by lavishing upon
the figures of *The Rainbow* and *Women in Love* all of the vivid stigmata of
normative personality. Birkin and Ursula may represent antithetical and uncanny
drives, but they develop and change as characters pondering their own pronouncements and reactions to self and others. The cost of a non-Shakespearean representation is enormous. Pynchon, in *The Crying of Lot 49* and *Gravity's Rainbow*,
evades the burden of the normative by resorting to something like Christopher
Marlowe's art of caricature in *The Jew of Malta*. Marlowe's Barabas is a marvelous
rhetorician, yet he is a cartoon alongside the troublingly equivocal Shylock. Pynchon's personages are deliberate cartoons also, as flat as comic strips. Marlowe's
achievement, and Pynchon's, are beyond dispute, yet they are like the prelude and
the postlude to Shakespearean reality. They do not wish to engage with our hunger
for the empirical world and so they enter the problematic cosmos of literary
fantasy.

No writer, not even Shakespeare or Proust, alters the available stock that we agree to call reality, but Shakespeare, more than any other, does show us how much of reality we could encounter if only we retained adequate desire. The strong literary representation of character is already an analysis of character, and is part of the healing work of a literary culture, which implicitly seeks to cure violence through a normative mimesis of ego, *as if it were stable,* whether in actuality it is or is not. I do not believe that this is a social quest taken on by literary culture, but rather that we confront here the aesthetic essence of what makes a culture *literary,* rather than metaphysical or ethical or religious. A culture becomes literary when its conceptual modes have failed it, which means when religion, philosophy, and science have begun to lose their authority. If they cannot heal violence, then literature attempts to do so, which may be only a turning inside out of the critical arguments of Girard and Bersani.

I conclude by offering a particular instance or special case as a paradigm for the healing enterprise that is at once the representation and the analysis of literary character. Let us call it the aesthetics of being outraged, or rather of successfully representing the state of being outraged. W. C. Fields was one modern master of such representation, and Nathanael West was another, as was Faulkner before him. Here also the greatest master remains Shakespeare, whose Macbeth, himself a bloody outrage, yet retains our imaginative sympathy precisely because he grows increasingly outraged as he experiences the equivocation of the fiend that lies like truth. The double-natured promises and the prophecies of the weird sisters finally induce in Macbeth an apocalyptic version of the stage actor's anxiety at missing cues, the horror of a phantasmagoric stage fright of missing one's time, of always reacting too late. Macbeth, a veritable monster of solipsistic inwardness but no intellectual, counters his dilemma by fresh murders, that prolong him in time yet provoke him only to a perpetually freshened sense of being outraged, as all his expectations become still worse confounded. We are moved by Macbeth, however estrangedly, because his terrible inwardness is a paradigm for our own solipsism, but also because none of us can resist a strong and successful representation of the human in a state of being outraged.

The ultimate outrage is the necessity of dying, an outrage concealed in a multitude of masks, including the tyrannical ambitions of Macbeth. I suspect that our outrage at being outraged is the most difficult of all our affects for us to represent to ourselves, which is why we are so inclined to imaginative sympathy for a character who strongly conveys that affect to us. The Shrike of West's *Miss Lonelyhearts* or Faulkner's Joe Christmas of *Light in August* are crucial modern instances, but such figures can be located in many other works, since the ability to represent this extreme emotion is one of the tests that strong writers are driven to set for themselves.

However a reader seeks to reduce literary character to a question of marks on a page, she will come at last to the impasse constituted by the thought of death, her death, and before that to all the stations of being outraged that memorialize her own drive towards death. In reading, she quests for evidences that are strong representations, whether of her desire or her despair. Such questings constitute the necessary basis for the analysis of literary character, an enterprise that always will survive every vagary of critical fashion.

EDITOR'S NOTE

This book brings together a representative selection of the best criticism devoted to Isabel Archer, the heroine of *The Portrait of a Lady,* by Henry James. I am indebted to Richard Fumosa for his skilled editorial assistance.

My introduction centers upon Isabel Archer's Emersonian quest for her own integrity and self-reliance.

A chronological series of critical extracts charts the history of Isabel's reception, from contemporary reviews to the present, including such crucial critics as Yvor Winters, F. R. Leavis, Richard Poirier, and Laurence Bedwell Holland.

Full-scale critical essays begin with Tony Tanner's analysis of the vulnerable elements in Isabel's self. Annette Niemtzow relates Isabel Archer's marriage to the problematics of being a "New Woman" in the Age of Henry James, while Nina Baym traces the subtle changes in Isabel created by James's textual revisions.

In Zephyra Porat's brilliant exegesis, the dialectic of Transcendental idealism and tragicomic realism in the portrayal of Isabel is fully worked through. In the mode of our current New Historicism, Jonathan Freedman relates Isabel to English Aestheticism, while Stephanie Smith emphasizes Henry James's paternalistic stance in regard to his heroine. This volume concludes with William Veeder's account of how James risked his own self-portrait in portraying the sublime Isabel Archer.

INTRODUCTION

There is a double tradition of fictional representation that leads on to a culmination in Isabel Archer, the superb heroine of what I would judge to be Henry James's masterwork, *The Portrait of a Lady*. One strand is that of the English heroines of the Protestant Will, commencing with Samuel Richardson's Clarissa Harlowe. Jane Austen's crucial protagonists carry Clarissa's line forward, until the English novel is distinguished by another eminence in George Eliot's *Middlemarch*, where Dorothea Brooke is clearly the legatee of Clarissa and of Austen's heroines. Though James was affected by George Eliot, his Isabel Archer owes more than he perhaps realized to the grandest characters of his American precursor, Nathaniel Hawthorne. Hester Prynne in *The Scarlet Letter* and Hilda in *The Marble Faun* anticipate elements of conflict in Isabel Archer, modalities that place intricate detours in the triumphant path of the Protestant Will, with its heroic drive towards accepting the esteem of others only to the degree that the heroine's self-esteem confers a saving esteem upon them. This curious kind of shared solipsism is subverted by the American religion of Emerson's self-reliance, a faith held (with subtle differences) both by Hester Prynne and by Isabel Archer. Isabel, truly "the heiress of all the ages," has become something close to the archetype of all those American young women, in life or in fiction, who become doom-eager through their transcendent (and transcendental) idealism, their need to find a total self-realization in their existence. Daughters of Emerson, even as James was in some sense his son, they demand victory, even as they suffer the great defeats of tragic marriages to inadequate men.

Richard Poirier remarks that Isabel's rejection of Warburton is a refusal of conventionalized society, and so reflects James's own societal freedom, both as person and as novelist. The novel's deepest irony is that James's self-portrait as a lady requires Isabel to choose a husband, and indeed requires her to choose badly; Osmond is humanly inferior on every count to Warburton and to Ralph Touchett, and even to the passionately obtuse American, Caspar Goodwood. Osmond, as I have ventured elsewhere, is a parody both of an Emersonian transcendentalist, and of a Paterian aesthete. The parody became much sharper when James revised the novel for his definitive New York Edition, but then nearly everyone except Isabel lost something of the author's regard in the quarter-century that passed between the first and final editions of *The Portrait of a Lady*. The Isabel of the New York Edition, now most readers' Isabel, is so subtle a consciousness that Osmond had to be made into an even grander monster in order initially to deceive her. James desired that Isabel's marriage was to be a parable both of the limitations and the final glory of American idealism. The strength of Hawthorne's Hester is repeated in Isabel, but in a finer tone necessarily, since *The Scarlet Letter* remains romance, whereas *The Portrait of a Lady* is closer to the conventions of *Middlemarch*.

Yet Isabel retains aspects of the heroine of romance, in that her consciousness is too large and free for any society, or its representative male, to accommodate her. Choosing correctly therefore is not an option for her: Ralph Touchett is too ill, Warburton too English, Goodwood too American, and Osmond neither a true transcendentalist nor an authentic aesthete. Since Osmond (particularly in the re-vised version) is the only one of these who lacks goodwill, there is a palpable blindness in Isabel. Her failures of perception and of judgment are crucial to the novel's action, and yet James cannot bear that we, or he, should consider them merely to be failures. They are the consequence of Isabel's powerful aestheticism and humane aspiration, and reflect the strength rather than the weakness of her own imagination. A true Emersonian (to her own partial ruin), there is for her no history, but only biography. Isabel's freedom is freedom from history, and as such proves to be a beautiful illusion. History would have shown her that Osmond's supposed disinterestedness was a failure's defense against reality, and that the feigned exquisiteness of his sensibility was only another repetition of an Epicurean fashion.

"Nothing is got for nothing" is the late Emersonian and rather grim recasting of the law of compensation. Repudiating history costs Isabel the terrible error of choosing the dreadful Osmond, but that almost not-less-than-everything catastro-phe does not destroy the sublime Isabel. She has learned what Emerson always knew, which is that there is a crack in everything that God has made, or as Emerson's admirer, Nietzsche, phrased it, that error about life is necessary for life. In returning to Osmond, she strengthens herself, and after all James does not prophesy how the marriage will end, although both Isabel and Osmond perma-nently cease to love one another. Her will is never purer nor more integral than when she chooses to return to her marriage. I do not think it accurate to charac-terize her decision as a renunciation of any kind. Rather, it is a frightening reaffir-mation of her own will, an extraordinary assertion of her magnificent and justified self-esteem. We know that she will go on making her own circumstances until she dies, and that Osmond will break long before she does. That is hardly in itself a cheerful prospect, but it is also not tragic. Isabel's Rome is not Hester Prynne's Boston, and all life is not closed to Isabel Archer as Mrs. Gilbert Osmond. For the truth about Isabel, as about Henry James, or about Emerson, is that none of them wanted to be loved, because authentic love, passion and possession, is the greatest of all threats to the freedom of the transcendent self, to the luminous self-perception of the aesthetic self. Isabel's revulsion from Goodwood is not just a turning away from his phallic intensity:

> "To get away from *you!*" she answered. But this expressed only a little of what she felt. The rest was that she had never been loved before. She had believed it, but this was different; this was the hot wind of the desert, at the approach of which the others dropped dead, like mere sweet airs of the garden. It wrapped her about; it lifted her off her feet, while the very taste of it, as of something potent, acrid and strange, forced open her set teeth.

To be the object of such a passion is precisely not to be free, and Isabel makes the Jamesian choice, which is also the Emersonian choice. No American elect spirit feels free if it is not alone, and no grand American self believes that it is any part of the creation. Isabel accepts her fate, and thereby secures a kind of freedom. James allows us, his readers, to speculate on just how much that balance of fate and freedom will achieve in Isabel's coming contention for power with the *poseur,* Osmond. One suspects that Osmond will not win.

—H. B.

CRITICAL EXTRACTS

HENRY JAMES

P. of a L. After Isabel's marriage there are *five* more instalments, and the success of the whole story greatly depends upon this portion being well conducted or not. Let me then make the most of it—let me imagine the best. There has been a want of action in the earlier part, and it may be made up here. The elements that remain are in themselves, I think, very interesting, and they only need to be strongly and happily combined. The weakness of the whole story is that it is too exclusively psychological—that it depends to[o] little on incident; but the complete unfolding of the situation that is established by Isabel's marriage may nonetheless be quite sufficiently dramatic. The idea of the whole thing is that the poor girl, who has dreamed of freedom and nobleness, who has done, as she believes, a generous, natural, clear-sighted thing, finds herself in reality ground in the very mill of the conventional. After a year or two of marriage the antagonism between her nature and Osmond's comes out—the open opposition of a noble character and a narrow one. There is a great deal to do here in a small compass; every word, therefore, must tell—every touch must count. If the last five parts of the story appear crowded, this will be rather a good defect in consideration of the perhaps too great diffuseness of the earlier portion. Isabel awakes from her sweet delusion—oh, the art required for making this delusion natural!—and finds herself face to face with a husband who has ended by conceiving a hatred for her own larger qualities. These facts, however, are not in themselves sufficient; the situation must be marked by important events. Such an event is the discovery of the relation that has existed between Osmond and Madame Merle, the discovery that she has married Madame Merle's lover. Madame Merle, in a word, is the mother of Pansy. Edward Rosier comes to Rome, falls in love with Pansy and wants to marry her; but Osmond opposes the marriage, on the ground of Rosier's insufficient means. Isabel favours Pansy—she sees that Rosier would make her an excellent husband, be tenderly devoted and kind to her—but Osmond absolutely forbids the idea. Lord Warburton comes to Rome, sees Isabel again and declares to her that he is resigned, that he has succeeded in accepting the fact of her marriage and that he is not

5

disposed, himself, to marry. He makes the acquaintance of Pansy, is charmed with her, and at last tells Isabel that he should like to make her his wife. Isabel is almost shocked, for she distrusts this sentiment of Lord Warburton's; and the reader must feel that she mistrusts it justly. This same sentiment is a very ticklish business. It is honest up to a certain point; but at bottom, without knowing it, Lord W.'s real motive is the desire to be near Isabel whom he sees, now, to be a disappointed, and unhappy woman. This is what Isabel has perceived; she feels that it would [be] cruel to Pansy, dangerous to herself, to allow such a marriage—for which, however, there are such great material inducements that she cannot well oppose it. Her position is a most difficult one, for by begging Lord Warburton to desist she only betrays her apprehension of him—which is precisely what she wishes not to do. Besides, she is afraid of doing a wrong to Pansy. Madame Merle, meanwhile, has caught a glimpse of Warburton's state of mind and eagerly takes up the idea of his marrying the girl. Pansy is very much in love with Rosier—she has no wish to marry Lord W. Isabel is [so] convinced at last of this that she feels absolved from considering her prospects with Lord W. and treats the latter with such coldness that he feels the vanity of hope and withdraws from the field, having indeed not paid any direct attention to Pansy, whom he cannot in the least be accused of jilting. Madame Merle, very angry at his withdrawal, accuses Isabel of having dissuaded him, out of jealousy, because of his having been an old lover of hers and her wishing to keep him for herself; and she still opposes the marriage with Rosier, because she has been made to believe by Lord Warburton's attentions that Pansy may do something much more brilliant. Isabel resents Madame Merle's interference, demands of her what she has to do with Pansy. Whereupon Madame Merle, in whose breast the suppressed feeling of maternity has long been rankling, and who is passionately jealous of Isabel's influence over Pansy, breaks out with the cry that she alone has a right—that Pansy is her daughter. (To be settled later whether this revelation is to be made by Mme Merle herself, or by the Countess Gemini. Better on many grounds that it should be the latter; and yet in that way I lose the 'great scene' between Madame Merle and Isabel.) In any event this whole matter of Mme Merle is (like Lord W.'s state of mind about Pansy) a very ticklish one—very delicate and difficult to handle. To make it natural that she should have brought about Isabel's marriage to her old lover—this is in itself a supreme difficulty. It is not, however, an impossibility, for I honestly believe it rests upon nature. Her old interest in Osmond remains in a modified form; she wishes to do something for him, and she does it through another rather than by herself. That, I think, is perfectly natural. As regards Pansy the strangeness of her conduct is greater; but we must remember that we see only its surface—we don't see her reasoning. Isabel has money, and Mme Merle has great confidence in her benevolence, in her generosity; she has no fear that she will be a harsh stepmother, and she believes she will push the fortunes of the child she herself is unable to avow and afraid openly to patronize. In all this Osmond sinks a little into the background—but one must get the sense of Isabel's exquisitely miserable revulsion. Three years have passed—time enough for it to have taken place. His worldliness, his deep snobbishness, his want of generosity, etc.; his hatred of her when he finds that she judges him, that she morally protests at so much that surrounds her. The uncleanness of the air; the Countess Gemini's lovers, etc. Caspar Goodwood of course must reappear, and Ralph, and Henrietta; Mrs. Touchett, too, for a moment. Ralph's helpless observation of Isabel's deep misery; her determination to show him nothing, and his inability to help her. This to be a strong feature in the situation. Pansy is sent back to the convent, to be kept from Rosier. Caspar Goodwood comes to Rome, because he has heard from Henrietta that Isabel is unhappy, and Isabel sends him away. She hears from Ralph at Gardencourt, that he is ill there (Ralph, himself), that indeed he is dying. (The letter to come from Mrs. Touchett who is with him; or even it would be well that it should be a telegram; it expresses Ralph's wish to see her.) Isabel tells Osmond she wishes to go; Osmond, jealously and nastily, forbids it; and Isabel, deeply distressed and embarrassed, hesitates. Then Madame Merle, who wishes her to make a *coup de tête,* to leave Osmond, so that she may be away from Pansy, reveals to her her belief that it was Ralph who induced her father to leave her the £70,000. Isabel, then, violently affected and overcome, starts directly for England. She reaches Ralph at Gardencourt, and finds Caspar Goodwood and Henrietta also there: i.e., in London. Ralph's death—Isabel's return to London, and interview with Caspar G.—His passionate outbreak; he beseeches her to return with him to America. She is greatly moved, she feels the full force of his devotion—to which she has never done justice; but she refuses. She starts again for Italy—and her departure is the climax and termination of the story.

With strong handling it seems to me that it may all be very true, very powerful, very touching. The obvious criticism of course will be that it is not finished—that I have not seen the heroine to the end of her situation—that I have left her *en l'air.*—This is both true and false. The *whole* of anything is never told; you can only take what groups together. What I have done has that unity—it groups together. It is complete in itself—and the rest may be taken up or not, later.

—I am not sure that it would not be best that the exposure of Mme Merle should never be complete, and above all that she should not denounce herself. This would injure very much the impression I have wished to give of her profundity, her self-control, her regard for appearances. It may be enough that Isabel should believe the fact in question—in consequence of what the Countess Gemini has told her. Then, when Madame Merle tells her of what Ralph has done for her of old—tells it with the view I have mentioned to precipitating her defiance of Osmond—Isabel may charge her with the Countess G.'s secret. This Madame Merle will deny—but deny in such a way that Isabel knows she lies; and *then* Isabel may depart.—The last (October) installment to take place wholly in England. At the very last Caspar Goodwood goes to Pratt's hotel, and is told that Mrs. Osmond has left it the night before. Later in the day he sees Henrietta who has the last word—utters the last line of the story: a characteristic characterization of Isabel.

—HENRY JAMES, Notebook entry (c. December 1880–January 1881),
The Complete Notebooks of Henry James, ed. Leon Edel
(New York: Oxford University Press, 1987), pp. 13–16

HORACE E. SCUDDER

The *Atlantic* may fairly claim to have exercised its critical function upon the just completed novels by Mr. James and Mr. Howells before the reader had begun to enjoy them, and to have reserved the right, when the reader should be in full possession, of explaining why and how much it liked them. Yet a book has, after all, a life distinct from the interrupted existence of a magazine serial, and it is quite possible to take up these comely volumes and receive a new impression of the integrity of the stories which they contain. Possibly, Mr. James's novel suffers less than some others might from being read in fragmentary form, for the minute finish of touch with which the lines in the portrait are applied meets the reader's eye with new power every time that he takes up the story after a fall upon other work; yet this very refinement of manipulation may lead one to overlook the larger consistency of the whole figure. It is worth while to step back a few paces, and fail for a moment to see each individual stroke of the brush.

Come, then, since we have been looking at the portrait of Isabel from the near point of monthly chapters, let us seat ourselves before the book, and, armed with an imaginative tin opera-glass to shut out all other pictures, renew our acquaintance with the portrait. How does it strike us as a whole? What is the impression finally left upon our minds? Have we added to our dream of fair women?

The artist gives us this advantage, that all the elaboration of his work looks distinctly to the perfection of the central figure. One can repeat almost in a single breath the incidental story of the book. That is dissolved immediately, if the incidents deposited are the critical ones of Isabel's meeting with her aunt, her rejection successively of Goodwood and Lord Warburton, her accession to wealth, her marriage with Osmond, her temporary separation, and her final return. A person hearing the narrative might be pardoned if he failed to see the making of a great novel in it, but only when one has recited it does he become aware how each step in the fatal series is a movement in the direction of destiny. By a fine concentration of attention upon the heroine, Mr. James impresses us with her importance, and the other characters, involved as they are with her life, fall back into secondary positions. It is much to have seized and held firmly so elusive a conception, and our admiration is increased when reflection shows that, individual as Isabel is in the painting, one may fairly take her as representative of womanly life today. The fine purpose of her freedom, the resolution with which she seeks to be the maker of her destiny, the subtle weakness into which all this betrays her, the apparent helplessness of her ultimate position, and the conjectured escape only through patient forbearance,—what are all these, if not attributes of womanly life expended under current conditions?

The consistency of the work is observable under another aspect. Mr. James's method is sufficiently well known, and since he has made it his own the critic may better accept it and measure it than complain of it. What renders it distinct from, say, Thackeray's method, with which it has been compared, or from George Eliot's, is the limitation of the favorite generalizations and analyses. If the reader will attend, he will see that these take place quite exclusively within the boundaries of the story and characters. That is to say, when the people in the book stop acting or speaking, it is to give to the novelist an opportunity, not to indulge in general reflections, having application to all sorts and conditions of men, of whom his *dramatis personæ* are but a part,—he has no desire to share humanity with them,—but to make acute reflections upon these particular people, and to explain more thoroughly than their words and acts can the motives which lie behind. We may, on general grounds, doubt the self-confidence or power of a novelist who feels this part of his performance to be essential, but there can be no doubt that Mr. James's method is a part of that concentration of mind which results in a singular consistency.

Yet all this carries an intimation of what is curiously noticeable in his work. It is consistent, but the consistency is with itself. Within the boundaries of the novel the logic of character and events is close and firm. We say this after due reflection upon the latest pages. There can be little doubt that the novelist suffers more in the reader's judgment from a false or ineffective scene at the close of his story than he gains from many felicitous strokes in the earlier development of plot or character. The impatient, undiscriminating objection, It does not end well, although it may incense the writer, is an ill-formulated expression of the feeling that the creation lacks the final, triumphant touch which gives life; the sixth swan in the story got a stitch-weed shirt, like the rest, but in the hurry of the last moment it lacked a few stitches, and so in the transformation the youngest brother was forced to put up with one arm and to show a wing for the other. Isabel Archer, with her fine horoscope, is an impressive figure, and one follows her in her free flight with so much admiration for her resolution and strong pinions that when she is caught in the meshes of Osmond's net one's indignation is moved, and a noble pity takes the place of frank admiration. But pity can live only in full communion with faith, and we can understand the hesitation which a reader might feel before the somewhat ambiguous passage of Isabel's last interview with Goodwood. The passage, however, admits of a generous construction, and we prefer to take it, and to see in the scene the author's intention of giving a final touch to his delineation of Goodwood's iron but untempered will, Isabel's vanishing dream of happiness, and her acceptance of the destiny which she had unwittingly chosen. We suspect that something of the reader's dissatisfaction at this juncture comes from his dislike of Goodwood, the jack-in-the-box of the story, whose unyielding nature seems somehow outside of all the events.

To return to our point. This self-consistency is a separate thing from any consistency with the world of reality. The characters, the situations, the incidents, are all true to the law of their own being, but that law runs parallel with the law which governs life, instead of being identical with it. In Andersen's quaint story of the Emperor's New Clothes, a little child discovers the unreality of the gossamer dress, and his voice breaks in upon the illusion from the outer world. Something of the same separation from the story, of the same unconscious naturalness of feeling, prompts the criticism that, though these people walk, and sit, and talk, and behave, they are yet in an illusionary world of their own. Only when one is within the charmed circle of the story is he under its spell, and so complete is the isolation of the book that the characters acquire a strange access of reality when they talk about each other. Not only so, but the introversion which now and then takes place deepens the sense of personality. In that masterly passage which occupies the forty-second section, where Isabel enters upon a disclosure of her changed life, the reader seems to be going down as in a diving-bell into the very secrets of her nature.

What is all this but saying that in the process of Mr. James's art the suggestion always seems to come from within, and to work outward? We recognize the people to whom he introduces us, not by any external signs, but by the private information which we have regarding their souls. The smiles which they wear—and one might make an ingenious collection of their variety—do not tell what is beneath the surface, but we know what they mean, because we already have an esoteric knowledge. Mr. James is at great pains to illustrate his characters by their attitudes, their movements, their by-play, yet we carry away but a slight impression of their external appearance; these are not bodily shapes, for the most part, but embodied spirits, who enjoy their materialization for a time, and contribute to a play which goes on upon a stage just a little apart from that great stage where the world's play, with men and women for actors, is carried forward.

—HORACE E. SCUDDER, *"The Portrait of a Lady* and *Dr. Breen's Practice,"*
Atlantic Monthly 49, No. 1 (January 1882): 126–28

MARGARET OLIPHANT

The one thing which the book is not, is what it calls itself. There are several portraits of subordinate ladies—of Mrs Touchett and Miss Stackpole, for example, both of which are admirable pictures; but of the heroine, upon whom the greatest pains have been expended, and to whom endless space is afforded for the setting forth of her characteristics, we have no portrait, nor, even with the enormous amount of material supplied by Mr James, do we find it easy to put together anything which will serve to supply the defect. We doubt much whether, in all the historical records that exist, we have as much material for the construction, let us say, of a recognisable portrait of Queen Elizabeth—no insignificant figure—as we have for that of Isabel Archer, the young lady who suddenly appears in the doorway of an old English country-house, inhabited like most other desirable places by American tenants—in this case her uncle and her cousin—fresh from her native country, prepared to take instant possession of her birthright as the explorer, discoverer, and conqueror of the old country,—and, in fact, reducing the gentlemen who meet her into instant subjection in the course of half an hour. How she does so, except by being very pretty, as we are told she is, we do not know; though the gentlemen in question are too experienced and clever in their own persons to be immediately subjugated by simple beauty. "Her head was erect, her eye brilliant, her flexible figure turned itself lightly this way and that, in sympathy with the alertness with which she evidently caught impressions. Her impressions were numerous, and they were all reflected in a clear, still smile," is Mr James's description of his heroine; and it is about the clearest view we get of the young lady. For once in a way he is outside of her: but as he goes on he gets more and more within the circle of this irresistible young woman's personality; and we have to receive both herself and her immediate surroundings, not so much as they actually are, but as they are seen through her eyes. This is always confusing; for self-knowledge at its closest has many limitations, and the most impartial student of his own mind will probably get more light upon it by overhearing one sharp characterisation from outside than by weeks of self-examination. Isabel's aspect from outside is conveyed to us only in the raptures of her adorers; for all the men she encounters fall in love with her: first, her cousin Ralph Touchett, then Lord Warburton, then Osmond, whom she marries: besides a persistent Boston man, who makes nothing of crossing the Atlantic to get a glimpse of her, and turns up again and again with a sort of dogged inappropriateness at every new stage of her career.

There is but little vicissitude, however, in her career; she comes to "Europe" with something of the intention which Mr James illustrated with, we think, a great deal more power, though less of the extremely refined and cultivated skill of which he is now master, in *The American,* the first work by which he was known in England; that is, to get everything she can out of her life and its opportunities,—all the sensation, the information, the variety of experience which it is possible it can convey. There is this difference between the young and visionary girl and the mature man, that whereas Mr James's first hero wanted practical satisfaction for his desires, and to get possession of all that was best, including, as the most indispensable article of all, the fairest and most costly flower of womanhood which was to be found or purchased anyhow,—Isabel prefers not to have anything but the sense of having—the wealth of spiritual possession. For this reason she likes to retain a hold upon the lovers whom she will not marry. The English lord with all his fine qualities—and it cannot be said that our American author and heroine do not do full justice to these qualities with a refined sense of the admirableness of the position, and the importance which attaches to so curious and desirable a specimen of humanity—gives her the most agreeable consciousness of power, though all his advantages do not tempt her to marry him, and she is sorry for vexing him—almost as sorry as she is agreeably excited by the incident altogether. Indeed it would appear that this accompaniment of homage is natural to the young American woman, and that she would feel herself to be treated unfairly if at least one English lord, besides innumerable other candidates of different descriptions, did not attest her power. This is very different from the more vulgar development of the American young woman, who is bent on securing a title for herself. Mr James's young ladies never do this. They are totally different from the Irene Macgillicuddys. Their curiosity about the English aristocrat is fresh and eager. They contemplate him attentively as the greatest novelty within their reach, and like and admire him as one of the wonders of the world; but they do not care to go any further. Isabel Archer passes through this phase very serenely, liking the new interest it puts into her life. But as a matter of fact she does not care for anything much except new interests. The adventures, or rather encounters, through which we are permitted to accompany her, are in reality but a small part of her career. There are gaps in which she travels far and wide—rapidly, eagerly, arduously. "She was like a thirsty person draining cup after cup," but always coming back again to the old investigation—the earnest study of all new phenomena—the consideration of how everything affected herself. Her desire for new experiences never fails, even when she gets into the dead block in which, as is natural, her perpetually increasing circle of moral enlightenment and sensation ends. "Take things more easily," her cousin advises:—

"Don't ask yourself so much whether this or that is good for you. Don't question your conscience so much; it will get out of tune, like a strummed piano. Keep it for great occasions. Don't try so much to force your character—it's like trying to pull open a rosebud. Live as you like best, and your character will form itself. . . . You have too much conscience," Ralph added. "It's out of all reason, the number of things you think wrong. Spread your wings—rise above the ground. It's never wrong to do that."

She had listened eagerly, as I say, and it was her nature to understand quickly.

. . . "What you say is very true," Isabel went on. "You could say nothing more true. I am absorbed in myself. I look at life too much as a doctor's prescription. Why, indeed, should we perpetually be thinking whether things are good for us, as if we were patients lying in a hospital? . . . I try to care more about the world than about myself, but I always come back to myself. It's because I am afraid." She stopped: her voice had trembled a little. "Yes; I am afraid. I can't tell you. A large fortune means freedom, and I am afraid of that. It's such a fine thing, and one should make such a good use of it. If one shouldn't, one would be ashamed. And one must always be thinking—it's a constant effort. I am not sure that it's not a greater happiness to be a pauper."

It was inevitable that such a heroine should end unhappily—even if it were not inevitable that all Mr James's books should break off with a sharp cut of arbitrary conclusion, leaving all the questions they so skilfully raise unsolved. Isabel, through the means of a wonderful woman whom she meets in her aunt's house, and who is a sort of symbol of unusual experience, as the younger woman is of the craving for it, falls under the fascinations of a certain æsthetic and beauty-loving American, Gilbert Osmond by name, who lives on one of the heights which surround Florence, a poor yet elegant *dilettante* life, "picking up" rarities of all kinds, making amateur drawings, surrounded by the faded silks and crafty embellishments of a collector, with a pretty little Dresden shepherdess of a daughter, newly returned from the convent, whose perfect conventional simplicity, freshness, and submission, afford Mr James the means of making one of his most finished and perfect sketches.

We confess to being quite unable to understand how it is that Isabel falls into Osmond's toils, unless it is because so elaborate and self-conscious a personality recoils instinctively, even though full of an abstract admiration for truth, from the downright and veracious, and finds in the complications of an elaborately conventional mind something that has the air of being larger and richer than the true. The reader is never for a moment taken in by the superiority of this most carefully dressed and posed figure, whose being altogether is mysterious, and of whom, notwithstanding the author's elaborate descriptions, we never penetrate the *fin mot.*

> "Success," says Mr James, "for Gilbert Osmond, would be to make himself felt; that was the only success to which he could now pretend. It is not a kind of distinction that is officially recognised, unless, indeed, the operation be performed upon multitudes of men. Osmond's life would be to impress himself not largely but deeply—a distinction of the most private sort: a single character might offer the whole measure of it. The clear and sensitive nature of a generous girl would make space for the record."

It is to be supposed, therefore, that this refined and philosophical *dilettante,* secluding himself among his faded silks and æsthetic ornaments, in his villa on Bellosguardo, is like a spider in his web awaiting the arrival of the fly which it shall be worth his while to capture. But, after all, these elaborate preparations were scarcely necessary for the capture of a young lady who was only Miss Archer, with a fortune of sixty thousand pounds. Had a Grand Duchess been his aim, it would have been comprehensible. There is far too great an effort for an insufficient result; and the almost immediate failure of their after relations is confusing and unaccountable. Something of the same curious failure we remember to have found in *Daniel Deronda,* where Gwendolen and her husband, after their elaborate drawing together, fly asunder the moment they are married, with a suddenness and bitterness—brutality on the man's part, and misery on the woman's—for which we find no adequate motive, since there was neither passion between them to die out, nor motive enough beforehand to force a union which was to end so abruptly. That Isabel should discover her husband to be, as he describes himself, not only conventional, but convention itself, when she believed him to be nobly superior to the world, is one thing; but that she should discover him to hate her is quite another; and his jealousy and tyranny in the one development seem out of character with his easy gracefulness and gentlemanliness in the other.

The last volume is full of the complete and utter failure to which the heroine's hopes and high desires have come; but it cannot be said that she acquits herself with the dignity that might have been expected of her under the disappointment. Not only does she allow her wretchedness to be taken for granted by all her friends, but it would almost seem as if, in the utter collapse of the world about her, this most abstract and intellectual of heroines is driven at last to the conclusion that the only good in life is to make a snatch at happiness anyhow—to take what is offered her at last in utter relinquishment of any better hope. She has left her husband to watch at the deathbed of the devoted cousin Ralph, who has loved her all through, and has been her best and most faithful friend; and when all is over, is suddenly brought face to face with the true American, the violent lover, with all the ardour and practical force of the New World, of whom, among the rest of her sensations, she has always been a little afraid. No trace of love for Caspar has ever appeared in her before; but he comes upon her suddenly, when she is weak with grief for Ralph, and contemplating with horror her return to the bitter round of her duties with Osmond. The American not only pours forth his passion, but proposes to her to fly with him from the wretchedness of her fate. "Why shouldn't we be happy?" he says; "the world is all before us, and the world is large," as—we are obliged to remind Mr James—a great many gentlemen in Mr Caspar Goodwood's position have said to a great many unhappy wives in the pages of fiction before.

Isabel gave a long murmur like a creature in pain: it was as if he were pressing something that hurt her. "The world is very small," she said at random; she had an immense desire to appear to resist. She said it at random to hear herself say something; but it was not what she meant. The world in truth had never seemed so large; it seemed to open out all around her, to take the form of a mighty sea, where she floated in fathomless waters. She had wanted help, and here was help; it had come in a rushing torrent. I know not whether she believed anything that he said; but she believed that to let him take her in his arms would be the next best thing to dying. This belief for the moment was a kind of rapture in which she felt herself sinking and sinking. In the movement she seemed to beat with her feet, in order to catch herself, to feel something to rest upon.

She does not yield, it is needless to say: our author could not have so far forgotten himself. But when this impetuous lover, by no means despairing of success, finds that she has returned to her home, he is consoled by her friend Miss Stackpole, with the significant words—the last in the book—"Look here, Mr Goodwood," she said; "just you wait!"

It is not very long since a respectable and gifted writer in another work of fiction permitted a young man of the highest virtue and honour to propose to a pure and honourable girl, utterly unprotected, that she should go away with him and be happy in a world which was large enough to conceal them, in much the same way; prefacing his proposal by the compliment that he knew she was not one of the prejudiced people who would be shocked by such a proposal: and so far was that spotless maiden from being shocked, that she took herself severely to task for her cruelty in refusing to make to her lover—poor fellow—the little sacrifice he asked. What do these gentlemen mean, we wonder? Isabel, so far as she has any body at all, is as free from fleshly stain as the purest imagination could desire. Is it only that in her search after experience her author felt it necessary that she should taste also the excitement of an unlawful passion? or is it his mind to preach that the world being so hollow and miserable, and devoid of hope, the best thing we can do is to eat and drink, for to-morrow we die? Anyhow, it is a most equivocal if not debasing conclusion, and brings us up sharp with a discord instead of the symphony of harmonising chords with which it has been the habit of art to accompany the end of every story. As a rule Mr James rejects symphonies, and attempts no harmonising conclusions. He leaves us usually tantalised, half angry with an end which is left to our imagination. But this is not a way of leaving matters to the imagination which we can at all consent to take from his hand. Abstract as is his heroine, a congeries of thoughts and questions rather than a woman, we cannot endure the possibility, even, of a future stain for her. It is a sort of insult to his own art, which is altogether out of accord with any such harsh effects. Let smaller workmen avail themselves of these easy means of startling the reader; from him we have a right to expect better things.

—MARGARET OLIPHANT, *Blackwood's Edinburgh Magazine* 131, No. 3
(March 1882): 374–81

HENRY JAMES

The house of fiction has in short not one window, but a million—a number of possible windows not to be reckoned, rather; every one of which has been pierced, or is still pierceable, in its vast front, by the need of the individual vision and by the pressure of the individual will. These apertures, of dissimilar shape and size, hang so, all together, over the human scene that we might have expected of them a greater sameness of report than we find. They are but windows at the best, mere holes in a dead wall, disconnected, perched aloft; they are not hinged doors opening straight upon life. But they have this mark of their own that at each of them stands a figure with a pair of eyes, or at least with a field-glass, which forms, again and again, for observation, a unique instrument, insuring to the person making use of it an impression distinct from every other. He and his neighbours are watching the same show, but one seeing more where the other sees less, one seeing black where the other sees white, one seeing big where the other sees small, one seeing coarse where the other sees fine. And so on, and so on; there is fortunately no saying on what, for the particular pair of eyes, the window may *not* open; "fortunately" by reason, precisely, of this incalculability of range. The spreading field, the human scene, is the "choice of subject"; the pierced aperture, either broad or balconied or slit-like and low-browed, is the "literary form"; but they are, singly or together, as nothing without the posted presence of the watcher—without, in other words, the consciousness of the artist. Tell me what the artist is, and I will tell you of what he has *been* conscious. Thereby I shall express to you at once his boundless freedom and his "moral" reference.

All this is a long way round, however, for my word about my dim first move toward *The Portrait,* which was exactly my grasp of a single character—an acquisition I had made, moreover, after a fashion not here to be retraced. Enough that I was, as seemed to me, in complete possession of it, that I had been so for a long time, that this had made it familiar and yet had not blurred its charm, and that, all urgently, all tormentingly, I saw it in motion and, so to speak, in transit. This amounts to saying that I saw it as bent upon its fate—some fate or other; *which,* among the possibilities, being precisely the question. Thus I had my vivid individual—vivid, so strangely, in spite of being still at large, not confined by the conditions, not engaged in the tangle, to which we look for much of the impress that constitutes an identity. If the apparition was still all to be placed how came it to be vivid?—since we puzzle such quantities out, mostly, just by the business of placing them. One could answer such a question beautifully, doubtless, if one could do so subtle, if not so monstrous, a thing as to write the history of the growth of one's imagination. One would describe then what, at a given time, had extraordinarily happened to it, and one would so, for instance, be in a position to tell, with an approach to clearness, how, under favour of occasion, it had been able to take over (take over straight from life) such and such a constituted, animated figure or form. The figure has to that extent, as you see, *been* placed—placed in the imagination that detains it, preserves, protects, enjoys it, conscious of its presence in the dusky, crowded, heterogeneous back-shop of the mind very much as a wary dealer in precious odds and ends, competent to make an "advance" on rare objects confided to him, is conscious of the rare little "piece" left in deposit by the reduced, mysterious lady of title or the speculative amateur, and which is already there to disclose its merit afresh as soon as a key shall have clicked in a cupboard-door.

That may be, I recognise, a somewhat superfine analogy for the particular "value" I here speak of, the image of the young feminine nature that I had had for so considerable a time all curiously at my disposal; but it appears to fond memory quite to fit the fact—with the recall, in addition, of my pious desire but to place my treasure right. I quite remind myself thus of the dealer resigned not to "realise," resigned to keeping the precious object locked up indefinitely rather than commit it, at no matter what price, to vulgar hands. For there *are* dealers in these forms and figures and treasures capable of that refinement. The point is, however, that this single small corner-stone, the conception of a certain young woman affronting her destiny, had begun with being all my outfit for the large building of *The Portrait of a Lady.* It came to be a square and spacious house—or has at least seemed so to me in this going over it again; but, such as it is, it had to be put up round my young woman while she stood there in perfect isolation. That is to me, artistically speaking, the circumstance of interest; for I have lost myself once more, I confess, in the curiosity of analysing the structure. By what process of logical accretion was this slight "personality," the mere slim shade of an intelligent but presumptuous girl, to find itself endowed with the high attributes of a Subject?—and indeed by what thinness, at the best, would such a subject not be vitiated? Millions of presumptuous girls, intelligent or not intelligent, daily affront their destiny, and what is it open to their destiny to *be,* at the most, that we should make an ado about it? The novel is of its very nature an "ado," an ado about something, and the larger the form it takes the greater of course the ado. Therefore, consciously, that was what one was in for—for positively organising an ado about Isabel Archer.

One looked it well in the face, I seem to remember, this extravagance; and with the effect precisely of recognising the charm of the problem. Challenge any such problem with any intelligence, and you immediately see how full it is of substance; the wonder being, all the while, as we look at the world, how absolutely, how inordinately, the Isabel Archers, and even much smaller female fry, insist on mattering. George Eliot has admirably noted it—"In these frail vessels is borne onward through the ages the treasure of human affection." In *Romeo and Juliet* Juliet has to be important, just as, in *Adam Bede* and *The Mill on the Floss* and *Middlemarch* and *Daniel Deronda,* Hetty Sorrel and Maggie Tulliver and Rosamond Vincy and Gwendolen Harleth have to be; with that much of firm ground, that much of bracing air, at the disposal all the while of their feet and their lungs. They are typical, none the less, of a class difficult, in the individual case, to make a centre of interest; so difficult in fact that many an expert painter, as for instance Dickens and Walter Scott, as for instance even, in the main, so subtle a hand as that of R. L. Stevenson, has preferred to leave the task unattempted. There are in fact writers as to whom we make out that their refuge from this is to assume it to be not worth their attempting; by which pusillanimity in truth their honour is scantly saved. It is never an attestation of a value, or even of our imperfect sense of one, it is never a tribute to any truth at all, that we shall represent that value badly. It never makes up, artistically, for an artist's dim feeling about a thing that he shall "do" the thing as ill as possible. There are better ways than that, the best of all of which is to begin with less stupidity.

It may be answered meanwhile, in regard to Shakespeare's and to George Eliot's testimony, that their concession to the "importance" of their Juliets and Cleopatras and Portias (even with Portia as the very type and model of the young person intelligent and presumptuous) and to that of their Hettys and Maggies and Rosamonds and Gwendolens, suffers the abatement that these slimnesses are, when figuring as the main props of the theme, never suffered to be sole ministers of its appeal, but have their inadequacy eked out with comic relief and underplots, as the playwrights say, when not with murders and battles and the great mutations of the world. If they are shown as "mattering" as much as they could possibly pretend to, the proof of it is in a hundred other persons, made of much stouter stuff, and each involved moreover in a hundred relations which matter to *them* concomitantly with that one. Cleopatra matters, beyond bounds, to Antony, but his colleagues, his antagonists, the state of Rome and the impending battle also pro-digiously matter; Portia matters to Antonio, and to Shylock, and to the Prince of Morocco, to the fifty aspiring princes, but for these gentry there are other lively concerns; for Antonio, notably, there are Shylock and Bassanio and his lost ventures and the extremity of his predicament. This extremity indeed, by the same token, matters to Portia—though its doing so becomes of interest all by the fact that Portia matters to *us.* That she does so, at any rate, and that almost everything comes round to it again, supports my contention as to this fine example of the value recognised in the mere young thing. (I say "mere" young thing because I guess that even Shakespeare, preoccupied mainly though he may have been with the passions of princes, would scarce have pretended to found the best of his appeal for her on her high social position.) It is an example exactly of the deep difficulty braved—the difficulty of making George Eliot's "frail vessel," if not the all-in-all for our attention, at least the clearest of the call.

Now to see deep difficulty braved is at any time, for the really addicted artist, to feel almost even as a pang the beautiful incentive, and to feel it verily in such sort as to wish the danger intensified. The difficulty most worth tackling can only be for him, in these conditions, the greatest the case permits of. So I remember feeling here (in presence, always, that is, of the particular uncertainty of my ground), that there would be one way better than another—oh, ever so much better than any other!—of making it fight out its battle. The frail vessel, that charged with George Eliot's "treasure," and thereby of such importance to those who curiously approach it, has likewise possibilities of importance to itself, possibilities which permit of treatment and in fact peculiarly require it from the moment they are considered at all. There is always the escape from any close account of the weak agent of such spells by using as a bridge for evasion, for retreat and flight, the view of her relation to those surrounding her. Make it predominantly a view of *their* relation and the trick is played: you give the general sense of her effect, and you give it, so far as the raising on it of a superstructure goes, with the maximum of ease. Well, I recall perfectly how little, in my now quite established connexion, the maximum of ease appealed to me, and how I seemed to get rid of it by an honest transposition of the weights in the two scales. "Place the centre of the subject in the young woman's own consciousness," I said to myself, "and you get as interesting and as beautiful a difficulty as you could wish. Stick to *that*—for the centre; put the heaviest weight into *that* scale, which will be so largely the scale of her relation to herself. Make her only interested enough, at the same time, in the things that are not herself, and this relation need n't fear to be too limited. Place meanwhile in the other scale the lighter weight (which is usually the one that tips the balance of interest): press least hard, in short, on the consciousness of your heroine's satellites, especially the male; make it an interest contributive only to the greater one. See, at all events, what can be done in this way. What better field could there be for a due ingenuity? The girl hovers, inextinguishable, as a charming creature, and the job will be to translate her into the highest terms of that formula, and as nearly as possible moreover into *all* of them. To depend upon her and her little concerns wholly to see you through will necessitate, remember, your really 'doing' her."

So far I reasoned, and it took nothing less than that technical rigour, I now easily see, to inspire me with the right confidence for erecting on such a plot of ground the neat and careful and proportioned pile of bricks that arches over it and that was thus to form, constructionally speaking, a literary monument. Such is the aspect that to-day *The Portrait* wears for me: a structure reared with an "architectural" competence, as Turgenieff would have said, that makes it, to the author's own sense, the most proportioned of his productions after *The Ambassadors*—which was to follow it so many years later and which has, no doubt, a superior roundness. On one thing I was determined; that, though I should clearly have to pile brick upon brick for the creation of an interest, I would leave no pretext for saying that anything is out of line, scale or perspective. I would build large—in fine embossed vaults and painted arches, as who should say, and yet never let it appear that the chequered pavement, the ground under the reader's feet, fails to stretch at every point to the base of the walls. That precautionary spirit, on re-perusal of the book, is the old note that most touches me: it testifies so, for my own ear, to the anxiety of my provision for the reader's amusement. I felt, in view of the possible limitations of my subject, that no such provision could be excessive, and the development of the latter was simply the general form of that earnest quest. And I find indeed that this is the only account I can give myself of the evolution of the fable: it is all under the head thus named that I conceive the needful accretion as having taken place, the right complications as having started. It was naturally of the essence that the young woman should be herself complex; that was rudi-mentary—or was at any rate the light in which Isabel Archer had originally dawned. It went, however, but a certain way, and other lights, contending, conflicting lights, and of as many different colours, if possible, as the rockets, the Roman candles and Catherine-wheels of a "pyrotechnic display," would be employable to attest that she was. I had, no doubt, a groping instinct for the right complications, since I am quite unable to track the footsteps of those that constitute, as the case stands, the general situation exhibited. They are there, for what they are worth, and as numerous as might be; but my memory, I confess, is a blank as to how and whence they came.

—HENRY JAMES, "Preface to the New York Edition" of *The Portrait of a Lady*
(New York: Scribner's, 1908), pp. x–xvii

CORNELIA PULSIFER KELLEY

Where, the critic is led to ask because of the great fondness of James for Isabel, had he obtained this "vivid individual?" Was she someone he actually knew—one of his many cousins? Had she grown out of the chance remark of a friend as Daisy had? Had he seen her in a boarding house? Had she come from his reading? The preface does not satisfy us on this point, and yet it gives a broadly general hint in the enumeration of the heroines of Shakespeare and George Eliot, who had been defrauded of mattering enough by their authors. And if one turns back to the critical article which James wrote in 1876 when *Daniel Deronda* completed its serial run, the hint is confirmed. From James's article more than from George Eliot's novel, it is clear that Gwendolen Harleth was the prototype of Isabel Archer, for the points which James noted about Gwendolen are the points which a critic must note about his heroine.

Isabel is similar to Gwendolen in nature, in basic characteristics:

Gwendolen is a perfect picture of youthfulness—its eagerness, its pre-sumption, its preoccupation with itself, its vanity and silliness, its sense of its own absoluteness. But she is extremely intelligent and clever, and therefore tragedy *can* have a hold upon her. Her conscience doesn't make the tragedy. . . . It is the tragedy which makes her conscience, which then reacts upon it.

If there is any difference between the two heroines, it is that of degree—an intensification in Isabel—and not of kind.

Isabel's story, broadly looked at, is the same as Gwendolen's:

> The universe, forcing itself with a slow, inexorable pressure into a narrow, complacent mind, and yet after all extremely sensitive mind, and making it ache with the pain of the process—that is Gwendolen's story. And it becomes completely characteristic in that her supreme perception of the fact that the world is whirling past her, is in the disappointment not of a base but of an exalted passion. The very chance to embrace what the author is so fond of calling a 'larger life' seems refused to her. She is punished for being narrow, and she is not allowed a chance to expand.

Of course in the particulars and details of plot there are differences, but in each novel, a young woman affronts her destiny. In each case, her purpose is noble, exalted, and pursued with passion, and *The Portrait* is, as James said of *Daniel Deronda* as a whole, "the romance of a high moral tone."

Again Isabel and her story are presented in the same manner:

> Gwendolen is a masterpiece. She is known, felt, and presented, psychologically, altogether in the grand manner . . . Gwendolen's whole history is superbly told. And see how the girl is known, inside out, how thoroughly she is felt and understood. It is the most *intelligent* thing in all George Eliot's writing, and that is saying much. It is so deep, so true, so complete; it holds such a wealth of psychological detail, it is more than masterly.

Truer words cannot be found to describe the portrait of Isabel and her history. Can it not be concluded that the desire, perhaps, too, the determination, to "do" thoroughly and completely, intelligently and feelingly, a similar heroine, had come to James in 1876 as he read and reviewed *Daniel Deronda?*

And the desire had been cherished and fostered. For this, James had experimented with American girls, trying out variations of the type, but hesitating to treat his "pious treasure" till he was sure of himself. For this, he had experimented with method, looking at his heroines through others, realizing that he must get at them and their minds directly if he was to do them justice, trying to on a small scale, but saving and storing up his energy for the service of Isabel. Thinking of this, he had probably tried to imagine other characters who might help him, and one day these characters had suddenly stepped before him with Isabel's story in their hands. Some of these, like Isabel, are like people he had met in George Eliot—Osmond's refined and distilled brutality is like that of Grandcourt's; Ralph's helpless devotion is related to that of Will Ladislaw's in *Middlemarch.* Others came from his own stories— Caspar is like Newman in his persistency; Pansy is like Aurora but with more delicacy due to her convent upbringing; Henrietta is related to Miranda Hope. Not a little of the greatness of *The Portrait* is due to the deep knowledge James had of all of his characters. He was thoroughly acquainted with them.

When, three years after writing the review, he turned to work on the portrait of Isabel, he probably had no consciousness of having borrowed her or her attendants. She was then *his* creature; like Gwendolen, to be sure, but there were many such in this world, and he had as much right to do her as he had to do Catherine, who was like Eugénie Grandet. Consider the following sentence from the review: "Gwendolen's history is admirably typical—as most things are with George Eliot: it is the very stuff that human life is made of." What happened to Gwendolen often happened. James saw that it happened to American girls as well as to English— especially when they came to Europe with the desire to meet life, and the idea of their own competence to deal with it; then the universe forced itself in with a slow, inexorable pressure. James not only felt free to take a similar heroine, he felt impelled to, for he had discovered long before from George Eliot and others, that it was the duty of the novelist to deal with the "very stuff" of life, and he had been proceeding with gradually increasing success ever since. He had even once tried a similar heroine of his own accord in Madame de Mauves. There were no basically new subjects, for human nature was as old as the hills. The American side of it, however, had not yet been adequately done. The same conclusions are to be applied in regard to the resemblance of Osmond to Grandcourt and of Ralph to Will. Such people existed; such "refined and distilled brutality," such handicapped and silent devotion were only too characteristic of life. If Isabel was to face life, she must meet and feel—ah, so emphatically feel—both.

Accordingly James sought a plot, or rather took the one his characters offered, where this would be possible in the highest degree. It was not thus possible in George Eliot's novel where not only Gwendolen's story was thrust behind Deronda's but Gwendolen's hands were tied by poverty. James decided to give his American girl the center of the stage, and then he contrived by the device of the inheritance, which Ralph's love and interest made possible, to make her rich, thus putting it into her power to be magnanimous, to marry a poor man in the wish to help him. He made her, in her own opinion a free agent, and the most bitter part of her tragedy occurs when she finds that she has not been free, only blind, and that others have "made" her life.

What was in *Washington Square* on a small scale, is in *The Portrait of a Lady* on an enlarged and heightened scale. Isabel is intelligent and clever, but she is surrounded by people, two in particular, who are not only clever but wicked, and hence her defeat at their hands. It must not be overlooked, however, that defeated though she is externally, Isabel achieves a moral victory for herself. Catherine did not; she sank into passive existence. Isabel, thus, is like Newman in *The American.* Behind it all is the influence of Turgénieff and his use of failure, now thoroughly absorbed by James as a dominating principle. When James wrote *The Portrait of a Lady,* he did not think of himself as working *under* George Eliot and Turgénieff, but as working along *with* them, even, indeed, as the preface indicates, of working *above* them.

He treated his heroine not only intelligently and truly and feelingly, he treated her artistically. He let Isabel matter *enough*. He gave the whole novel to her. He not only placed her in the center, he placed the center in her consciousness, in her view of herself and of life. However, he did not stay in her mind all of the time, as he had stayed in Mallet's and Newman's, for Isabel, like Catherine, was not to see the conniving about her. But he looked at the others *only* as their plotting involved her, and except for Ralph, who was lovingly watching and seeing all, he stayed as much as possible out of the minds of those surrounding her. He kept everything focussed upon her; then he looked at everything as she saw it. The method which James used in *The Portrait of a Lady* was a combination of his method of using a mind as his glass and the direct approach which he used in *Washington Square*—it was his method made more flexible, adapted to his material, not ruthlessly applied despite the wisdom of the situation. James had control of it.

Then he put everything together, brought it out as he proceeded, built it up increasingly to a climax with an "architectural completeness" which only once again did he feel that he equalled. In this regard, he mentioned in the preface, one thing which he regretted and another thing of which he was most proud. He regretted that he had brought in Henrietta, that "light ficelle" who runs beside Isabel, listens to her ideas, and often takes her to task, but plays no essential part in the story. He was pleased with the way in which he had converted Isabel's sense of and for mild adventures into the very "stuff" of story. By giving Isabel a premonitory feeling when she first sees Madame Merle that this grand lady is to play a part in her life, he had been able to produce "the maximum of intensity with the minimum of strain." He was proud, especially, of Isabel's vigil with herself half way through the book, when she spends the night viewing and reviewing the situation. That, brought in where it is, picks up and moves forward the action, accomplishes vividly in one chapter an account of three years of Isabel's life. "It was designed to have all the vivacity of incident and all the economy of picture." It *is* good, perhaps the best thing in the book, where everything is well-nigh superlative. No wonder James was proud.

There are details of treatment which James did not mention in the preface but left to the reader to discern from the book. The "architecture" which he was conscious of using enters on the first page and supports the novel through to the last. James set the stage for Isabel to appear—the spreading lawns at Gardencourt, the three men idly speculating—then brought her in, plunging her into a new world, a new kind of existence. What led to this, the antecedent action, he deferred for two chapters, and then recounted it rapidly securing thus an advantage artistically over *Washington Square* where he had followed Balzac. At the end, he left Isabel turning, back to Rome to a scene which will be more unpleasant than any in the book, and he gave Henrietta the task of informing Caspar. Though it is stopped short by the author, Isabel's story is by no means finished; she must continue to live and suffer for many years, but there is no need for her story to be finished completely as James had felt compelled to finish the story of Catherine. The reader knows how Isabel will now act and feel, with her eyes opened and Ralph's love sustaining her and making life a bit more endurable. In the middle of the novel, James made everything lead to something else, and not only this, but intentionally gave Isabel premonitions of her unhappiness, vague foresight as to her future. The use of the direct approach not only enabled him to see the plotting of others, but it allowed him to look at Isabel from the outside as well as from the inside. The advantage of this he realized when he resumed Isabel's story after her marriage and wisely revealed the state of her mind indirectly by telling what others see and guess, before approaching it directly in the midnight vigil. All this shows the hand of an artist and a master as well, for though James trusted the stage to others temporarily, the glance of author, characters, and reader is kept focussed upon the mind of Isabel.

The finish of the novel is no less perfect than its architecture. It is narrative as James had never written it before—a blending of incident, dialogue, description—one running into the other so that the result is constant fluidity of motion. The portions of straight narrative—for want of a word one must so distinguish what is not dialogue or description—run smoothly, but because the nature of the story demands it, often slowly, becoming quite analytical and expository in places. Still there is always, even in the most expositional of the parts, movement of a sort. James's concern was the *development* of a mind. The narrative portions frequently melt into dialogue, which easily assumes the burden of furthering the action, notably when Isabel and Osmond are conversing, or of telling what has happened, as in Isabel's facing Caspar after she has accepted Osmond. The dialogue operates still further in revealing character, both directly and indirectly. Much of the analysis of Isabel comes from the mouth of Ralph or of Henrietta—who looked at thus seems to have a function after all—as they talk with Isabel, criticize her, and lead her to expose herself. Because of this, little description of a pure, unmixed sort was needed, and there are no sustained passages of description, no large blocks of it such as James, following Balzac, had used in *Washington Square*. It is wrought into the dialogue, into the incident. One can say both that there is no description and that there is description on every page, achieved by a short remark, a phrase, or even one word as it accompanies dialogue or is worked into incident. The portrait of Isabel is the portrait of a mind rather than that of a person with physical form and body, and it takes the whole novel to give the complete portrait. The description of place is likewise wrought into the story, and the mention of place brings us to a discovery which is to be made in this novel as to the changing trend in James's interests.

—CORNELIA PULSIFER KELLEY, *The Early Development of Henry James*
(University of Illinois Studies in Language and Literature 15, Nos. 1–2)
(Urbana, 1930), pp. 293–99

YVOR WINTERS

James displays in all of his more serious work an unmistakable desire to allow his characters unrestricted freedom of choice and to develop his plots out of such choice and out of consequent acts of choice to which the initial acts may lead. Now absolutely considered, no human complex is ever free from a great many elements which are without the control and even the understanding of the human participants. We may discover this fact very simply if we consider for a moment *The Portrait of a Lady.*

We may fairly say that it is chance which brings Madame Merle into the life of Isabel Archer: at any rate, the entrance of Madame Merle is a fact in itself of absolutely no ethical antecedents or significance. On the other hand, we may say that the actions of Isabel Archer are in certain respects and up to a certain point determined: she is first of all human, and is subject to the fundamental necessities of humanity; being a normal young woman, she is fairly certain to marry, for example. And if she marries, she will in the matter of choice be limited by chance— that is, she will have to choose from among the men whom she happens to know, even if we suppose it to be within her power to attract any man whom she desires. Her choice within these limits may in a sense be said to be determined—as perhaps it actually was—by a temperamental bent of her own which she fails to understand and consider, or by the facts of her personal history, which result in certain forms of knowledge and certain forms of ignorance, and which may consequently lead her to judge a situation on the basis of imperfect knowledge. The initial tragic error of Hyacinth Robinson, of *The Princess Casamassima,* for example, is conceived as a free choice made in ignorance of the essential knowledge which would have prevented it; similarly, Mrs. Wharton's finest short work, "Bunner Sisters," is conceived as a sequence of steps taken by the two protagonists into tragic knowledge, each step being made freely and apparently wisely on the basis of the imperfect knowledge held at the time it is taken.

Elements of this sort are what we call the given facts of the plot: they are the ineliminable facts of character and of initial situation. We have a certain group of particularized individuals in juxtaposition; the particularity is destiny, the juxtaposition chance. But the understanding and the will may rise in some measure superior to destiny and to chance, and when they do so, we have human victory; or they may make the effort and fail, in which case we have tragedy; or the failure having occurred, there may be a comprehension of the failure and a willed adjustment to it, in which case we have the combination of tragedy and victory. It is this combination, the representation of which Henry James especially strives to achieve.

—YVOR WINTERS, "Maule's Well, or Henry James and the Relation of Morals to Manners" (1937), *Maule's Curse: Seven Studies in the History of American Obscurantism* (Norfolk, CT: New Directions, 1938), pp. 176–77

EDWARD SACKVILLE WEST

The code of ladyhood received its first attacks (from within) just before the last war. After the war it was generally buffeted, both from within and from without; now there are few representatives of the species still extant, and they are mostly

old, living apart and—as a standard—generally unregarded. Where a lady is detected, her vulnerability is contemptuously exploited. Virtue may be its own reward, but the adage comes ill from those who flout it. What is—what was—that
virtue? To be a lady meant to possess a high degree of social responsibility and a
sensitiveness to *taste* in behaviour. It was primarily an aesthetic, only secondarily a
moral, position: the lady did certain good things because to do them was implied
by her condition, and she avoided certain others because they were (to her)
obviously ugly. If she was kind it was because she was, in the nature of her case,
disinterested. She was not expected to be an angel, but was continuously required
to be something of an artist.

In 1881 ladies were the rule, and in drawing the portrait of one of the
middle-aged, cosmopolitan man of letters that was Henry James set himself to
make explicit what novelists like Disraeli and Meredith took for granted, and to
isolate and set in relief the specific qualities of the situation. The result is by the
highest standard a most beautiful and distinguished piece of work. If, as a novel,
it is not quite in the first class, the reason lies, not in any failure to realise the
chief end, but rather in the relative weakness of two of the other characters.
Nevertheless the standard of conduct represented by Isabel Archer will not soon
be matched by any code of social behaviour we are likely to see emerge from
the opening era. Indeed, to read *The Portrait of a Lady* to-day is to take the
measure of the relational poverty to which modern men and women have condemned themselves.

Perhaps I can best establish this by reminding you briefly of the plot, which is,
generally speaking, that of almost all James's larger fictions. A beautiful young girl,
brought up in a happy, but strict, New England home, comes to England at the
invitation of her aunt, the selfish but intelligent wife of a rich old Anglo-American
banker. At the latter's country house Isabel receives attentions, first from her
cousin, Ralph Touchett, a prematurely wise and very kind invalid who hopes for
nothing but friendship from her; secondly from the local landowner, Lord Warburton, who is as good as the gold of which he disposes in so large a quantity;
thirdly from an old admirer, Caspar Goodwood, a strong silent business man who
has followed her from America and does not intend to be shaken off. But Isabel
refuses all three. Why? Because none of them touches her imagination. The Young
Girl is still in the ascendant; the Lady awaits the test of experience. This is not long
in coming. While yet in England Isabel meets a friend of her aunt's, a clever,
charming, accomplished, somewhat mysterious woman of the world, Madame
Merle—and succumbs to the romance of charm. Later, when she accompanies her
aunt to Florence, she is taken by Madame Merle to visit a friend of hers, one Gilbert
Osmond, a dilettante living in distinguished poverty with a young daughter in a
beautiful house full of precious objects picked up "on the cheap." Against the advice
of everyone, in spite of the horrified warnings of Ralph Touchett, the more discreet
approaches of Lord Warburton, and the overt attacks of Caspar Goodwood, Isabel
insists upon marrying Osmond, who, primed by Madame Merle with the information that Isabel is her uncle's heiress, has alone guessed how to appeal to her

imagination. Defiant, persuaded she is doing a fine thing, Isabel marries in haste and repents at gradual, dreadful leisure. She is not long in discovering that her husband is heartless, pig-selfish, a snob, and pettily cruel; but it takes her longer to realise that his low mind which always attributes the base motive, actually hates her for being what she is—a lady. The climax is only reached when she discovers that Pansy Osmond is her husband's illegitimate child by Madame Merle, who married Isabel to her old lover for the sake of a common convenience. At this point Isabel's isolation is complete, for she has deliberately cut herself off from all those who could, and would, help her. After Ralph Touchett's death, Goodwood makes a last appeal to Isabel to leave her odious husband and return to America with him; but she refuses, preferring to lie on the bed she has made for herself.

Such is the story, which is unfolded with Victorian leisureliness but with a serpentine guile in the "placing" of events and the juxtaposition of characters. As far as the creation of living character goes, James's later elaboration of method never enabled him to do better than here. As the years went on he took mother-of-pearl opera-glasses to look at things he could already see quite clearly. The result was a fascinatingly absolute completeness of detail and a soft yet bright light beautifully diffused over the whole canvas—but at the cost of lively impact and of clear-cut dialogue. It is possible that at least once (in *The Wings of the Dove*) James treated a situation with wider and deeper implications and an even greater intrinsic pathos; he never told a more poignant story with more perception and directness.

The poignancy lies in the sweetness of Isabel's character and the brutal disillusionment to which her Bovarysme exposes it. She may have "enjoyed puzzling a lord," but she declined to marry even the nicest of them. To have chosen so much—so very much—worse would seem to argue a failure of intelligence. But this is exactly the crux of James's vision of Isabel's character, for we are told quite early in the book that her view of life reposed on a considerable self-esteem. Now innocence such as hers is made doubly vulnerable by this quality, which creates a vicious time-lag after innocence has been destroyed. So that, even when Osmond sneered most outrageously at her, "she still wished to justify herself; he had the power, in an extraordinary degree, of making her feel this need. *There was something in her imagination he could always appeal to against her judgment.*" (Italics mine.) That something was the romantic dream which such characters as Isabel never wholly relinquish.

Such dreams, however, have nothing to do with being a lady, and life would in any case have posed Isabel some problem or other involving that conception of how to behave. It was not for nothing that James was steeped in French literature, and this novel in especial rings with the sharp, clear voices of La Bruyère and La Rochefoucauld, as well as the graver tones of Corneille. For the Lady is a Cornelian conception and *The Portrait* a typically Cornelian tragedy. Yet these sacrifices have concomitant satisfactions, and Isabel rightly felt herself to be "in a better position for appreciating people than they are for appreciating you." And even in the ultimate abyss of disillusion, during her last meeting with the woman who had grossly betrayed her friendship, she enjoyed the luxury of silence, where mere words would have spelt a vulgar revenge. Such private subtleties are the reward of a Cornelian conception of duty being to embrace danger and unhappiness in the aesthetic fulfillment of personality.

"L'esthétique est une justice supérieure," said Flaubert. Superior or not, Henry James is a novelist who never flinches from judging his characters. Neither in this book nor elsewhere does he pretend to impartiality; we are told, in no uncertain terms, as La Rochefoucauld would have told us, what to think of his people. This, where the novelist is quite certain of his ground, may be a gain; where he is not, it merely creates prejudice. No one is likely to object to the way in which the Touchetts, Madame Merle, Henrietta Stackpole, the Warburton family, or Isabel herself are presented. Caspar Goodwood and Gilbert Osmond are less completely successful. The former, intended to seem stiff, is in effect wooden; while in Osmond, carefully and fairly as he is drawn, we are conscious of being led up the garden path of an ever so dim theatricality; which is, of course, disappointing. In fact the best portrait of Osmond is the shadow he casts on Isabel herself. Evil is contagious, and what we are permitted to see of Osmond's ill effects on his wife is among the many evidences we possess of James's sensitiveness to what Hazlitt called "the air of truth."

To quote La Rochefoucauld: "When loyalty in love does violence to our feelings, it is no better than disloyalty." This is very un-Cornelian and no lady would agree with it; yet Isabel (and here is one of the incidental beauties of this rich novel) allowed poor Ralph, on his deathbed, to perceive, though not to hear, that she loved him more than anyone, at long last. They discuss death and Ralph says: "Dear Isabel, life is better, for in life there is love. Death is good—but there's no love."

So Isabel chose life, and the love that is disclosed by the renunciation of love. There is no "full close" to this novel and the scene of Goodwood's final appeal is not among the best in the book. The last page flings open the door on to a room as empty as the heart that has just left it. We are left to imagine the years of silent resignation and gnawing doubt—for she will sometimes have doubted—that must have followed Isabel's return to Italy and her husband. Here, in this unresolved and diminishing chord, we feel some of that ineffable quality of mystery that envelops two of Balzac's finest stories—"Le Lys dans la vallée" and "Le Curé de village." Mme. de Mortsauf ended by preferring death to the "love" of her impossible husband (a better man, however, than Gilbert Osmond); but Mme. Graslin, fortified by the Catholic religion and the ruthless support of the priest who knew her secret, found a better way of sticking it out. We may indulge the hope that, on her return to Italy, Isabel may have solaced her loneliness with care for the peasants around her. In any case, all these heroines have one important quality in common: they are, first and foremost, ladies, and know how not to notice the rolling eye of the Devil, even when he speaks sweetest reason.

—EDWARD SACKVILLE WEST, "Books in General," *New Statesman and Nation,*
April 17, 1943, p. 259

GRAHAM GREENE

'The conception of a certain young lady affronting her destiny'—that is how Henry James described the subject of this book, for which he felt, next to *The Ambassadors,* the greatest personal tenderness. In his wonderful preface (for no other book in the collected edition of his works did he write a preface so rich in revelations and memories) he compares *The Portrait of a Lady* several times to a building, and it is as a great, leisurely built cathedral that one thinks of it, with immense smooth pillars, side-chapels, and aisles, and a dark crypt where Ralph Touchett lies in marble like a crusader with his feet crossed to show that he has seen the Holy Land; sometimes, indeed, it may seem to us too ample a shrine for one portrait until we remember that this master-craftsman always has his reasons: those huge pillars are required to bear the weight of Time (that dark backward and abysm that is the novelist's abiding problem): the succession of side-chapels are all designed to cast their particular light upon the high altar: no vista is without its ambiguous purpose. The whole building, indeed, is a triumph of architectural planning: the prentice hand which had already produced some works—*Roderick Hudson* and *The American*—impressive if clumsy, and others—*The Europeans* and *Washington Square*—graceful if slight, had at last learnt the whole secret of planning for permanence. And the subject? 'A certain young woman affronting her destiny.' Does it perhaps still, at first thought, seem a little inadequate?

The answer, of course, is that it all depends on the destiny, and about the destiny Henry James has in his preface nothing to tell us. He is always something of a conjurer in these prefaces: he seems ready to disclose everything—the source of his story: the technique of its writing: even the room in which he settles down to work and the noises of the street outside. Sometimes he blinds the reader with a bold sleight of hand, calling, for example, *The Turn of the Screw* 'a fairy-tale pure and simple'. We must always remain on our guard while reading these prefaces, for at a certain level no writer has really disclosed less.

The plot in the case of this novel is far from being an original one: it is as if James, looking round for the events which were to bring his young woman, Isabel Archer, into play, had taken the first to hand: a fortune-hunter, the fortune-hunter's unscrupulous mistress, and a young American heiress caught in the meshes of a loveless marriage. (He was to use almost identically the same plot but with deeper implications and more elaborate undertones in *The Wings of the Dove.*) We can almost see the young James laying down some popular three-decker of the period in his Roman or Venetian lodgings and wondering. 'What could I do with even that story?' For a plot after all is only the machinery—the machinery which will show the young woman (what young woman?) affronting her destiny (but what destiny?). In his preface, apparently so revealing, James has no answer to these questions. Nor is there anything there which will help us to guess what element it was in the melodramatic plot that attracted the young writer at this moment when he came first into his full powers as a novelist, and again years later when as an old man he set to work to crown his career with the three poetic masterpieces, *The Wings of the Dove, The Ambassadors,* and *The Golden Bowl.*

The first question is the least important and we have the answer in Isabel Archer's relationship to Milly Theale in *The Wings of the Dove:* it is not only their predicament which is the same, or nearly so (Milly's fortune-hunter, Merton Densher, was enriched by the later James with a conscience, a depth of character, a dignity in his corruption that Gilbert Osmond lacks: indeed in the later book it is the fortune-hunter who steals the tragedy, for Milly dies and it is the living whom we pity): the two women are identical. Milly Theale, if it had not been for her fatal sickness, would have affronted the same destiny and met the same fate as Isabel Archer: the courage, the generosity, the confidence, and inexperience belong to the same character, and James has disclosed to us the source of the later portrait— his young and much-loved cousin Mary Temple who died of tuberculosis at twenty-four. This girl of infinite potentiality, whose gay sad troubled letters can be read in *Notes of a Son and Brother,* haunted his memory like a legend; it was as if her image stood for everything that had been graceful, charming, happy in youth—'the whole world of the old New York, that of the earlier dancing years'—everything that was to be betrayed by life. We have only to compare these pages of his autobiography, full of air and space and light, in which the figures of the son and brother, the Albany uncles, the beloved cousin, move like the pastoral figures in a Poussin landscape, with his description of America when he revisited the States in his middle age, to see how far he had travelled, how life had closed in. In his fiction he travelled even farther. In his magnificent last short story, 'The Jolly Corner,' Brydon, the returned expatriate, finds his old New York house haunted by the ghost of himself, the self he would have become if he had remained in America. The vision is pursued by the unwitting Brydon from room to room until finally it is brought to bay under the fanlight in the hall and presents a face 'evil, odious, blatant, vulgar'. At that moment one remembers what James also remembered: 'the springtime of '65 as it breathed through Denton streets', the summer twilight sailing back from Newport, Mary Temple.

> In none of the company was the note so clear as in this rarest, though at the same time symptomatically or ominously palest, flower of the stem; who was natural at more points and about more things, with a greater sense of freedom and ease and reach of horizon than any of the others dreamed of. They had that way, delightfully, with the small, after all, and the common matters—while she had it with those too, but with the great and rare ones over and above; so that she was to remain for us the very figure and image of a felt interest in life, an interest as magnanimously farspread, or as familiarly and exquisitely fixed, as her splendid shifting sensibility, moral, personal, nervous, and having at once such noble flights and such touchingly discouraged drops, such graces of indifference and inconsequence, might at any moment determine. She was really to remain, for our appreciation, the supreme case of a taste for life as life, as personal living; of an endlessly active and yet

somehow a careless, an illusionless, a sublimely forewarned curiosity about it: something that made her, slim and fair and quick, all straightness and charming tossed head, with long light and yet almost sliding steps and a large light postponing, renouncing laugh, the very muse or amateur priestess of rash speculation.

Even if we had not James's own word for it, we could never doubt that here is the source: the fork of his imagination was struck and went on sounding. Mary Temple, of course, never affronted her destiny: she was betrayed quite simply by her body, and James uses words of her that he could as well have used of Milly Theale dying in her Venetian palace—'death at the last was dreadful to her; she would have given anything to live', but isn't it significant that whenever an imaginary future is conceived for this brave spontaneous young woman it always ends in betrayal? Milly Theale escapes from her betrayal simply by dying; Isabel Archer, tied for life to Gilbert Osmond—that precious vulgarian, cold as a fishmonger's slab—is deserted even by her creator. For how are we to understand the ambiguity of the closing pages when Isabel's friend, Henrietta Stackpole, tries to comfort the faithful and despairing 'follower' (this word surely best describes Caspar Goodwood's relationship to Isabel)?

> 'Look here, Mr. Goodwood,' she said; 'just you wait!'
> On which he looked up at her—but only to guess, from her face, with a revulsion, that she simply meant he was young. She stood shining at him with that cheap comfort, and it added, on the spot, thirty years to his life. She walked him away with her, however, as if she had given him now the key to patience.

It is as if James, too, were handing his more casual readers the key to patience, while at the same time asserting between the lines that there is no way out of the inevitable betrayal except the way that Milly Theale and Mary Temple took involuntarily. There is no possibility of a happy ending: this is surely what James always tells us, not with the despairing larger-than-life gesture of a romantic novelist but with a kind of bitter precision. He presents us with a theorem, but it is we who have to work out the meaning of x and discover that x equals no-way-out. It is part of the permanent fascination of his style that he never does all the work for us, and there will always be careless mathematicians prepared to argue the meaning of that other ambiguous ending, when Merton Densher, having gained a fortune with Milly Theale's death, is left alone with his mistress, Kate Croy, who had planned it all, just as Mme Merle had planned Isabel's betrayal.

> He heard her out in stillness, watching her face but not moving. Then he only said: 'I'll marry you, mind you, in an hour.'
> 'As we were?'
> 'As we were.'
> But she turned to the door, and her headshake was now the end. 'We shall never be again as we were!'

Some of James's critics have preferred to ignore the real destiny of his characters, and they can produce many of his false revealing statements to support them; he has been multitudinously discussed as a social novelist primarily concerned with the international scene, with the impact of the Old World on the New. It is true the innocent figure is nearly always American (Roderick Hudson, Newman, Isabel and Milly, Maggie Verver and her father), but the corrupted characters—the vehicles for a sense of evil unsurpassed by the theological novelists of our day, M. Mauriac or M. Bernanos—are also American: Mme Merle, Gilbert Osmond, Kate Croy, Merton Densher, Charlotte Stant. His characters are mainly American, simply because James himself was American.

No, it was only on the superficial level of plot, one feels, that James was interested in the American visitor; what deeply interested him, what was indeed his ruling passion, was the idea of treachery, the 'Judas complex'. In a very early novel which he never reprinted, *Watch and Ward,* James dealt with the blackmailer, the man enabled to betray because of his intimate knowledge. As he proceeded in his career he shed the more obvious melodramatic trappings of betrayal, and in *The Portrait of a Lady,* melodrama is at the point of vanishing. What was to follow was only to be the turning of the screw. Isabel Archer was betrayed by little more than an acquaintance; Milly Theale by her dearest friend; until we reach the complicated culmination of treacheries in *The Golden Bowl.* But how many turns and twists of betrayal we could follow, had we space and time, between *Watch and Ward* and that grand climax!

This then is the destiny that not only the young women affront—you must betray or, more fortunately perhaps, you must be betrayed. A few—James himself, Ralph Touchett in this novel, Mrs. Assingham in *The Golden Bowl*—will simply sadly watch. We shall never know what it was at the very start of life that so deeply impressed on the young James's mind this sense of treachery; but when we remember how patiently and faithfully throughout his life he drew the portrait of one young woman who died, one wonders whether it was just simply a death that opened his eyes to the inherent disappointment of existence, the betrayal of hope. The eyes once open, the material need never fail him. He could sit there, an ageing honoured man in Lamb House, Rye, and hear the footsteps of the traitors and their victims going endlessly by on the pavement. It is of James himself that we think when we read in *The Portrait of a Lady* of Ralph Touchett's melancholy vigil in the big house in Winchester Square:

> The square was still, the house was still; when he raised one of the windows of the dining-room to let in the air he heard the slow creak of the boots of a lone constable. His own step, in the empty place, seemed loud and sonorous; some of the carpets had been raised, and whenever he moved he roused a melancholy echo. He sat down in one of the armchairs; the big dark dining table twinkled here and there in the small candle-light; the pictures on the wall, all of them very brown, looked vague and incoherent. There was a ghostly presence as of dinners long since digested, of table-talk that had lost

its actuality. This hint of the supernatural perhaps had something to do with the fact that his imagination took a flight and that he remained in his chair a long time beyond the hour at which he should have been in bed; doing nothing, not even reading the evening paper. I say he did nothing, and I maintain the phrase in the face of the fact that he thought at these moments of Isabel.

—GRAHAM GREENE, "Introduction" to *The Portrait of a Lady* (Oxford: Oxford University Press, 1947), pp. iv–ix

F. R. LEAVIS

⟨. . .⟩ *The Portrait of a Lady* is not only a great and brilliant novel; it belongs, where the critical study and discussion of fiction are concerned, to the list of essential texts. Its value in such use—in discussion directed at establishing the nature and procedures of intelligent criticism—is rich and diverse. For an elementary exercise, compare *The Portrait of a Lady* with *The Egoist:* there is no better way of putting Meredith (now being revived as the poet-novelist of 'high civilization') in his place. The difference between supremely intelligent art, with its genuine and functional wit and poetry, and what Meredith offers is sufficiently plain: the judgments are inevitable.

It is only for the sake of an elementary exercise that one brings *The Portrait of a Lady* and *The Egoist* together. The comparison with *Daniel Deronda* is another matter. That there is an essential relation between the two books will hardly be disputed by anyone who knows them both. James had, and retained throughout his life, an intense admiration for *Daniel Deronda,* and within three years of writing his critique of it, the 'Conversation', began *The Portrait of a Lady.* But no such extraneous knowledge is necessary to make the fact of the relation obvious to anyone in whose mind the two novels are present together. To explore that relation is to contemplate an illuminating instance of 'influence', involving two great books by very unlike authors; to open for study a central line of tradition; and to be challenged to make comparative judgments of a most delicate kind.

What James does with the Gwendolen-Grandcourt theme is highly characteristic. Gwendolen Harleth is driven into accepting Grandcourt by economic pressure, and incurs, in consequence, remorse and a painful initiation into moral maturity. James eliminates the economic pressure and the agonized conscience together. Isabel Archer, as a result of Ralph Touchett's intervention with his dying father, is made independent: Ralph, in love with her love of life, her high (if necessarily vague) expectation of it, and her self-confident vitality of the ideal American girl, wants to 'see what she will do'. Mr. Yvor Winters, in *Maule's Curse,* sees her as representing James's preoccupation with pure 'ethical sensibility': she is to make a free 'ethical choice'. Actually, of course, there is a patent irony. Ralph

Touchett has to recognize that the arrangement that was to set her free for flight has made her worth acquiring, for cage-life, by the petty æsthete-egotist whom he has never thought of as capable of interesting her. Isabel herself has to recognize that when she thought she was supremely the free agent she was being made use of, and that her choice was something managed for their own convenience, and at her expense, by Gilbert Osmond and Madame Merle. Further, Mr. Matthiessen, I think, is undoubtedly right in his view (see *Henry James: The Major Phase*) that James intends a more general irony—an irony directed against the optimistic idealism of the American transcendental tradition.

The weakness of the book (I have suggested, in discussing George Eliot earlier in these pages) is that this intention has lost its force in a radical ambiguity or inconsistency. James admires his American heroine too much to permit himself a clear and consistent irony. It isn't unfair to say that she behaves like a silly and wilful girl. She isn't urged into her disastrous marriage, as Gwendolen Harleth is, by the pressure of all those whom she most loves and respects. On the contrary, all Isabel Archer's friends warn her against Osmond: Ralph Touchett's quietly contemptuous placing of him should, we feel, have been sufficient. But she persists in her sublime confidence that she knows better. Yet we are not allowed to feel that the sympathy claimed for her is to have any critical or ironical admixture. When, after her marriage, the disastrous nature of her mistake has become generally known, she is regarded by everyone as an exalted tragic victim, an object for pure compassion; there is no hint of any qualifying criticism. In short, the implicit valuation of her that we are expected to endorse is at odds with the general ironic intention we must suppose James to have entertained.

When we ask how he can have rested in such a radical incoherence, the answer lies, I think, in his unawareness of his relation to George Eliot. He had been profoundly impressed by the irony of Gwendolen's situation after her marriage, and he failed to recognize how large a part of his 'inspiration' in *The Portrait of a Lady* was the desire to produce a similar irony. The unrecognized impulsion had a determining imaginative influence; he reproduced the ironic situation, but failed to ground it in a justifying fable. If we don't put our finger on the inconsistency at first, it is because of the way in which James works in terms of brilliant dramatic scenes, cunningly chosen; scenes done with a characteristic art, all the resources of which are devoted to satisfying us with very little in the way of inward realization of Isabel and to keeping us interested in guessing from outside what is going on inside—in trying to construct the psychological and moral substance of the action from a minimum of data.

The weakness revealed in *The Portrait of a Lady* when we focus on the heroine and ponder the theme as it immediately concerns her might seem to be fatal to the claims of the book as a work of art. It is, nevertheless, a great novel: not only is it brilliant and full of life; when all qualifications have been urged, we can still see close and coherent organization—we have still a significant whole. To produce adequate grounds for this judgment we have only to consider *The Portrait of a Lady* in its quality of Jamesian drama on the 'international theme'—for it is that; it belongs with its predecessors, *Roderick Hudson* and *The Europeans*. Its greatness is a matter of the inclusive harmony it represents—the vital poise between the diverse tendencies and impulsions that make up James's complex reaction to the interplay, in his experience, of the differing civilizations.

In Isabel Archer we have again the supremacy of the American girl; but in her we can recognize a real superiority, even if, pondering it critically, we judge it to depend on a large measure of idealization. Her freedom in the face of English conventions appears—and she is a firmly realized presence for us—as a true emancipation of spirit. Unlike Daisy Miller she has her own superior code, in her scruple, her self-respect and her sensitiveness; she is educated and highly intelligent. She is more idealized, it is true, than Bessie Alden. Nevertheless, however idealized, and whatever I may have said in comparing her with Gwendolen Harleth, she is convincing and impressive: the idealization stands for a true fineness, worthily imagined by James.

Lord Warburton, on the other hand, is very much superior to Lord Lambeth of 'An International Episode'. He is far from stupid or impermeable to ideas ('he had a lively grey eye'), and he sees the order to which he belongs as standing for something more than precedence and privilege. In fact, that order is still in some ways idealized in *The Portrait of a Lady,* and the presentation of it has a mellow fulness that has much to do with the effect of rich beauty characterizing the book. The opening scene, on the lawn, giving us, with a ripe and subtle art that at once proclaims a great master, the old American banker and his company against the background of country-house, sets the tone. He admires and respects Lord War-burton and Lord Warburton's world, while, at the same time, the quite different standards he himself represents (he remains an American after thirty successful years in England), and the free play of mind and spirit that, with his son, he introduces into that world, constitutes an implicit criticism of it. We have here a sufficient hint at the way in which, in the total effect of the book, the idealization and the criticism are reconciled.

The admirableness of Lord Warburton and the impressiveness of his world, as we are made to feel them, are essential to the significance of Isabel's negative choice. That her rejection of them doesn't strike us as the least capricious, but as an act of radically ethical judgment, is a tribute to the reality with which James has invested her (she is *not,* we must concede, Gwendolen Harleth):

> At the risk of adding to the evidence of her self-sufficiency it must be said that there had been moments when this possibility of admiration by a personage represented to her an aggression almost to the degree of an affront, quite to the degree of an inconvenience. She had never yet known a personage; there had been no personages, in this sense, in her life; there were probably none such at all in her native land. When she had thought of individual eminence she had thought of it on the basis of character and wit—of what one might like in a gentleman's mind and in his talk. She herself was a character—she couldn't help being aware of that; and hitherto her visions of a completed conscious-ness had concerned themselves largely with moral images—things as to which

the question would be whether they pleased her sublime soul. Lord Warburton loomed up before her, largely and brightly, as a collection of attributes
and powers which were not to be measured by this simple rule, but which
demanded a different sort of appreciation—an appreciation that the girl, with
her habit of judging quickly and freely, felt she lacked the patience to bestow.
He appeared to demand of her something that no one else, as it were, had
presumed to do. What she felt was that a territorial, a political, a social
magnate had conceived the design of drawing her into the system in which he
rather invidiously lived and moved. A certain instinct, not imperious, but
persuasive, told her to resist—murmured to her that virtually she had a
system and an orbit of her own.

James goes on immediately to tell us that there was 'a young man lately come
from America who had no system at all'. This, in the guise of Caspar Goodwood
from New England, is the American business-man. He represents what America
has to offer Isabel—stark unpliant integrity and self-reliant practical will, as opposed
to 'system' and the civilized graces. 'His jaw was too square and set and his figure
too straight and stiff: these things suggested a want of easy consonance with the
deeper rhythms of life'. But in spite of this promising description he is
sentimentalized—in so far as he is 'there' at all—and he is one of the weaknesses
of the book. However, the ineffectualness of the intention he stands for leaves
Isabel's rejection of Lord Warburton all its significance.

This significance is beautifully intimated in such touches as the lapse (it is not
unique) that Lord Warburton is guilty of on the occasion of Mrs. Touchett's forbidding Isabel to stay up alone with the gentlemen (Chapter VII):

> 'Need I go, dear aunt? I'll come up in half an hour.'
> 'It is impossible I should wait for you,' Mrs. Touchett answered.
> 'Ah, you needn't wait! Ralph will light my candle,' Isabel gaily engaged.
> 'I'll light your candle; do let me light your candle, Miss Archer!' Lord
> Warburton exclaimed. 'Only I beg it shall not be before midnight.'
> Mrs. Touchett fixed her bright little eyes upon him a moment and
> transferred them coldly to her niece.

Warburton would not have used this tone to an English girl. Perceiving that she
has the American freedom where the English *convenances* are concerned, he
immediately classifies her as 'an American girl', and slips into a manner that would
have been in place with Henrietta Stackpole, the bright young journalist who
habitually 'walks in without knocking at the door'. It shocks us, such is the power of
James's art. It shocks us more than it shocks Isabel, and it serves none the less for
that to bring to a concrete point for us the rightness of her decision against him. For
it reveals to us an obtuse complacency, in assuming which for a moment Lord
Warburton seems to reveal the spirit of the 'system' he belongs to.

This passage has its retro-active parallel in the later exchange (Chapter X)
between Ralph Touchett and Henrietta, in which he pretends, to her confusion, to
think that she is making love to him. Ralph's 'lapse' doesn't matter. It merely leads

us to say that he knows how to treat Henrietta, just as he knows how to treat everyone. For Ralph Touchett is the centre, the key-figure, of James's 'system'—the poise or harmony I have spoken of as characterizing *The Portrait of a Lady*. He is neither American nor English—or he is both: that is, he combines the advantages, while being free from the limitations. He can place everyone, and represents the ideal civilization that James found in no country.

He understands why Isabel likes Henrietta, but, when told that Henrietta carries in her garments 'the strong, sweet, fresh odour' of her great country, he replies: she 'does smell of the Future—it almost knocks one down!' For her he is just another expatriate, like Osmond. And when Isabel asks the Parisian Americans, whom, in their obviousness, she *can* place, 'You all live this way, but what does it lead to?', Mrs. Touchett, placing herself, 'thought the question worthy of Henrietta Stackpole'. The discriminations, in fact, are established with beautiful precision all along the scale. Isabel herself notices that Ralph seems to resemble Osmond in having a fastidious taste—and that yet there is a difference. Ralph himself, in placing Osmond for her (she, of course, doesn't take it in, and that is the tragic irony), explains what it is: 'He has a great dread of vulgarity; that's his special line; he hasn't any other that I know of'. He places Madame Merle too—again without effect:

'Ah, with Madame Merle you may go anywhere *de confiance,'* said Ralph. 'She knows none but the best people.'

This will suffice to indicate the kind of essential organization that makes *The Portrait of a Lady,* for all the critical points I made about it in discussing George Eliot, a great book. Its greatness derives from his peculiar genius and experience, and it embodies an organization of his vital interests. These interests inform everything in it: the wit, the dialogue, the plot, the characterization.

The creative wealth of the book is all distinctively Jamesian. Madame Merle, for instance, couldn't have been done by George Eliot. The vision here is Isabel's, who hasn't yet seen through her:

She had become too flexible, too useful, was too ripe and too final. She was in a word too perfectly the social animal that man and woman are supposed to have been intended to be; and she had rid herself of every remnant of that tonic wildness which we may assume to have belonged even to the most amiable persons in the ages before country-house life was the fashion. Isabel found it difficult to think of her in any detachment or privacy, she existed only in her relations, direct or indirect, with her fellow mortals. One might wonder what commerce she could possibly hold with her own spirit. One always ended, however, by feeling that a charming surface doesn't necessarily prove one superficial; this was an illusion in which, in one's youth, one had but just escaped being nourished. Madame Merle was not superficial—not she. She was deep . . .

She represents, that is, a social 'civilization' ('the great round world itself') that is not of the kind James himself is after (just as she is, with Osmond, the complete expatriate who has none of the American virtues). Then there is Mrs. Touchett, who reminds us of an American type we meet in some of Lawrence's best work (*St. Mawr*, for instance). James presents her with his characteristic wit—which, as I have said, is no mere surface-habit of expression: 'The edges of her conduct were so very clear-cut that for susceptible persons it sometimes had a knife-like effect'. Henrietta Stackpole is another American type, perfectly done—marvellously escaping the effect of caricature, and remaining for all her portentous representativeness, sufficiently sympathetic. Then there is Osmond's sister, the Countess Gemini, 'a lady who had so mismanaged her improprieties that they had ceased to hang together at all . . . and had become the mere floating fragments of a wrecked renown, incommoding social circulation', and who would plunge into a lucid conversation 'as a poodle plunges after a thrown stick'.

The Countess Gemini, though so well done, is a weakness in the book, in the sense that she is too simply there to serve as a piece of machinery. She alone can reveal to Isabel the clandestine relations of Osmond and Madame Merle, and the fact that Pansy is their daughter, and she is given no sufficient motives for performing the service. Pansy herself raises the question of James's attitude toward the pure protected *jeune fille* (the 'blank page'), a type to which he seems curiously drawn. In *The Awkward Age* he shows the good little Aggie, the foil to Nanda, developing after marriage into something approaching, at the level of Edwardian smart society, a vulgar trollop: and we readily accept the implication that, in such a *milieu*, the development follows naturally out of such 'innocence'. In *The Ambassadors* he seems to confirm this implication by giving the decidedly not innocent Madame Vionnet another carefully guarded 'blank page' for daughter.

Though Pansy serves obvious functions as machinery in the relations between Isabel and Osmond, her presence in the book has, in addition, some point. As a representative figure, 'the white flower of cultivated sweetness', she pairs in contrast with Henrietta Stackpole, the embodiment of a quite different innocence—a robust American innocence that thrives on free exposure to the world. She brings us, in fact, to the general observation that almost all the characters can be seen to have, in the same way, their values and significances in a total scheme. For though *The Portrait of a Lady* is on so much larger a scale than *The Europeans,* and because of its complexity doesn't invite the description of 'moral fable', it is similarly organized: it is all intensely significant. It offers no largesse of irrelevant 'life'; its vitality is wholly that of art.

—F. R. LEAVIS, "*The Portrait of a Lady* Reprinted," *Scrutiny* 15, No. 3
(Summer 1948): 235–40

RICHARD CHASE

Without attempting any sort of full discussion of Isabel and her troubles, one may note that she sees reality as the romancer sees it. This is obvious as a general proposition, since Isabel is patently romantic in the sense that she has highly imaginative dreams which prove to be beyond the possibility of fulfillment. A realistic young woman, or, for that matter, a conventionally romantic one, would have accepted Lord Warburton as a good catch, for he is, after all, an excellent man as well as a rich and noble lord. But Isabel has higher ideals than any she thinks can be realized by a life with Lord Warburton. Her personal romance includes strenuous abstractions that lead her to aspire to far more than the conventional romance of marrying an English nobleman. She therefore perversely and no doubt quite mistakenly decides that to marry Lord Warburton would be to "escape" her "fate." "I can't escape unhappiness," she says. "In marrying you I shall be trying to." And she continues by saying that by marrying Lord Warburton she would be "turning away," "separating" herself from life, "from the usual chances and dangers, from what most people know and suffer." Lord Warburton's answer is one that would in the main turn out to be true: "I don't offer you any exoneration from life or from any chances or dangers whatever." He is brought by Isabel's behavior to a true understanding of her, and he exclaims, "I never saw a person judge things on such theoretic grounds." Her theory is that he is merely "a collection of attributes and powers," but this is clearly a false theory. Despite his being a hereditary nobleman and so, bound to the formalities and duties of his station in life, he presents himself to her with perfect candor as a man, and not a lord, who needs and desires her. Thus Isabel's vague democratic objections to English aristocracy, which in any case she seems generally to admire, are not the real reason why she rejects Lord Warburton. Nor when she does marry does she choose a man notable for democracy. She rejects Lord Warburton at the behest of her puritan spirituality, which leads her to flee from the mere physical and social realities of life as these would be should she marry him. Perversely and mistakenly, her argument is that marriage to Lord Warburton would exempt her from life. Better a collection of attributes and powers (which in any case Lord Warburton is not) than a collection of sterile tastes and appetites, which Gilbert Osmond certainly is. But Isabel does not see Osmond for what he is until too late. (I am assuming here as elsewhere that Isabel's choice is, for all practical purposes, between Warburton and Osmond. Ralph is in love with her, but his illness disqualifies him. The persistent Caspar Goodwood presents himself at intervals, but Isabel does not see him as an actual possibility. She seems to conceive of him as worthy but as rather stodgy in his conventional Massachusetts way. She scarcely thinks of him as being momentously on the scene until at the very end of the novel when he proposes to rescue her from Osmond and, in his vehemence, frightens her with his masculine aggressiveness by giving her, so far as the reader knows, her only kiss.)

How is it that the image Osmond presents to the world so easily commands Isabel's assent? This is a hard problem, but the answer may be suggested by observing that although Isabel's vision of things is neither that of self-interested common sense nor that of worldly romance in which poor girls marry great lords, it emphatically is that of the romance associated with the American tradition of puritanism and transcendentalism. Isabel subscribes to the American romance of the self. She believes that the self finds fulfillment either in its own isolated integrity or on a more or less transcendent ground where the contending forces of good and evil are symbolized abstractions. She sees her fate as a spiritual melodrama. Her grasp of reality, though manifold in its presumptions, is unstable, and her desire for experience is ambivalent. She rejects Lord Warburton ostensibly because she fears that marrying him will exempt her from life. But Ralph Touchett, who often speaks with the wisdom of the author, has no trouble in securing a contradictory admission from his amusing and perplexing cousin. At the end of a lengthy dialogue about her rejection of Lord Warburton, Ralph conjectures, "You want to drain the cup of experience," and gets out of Isabel this surprising answer, "No, I don't wish to touch the cup of experience. It's a poisoned drink! I only want to see for myself." To which Ralph adds a comment in the partial truth of which we may see a link between Isabel and Osmond: "You want to see, but not to feel."

Ralph has hit upon a truth about his cousin. The kind of cold, amoral aloofness, the possibly morbid passion for observing life at a distance—these are real traits of Isabel's character. True, they are no more than strong strands in her fabric. But they are strong enough so that she responds to Osmond's talk about how "one ought to make one's life a work of art," without being aware of the inhumanity and the withering aestheticism such an idea may imply. Only when it is too late does she discover the cold malignancy of her husband. Only too late does she see that, apart from his need of the money she has inherited from her uncle, she is cherished by Osmond only to the extent that he can consider her another art object in his collection. Only too late does she understand the subtle corruption that leads Osmond to try to arrange his daughter's education so as to make her life "a work of art." Listening to Osmond's plans for Pansy's schooling, Isabel seems to see at last "how far her husband's desire to be effective was capable of going—to the point of playing theoretic tricks on the delicate organism of his daughter." In this way Isabel, who is herself every bit the theorist Lord Warburton accused her of being, comes to understand the perverse puritan impulse which Hawthorne called "the Unpardonable Sin." The sin is the same whether one's cold, theoretical manipulation of others has an aesthetic motive or as with Hawthorne's Chillingworth or Ethan Brand a quasi-scientific one.

Isabel's romance of the self, as was suggested above, requires that self-fulfillment shall take place only at a high level of abstraction, where the disinterested pursuit of perfection may be carried on. And although Ralph Touchett warns his cousin that Osmond is a "sterile aesthete," she sees in him at once the high priest, the devoted custodian, and martyr of the life of perfection. She is very far from believing that the ordinary vulgar circumstances of one's life have anything to do with one's self. She finds it inconceivable and rather degrading that anyone should suppose the self to be in any sort of dialectic with the mere things one is surrounded by. In Chapter 19 there occurs an important exchange between Madame Merle and Isabel on this point. They have been talking about the inevitable "young man with a mustache" who must figure in some way in every young woman's life. Madame Merle speculatively inquires whether Isabel's "young man with a mustache" has a "castle in the Apennines" or "an ugly brick house in Fortieth Street." And when

Isabel says characteristically, "I don't care anything about his house," Madame Merle replies, "That's very crude of you." And she continues by saying,

> There's no such thing as an isolated man or woman; we're each of us made up of some cluster of appurtenances. What shall we call our "self"? Where does it begin? where does it end? It overflows into everything that belongs to us—and then it flows back again. I know a large part of myself is in the clothes I choose to wear. I've a great respect for *things!* One's self—for other people—is one's expression of one's self; and one's house, one's furniture, one's garments, the books one reads, the company one keeps—these things are all expressive.

This bit of worldly wisdom strikes Isabel as being worldly, all too worldly, but not as being wisdom. "I don't agree with you," she says. "I think just the other way. I don't know whether I succeed in expressing myself, but I know that nothing else expresses me. Nothing that belongs to me is any measure of me; everything's on the contrary a limit, a barrier, and a perfectly arbitrary one." To find the fulfillment of self through superiority to mere things and without attention to what others may think about what one does—this is the feat Isabel supposes Osmond to have accomplished. Actually as she comes tragically to see, Osmond is above all men enslaved by things and by what he supposes others to be thinking of him. "She had thought it a grand indifference, an exquisite independence. But indifference was really the last of his qualities; she had never seen anyone who thought so much of others."

The moral world shared by Isabel and Osmond—a world in which Lord Warburton has no place—is that of the high Emersonian self-culture. In the sordid elegance of Osmond's implacably willed hedonism we discover the final possibilities of corruption in this culture, which is of course no less subject to corruption than any other moral idealism. In Isabel's unhappy career we estimate the tragic implications of an idealism that in effect directs one to seek the rewards of the fully "lived life" without descending from one's high pedestal into its actual conditions. In Isabel's sincere presentation of her essentially spiritual quest as a quest for a real involvement in "the usual chances and dangers" of life lies the tragic irony of the story. And it has, furthermore, the advantage of verisimilitude since that is how an ambitious young woman in the latter part of the nineteenth century—spiritual puritan though she might be—would conceive of her quest, knowing it to be no longer inevitably the part of woman to isolate herself from the world either because of religious conviction or in acquiescence to the conventions about woman's place.

Isabel Archer may be said to have the imagination of romance most notably in the sense that she responds to character intensely only when it conceives of itself at a high level of abstraction and when its acts are symbolic of ideal values. When this imagination is confronted by an appealingly complex human being, such as Lord Warburton, it sees only "a collection of attributes and powers." Like the romancer, Isabel refuses to impute significance to human actions unless they are conceived as being exempt from the ordinary circumstances of life, whereas the genuine novelist sees in ordinary circumstances the inescapable root condition of significant actions.

So, to carry the analogy only one step along, James in the end brings Isabel's point of view around from that of the romancer to that of the novelist. Like *The Blithedale Romance, The Portrait of a Lady* explores the limits of romance. But whereas Hawthorne seems to admit that he cannot be the true novelist and thus surrenders the imagination of the novelist to that of the romancer, James does the opposite, affirming the primacy of the novelist's imagination. But though he rejects romance as a moral view of the world, he assimilates into the very substance of the novel, by means of metaphor and the charm of the heroine herself, the appeal of romance. Thus he is able to meet superabundantly the requirement for the novel which he calls in the Preface to *The American* satisfying "our general sense of the ways things happen" and at the same time he is able to provide the novel with the poetry of romance.

—RICHARD CHASE, "The Lesson of the Master: *The Portrait of a Lady,"*
The American Novel and Its Tradition (Garden City, NY: Doubleday, 1957),
pp. 129–35

WILLIAM H. GASS

The Portrait of a Lady is James's first fully exposed case of human manipulation; his first full-dress investigation, at the level of what Plato called "right opinion," of what it means to be a consumer of persons, and of what it means to be a person consumed. The population of James's fictional society is composed, as populations commonly are, of purchasers and their purchases, of the handlers and the handled, of the users and the used. Sometimes actual objects, like Mrs. Gareth's spoils, are involved in the transaction, but their involvement is symbolic of a buying and a being sold which is on the level of human worth (where the quality of the product is measured in terms of its responsiveness to the purchaser's "finest feelings," and its ability to sound the buyer's taste discreetly aloud), and it is for this reason that James never chooses to center his interest upon objects which can, by use, be visibly consumed. In nearly all of the later novels and stories, it is a human being, not an object—it is first Isabel Archer, then Pansy—who is the spoil, and it is by no means true that only the "villains" fall upon her and try to carry her off; nor is it easy to discover just who the villains really are.

Kant's imperative governs by its absence—as the hollow center. It is not that some characters, the "good" people, are busy being the moral legislators of mankind and that the others, the "bad" people, are committed to a crass and shallow pragmatism or a trifling estheticism; for were that the case, *The Portrait* would be just another skillful novel of manners and James would be distinctly visible, outside the work, nodding or shaking his head at the behavior of the animals in his moral fable. He would have managed no advance in the art of English fiction. James's examination of the methods of human consumption goes too deep. He is concerned with all of the ways in which men may be reduced to the status of objects, and because James pursues his subject so diligently, satisfying himself only when he has unraveled every thread, and because he is so intent on avoiding in himself what he has revealed as evil in his characters and exemplifying rather what he praises in Hawthorne, who, he says, "never intermeddled," the moral problem of *The Portrait* becomes an esthetic problem, a problem of form, the scope and course of the action, the nature of the characters, the content of dialogue, the shape and dress of setting, the points-of-view, the figures of speech, the very turn and tumble of the sentences themselves directed by the problem's looked-for solution, and there is consequently no suggestion that one should choose up sides or take to heart his criticism of a certain society nor any invitation to discuss the moral motivations of his characters *as if* they were surrogates for the real.

The moral problem, moreover, merges with the esthetic. It is possible to be an artist, James sees, in more than paint and language, and in *The Portrait,* as it is so often in his other work, Isabel Archer becomes the unworked medium through which, like benevolent Svengali, the shapers and admirers of beautifully brought out persons express their artistry and themselves. The result is very often lovely, but it is invariably sad. James has the feeling, furthermore, and it is a distinctly magical feeling, that the novelist takes possession of his subject through his words; that the artist is a puppeteer; his works are the works of a god. He constantly endeavors to shift the obligation and the blame, if there be any, to another: his reflector, his reverberator, his sensitive gong. In *The Portrait* James begins his movement toward the theory of the point-of-view. The phrase itself occurs incessantly. Its acceptance as a canon of method means the loss of a single, universally objective reality. He is committed, henceforth, to a standpoint philosophy, and it would seem, then, that the best world would be that observed from the most sensitive, catholic, yet discriminating standpoint. In this way, the esthetic problem reaches out to the metaphysical. This marvelous observer: what is it he observes? Does he see the world as it really is, palpitating with delicious signs of the internal, or does he merely fling out the self-capturing net? James struggles with this question most obviously in *The Sacred Fount* but it is always before him. So many of his characters are "perceptive." They understand the value of the unmolded clay. They feel they know, as artists, what will be best for their human medium. They will *take up* the young lady (for so it usually is). They will *bring* her *out.* They will *do for* her; *make something of* her. She will be *beautiful* and *fine,* in short, she will inspire *interest, amusement,* and *wonder.* And their pursuit of the ideally refractive medium parallels perfectly Henry James's own, except he is aware that his selected lens dare not be perfect else he will have embodied a god again, and far more obnoxious must this god seem in the body of a character than he did in the nib of the author's pen; but more than this, James knows, as his creations so often do not, that this manipulation is the essence, the ultimate germ, of the evil the whole of his work condemns, and it is nowhere more brutal than when fronted by the kindest regard and backed by a benevolent will.

The Portrait of a Lady, for one who is familiar with James, opens on rich sounds. None of his major motifs is missing. The talk at tea provides us with five, the composition of the company constitutes a sixth, and his treatment of the setting satisfies the full and holy seven. The talk moves in a desultory fashion ("desultory" is a repetitive word) and in joking tones ("That's a sort of joke" is the repetitive phrase) from health and illness, and the ambiguity of its value, to boredom, considered as a kind of sickness, and the ambiguity of its production. Wealth is suggested as a cause of boredom, then marriage is proposed as a cure. The elder Touchett warns Lord Warburton not to fall in love with his niece, a young lady recently captured by his wife to be exhibited abroad. The questions about her are: has she money? is she interesting? The jokes are: is she marriageable? is she engaged? Isabel is the fifth thing, then—the young, spirited material. Lord Warburton is English, of course, while the Touchetts are Americans. Isabel's coming will sharpen the contrast, dramatize the confrontation. Lastly, James dwells lovingly on the ancient red brick house, emphasizing its esthetic appeal, its traditions, its status as a work of art. In describing the grounds he indicates, too, what an American man of money may do: fall in love with a history not his own and allow it, slowly, to civilize him, draw him into Europe. Lord Warburton is said to be bored. It is suggested that he is trying to fall in love. Ralph is described as cynical, without belief, a condition ascribed to his illness by his father. "He seems to feel as if he had never had a chance." But the best of the ladies will save us, the elder Touchett says, a remark made improbable by his own lack of success.

The structure of the talk of this astonishing first chapter foreshadows everything. All jests turn earnest, and in them, as in the aimless pattern of the jesters' leisure, lies plain the essential evil, for the evil cannot be blinked even though it may not be so immediately irritating to the eye as the evil of Madame Merle or Gilbert Osmond. There is in Isabel herself a certain willingness to be employed, a desire to be taken up and fancied, if only because that very enslavement, on other terms, makes her more free. She refuses Warburton, not because he seeks his own salvation in her, his cure by "interest," but rather because marriage to him would not satisfy her greed for experience, her freedom to see and feel and do. Neither Warburton nor Goodwood appeals as a person to Isabel's vanity. She is a great subject. She will make a great portrait. She knows it. Nevertheless Isabel's ambitions are at first naïve and inarticulate. It is Ralph who sees the chance, in her, for the really fine thing; who sees in her his own chance, too, the chance at life denied him. It is Ralph, finally, who empowers her flight and in doing so draws the attention of the hunters.

Ralph and Osmond represent two types of the artist. Osmond regards Isabel as an opportunity to create a work which will flatter himself and be the best testimony to his taste. Her intelligence is a silver plate he will heap with fruits to decorate his table. Her talk will be for him "a sort of served dessert." He will rap her with his knuckle. She will ring. As Osmond's wife, Isabel recognizes that she is a piece of property; her mind is attached to his like a small garden plot to a deer park. But Ralph obeys the strictures *The Art of Fiction* was later to lay down. He works rather with the medium itself and respects the given. His desire is to exhibit it, make it whole, refulgent, round. He wants, in short, to make an image or to see one made—a portrait. He demands of the work only that it be "interesting." He effaces himself. The "case" is his concern. *The Portrait*'s crucial scene, in this regard, is that between Ralph and his dying father. Ralph cannot love Isabel. His illness prevents him. He feels it would be wrong. Nevertheless, he takes, he says, "a great interest" in his cousin although he has no real influence over her.

> "But I should like to do something for her. . . . I should like to put a little wind in her sails. . . . I should like to put it into her power to do some of the things she wants. She wants to see the world for instance. I should like to put money in her purse."

The language is unmistakable. It is the language of Iago. Ralph wants her rich.

> "I call people rich when they're able to meet the requirements of their imagination. Isabel has a great deal of imagination."

With money she will not have to marry for it. Money will make her free. It is a curious faith. Mr. Touchett says, "You speak as if it were for your mere amusement," and Ralph replies, "So it is, a good deal." Mr. Touchett's objections are serenely met. Isabel will be extravagant but she will come to her senses in time. And Ralph says,

> ". . . it would be very painful to me to think of her coming to the consciousness of a lot of wants she should be unable to satisfy. . . ."
> "Well, I don't know. . . . I don't think I enter into your spirit. It seems to me immoral."
> "Immoral, dear daddy?"
> "Well, I don't know that it's right to make everything so easy for a person."
> "It surely depends upon the person. When the person's good, your making things easy is all to the credit of virtue. To facilitate the execution of good impulses, what can be a nobler act? . . ."
> "Isabel's a sweet young thing; but do you think she's so good as that?"
> "She's as good as her best opportunities . . ."
> "Doesn't it occur to you that a young lady with sixty thousand pounds may fall a victim to the fortune-hunters?"
> "She'll hardly fall victim to more than one."
> "Well, one's too many."
> "Decidedly. That's a risk, and it has entered into my calculation. I think it's appreciable, but I think it's small, and I'm prepared to take it. . . ."
> "But I don't see what good you're to get of it. . . ."
> "I shall get just the good I said a few moments ago I wished to put into Isabel's reach—that of having met the requirements of my imagination. . . ."

The differences between Gilbert Osmond and Ralph Touchett are vast, but they are also thin.

Isabel Archer is thus free to try her wings. She is thrown upon the world. She becomes the friend of Madame Merle, "the great round world herself": polished, perfect, beautiful without a fault, mysterious, exciting, treacherous, repellent, and at bottom, like Isabel, identically betrayed; like Isabel again, seeking out of her own ruin to protect Pansy, the new subject, "the blank page," from that same round world that is herself. It is irony of the profoundest sort that "good" and "evil" in their paths should pass so closely. The dark ambitions of Serena Merle are lightened by a pathetic bulb, and it is only those whose eyes are fascinated and convinced by surface who can put their confident finger on the "really good." Ralph Touchett, and we are not meant to miss the appropriateness of his name, has not only failed to respect Isabel Archer as an end, he has failed to calculate correctly the qualities of his object. Isabel is a sweet, young thing. She is not yet, at any rate, as good as her best opportunities. The sensitive eye was at the acute point blind. Ralph has unwittingly put his bird in a cage. In a later interview, Isabel tells him she has given up all desire for a general view of life. Now she prefers corners. It is a corner she's been driven to. Time after time the "better" people curse the future they wish to save with their bequests. Longdon of *The Awkward Age* and Milly Theale of *The Wings of the Dove* come immediately to mind. Time after time the better artists fail because their point-of-view is ultimately only *theirs,* and because they have brought the esthetic relation too grandly, too completely into life.

—WILLIAM H. GASS, "The High Brutality of Good Intentions" (1958), *Fiction and the Figures of Life* (New York: Knopf, 1970), pp. 181–89

RICHARD POIRIER

Each of the early novels has revealed a considerable autobiographical tendency, seldom apparent in the external action but distinctly implied in the qualities of literary expression, particularly in the comedy. It can be said in general that the comedy in these novels is always a reflection of James's commitment to the ideal of individual freedom. In using the word 'freedom' so often, he has in mind something more complicated than the condition of being able to act entirely as one sees fit. When Ralph, discussing Isabel's inheritance with his father, remarks that 'your bequest will make her free', he gives an indication of the significance of freedom by saying that he wants to make Isabel rich because she has a great deal of 'imagination': 'People [are] rich when they are able to gratify their imagination'. The extremely high demands which James puts upon the word 'imagination' are apparent in this and in all the early fiction, and his discriminating awareness of its significance is everywhere observable, notably in the revisions, where he is especially careful in his use of the word. F. O. Matthiessen has noticed, for example, that in the revision of *The Portrait of a Lady,* even so admired a figure as Warburton is denied Ralph's original commendation as a 'man of imagination' and is instead referred to as 'a man of a good deal of charming taste'. Matthiessen is somewhat mistaken, however, in deciding that the word is used to designate an ability to judge things properly. Rather, it has to do with a capacity that often flouts good judgment, and it refers, generally, to reverently eager expectations, which Warburton lacks, about the unplumbed opportunities that life offers. Thus, even the individuality of Warburton's radicalism is a reaction *within* the social system of which, for Isabel's taste, he is too conspicuously a part. 'Imagination' in James is always connected with a conception of the future and with a desire to achieve more than the rewards which could be had if one accepted what organized society considers pre-eminently valuable.

Ralph, through a gift of money, tries to give Isabel the power to act upon her imaginations of freedom. He hopes that her imagination might range so freely that she need not bother to consult customary restrictions on possibility and need not fear the intimidation of other people's opinion. Money puts her beyond the need to respond conventionally to such opportunities as Warburton offers. But with the design of making her capacity for freedom not contingent merely upon wealth, James lets her reject Warburton long before her inheritance. His stylistic manœuvering so conditions us to the act that we are not likely to join the 'more quickly judging half of man-kind' in deciding that as a poor girl she ought to have accepted him. Therein we see the essential Americanism of this novel—how much it affirms her aspirations against what it shows to be ordinary social expectation. The attitudes towards experience here are very similar to those we found in *Roderick Hudson*. If Ralph is 'an apostle of freedom', then so is Rowland Mallet, who has his Roderick just as Ralph his Isabel, and if Mr. Striker is a kind of 'fool', who is at the same time fairly right about things, then so is Henrietta. In James's first novel as in this, the essential conflict is between 'fixed' and 'free' characters. The conflict is relatively simple in *Roderick Hudson* in that it depends upon James's categorization of the minor characters and of their relationship with the major ones. This cannot be said of *The Portrait of a Lady*, written, astonishingly, only five years later. The theme it shares with the novels that precede it has become by then so extremely complicated by James's developing attitudes that he temporarily leaves it for the new directions apparent in *The Bostonians.*

These complications are apparent in yet another manifestation of that defensiveness about his heroine which we have been considering. In his attempt to preserve the integrity of her Quixotic imaginings he shows us how each of them has an extreme and comic version, the excesses of which she manages to escape. Isabel's opinions, are, more often than not, theoretical, and they develop less from responses to specific things than as conceptions of how one ought to respond, derived from observations of the kind of person she imagines she would like to be. On her arrival in England she talks in a way similar to what we later find in Henrietta Stackpole, and she has an equally touristic attitude towards England and Europe. Henrietta remarks, soon after arrival at Gardencourt, that she intends to describe Ralph in one of her articles because 'there is a great need just now for the alienated American, and your cousin is a beautiful specimen'. Isabel's pained superiority to this should not make us forget that not twenty pages earlier she herself had spoken to

Ralph about ' "specimens"; it was a word that played a considerable part in her vocabulary; she had given him to understand that she wished to see English society illustrated by figures'. The change in Isabel is to be ascribed to a temporary and, again, theoretical change of allegiances from the point of view of an earlier friend, Henrietta, to that of a later one, Mrs. Touchett.

The technique of characterization by which James reveals similarities between Isabel and characters who seem otherwise quite unlike her has gone unnoticed. This has happened largely because criticism has paid too little attention to the surface of Isabel's conversation, and too much to what is wrongly assumed to be its depth, as if it were a dramatic paraphrase of what James himself 'means'. The point, more often, is that the opinions she spouts are merely trial balloons which she has borrowed from others for purposes of investigating the misty reaches of her own mind. As a result, her conversation has about it the ring of parody. With the reference to 'her aunt' left out, for example, even those well acquainted with the novel might ascribe the following speech to Henrietta rather than to Isabel:

> 'Now what is your point of view?' she asked her aunt. 'When you criticize everything here, you should have a point of view. Yours doesn't seem to be American—you thought everything over there so disagreeable. When I criticize, I have mine; it's thoroughly American!'
>
> 'My dear young lady,' said Mrs. Touchett, 'there are as many points of view in the world as there are people of sense. You may say that doesn't make them very numerous! American? Never in the world; that's shockingly narrow. My point of view, thank God, is personal!'
>
> Isabel thought this a better answer than she admitted; it was a tolerable description of her own manner of judging.

The substance of this conversation concerns the making of criticisms and judgments without having as a standard some official or institutional commitment such as America. Concern with the making of judgments that are at once personal and beyond provincial loyalties is the central circumstance behind the style and tone of the novel and the determining factor for the dramatic situations in which Isabel finds herself. In the interests of becoming a better 'judge', Isabel unhesitatingly, if silently, gives up an old vocabulary in this conversation for a new one. By this characteristic act, she leaves Henrietta alone to absorb James's satire on provincial Americanism. Being at the centre of the action, Isabel is surrounded, so to speak, by the various people whose attitudes she has at one time adopted, momentarily bringing one or another to the centre with her, but only to send him back to the periphery, there to represent through the rest of the novel a fixity of attitude from which she herself has escaped. The only important exception to this is Ralph, whose wholeness of perception becomes hers only through experience. It is not available, as are the more limited perspectives of Henrietta, Mrs. Touchett, Madame Merle, or Osmond, through the self-conscious selection of a social manner.

This is not to say that there is any falsity in Isabel's various imaginations of herself. Indeed, there is a high consistency in the evolution of her point of view and

its consequences in the choices she makes. Her progress from one kind of discourse to another is measured by a straight line on which she may be thought to
move as far as she can away from any attitude which seems to her constricted by
external circumstances such as nationality or social convention. Isabel is able to
justify what Henrietta calls her 'change' by telling her friend how the actual conditions of her life, with or without the various personal influences to which she
submits, would dispose her to a natural independence of institutional points of view:

> 'I can do what I choose—I belong quite to the independent class. I have
> neither father nor mother; I am poor; I am of a serious disposition and not
> pretty. I therefore am not bound to be timid and conventional'.

One gets a sense of the peculiarity of this novel, within the tradition of English
fiction which deals with ambitious orphans, by thinking of Isabel as an Emersonian
Becky Sharp. Her particular situation frees her from allegiance to social hierarchy,
but the advantage she sees in this has nothing to do with the freedom to act
indiscriminately in the pursuit of wealth and social position. Quite the contrary, she
wants a sort of enlightenment, a spiritual and by no means discernible grandeur. To
her mind, as to that of James's most conspicuous orphan, Hyacinth Robinson of *The
Princess Casamassima*, the ideal of an 'aristocratic situation' has ultimately nothing to
do with class. It is a matter of being in a position to appreciate more and to see
more than the members of any particular class, even the aristocracy, are allowed.
Isabel has no trouble finding more evidences of what she considers 'aristocracy' in
Madame Merle than in Lord Warburton. Yet, from the beginning, she suspects that
even Madame Merle is less admirable than she might be simply because she cares
too much for the world's opinion and approval. They have their first disagreement,
in fact, over the older woman's belief that 'we are each of us made up of a cluster
of appurtenances'. Isabel, with all the overstatement of a young person in a moment
of frustrated loyalty to a beloved and presumably wiser adult, grandly responds:

> 'I think just the other way. I don't know whether I succeed in expressing
> myself, but I know that nothing else expresses me. Nothing that belongs to me
> is any measure of me; on the contrary it's a limit, a barrier, and a perfectly
> arbitrary one. Certainly the clothes which, as you say, I choose to wear, don't
> express me; and heaven forbid they should! To begin with it's not my choice
> that I wear them; they are imposed upon me by society.'

If Isabel would be a Thoreau, she does not find a Canadian woodsman's
congeniality in Madame Merle's immediate reply: 'Should you prefer to go without
them?' Later, to Madame Merle's warning that people will draw conclusions if she
goes alone to the house of a handsome bachelor like Osmond, she reacts with the
thought: 'What cared Isabel Archer for the vulgar judgments of obscure people'. By
ignoring such judgments when she finally accepts Osmond's proposal of marriage,
she is, according to her statement to Henrietta, being perfectly natural. She belongs,
as she says, 'quite to the independent class', meaning that she belongs to no class at
all in the commonly accepted meaning of the term.

It is a fact easily ignored that Isabel's marriage to Osmond is precisely the most predictable and consistent thing that could happen to her even if she did not have the fortune which attracts him and which allows her the flattering sense that she is at last giving something instead of taking it. In her conception of him and, indeed, in all that seems to us apparent in his situation, he is a man without social identity. That is why she loves him. She assures Caspar Goodwood that she is 'marrying a nonentity', readily agrees with Mrs. Touchett that he has no money, no name, no importance, and tells Ralph that, unlike Lord Warburton, Osmond has

> 'no property, no title, no honours, no houses, nor lands, nor position, nor reputation, nor brilliant belongings of any sort. It is the total absence of these things that pleases me. Mr. Osmond is simply a man—he is not a proprietor'.

She exults in the fact that he is 'a specimen apart', and with a brilliant daring James even allows him to lay claim to the Jamesian virtue of renouncing practical social ambitions and advantages. In permitting this, James indicates in yet another way how Isabel's imagination responds to those very conditions of life to which his own is romantically but less sentimentally drawn. Osmond tells her that his life has affirmed 'not my natural indifference—I had none. But my studied, my wilful renunciation'. So great is the appeal of his separateness, of his 'originality', by which she means his exclusiveness of any socially observed types, that she cannot heed even his own explicitness when he tells her before the marriage: 'No, I am not conventional. I am convention itself'. It is remarkable how little he actually deceives her about the fact that his life is a matter of forms, of calculated attitudes. She is totally absorbed in the heroism of her choice. Osmond has so polished his aloofness that she sees in it a reflection of her own idealized aspirations. She hopes the marriage will lead to 'the high places of happiness from which the world would seem to lie below one', indicating that desire for elevation of view which, as we saw in Chapter II, is expressed in the imagery not only of several of the novels but also of passages from letters and essays where James talks admiringly about himself and the writers he likes.

James had a tolerant but patronizing conception of the narrowness of Emerson's intelligence, but it is hard not to see in the relationship between Isabel and Osmond a dramatization of what James was later to praise as the Emersonian vision 'of what we require and what we are capable of in the way of aspiration and independence'. The consummate irony of *The Portrait of a Lady* is the degree to which Osmond is a mock version of the transcendentalist. He fits, so far as Isabel has any opportunity of knowing him, almost perfectly into the characterization which Emerson gives of the transcendental personality:

> It is a sign of our times, conspicuous to the coarsest observer, that many intelligent and religious persons withdraw themselves from the common labors and competitions of the market and the caucus, and betake themselves to a certain solitary and critical way of living, from which no solid fruit has yet appeared to justify their separation. They hold themselves aloof: they feel the

disproportion between their faculties and the work offered them, and they prefer to ramble in the country and perish of ennui, to the degradation of such charities and such ambitions as the city can propose to them . . . this part is chosen both from temperament and from principle; with some unwillingness too, and as a choice of the less of two evils. . . . With this passion for what is great and extraordinary, it cannot be wondered at that they are repelled by vulgarity and frivolity in people.

The closeness of this description to the career of Osmond, even to his scorning the city of Rome to live in Florence, needs no comment in view of the quotations already made from the novel about him. To be aware of the similarity here is to make it less surprising that Isabel, whose mental processes are authentically Emersonian, should see an image of herself in the man she marries. Again, Emerson's description is a suitable characterization, but it is significant that the part of his essay which applies to Isabel is a description of mentality, while that which is relevant to Osmond describes merely the public evidences of such mentality:

> His [the transcendentalist's] thought,—that is the Universe. His experience inclines him to behold the procession of facts you call the world, as flowing perpetually outward from an invisible, unsounded centre in himself, centre alike of him and of them and necessitating him to regard all things as having a subjective or relative existence, relative to that aforesaid Unknown Centre of him.
>
> From this transfer of the world into the consciousness, this beholding of all things in the mind, follow easily his whole ethics. It is simpler to be self-dependent. The height, the deity of man is to be self-sustained, to need no gift, no foreign force. Society is good when it does not violate me, but best when it is likest to solitude. Everything real is self-existent.

The first of these passages is a version of Isabel's difference with Madame Merle ('nothing else expresses me') when that lady, far from regarding 'all things as having a subjective or relative existence', declares that she has 'a great respect for *things'*. The second, with its reference to 'the height' of man as being the condition of his self-subsistence, is not only a description of Isabel's 'aristocratic situation', but also a paraphrase of the idea of freedom, and its attendant imagery, which concerns James in most of the works we have considered. Given all this, it is extremely appropriate that when Mrs. Touchett finds Isabel in Albany the girl is 'trudging over the sandy plains of a history of German thought'. At the time, no history of German philosophy would fail to make Kant as conspicuous to an American audience as Emerson already had.

This connection between James and Emerson is worth attention because, as it has already been shown, the idealistic and romantic attitudes towards experience which are to be found in Emerson's essays are observable as well in the whole body of significant American fiction from Melville and Hawthorne to Faulkner. The relationship between James and Emerson is important within the larger fact that both of them subscribe to attitudes which are discernibly American, regardless of whether the literature derives from New England, New York, the South, or the West. It has often been said that Isabel Archer is an imitation of George Eliot's Dorothea Brooke, but it is apparent from all the novels of James which have no resemblance to *Middlemarch,* and from their Emersonian echoes, that *The Portrait of a Lady* could have brought the theme of aspiration to the point it does without the help of George Eliot.

Comparing, for example, the scenes wherein the heroine of each novel discovers within the atmosphere and landscape of the city of Rome a representation of her own feelings of disappointment, we can remark on the substantially greater vividness and resonance of George Eliot's imagery. In *Middlemarch* Rome *can* objectify and symbolize the nature of Dorothea's inner turmoil, and it can do so in a way that considerably extends the historical as well as the personal significance of the failure of her marriage. By comparison, James's descriptions of the city in *The Portrait of a Lady* are misty, sentimental, and weakly suggestive. The city cannot adequately reflect the quality or the representative importance of Isabel's sense of failure and possible betrayal. A comparison between James and George Eliot along the lines being briefly sketched would require another study as full as this one. What I am offering is merely a specific instance to illustrate the literary consequences of James's temperamental bias towards a specifically American view of tragic experience—the discovery of the unsatisfactory correlation between the internal world of heroic imagination and the external, historical world. Santayana, speaking of American philosophers, including William James, summarizes the dilemma in ways that give Isabel's part in it a wider context. 'Each of them,' he writes in *Character and Opinion in the United States,* 'felt himself bound by two different responsibilities, that of describing things as they are, and that of finding them propitious to certain human preconceived desires'. In James's novels, very often, the second of these is the happy prelude to the first. This, at least, is the experience of his heroic characters, and it is ours in reading about them. For us as for Newman, Eugenia, Isabel, and Milly, there is the entertainment before there is the knowledge, the romance before the reality. In heading, as we are, towards a discussion of artful manners and glamorous deception in this novel, it is well to recall James's definition of 'romantic': '. . . the things that can reach us only through the beautiful circuit and subterfuge of our thought and desire'.

—RICHARD POIRIER, *"The Portrait of a Lady," The Comic Sense in Henry James: A Study of the Early Novels* (New York: Oxford University Press, 1960), pp. 213–22

LEON EDEL

The Portrait of a Lady was the third of Henry James's large studies of the American abroad and twice as long as either of its predecessors. In *Roderick Hudson* he had posed the case of the artist, the limitations of his American background, and the frustration of his creative energy from the moment it was confronted by passion.

In *The American* he had pictured an ambitious businessman, bent on civilizing himself, proud enough to know his worth, and arrogant enough to think that the best of Europe was none too good for him. *The Portrait* was envisaged as a kind of feminine version of *The American,* and James began with the thought that his Isabel Archer would be a female Christopher Newman. Indeed this may be why he named her Isabel; there is a certain logic in moving from Christopher to the Queen who sent him faring across the ocean. And Isabel Archer deems herself good enough to be a queen; she embodies a notion not unlike that of Isabella of Boston, whose motto was *C'est mon plaisir.*

In Isabel Archer, Henry wished to draw "the character and aspect of a particular engaging young woman," and to show her in the act of "affronting her destiny." Like her male predecessors she goes abroad a thorough provincial, with her "meagre knowledge, her inflated ideals, her confidence at once innocent and dogmatic, her temper at once exacting and indulgent." A person who is dogmatic and exacting on the strength of meagre knowledge can only be characterized as presumptuous; and there is presumption in Isabel, for all the delicacy of her feeling: presumption suggests also a strong measure of egotism. James presents her to us as a young romantic with high notions of what life will bring her; and also as one who tends to see herself in a strong dramatic light. She pays the penalty of giving "undue encouragement to the faculty of seeing without judging"; she takes things for granted on scanty evidence. The author confesses that she was "probably very liable to the sin of self-esteem; she often surveyed with complacency the field of her own nature." He speaks of her "mixture of curiosity and fastidiousness, of vivacity and indifference, her determination to see, to try, to know, her combination of the desultory flame-like spirit and the eager and personal creature of her conditions." And he adds: "She treated herself to occasions of homage."

The allusion to her "flame-like spirit" suggests that Isabel images Henry's long-dead cousin Minny Temple, for he was to describe her in the same way. He was to confess that he had actually thought of Minny, in creating the eager imagination and the intellectual shortcomings of his heroine. But Minny, as he pointed out to Grace Norton, had been "incomplete." Death had deprived her of the trials—and the joys—of maturity. Henry, as artist, could imagine and "complete" that which had been left undone. Nevertheless, if Isabel has something of Henry's cousin in her make-up, she has much of Henry himself. He endows her, at any rate, with the background of his own Albany childhood, and as in *Washington Square* he interpolates a section wholly autobiographical, depicting his grandmother's house, the Dutch school from which he himself had fled in rebellion (as Isabel does), the "capital peach trees," which he had always sampled and always remembered. The scene is re-evoked years later in the autobiographies.

The most Jamesian of Henry's heroines is thus closely linked by her background and early life to her creator. And when Henry sends Isabel to Europe and makes her into an heiress, he places her in a predicament somewhat analogous to his own. Henry was hardly an "heir"; but his pen had won him a measure of the freedom which others possess through wealth. In posing the questions: what would

Isabel do with her new-found privileges? where would she turn? how behave? he was seeking answers for himself as well as for her. The questions are asked in the novel by Ralph Touchett, Isabel's cousin, a sensitive invalid who has silently transferred his inheritance to her. He knows he has not long to live; and he wishes to see how Isabel's large nature will profit by endowment. If this is a sign of his love for her, and the sole way in which he can be symbolically united to her, it is also Ralph's way of living vicariously in Isabel's life and participating in whatever fate her temperament may reserve for her. He, too, has a substantial fund of egotism.

Like her early predecessor in *Watch and Ward,* Isabel presently finds herself with three suitors. The first is a young man of very respectable fortune and family, from the United States, who has pursued her abroad. His name is Caspar Goodwood. He is an individual who has a "disagreeably strong push, a kind of hardness of presence, in his way of rising before her." He insists "with his whole weight and force." He is in short monotonously masculine; and if Isabel finds his sheer sexual force attractive it is also terrifying. Passion, or sex, as with Roderick, is not freedom. She rejects Goodwood several times during the novel and flees from him at the end when she finds his kiss to be like "white lightning." When "darkness returned she was free."

The second suitor is less dull and much less terrifying. He is a British lord named Warburton, a fine upstanding liberal, without too much imagination, one of the types Henry has met at his club or in country houses, fortunate heir of a position in a hierarchical society and the substantial means by which to sustain it. He inspires a different kind of fear in Isabel. "What she felt was that a territorial, a political, a social magnate had conceived the design of drawing her into the system in which he rather invidiously lived and moved. A certain instinct, not imperious, but persuasive, told her to resist—murmured to her that virtually she had a system and an orbit of her own." Social position in a word was also not freedom; moreover, social position in a hierarchical society represented a strong threat to a woman powerful enough and egotistical enough to believe that she has "an orbit of her own."

Isabel is romantic, and young. "I'm very fond of my liberty," she says early in the book, and she says also, "I wish to choose my fate," quite as if the ultimate choice were hers. If we see this as containing a measure of the egotism of youth, we must recognize that in her case it has its ingenuous charm. Nevertheless Henrietta Stackpole, an energetic and rather meddlesome newspaperwoman, recognizes it for what it is—for she is endowed with not a little egotism herself. She reminds Isabel: "You can't always please yourself; you must sometimes please other people."

At this stage Henry's heroine is still full of her hopes and dreams. Asked to define success—a matter of some interest to her author—she replies that it is to see "some dream of one's youth come true." And asked to define her idea of happiness, she offers a vision of a journey into the unknown—"A swift carriage, of a dark night, rattling with four horses over roads that one can't see." The concept is largely that of a girl who reads novels. However the young lady from America does not really mean what she says. She tries very hard to see, at every turn, the roads before her—and in broad daylight. She is supremely cautious in action, for one so daring in her fancy. And what she discovers is that even in daylight on a clear highway, it is possible to take a wrong turning.

Isabel's wrong turning occurs without her knowledge, when she meets a woman of a certain age who is worldly-wise and accomplished, the last word in refinement, an American expatriate of long standing, who has absorbed Europe into her being and bestrides the Continent with that appearance of freedom and insouciance to which Isabel aspires. The charm she exhibits, the deep attraction Isabel feels for her, are founded in part on the girl's inexperience of people and her inability to recognize the treacheries of life. The woman's name is Madame Merle. The *merle* is a blackbird. Serena Merle introduces Isabel to another American expatriate, who lives in a thick-walled villa in Florence on Bellosguardo, with his young daughter. At this point Henry places in his novel his early vision of Francis Boott and Lizzie, recorded in his travel sketch of 1877, when he had mused on the "tranquil, contented life" of the father and daughter, and the exquisite beauty that was a part of their daily existence. He had spoken of Frank and Lizzie as "figures in an ancient, noble landscape," and Gilbert Osmond and his daughter Pansy are such figures. Pansy, though pictured at a younger age than Henry had ever known Lizzie, is re-imagined as having the same cultivated qualities of the *jeune fille,* the *achieved* manners of an old civilization. Osmond, however, bears no resemblance to Boott, who was an open, generous, naïve and easy-laughing amateur of life. Osmond's sinister character derives from other sources, and in all critical speculation as to who was his "original," the principal original has been overlooked. To discover him we must compare him first with Catherine Sloper's father in *Washington Square.* He has the same intelligence and the same piercing sarcasm. As a father, Osmond is capable of the same coldness to his daughter's feelings. But he is an infinitely more malign father, and his will to power is infinitely greater than Dr. Sloper's self-aggrandizement in the Square.

"There were two or three people in the world I envied," Osmond tells Isabel shortly after meeting her, "—the Emperor of Russia, for instance, and the Sultan of Turkey! There were even moments when I envied the Pope of Rome—for the consideration he enjoys." Nothing less than the Tsar of all the Russias, and the man who could claim to be holier than all others. We grant Osmond his fine irony, as he says this, but we must nevertheless recognize what it expresses. Since he cannot be Tsar or Sultan or Pope, Osmond has consoled himself with being "simply the most fastidious young gentleman living." By now he is no longer young; he is confirmed, however, in his own private domain of power, as the perfect collector of bric-à-brac and *objets d'art,* and a subtle manipulator of persons as well as things. Pansy has been made into one of these objects: and Isabel is to be added to the collection. Strange as it may seem, Osmond clearly expresses one side of Henry James—the hidden side—not as malignant as that of his creation, but nevertheless that of the individual who abjures power by clothing it in meekness and deceptive docility. In this sense, Henry is the "original" of his villain. Osmond is what Henry might, under some circumstances, have become. He is what Henry could be on occasion when snobbery prevailed over humanity, and arrogance and egotism over his urbanity and his benign view of the human comedy. Perhaps the most accurate way of describing this identification with Osmond would be to say that in creating him Henry put into him his highest ambition and drive to power—the grandiose way in which he confronted his own destiny—while at the same time recognizing in his villain the dangers to which such inner absolutism might expose him. In the hands of a limited being, like Osmond, the drive to power ended in dilettantism and petty rages. In Henry's hands the same drive had given him unbounded creativity.

Isabel and Osmond are then, for all their differences, two sides of the same coin, two studies in egotism—and a kind of egotism which belonged to their author. For Isabel, generous high-minded creature though she is, in pursuit of an abstraction she calls "freedom," insists self-centeredly (in spite of grim warnings from all her friends) that she has found it in Osmond. She sees "a quiet, clever, sensitive, distinguished man . . . a lovely studious life in a lovely land . . . a care for beauty and perfection." He is the "elegant complicated medal struck off for a special occasion" and she feels it to be her occasion. Has she not always felt she was rather "the special thing" herself—a subject of her personal homage? And now, possessed of her wealth, it is as if she could combine her own power with the quiet existence of this individual and his exquisite flower-like daughter. When she marries him she believes that it is she who brings powerful elements into the union: "she would launch his boat for him; she would be his providence." This is indeed an exalted notion of her role, and it suggests the role she assigned to Osmond. Thinking back on this later, she wonders at the "kind of maternal strain" she had possessed in her passion; she believes that her money had been her burden. But this is rationalized after the fact. Isabel and Osmond had been attracted to one another because each saw in the other a mirror-image of self. The two had experienced an irresistible need for each other and in the end they cannot suffer each other. Power may be attracted to power, but it cannot endure it. Each insists on supremacy. Osmond tries to bend Isabel to his will. She cannot be bent. Her kind of power refuses to be subjugated: it exerts its own kind of subjugation. His, more devious, returns perpetually to the assault. The impasse is complete.

Henry had written into this work two aspects of himself: there was his legitimate aspiration to freedom, and his covert drive to power hidden behind his compliance, docility and industry. In the largest sense, egotism and power are the real subjects of *The Portrait of a Lady,* concealed behind a mask of free will and determinism. How was one to possess the power and arrogance of one's genius and still be on good terms with oneself and the world? How was one to establish relationships with people when one felt—and knew—one was superior to them? Yet how avoid loneliness and isolation? Above all, how enjoy one's freedom and not make mistakes in the exercise of it? Ralph watches Isabel make her mistakes: and it is he who in the end delivers the uncomfortable verdict that she has been "ground in the very mill of the conventional." Ralph thereby accepts Isabel at her own evaluation; he believes, as she did, that she was worthy of something more than the conventional. And beyond the unhappiness of Isabel's marriage lies the revelation that she has been the victim of a carefully-laid plot: that Madame Merle had been the mistress of Osmond; Pansy is their child; and the marriage had been arranged by the wily "blackbird" to endow Pansy with Isabel's fortune.

It is possible in this light to see that Isabel's rejection of Goodwood and Warburton went beyond the mere sense that they threatened her freedom. They would have inhibited her freedom to exercise her power. Goodwood would have imposed his masculinity and the power of his passion; Warburton would have involved Isabel in a society where the determinants of power had been fixed long before. She had looked upon one aspect of herself in Osmond and had fallen in love with it. He had done the same in looking at her. The other image, that of Osmond's selfishness and his "demonic imagination," belong in all probability to Henry's "buried life," some part of which he concealed even from himself, but which emerged from the depths in the writing of this character.

In *The Portrait of a Lady* there is a kind of continuous endowment of the characters with aspects of their author and the questions arising in his life even as he was writing the book—as if he were putting on different hats and different neckties and looking at himself in a series of mirrors. Curiously enough this observation was made long before the biographical knowledge we possess today enables us to identify this process of character infiltration. James Herbert Morse, writing in the *Century Magazine* a year after the publication of the novel, observed that there was in nearly every personage of *The Portrait* "an observable infusion of the author's personality." He went on:

> The men and women are almost equally quick-witted, curt and sharp. While each has a certain amount of individuality, the sharpness is one of the elements in common, preventing a complete differentiation. It is not wit alone, and repartee, but a sub-acid quality which sets the persons to criticising each other. One does not like to call it snarling. Mr. James is too much of a gentleman to admit snarling among ladies and gentlemen; and yet every leading person in the book does, in a polite way, enter frequently into a form of personal criticism of somebody else.

Since Morse wrote these lines we have come to understand the technique by which James sought to cover up what he was doing; his method of using shifting angles of vision so as to make us feel the way in which people see one another. We see Osmond through the eyes of all the principal characters, and this dramatizes even more Isabel's blindness to his faults during the period when she is debating whether she will marry him. Morse was right, however, in feeling that in a certain sense the various speakers in the novel were "engaged in the business of helping the author develop his characters." On the level of technique, this was one of James's brilliant devices: and later he was even to boast that he created artificial characters for this purpose and managed to endow them with the attributes of life. For biography, however, this method has the unusual effect of throwing a personal shadow behind the impersonal puppets projected and fashioned by the artist's imagination. "We cannot escape the conviction," said Morse, "that he has at least so far written himself into his books that a shrewd critic could reconstruct him from them." And he went on to be the shrewd critic: "The person thus fashioned would be one of fine intellectual powers, incapable of meannesses; of fastidious tastes, and of limited sympathies; a man, in short, of passions refined away by the intellect."

This needs amendment today. The visage of the writer reflected in *The Portrait* is rather that of a man of large sympathies and powerful passions, which are in some degree inhibited, and which are struggling to be set free, indeed which are using all kinds of indirection to find some liberating channel. And it is in the relationship between Isabel and Osmond that we can best observe this at work.

In the end one feels that Isabel's disillusionment, the damage to her self-esteem and the crushing effect of her experience, reside in the shock she receives that so large a nature should have been capable of so great a mistake; and in her realization that instead of being able to maneuver her environment, as her freedom allowed, she had been maneuvered by it. Christopher Newman had had a similar shock, in the Faubourg St. Germain. But he could write it off as the corruption and deceit of the French nobility. The deeper illusion here resides in the fact that Serena Merle and Gilbert Osmond are Americans, and the implications are that as expatriates, long divorced from their native soil, they also have been corrupted: they conceal a world of evil unknown to Isabel. America had ill prepared her for this. The American and the Americana, in Henry's two novels, represented—in the larger picture—the New World's concept of its own liberties, the admixture of freedom and of power contained in America's emerging philosophy, and in the doctrines of pragmatism of which Henry's brother William was to be a founder. In drawing his novel from the hidden forces of his own experience into the palpable world of his study and observation, Henry James had touched upon certain fundamental aspects of the American character.

—LEON EDEL, "A Band of Egotists," *Henry James 1870–1881: The Conquest of London* (Philadelphia: J. B. Lippincott, 1962), pp. 421–30

DOROTHEA KROOK

⟨...⟩ it may be useful to set out explicitly Isabel Archer's principal reasons for choosing to marry Gilbert Osmond. For in view of what happens to the marriage, it is important that these reasons should be 'good' or 'creditable' enough to save Isabel from being condemned as a mere simpleton who deserves what she gets for being such a fool as to marry a man like Osmond. Nor is it merely gratuitous to urge that these reasons *are* sufficiently good or creditable, since this very point has been disputed by some modern critics of *The Portrait of a Lady:* who have seen in Isabel Archer nothing but a half-educated American girl with a head stuffed full of sentimental nonsense about life and art and Europe and gracious living—the sort of 'sentimental idealism' which, as everyone knows, is the weaker side of the American national character, and therefore needs to be exposed rather than condoned as (according to these critics) James condones it in *The Portrait of a Lady*.

To take this view is, of course, to drain the whole central relationship of the book of its tragic meaning, and *a fortiori* to diminish almost out of existence Isabel Archer's stature as a tragic heroine. It is accordingly important for those who believe that this central relationship *is* tragic in the fullest sense of the word to establish the moral sufficiency of the reasons that led Isabel Archer to enter into her tragically disastrous marriage.

It has already been noted that what pre-eminently draws Isabel to Osmond is his sovereign personal distinction—the single quality that for her subsumes all his other qualities. But to this power of his to satisfy the requirements of her imagination must be added two vital elements of her own nature. The first is her ardent desire to develop her mind and her sensibilities: her need, that is, to give direction and form to her vague aspiration after knowledge and virtue—'experience' in the largest, noblest sense of the word. This, James desires us to understand, is one of the most engaging characteristics of his engaging young woman Isabel Archer; and for the reason chiefly that it argues the presence of that intellectual energy and moral spontaneity, so lamentably lacking in the English and Europeans, which James had already remarked as one of the most inspiring features of the American national character.

To take this view of Isabel Archer's American 'idealism' helps us to understand, among other things, what James is referring to in a frequently misunderstood passage in the Preface in which he speaks of Isabel's *presumption*. The word is used, I believe, with an irony at once comic and tragic, and in both aspects with a mitigating tenderness. The comic emphasis lies nearest the surface. It is to be detected in the many references to the vanity, self-centredness, even arrogance of his engaging young woman, which James exposes with so much pleasant wit in the earlier portions of the book. Even here, however, the irony is not directed so much against the vanity, self-centredness, arrogance as such, but is intended rather to direct our amused attention to the perpetual struggle in Isabel between these frailties of her all too feminine nature and the high moral principles to which she is, both by temperament and training, whole-heartedly committed. The struggle is genuine and equal because both sides are equally real and powerful: in Henry James's view of man's nature we will not find a trace of the shallow realism which proceeds on the axiom that the baser elements in a human soul are always more real because more base; and its interest and amusement for us is precisely in the fact that it is exhibited as so thoroughly equal.

In its more serious aspect, Isabel Archer's 'presumption' may be seen as the natural concomitant of her passionate desire to grow in knowledge and virtue in a society which holds both in small esteem. It appears presumptuous to those around her (that is what *they* would call it, James is saying) because they are themselves so little moved by any passion of this kind, and can therefore barely recognise it for what it is; and the tenderness of James's irony is accordingly for all that is beautiful and noble in his heroine's spirit, and the irony itself for what she will have to suffer for being what she is in the society in which she finds herself.

But besides this, the irony has still another, deeper meaning. It suggests, first, that this kind of 'presumption' belongs inescapably to every genuinely adventurous, enquiring, questing mind—is in fact almost only another name for these admirable qualities; and, second, that it is the more dangerous for being a part of something essentially good and noble. Knowledge puffeth up, warned St Paul, meaning that knowledge need not but, alas, too often does make a man proud, vainglorious, 'presumptuous'; and for a young person especially (James, particularising Paul's wisdom, tells us) it is difficult not to feel the kind of pride or 'vainglory' in her growing knowledge which is, or may be, inimical to the soul's health. So Isabel Archer's love of appearances struggles with her love of truth and reality, and her disinterested passion for knowledge with her sense of personal power in the acquisition of it; and all this too is exhibited in those opening portions of the book with an irony equally penetrating and tender. ⟨. . .⟩

⟨. . .⟩ it is the discovery of Osmond's base worldliness and the corrupt values springing from it that first undermines and finally destroys the loving trust in his essential goodness with which Isabel entered into the marriage; and it is this, along with Osmond's egotism, coldness and brutality, that constitutes the betrayal which is the heart of the tragedy. Nevertheless, if this were in fact the whole tragedy of *The Portrait of a Lady* there would be, paradoxically, no tragedy in the proper sense of the word. The heroine, Isabel Archer, would be the totally innocent and helpless victim of a cruel combination of circumstances which she had been powerless to avert; and she would then bear no responsibility for the disaster following from them. The story of *The Portrait of a Lady* would in that case be a story pitiful and heart-breaking indeed, as a story of human suffering always is; but it would not be a tragedy, for a mere victim cannot be a tragic hero or heroine: the tragic effect in drama depends upon our recognising that the hero shall be in some sense and in some degree responsible for the fate that overtakes him.

Now Isabel Archer, we discover, is not in fact a mere victim. On the contrary, she carries a proper share of the moral responsibility for the disaster that overtakes her. Nor is Osmond, on his side, merely a vicious brute. He too (we discover) has been deceived, in a subtly interesting way; he too has been misled into a fatal error of judgement which has helped to precipitate the catastrophe; and it is in James's dramatic exposé of this joint responsibility for the tragic catastrophe that his gift of moral analysis is perhaps at its most brilliant.

What we discover first is that Osmond's original motives for wishing to marry Isabel had not been as base as might be supposed. He had certainly not been a mere adventurer who was marrying her for her money—like another Morris Townsend in *Washington Square* who was only less crude in his tactics. If Isabel, we are made to understand, had been in the least (for instance) like her impossible friend Henrietta Stackpole, he would not have married her were she ten times the heiress she was. Nor had he been merely the aesthetic dilettante (as some critics have thought him), who merely desired to possess Isabel Archer as the finest piece in his collection of 'fine things'. The money-motive had indeed not been absent, and the aesthetic motive had certainly been present; but his main reason for wanting to marry her was, simply, that he liked her: that he found her really charming and graceful (as he tells Madame Merle); that he was in fact, to his capacity, in love with Isabel—genuinely, even ardently, in love.

—DOROTHEA KROOK, *"The Portrait of a Lady," The Ordeal of Consciousness in Henry James* (Cambridge: Cambridge University Press, 1962), pp. 41–43, 50–52

LAURENCE BEDWELL HOLLAND

So intimately is James implicated in the action of his novel that letters he was writing while working on the *Portrait* are echoed in the passages where Osmond's mind and feelings are stirred by the workings of the plot and he proposes marriage to Isabel. James wrote that he was "much more interested in my current work than anything else," that he was "working with great ease, relish, and success," that his work would bring $6,000 from serialization alone, that it would "rend the veil" which covered his "ferocious ambition," that it would be from the finished *Portrait,* his most ambitious early effort, "that I myself shall pretend to date." It is Ralph who notices that the costumed "fine lady" which the once "free, keen" Isabel has become "represented Gilbert Osmond," who now "was in his element; at last he had material to work with." His calculated effects "were produced by no vulgar means, but the motive was as vulgar as the art was great. . . . 'He works with superior material,' Ralph said to himself; 'it's rich abundance compared with his former resources.'" It is the excitement of such opportunities that earlier had awakened Osmond. Just before his proposal Osmond finds himself pleased with his newly aroused "sense of success," feeling that his earlier successes had rested "on vague laurels," and that his present success was "easy . . . only because he had made an altogether exceptional effort." While the "desire to have something or other to show for his 'parts' . . . had been the dream of his youth," now it was to materialize with Isabel's help and at her expense: "If an anonymous drawing on a museum wall had been conscious and watchful it might have known this peculiar pleasure of being at last . . . identified—as from the hand of a great master—by the so high and so unnoticed fact of style. His 'style' is what the girl had discovered with a little help; and now, beside herself enjoying it, she should publish it to the world without his having any of the trouble. She would do the thing for him and he would not have waited in vain." In this view of Osmond are joined both the finished work of art—the drawing with which Osmond is associated so intimately—and the master whose style was displayed in making it.

The useful girl is Isabel with her combination of caution and curiosity, inexperience and alertness, and the strength of will which leads her to confront life's options " 'So as to choose.' " Her suspicion of the poisoned cup of experience and her fear of suffering are countered by her desire to join in what ordinary " 'people know and suffer.' " Her desire "to leave the past behind her" and encounter always fresh beginnings is balanced by her deepening response to the appeal of the past and tradition. Her acknowledged ignorance "about bills" or " 'anything about money' " is countered by the definiteness of her aversion " 'to being under pecuniary obligations' " and the assurance of her delusion that in going to Europe she is literally " 'travelling at her own expense.' " The "something cold and dry in her temperament" which an "unappreciated suitor" would notice is countered by the boldness of her "ridiculously active" imagination which renders her vulnerable to delusions, being so "wide-eyed" as to suffer from "seeing too many things at once" and incurring the "penalty of having given undue encouragement to the faculty of seeing without judging." Her mind in sum is a "tangle of vague outlines at the start," but the interaction of her capacity for experience with the plot which forms that experience joins her conscience and her imagination and fills in the outlines of both Isabel's and the *Portrait*'s visions.

In the course of experiencing the lures and pressures that shape her destiny in the novel, the action brings her maternal instincts into the foreground. Mrs. Touchett's taunting fear that Isabel may decide that her " 'mission in life's to prove that a stepmother may sacrifice herself—and that, to prove it, she must first become one' " is confirmed by Isabel's feeling toward Pansy and by her eventual actions, and it is given another dimension by Isabel's late recognition that her feeling for Osmond himself contained "a maternal strain—the happiness of a woman who felt that she was a contributor, that she came with charged hands."

Moreover, the plotted action which involves her with Osmond and Pansy dissociates both Isabel and finally Pansy from the securities and settled conventions of the strictly aristocratic tradition, embodied in Lord Warburton, and involves each instead in something more problematical and hazardous. For Pansy it is the prospect of a marriage founded on no more than sheer mutual affection and a great sufficiency of cash; Pansy herself, whom Isabel feels to be a blank page she hopes will be filled with "an edifying text," displays nothing but her fragile charm and the genuineness of her devotion; Ned Rosier has neither settled status nor job and office, his mind and tastes are not exceptional, and his only recommendation is the genuine commitment defined by his courtship and the sale of his prized treasures.

Isabel's involvement is with the actual form of her strange marriage with Osmond. Within that form Isabel's and Osmond's child is born (he dies at the age of six months) and Isabel acquires her stepdaughter. Within a few years, however, it is clear that intimacy between Isabel and Osmond has ceased, and by the end his attitude is one of contempt; as Isabel finally tells him, " 'It's malignant.' " Yet the form, as a sheer institutional form, still holds and within it takes place a striking confrontation when Isabel distinguishes between her own and her husband's conceptions of aristocracy and tradition. It is not only striking but significant because their different attitudes together reveal conflicting tendencies that are widespread in American culture but which are particularly pressing in the Genteel Tradition, and these tendencies are embodied in the marriage which the plot has figured for them.

Isabel's view of aristocracy is distinguished by being ethical and experiential and envisions the reconciliation of duty with enjoyment: the "union of great knowledge with great liberty; the knowledge would give one a sense of duty and the liberty a sense of enjoyment." Osmond's is at once more formal and more active; it is "altogether a thing of forms, a conscious, calculated attitude." And while both characters respect tradition, the "old, the consecrated, the transmitted," and both speak as if dissociated from it and encountering it from some distance, Isabel's attitude is eclectic and based on her determination "to do what she chose with it." Osmond's view is at once more conservative in its deference to older social patterns, more desperate in his sense of alienation from them, and more radical in his means to attain them, as befits the prince in exile from America and would-be pope who longs for the deference paid an aristocrat but has not inherited the traditional aristocratic forms. He has a "large collection" of traditions and feels that the "great thing was to act in accordance with them" rather than to choose among them; and his proprietorship, like his manner, is founded on the realization that distinguishes him from the European who could simply find or tranquilly inherit his traditions: Osmond, the American expatriate, knows that "if one was so unfortunate as not to have [tradition] one must immediately proceed to make it."

Isabel's determination to "choose," and Osmond's to construct or "make," are sharply delineated by the mutual antagonism of the two characters, but they are joined in perilous proximity by the bond of their marriage and both are related to other social realities which are part of their American background. These are the money economy and obsessive attitudes toward money, which characterize the culture of American capitalism, and characteristic American attitudes (one utilitarian, the other guilt-ridden) toward inherited wealth.

Osmond, the son of a "rich and wild" father and a mother who combined a practical "administrative" view with a talent for poor poetry, has made in his expatriation a " 'wilfull renunciation' " which is nonetheless a social construct; it is founded on the habitual intent to utilize economic resources without creating them and is centered on his immediate family. Determined " 'not to strive nor struggle' " in the business world, yet content with the independent income derived therefrom (though he thinks it " 'little' "), he carefully harbors and manages his economic resources, buys and builds his collection and refines his tastes, buys and constructs his walled substitute for a world of forms which he might prefer to have inherited. Making his " 'life an art' " as he advised Isabel to do, he attempts to mold Pansy, with his "artistic" or "plastic view" of her capacities, in accordance with his desire for dominance. He is the genteel embodiment of "convention" in a strikingly modern version recognizable since 1789: convention become conscious and deliberate, the result less of habit and tacit agreement than of calculated control, deliberate formulation, and the determination not simply to order life as it is but to shape it more firmly and actually change it. When the opportunity to gain Isabel and her fortune presents itself, he is happy for the opportunity to put it and her to use.

Isabel and her fortune come to be as closely associated in her own mind as they are in Osmond's and as they are throughout the novel. In Chapter I Daniel Touchett, after reading the reference in his wife's telegram to Isabel's being " 'independent,' " asks this question: is the word " 'used in a moral or in a financial sense?' " His question proves to have point. After Isabel has accustomed herself to the fact that she is rich, she is enchanted by a "maze of visions" of what a generous, independent, responsible girl could do with such resources, and her fortune "became to her mind a part of her better self; it gave her importance, gave her even, to her own imagination, a certain ideal beauty." Her attitude has less conscious origins in her temperament and in her environment, the attitudes toward experience and money being so intimate that the novel renders the one the image of the other. When Osmond proposes, Isabel is checked by a sense of dread, her hesitancy being founded on "the force which . . . ought to have banished all dread—the sense of something within herself, deep down, that she supposed to be inspired and trustful passion." Yet that fount of passion is one which Isabel inclines to save as against the alternative she anticipates, that of spending it entirely: "It was there like a large sum stored in a bank—which there was a terror in having to begin to spend. If she touched it, it would all come out." (This analogy between a bank and Isabel's capacity for passion was added in revision.) By the time she is engaged, her consent is taking the form of an act of absolution and benefaction but also of proprietorship.

She is gratified by Pansy's affection, for "Pansy already so represented part of the service she should render," and if she feels "humility" in surrendering to Osmond, she feels also "a kind of pride" in the knowledge that "she should be able to be of use to him" and that "she was not only taking, she was giving." When Isabel looks back on her decision later, she recognizes that she never would have married him "but for her money." Her money had been the contribution to the marriage that appealed to her "maternal strain," yet the indelicacy of having merely inherited it was also a "burden" on her conscience which she longed to transfer to someone else. "What would lighten her own conscience more effectually than to make it over to the man with the best taste in the world" when she could think of no charitable institution as interesting as he? "He would use her fortune in a way that would make her think better of it and rub off a certain grossness attaching to the good luck of an unexpected inheritance." Moreover, she had felt that the "subtlest . . . manly organism she had ever known had become her property, and the recognition of having but to put out her hands and take it had been originally a sort of act of devotion."

These divergent views—of proprietorship, the propriety of money, domestic economy, parental care, tradition, and aristocratic forms and values—are held juxtaposed within the bond of Isabel's and Osmond's marriage. Their variety, their tension, and their proximity are an indication that not only the separate views themselves but their interconnections are being examined, and that the form which joins them, the marriage, is being subjected to a test under the pressures shaped by the plot. Indeed, the marriage institution as displayed is not a settled institutional mold but is a form in the process of being shaped. The terms "experiment" for the Touchetts' marriage and "undertaking" for matrimony in general are decidedly apt in the context of the *Portrait*—and with them the term "form," which is used by Caspar when condemning the " 'ghastly form' " which Isabel's marriage has become and is used also when Osmond, urging Isabel not to leave, is said to speak "in the name of something sacred and precious—the observance of a magnificent form."

For the *Portrait* reveals in the institution the principal functions of a form: the capacity to sustain a fully developed relationship; but also the capacity to precede the full development of a process or experience while yet prefiguring it, and thus to shape the plans and aspirations for personal and social experience, to embody emerging possibilities as well as actual achievements; and the capacity to survive the process or experience itself, remaining a skeletal but nonetheless real image of possibilities no longer (or not yet again) actual. Within the context of the *Portrait*, the marriages of the Countess and much later of Warburton image the institution reduced to its most factitiously conventional status, while Daniel Touchett's hopes for Ralph's and Isabel's marriage, and earlier for Warburton's, and Isabel's hopes for Pansy's, view the institution as a form of aspiration and commitment, with the Touchetts' marriage (and Henrietta Stackpole's) falling in between.

Indeed, the *Portrait* gives body to ambivalent remarks James made in letters to his brother and Grace Norton, in 1878 and 1881, on the subject of marriage, confirming his intention not to marry but insisting on the importance of the institution, associating the form of marriage with commitments of the profoundest sort, and displaying a firm regard for the institution despite his own decision. He wrote that "I believe almost as much in matrimony for most other people as I believe in it little for myself," and that "one's attitude toward marriage is . . . the most characteristic part doubtless of one's general attitude toward life. . . . If I were to marry I should be guilty in my own eyes of inconsistency—I should pretend to think quite a bit better of life than I really do." These letters make the form of marriage an image of commitments to life itself, whether within or beyond the range of one's actual conduct. These are commitments which James's imagination entertained and made in his fiction, if nowhere else, and they are at issue in the *Portrait*.

There the plot—like the world it represents endowing and then drawing on Isabel's banked resources of temperament and inheritance—focuses first on the prospective form of her marriage; then as that becomes a hollow shell it widens its focus to include the prospects for Pansy's. In the process, Isabel's acts of confronting and imagining experience become acts of paying and suffering and responsible commitment as she is led by her husband "into the mansion of his own habitation" and made a victim of her world (including her own temperament and illusions) and of the *Portrait* which creates and paints her.

—LAURENCE BEDWELL HOLLAND, "The Marriage," *The Expense of Vision: Essays on the Craft of Henry James* (Princeton: Princeton University Press, 1964), pp. 35–42.

MANFRED MACKENZIE

Although we are so familiar with the social observer and critic in Henry James, I doubt if we have ever asked what *kind* of society it is that he typically imagines. This, therefore, is the question asked here: whether there is a "sociology" implicit in James's international situations.

In order to answer this question, we might invent a generic Jamesian situation (one that is based on the international stories and that is, I hope, fairly unexceptionable). Thus the hero leaves America generally on the grounds that his society is insufficient for him and that he can best complete himself in Europe. If he succeeds, his story will end with his marriage: in the international comedy, he marries in Europe, is "married" to "Europe" ("Europe" understood as a style of life). But, even at best, James's hero will have met a complex fate. On account of his craving for completion he has risked, perhaps forfeited, American social possibilities—life-feeling and identity and power, without, however, becoming eligible to earn any corresponding social identity in Europe. Indeed, all that he can become is what may be called a "social aesthete": he cannot participate in any conventional modes of social power, only in terms of *seeing*, of *knowledge*, or of *consciousness*.

One can put this situation in another way. While his own society seems to preclude him from all but a "light ornamental" identity (*Roderick Hudson*), he has gone on to find an only apparently accessible Europe. In fact, he encounters in Europe a kind of sphere of protection, a graduated secrecy, around an innermost social essence. Even when he succeeds with mediators, he finds that their function is ultimately to confirm this sphere of protection. What is complex about his social fate is that he is initiated exoterically, but never esoterically, into a group that takes on the character of a secret society.

If this development is an elusive one, it is intensified by the hero's reaction. Initiated only the more gallingly to be precluded, he is threatened with the total forfeit of a social personality which, while incomplete, has at least been reliable. He is in a critical false position. Now, out of an inevitable resentment, he looks for compensation. He will possess a secret of his own, even if he has forcibly to dispossess those who preclude him from their secret.

At this point, one can distinguish a further stage in the Jamesian hero's reaction. He may be compelled not only to possess himself of a secret but also to make use of this secret—*to use secrecy*—in order to assert himself. He resorts to the lie; or he conspires. In the latter event, he forms his own cabal, a schismatic, a "secretive," society—"communities of knowledge," as a phrase from "The Jolly Corner" puts it. Only when the hero can bring himself to accommodate his false position, and gain social sufficiency, does this essentially revengeful conspiracy dissolve in any way. ⟨. . .⟩

Thus Isabel Archer begins by voluntarily forfeiting something of her American social identity in favour of what she calls "the infinite vista of a multiplied life" in Europe. She wants to complete an insufficient self in terms of limitless consciousness. The consequence of this forfeit, the novel now discovers, is an extraordinary social freedom. Indeed, positioned between two societies, Isabel comes to have too much autonomy, a false freedom that arises from a false social position. This in turn leads her to seek a compensation that is not easy to distinguish from revenge. By the end, at least, *The Portrait of a Lady* is developing into a Jamesian revenge cycle.

The problem of Isabel's social identity is focussed in her relationships with her suitors. What is less obvious, perhaps, is that her suitors appear in a definite sequence, a sequence that the novel repeats several times.

Leaving aside the proposal from Goodwood to which James makes passing reference early on (Chapter 4), we can say that Isabel's first important opportunity to marry is afforded by Lord Warburton. In her naive view he is "a specimen," English society illustrated by an eminent case. And, indeed, she encounters in him social essence or power (something that is all the more defined for her by his open "radical" apology for it): she suffers "an appreciable shock," and reacts to his as yet implicit appeal with "a certain fear." It is clear that her whole social personality is at issue: can she forfeit to such an extent an American self that might have Caspar Goodwood for the asking?

It is surely to underscore this question that James now introduces Henrietta Stackpole, who functions both as a measure of Isabel's lapse from her American "faith" and as a cue to return to that faith. Henrietta has, it turns out, enlisted in Caspar Goodwood's cause, perhaps even to the extent of encouraging him to write directly to Isabel. It is precisely at this point—Isabel is reading Goodwood's letter—that she encounters her English specimen once more: "Lord Warburton loomed up before her, largely and brightly, as a collection of attributes and powers. ... What she felt was that a territorial, a political, a social magnate had conceived the design of drawing her into the system in which he rather invidiously lived and moved." Again she betrays anxiety, leaving Warburton "really frightened at herself." And again it is reasonable to suppose that she feels threatened in her social (as well as sexual) identity.

She is threatened in her social identity from two sides. She might be said to have an exposed "front" and "back." Because marriage to Warburton might mean too drastic a forfeit of an American "system of her own," she prefers to forfeit this chance of an alternative social identity, of association with "Great responsibilities, great opportunities, great consideration, great wealth, great power, a natural share in the public affairs of a great country" (Ralph Touchett). She also prefers to forfeit whatever Warburton can offer on account of her imminent American captain of industry, who is just as much a specimen of social essence and power: "more than any man she had ever known ... Caspar Goodwood expressed for her an energy—and she had always felt it as a power—that was of his very nature." But this is also the Caspar Goodwood whom she has already rejected in America, and whom she now, immediately after rejecting Lord Warburton, rejects once again. If Warburton cannot be the real right thing on account of the presence of Goodwood, Goodwood is less than ever the real right thing for appealing to her after she has encountered Warburton. It turns out, then, that Isabel does not avoid forfeiting her American identity by forfeiting an English marriage. Indeed, the opposite is the case, and the encounter with Warburton may be seen as being nothing less than a burning of her boats to America. Strether is in exactly this situation in *The Ambassadors*.

Isabel has refined her position to the extent of separating herself from the different kinds of vitality that are concentrated in a Goodwood, a Warburton. She is now "free." Her freedom, however, is very much the special and temporary advantage of a social aesthete who has a "seeing" relationship, as it were, not an organic and vital one, to the society in which she finds herself placed. The series of non-sequiturs in the conversation she has with Ralph Touchett after rejecting Warburton and Goodwood makes this clear:

"You want to see life—you'll be hanged if you don't, as the young men say."
"I don't think I want to see it as the young men want to see it. But I do want to look about me."
"You want to drain the cup of experience."
"No, I don't wish to touch the cup of experience. It's a poisoned drink! I only want to see for myself."
"You want to see, but not to feel," Ralph remarked.
"I don't think that if one's a sentient being one can make the distinction. I'm a good deal like Henrietta. The other day when I asked her if she wished to marry she said: 'Not till I've seen Europe!' I too don't wish to marry till I've seen Europe."

It takes little imagination to see how these non-sequiturs might just as easily express the disadvantages as the advantage of a false position. And, indeed, this very desire so to *see* Europe betrays a false position: Isabel has a Jamesian social aesthete's need for compensatory access to social essence. As she has told Ralph Touchett very early on at Gardencourt, she wants to see the castle "ghost." She wants more than exoteric social "knowledge" (the picturesque, the "castle" that would satisfy a Henrietta Stackpole, who is so ironically said to be in search of "the inner life"), she wants an esoteric social consciousness. No longer quite sure of her own value, she needs a "secret."

Isabel's problematic social aestheticism explains, I believe, her relationship with Mme Merle and Gilbert Osmond, to whom she is now drawn. Endowed with a fortune that only increases her sense of freedom, she falls under the influence of a *deracinée* American for whom social aestheticism has become virtually "metaphysical":

"When you've lived as long as I you'll see that every human being has his shell and that you must take the shell into account. By the shell I mean the whole envelope of circumstances. There's no such thing as an isolated man or woman; we're each of us made up of some cluster of appurtenances. What shall we call our 'self'? Where does it begin? where does it end? It overflows into everything that belongs to us—and then it flows back again. I know a large part of myself is in the clothes I choose to wear. I've a great respect for *things!* One's self—for other people—is one's expression of one's self; and one's house, one's furniture, one's garments, the books one reads, the company one keeps—these things are all expressive."

—Madame Merle, whom Mrs. Touchett describes as knowing "absolutely everything on earth there is to know," and as being "too fond of mystery . . . that's her greatest fault." And, through Mme Merle, she falls under the spell of an expatriate aesthete who likewise makes a metaphysic of his social apostasy by advocating that one should live as a work of art, and who adorns himself accordingly by collecting "tradition":

> His ideal was a conception of high prosperity and propriety, of the aristocratic life.... He had never lapsed from it for an hour; he would never have recovered from the shame of doing so.... But for Osmond it was altogether a thing of forms, a conscious, calculated attitude.... He had an immense esteem for tradition; he had told her once that the best thing in the world was to have it, but that if one was so unfortunate as not to have it one must immediately proceed to make it. She knew then that he meant by this that she hadn't it, but that he was better off; though from what source he had derived his traditions she had never learned. He had a very large collection of them, however; that was very certain....

—and who then uses his self-adornment, the esotericism of which he is the absolute arbiter, as a way of mystifying society into paying him the recognition it refuses him:

> It was the mask, not the face of the house. It had heavy lids, but no eyes; the house in reality looked another way.... The windows of the ground floor, as you saw them from the piazza, were, in their noble proportions extremely architectural; but their function seemed less to offer communication with the world than to defy the world to look in.

One can go further; not only is Isabel drawn to these conspirators because they embody and supply an ideology for her own reaction to her untenable false position, she actually finds in them *compensation* for it. At a time when she feels herself extraordinarily exposed, she senses her community with them, a community of suppressed revenge-feeling. Of course, in saying this one has to distinguish her need for compensation from the conspirators', which, after a lifetime of preclusion, amounts to a need for specific revenge. Isabel may be on the point of entering a revenge-cycle, they are so deeply imbued with revenge-feeling as to be ever-ready to seek an outlet for it. The touchstone for Isabel's and the conspirators' respective attitudes is Lord Warburton, whom Isabel refuses for fear of apostasy but whom Mme Merle, whose life (according to Osmond) is identical with her social ambitions, wants urgently to "have" in order to complete her apostasy. Indeed, Mme Merle's "having" Warburton is the aim of her part in the conspiracy to marry Isabel. Mme Merle's supreme motive is to have a compensatory "second go" through an exalted Pansy, and she would "have" Isabel in order one day to "have," if not Warburton, then the likes of him. For his part, Osmond can take a secret revenge for the secret injury a personage like Warburton inflicts on him simply by existing. Gilbert Osmond will marry the woman Lord Warburton wants:

> ... and now that he had seen Lord Warburton, whom he thought a very fine example of his race and order, he perceived a new attraction in the idea of taking to himself a young lady who had qualified herself to figure in his

collection of choice objects by declining so noble a hand. Gilbert Osmond had a high appreciation of this particular patriciate; not so much for its distinction, which he thought easily surpassable, as for its solid actuality. He had never forgiven his star for not appointing him to an English dukedom, and he could measure the unexpectedness of such conduct as Isabel's. It would be proper that the woman he might marry should have done something of that sort.

By marrying Isabel Osmond can do more than "have" Warburton, and thereby collect "tradition." He says of the quite ludicrous variety of people he envies, the Pope, the Emperor of Russia, the Sultan of Turkey and, here, an English duke, "I only want to *be* them," and now, out of his enormous existential envy, he can in a manner *be* Lord Warburton. He can complete his social apostasy, once and for all revenge himself on his unacceptable American past.

Finally the distinction between Isabel and the conspirators has to do with their differing sense of their identities. They are at either extreme of a revenge cycle because Isabel is only beginning to forfeit her cherished self-conception while the conspirators, as the novel insists several times over, are inveterate non-entities, are by now essentially impotent in respect to their self-conceptions. So it is appropriate to say that, while Isabel is seeking no more than an as yet indefinable compensation, the conspirators are ridden with *ressentiment: ressentiment,* or generalized revenge-feeling that is so much associated with feelings of weakness as to be deeply suppressed for fear of betraying this weakness, and as to seek as a result only delayed and ambiguous outlets. This is why we can view the intrigue in the second half of the novel to "have" Warburton as the ultimate end of the original conspiracy to "have" Isabel. Given Mme Merle's kind of revenge-feeling, association with Lord Warburton is the necessarily secret intention within the secret intention—so much so that even Osmond does not seem to be aware of his fellow conspirator's motives when she recommends Isabel to him as worth his effort to marry (Chapter 22).

The view that Isabel enters into a Jamesian revenge-cycle is, I think, confirmed by the fact that the novel repeats the sequence in which her suitors appear. Even as Osmond courts her in Rome (Chapters 24–29), Warburton appears (Chapters 27–28); and then Goodwood too appears sometime before her marriage (Chapter 32): if anything, their appearance simply determines Isabel in her intention to marry Osmond. Again, after her marriage, Warburton arrives on his visit to Florence with Ralph and, in order to approach Isabel, pays equivocal attention to Pansy (Chapters 38–46); and then Goodwood arrives (Chapters 47–48) and departs after a further appeal to Isabel. Yet again, after her rupture with Osmond and return full circle to Gardencourt, Isabel encounters Warburton and then Goodwood; even though he is on the point of marrying, Warburton can still make an implicit appeal to her, while Goodwood demands violently that she leave Osmond. For all this, Isabel is as consistent as ever with herself. She reacts towards Osmond: "She had not known where to turn; but she knew now. There was a very straight path."

Why? If it is true that Isabel originally married Osmond in order to compensate for any loss of social identity, in what way can her return be said to be consistent with her marriage? If Isabel knows, she does not say what she knows. One can only speculate that whereas she had previously sought compensation *in* Osmond for the partial forfeit of her social identity, she now intends to seek compensation *from* him for his failure to compensate her, indeed for having deprived her of identity. She returns to Florence as another Madame de Mauves, as Isabel *vindex*, there to bring home to Osmond the force of her cherished but now forfeited self-conception. Like Mme Merle, she has determined on "a second go." And as such a second go is likely to be a secret matter if at all revengeful in spirit—Mme Merle demonstrates this amply—she shows nothing. Isabel does know, but does not say what she knows. James himself will not say what he knows, indeed leaves the story *"en l'air"* (*Notebooks*)—as if he were finding a form that would express his characterization. His story about conspiracy turns into its own secret, makes a formal use of secrecy.

The events of the second half of the story substantiate this speculation. We have seen that, in marrying Osmond, Isabel is drawn into a revenge cycle. But then both Mme Merle and Osmond find that the instrument of their revenge is unconsciously humiliating them with her American "good faith." Mme Merle is steadily displaced by Isabel in her own child's affections, Osmond finds not only that he remains intrinsically a "perfect nonentity" in comparison with a Lord Warburton, but also that he is a perfect social nonentity in comparison with his American wife. It is as if, after years of having to endure a painful "front" in Europe, the *deraciné* should now be made painfully aware by Isabel of a "back," of the full extent of his social deprivation. Infinitely humiliated, he begins consciously to humiliate Isabel in his turn. The social aesthete invokes his "traditions," and tries to show Isabel up as a Yankee provincial having "no traditions." Something of this *ressentiment* emerges in his treatment of Caspar Goodwood:

> "Now we've *liked you*—!... We've liked you because—because you've reconciled us a little to the future.... I'm talking for my wife as well as for myself, you see. She speaks for me, my wife; why shouldn't I speak for her? We're as united, you know, as the candlestick and the snuffers. Am I assuming too much when I say that I think I've understood from you that your occupations have been—a—commercial? There's a danger in that, you know; but it's the way you have escaped that strikes us.... What I mean is that you *might have been*—a—what I was mentioning just now. The whole American world was in a conspiracy to make you so. But you resisted, you've something about you that saved you. And yet you're so modern, so modern; the most modern man we know!"

It is difficult to imagine a more comprehensive, infiltrating and ambiguous malice. It is the perfect malice of a perfect might-have-been.

Finally, finding no outlet for his *ressentiment* in a marriage between Pansy and Warburton, Osmond makes use of his "traditions"—actually, they are what

the novel elsewhere calls "elaborate mystifications." In his characteristically ambiguous way, he banishes Pansy to the convent. Then, invoking their marriage as
an absolute tradition, he refuses to let Isabel visit the dying Ralph in England:
"Because I think we should accept the consequences of our actions, and what I
value most in life is the honour of the thing!" The *ressentiment* man who feels
he is of no intrinsic value, who can experience value only through perpetual
comparison of himself with others, thus revenges himself upon all those who are
of value. And Mme Merle, who likewise can find no outlet for herself in a marriage of Pansy and Warburton, inflicts all her secret knowledge on Isabel, including as a last stroke the knowledge that it is her beloved Ralph who is
ultimately responsible for her disaster.

Isabel is utterly displaced from her identity. Considering her false position,
it is difficult not to speculate that she must feel resentful in proportion to its
seriousness. It is true that her feeling is initially one of "infinite sadness," and that
she exhibits none of the theatrical resentment the Countess Gemini expects of
her. But there may be all the difference between feeling and actually showing
resentment. Isabel may show nothing because she is at first rendered powerless
in her being, is in a state of comprehensive shock. Besides, as someone who
always presumptuously insists that "people suffer too easily ... It's not absolutely
necessary to suffer; we were not made for that" (Chapter 5), that "It couldn't be
she was to live only to suffer ... To live only to suffer—only to feel the injury
of life repeated and enlarged—it seemed to her she was too valuable, too capable, for that" (Chapter 53), she may be expected both to resist admitting injury and, consequently, to suppress any revenge-feeling. Then again, she is able
to see the full extent of her false position only at Gardencourt, to see exactly
what she has forfeited—not even for the right reasons. Only there does she see
the "ghost," realise that her lifetime is to be "ghosted" by a fruitful life that might
have been.

Isabel has ample cause for resentment. And up to a point she has cause not
to show any resentment. But that she should seem compelled to return to Osmond
without the slightest sign of forgiveness or renunciation, indeed without putting out
any reason, is disturbing. We must, I think, imagine that she has determined merely
to suppress her revenge-feeling for the time being, determined upon a secret
redress for an injury she would keep secret if she is ever to reestablish her original
self-conception. So there is no open rupture with Osmond. On the contrary, Isabel
will return to him and uphold the "honour" of their marriage. In one way or
another, she will have her golden bowl. At the same time she will "know" Osmond
in his insufficiency and impotence, "know" him without saying what she knows. By
this use of secrecy she will be a permanent reproach to the man "who was once
so fine." In short, we may see her return to Osmond not just as a seeking for
compensation, but as an act of resentment, an act that is presumably a prelude to
a life of taking revenge through righteousness.

—MANFRED MACKENZIE, "Communities of Knowledge: Secret Society in
Henry James," *ELH* 39, No. 1 (March 1972): 147–48, 152–60

LISA APPIGNANESI

The Portrait of a Lady is in many ways a transitional novel. It reveals James moving from a stage in which his not as yet fully controlled art explores the inner sensibility attached to the fairy-tale realm to a phase where he is complete master of his craft and involved with the repercussions the outward social and political world have on the private sensibility. The break, however, is by no means a clean one and *The Portrait* illuminates precisely the tensions between these two modes of feeling and being. James himself realised the importance of this book in his development and wrote to his mother that it would be, in comparison to his earlier works, as 'wine is to water'. His claims for the novel's 'seriousness' and 'bigness' seem to suggest that he was well aware, even before he had begun the writing of it, that *The Portrait* would be a book which included all his former tendencies as well as pointing the way to new ground. Indeed, the book reveals the main trends in the development of James's vision up to this point and directs his feminine orientation to the realistic and eventually masculine world of the middle period.

Philip Rahv calls Isabel the 'American Cinderella', but in Isabel the Cinderella character is not brought to its ultimate development. Isabel does not see the invisible; she does not in James's terminology, achieve 'consciousness'. In this she is the perfect receptacle of James's art and vision at this period of his career. Leon Edel, James's biographer, notes that *The Portrait* is 'pure fairy-tale: a rich uncle, a poor niece, an ugly sick cousin who worships her from a distance, three suitors, a fairy godfather who converts the niece into an heiress, and finally her betrayal by a couple of cosmopolitan compatriots into a marriage as sinister as the backdrop of a Brontë novel.' Yet a close examination of Isabel's unfolding character would seem to lead the novel further from the intensely inward world of the fairy-tale than any major work of James thus far. In *The Portrait* James seems to be relocating his forces and directing the reader's eyes toward the fixity of those external powers which will not permit the magic of the fairy world to function for the full flowering of the Cinderella figure.

Isabel, of course, begins with all the necessary qualifications of the Cinderella heroine. She is an innocent, virtually an orphan whose full imaginative life leads her to see everything as being 'just like a novel'. Although James claims her to be a 'frail vessel', he seems quite willing to satirize her innocence and her delusions. In fact, all the characters in the book, except Isabel herself, seem to be aware of her naiveté and illusions, for our Cinderella has been, in many ways, lifted out of the fairy sphere into the cold eye of a critical reality. Fairy godmother Touchett has taken on a critical air and states, 'It occurred to me that it would be a kindness to take her about and introduce her to the world. She thinks she knows a great deal of it—like most American girls; but like most American girls she's ridiculously mistaken.' James, with superb irony echoes this criticism of the unsuspecting Isabel, while in the same breath lauding her fineness.

Altogether, with her meagre knowledge, her inflated ideals, her confidence at once innocent and dogmatic, her temper at once exacting and indulgent, her mixture of curiosity and fastidiousness, of vivacity and indifference, her desire to look very well and to be if possible even better, her determination to see, to try, to know, her combination of the delicate, desultory, flame-like spirit and the eager and personal creature of conditions: she would be an easy victim of scientific criticism if she were not intended to awaken on the reader's part an impulse more tender and more purely expectant.

Isabel, with her romantic illusions, her penchant for grand definitions and her innocent belief in an ideal of happiness, certainly provides an easy victim for the factual and conventional society in which she finds herself. 'I'm very fond of my liberty', she says, in the strain of all James's Cinderella heroines, yet the world she is thrown into is not the fairy-tale realm where this independence can result in successful fulfillment. The old world for James is the realistic sphere of corruption and frustration, which forces innocent and presumptuous idealists to succumb to its decadent framework. It is a static and defined sphere, old in its worldly wisdom, a climate unfavourable to the retention of innocence. The Palazzo Roccanera, home of Osmond's perversity, stands solid and dungeon-like, firmly fixed in the still centre of this old world. Yet it is Isabel's own lack of awareness, her inability truly to see, as well as the inclement atmosphere, which is responsible for her victimisation. James seems to give her freedom precisely to see how far innocence can be stretched before it breaks down in the face of a public order which beckons the individual to gaze outward at the standards of the external world rather than inward to the heart of full being.

Isabel contains a tension within her own nature which makes her kin both to the Cinderella heroine, like Mary Garland, and to the more defined and predictable Christina Light. It is her similarity to this latter figure which leads her to her downfall. The picture which Madame Grandoni draws of Christina has many points in common with James's early depiction of Isabel, although, of course, Isabel has none of Christina's worldly lucidity. 'She had an unquenchable desire to think well of herself . . . Her life should always be in harmony with the most pleasing impression she should produce.' And later, 'Isabel's chief dread in life at this period of her development was that she should appear narrow-minded; what she feared next afterwards was that she should really be so'. Isabel's high regard for appearances, her willingness to play at the great lady, are similar to Christina's taste for histrionics and her willingness to do only those things which will contribute to her grandeur. Although Isabel's values are in many ways different from Christina's, the respect for appearances which lies dormant in her character at the start, but which gradually expands, is precisely what leads her so willingly to Osmond's altar and to a betrayal of her great desire for inner and external freedom. This aspect of her character is what allows her to be so greatly drawn to Madame Merle, who is in many ways an older Christina and hence an older and wiser Isabel. We remember that Madame Merle in her youth similarly had grandiose ambitions and illusions.

Madame Merle is totally a being of appearances, a perfect picture. Isabel's fallacy lies in admiring these qualities which make up the static, the fixed, and hence prevent eternal fluidity and flexibility of the being who is to experience the 'felt life'. Madame Merle is indeed a perfect picture, a totally outward-looking woman, circumscribed by a social frame.

> Her nature had been too much overlaid by custom and her angles too much rubbed away. She had become . . . too final. She was in a word too perfectly the social animal that man and woman are supposed to have been intended to be; and she had rid herself of every remnant of that tonic wildness . . . Isabel found it difficult to think of her in any detachment or privacy, she existed only in her relations, direct or indirect, with her fellow mortals. One might wonder what commerce she could possibly hold with her own spirit.

Yet Isabel excuses these elements in Madame Merle, thereby prophesying her own ultimate turn to this external world of appearances. She reacts against Madame Merle's pronouncement, 'we're each of us made up of some cluster of appurtenances. . . . I know a large part of myself is in the clothes I choose to wear. I've a great respect for *things!* One's self—for other people—is one's expression of one's self; and one's house, one's furniture, one's garments, the books one reads, the company one keeps—these things are all expressive'. However, she ends by marrying these 'things'. This is the expression of the doctrine of an arch materialist, with no respect for the spirit, the inner side of man. Isabel proceeds to marry Osmond precisely because his taste is expressed so exactly by his *things*.

The tension within Isabel between the Cinderella qualities of imagination and her respect for outwardness and absolute values, is resolved in the direction of the latter. She is less of a victim than Catherine, for her fate is in many ways the direct outcome of her inner make-up. Although she has sensitivity enough to recognise the fixing and stultifying elements of Osmond's house and hence of himself, she is attracted to it none the less. 'There was something brave and strong in the place; it looked somehow as if, once you were in, you would need an act of energy to get out.' Osmond's inertia, his affirmed indifference, his studied and wilful renunciation, his admission to these qualities and to the fact that he is 'convention itself' before his marriage to Isabel does nothing to deter her. Isabel feels she has a mission to perform. She wishes to be selfless in her marriage, to give not only to Osmond but also to his daughter Pansy. Her ideals fully distort any critical powers she may have and she wilfully gives up that openness of spirit which comprises the basis of Jamesian femininity in order to serve in a small way. 'The desire for unlimited expansion had been succeeded in her soul by the sense that life was vacant without some private duty that might gather one's energies to a point'. Moreover, the idea of totally filling the role of being 'the most important woman of the world' for someone, strongly appeals to Isabel, since she measures her own value in the eyes of others. Slightly frightened, but more than a little enticed by Osmond's pronouncements, she blindly marries herself to 'convention'—a convention based on empty forms, on exquisite taste and external values. She is prepared to pay homage, to do her duty—a word she holds in high esteem—to the sterility of convention; to take a 'pose' which is lived exclusively for the world.

If Isabel's attraction to Osmond can be explained away before her marriage by the fact of her innocence, this innocence does not justify her final action in the book. As we see in her reverie by the fire, she is now fully aware of Osmond's sterility and egotism. However, her recognition does not penetrate far enough into herself to allow her to see what lies at the core of the 'felt life'. Isabel sets limits of propriety for herself; she is afraid to bring the full brunt of her sensibility into the open and thus she cannot fully *be* in the Jamesian sense. Unlike Maggie in *The Golden Bowl*, she never attains self-consciousness, precisely because of the tendency in her own nature to overvalue appearances. Her faulty vision always sees further outwards than inwards. She recognises that both she and Osmond have been deceived in their marriage, yet ultimately she once again turns toward a form, a fixity which Osmond calls 'magnificent' and which she herself views as 'something transcendent and absolute like the sign of the cross or the flag of one's own country'.

Isabel leaves the feminine orientation of the inward-looking Cinderella behind her; she mistakes professional connoisseurship for true artistic imaginativeness. She accepts the superficial as profound. Thus she does not transgress the grounds of her own portrait of a *lady* to become a full-fledged feminine principle with the possibility of a creative or transformative effect. She emerges at the end of the book merely as a 'lady'—a finished social product in which imagination and freedom have given way to the rigidity of forms. James has the child of her marriage to Osmond die, thereby suggesting the barrenness of the life she has chosen.

By succumbing to the bounds of her portrait and returning to the ritual and form of marriage with Osmond, there is a suggestion that Isabel suffers the fate of one of Osmond's earlier victims, Madame Merle, who says to Osmond:

> You've not only dried up my tears; you've dried up my soul . . . I don't believe at all that it's an immortal principle. I believe it can perfectly be destroyed. That's what has happened to mine, which was a very good one to start with; and it's you I have to thank for it. You're very bad.

This, in the 'cool' Jamesian world is tantamount to damnation and the paradise lost imagery of this part of the book seems quite in keeping with the idea of Osmond, the serpent, as a destroyer of souls. It seems quite unlikely that Isabel at the end of her tale is returning to Osmond in order to create a fresh version of an inward paradise. She *has* succumbed to definition, to the inflexibility and static quality of an absolute, a portrait.

Her final scene with Caspar Goodwood testifies to this as she is fixed into the mould of Diana—the female archer, whose sign is the sterility and purity of the moon. Isabel's fear of passion, of that which will disturb her to the core of her being and thus force her to see herself fully, is suggested throughout her portrait. Her putting off of Warburton is based on this fear, and it is once again illustrated in this description James gives us. 'Deep in her soul—it was the deepest thing there—lay the belief that if a certain light should dawn she would give herself completely; but this image on the whole was too bookish to be attractive.' Cargill is certainly right in saying:

> Bookish and without passional experience, she had married Osmond out of illusion, but even though she had given him a child, he had never really touched the core of her nature—it needed Goodwood's kiss to do that, and Matthiessen is right in testifying to its effectiveness in revealing the virginal nature of the heroine.

Isabel runs away from Goodwood and in doing so she renders her portrait complete. She emerges as the slightly ascetic Diana who lives, as she herself puts it, in the mind of Osmond, the moon. She has become another masculine emanation, a static figure, whose outlines are complete, defined, and whose possibility for expanding the circuit of 'felt life' and attaining consciousness is closed.

There is nothing to say that James approved of Isabel's actions. Indeed his ironic approach to her should make us wary of idealising her as the consummate Jamesian heroine. If we rid ourselves of this assumption, we see that Isabel emerges as the first Jamesian venture into the realistic world of his middle period, when he holds the tools of his craft well under control and explores the various dead ends of static and outward definition of character. James's orientation in this period may be 'feminine' as it has been before, yet what he is essentially examining is the defeminized world which tends towards absolutes, toward extra-personal definitions of the self rather than to the flexibility and openness of personalism and the fairy-tale.

—LISA APPIGNANESI, "Henry James: Femininity and the Moral Sensibility,"
*Femininity and the Creative Imagination: A Study of Henry James,
Robert Musil and Marcel Proust* (London: Vision Press, 1973), pp. 40–46

RONALD WALLACE

When Frederick Crews calls Isabel Archer an "unimpeachable heroine," we must suspect that he has missed the essentially comic tradition to which she, as heroine, belongs. As admirable and perceptive as Isabel Archer may at times be in *The Portrait of a Lady*, she is dogmatic, her ideals are inflated, and her self-knowledge is meager throughout. As Leon Edel suggests, she is, in fact, a female Christopher Newman, and like Newman, for all her delicacy of feeling, she is presumptuous and egotistical. Although Isabel has a larger fund of self-awareness than Newman, her awareness reverses repeatedly in the novel. "She had an unquenchable desire to think well of herself," James tells us. She believes that "one should try to be one's own best friend and to give one's self, in this manner, distinguished company." "Sometimes she went so far as to wish that she might find herself some day in a difficult position, so that she could have the pleasure of being as heroic as the occasion demanded."

Northrop Frye observes that "comedy is designed not to condemn evil, but to ridicule a lack of self-knowledge." Isabel Archer belongs to a long tradition of characters whose self-knowledge exposes them to ridicule. Oscar Cargill refers to the tradition as that of the "limited heroine," but a more precise term, perhaps, is "self-deceived protagonist." James, himself, in the preface to *The Portrait* refers to several other female characters in this tradition; George Eliot's Hetty Sorrel and Rosamond Vincy are both rank egotists. Other heroines in this tradition, more closely related to Isabel than the extreme Hetty and Rosamond, are Jane Austen's Emma Woodhouse, and George Eliot's Dorothea Brooke. To see Isabel's place in this tradition, as Cargill points out, is to correct the wrong assumption that she is the ideal type of James's cousin Minny Temple.

Like Emma, Isabel is obviously misguided, selfish, egotistical, and stupidly naive, yet at the same time sympathetic and potentially intelligent. And, like Dorothea, she is the victim of her own headlong enthusiasms, her ignorance of the world and of herself, and her misplaced devotion. But Isabel is left much more alone in her self-delusion than either Emma or Dorothea. Jane Austen provides her heroine with a clear representative of right action in Knightley. Both he and the pastoral world of Highbury itself guide Emma toward a wisdom and self-knowledge symbolized by her final union with Knightley, the moral norm and emblem of an ideal society.

Dorothea's standard of conduct is much less clear to the reader or to herself. But if Dorothea lacks the objective correlative of the moral norm which Knightley provides, she is saved by the *deus ex machina* of death, and in the end marries happily, for love. Both Dorothea and Isabel, however, have principles which are inadequate for confronting the complexities of life. Dogmatism and egotism are their main obstacles to moral enlargement. And the irony which overtakes them both is that in seeking escape from narrowing influences (Dorothea wants to escape her provincial town and Isabel rejects the confinement of Warburton or Goodwood) they submit themselves to a marital narrowness far more malevolent. But whereas Casaubon dies, Osmond lives, and Isabel must accept responsibility for her own actions. She cannot marry Ralph as Emma marries Knightley and Dorothea marries Will Ladislaw.

If Emma's situation is rendered less difficult because Knightley represents the moral norm which she must merely perceive, and if Dorothea's final creation of moral value requires a *deus ex machina,* Isabel's circumstances emphasize her inability or unwillingness to rely on external help. She, like Emma, is provided a version of the ideal in Ralph. But Ralph is sick, Isabel cannot take his joking seriously, and she remains unable to adopt his perspective on life. In the end, Isabel is perhaps morally stronger than either of her predecessors when she rejects her own *deus ex machina,* Caspar Goodwood, and affirms her decision to create her own moral norm.

But despite Isabel's strength, James emphasizes her weaknesses. He intrudes to inform the reader that "the love of knowledge coexisted in her mind with the finest capacity for ignorance." And even when he warns the reader not to be too harsh with Isabel he comically undercuts her in the manner of George Eliot:

Smile not, however, I venture to repeat, at this simple young woman from Albany who debated whether she should accept an English peer before he had offered himself and who was disposed to believe that on the whole she could do better. She was a person of great good faith, and if there was a great deal of folly in her wisdom those who judge her severely may have the satisfaction of finding that, later, she became consistently wise only at the cost of an amount of folly.

James earlier insists that despite her "meager knowledge, her inflated ideals," and her "dogmatic" confidence, she is "intended to awaken on the reader's part an impulse more tender and more purely expectant." George Eliot uses a similar technique to expose the pedantic Casaubon, repeatedly intruding in *Middlemarch* to protest that Casaubon isn't really as bad as he seems. But in protesting, she lists all of Casaubon's faults, making doubly sure that the reader has not missed them. James uses the same method when he lists Isabel's defects and then insists that they are not so bad.

Isabel's approach to life, like that of Emma and Dorothea, is romantic, idealistic, and theoretic. Henrietta Stackpole correctly analyzes Isabel's main fault when she tells her friend that she lives "too much in the world of your own dreams. You're not enough in contact with reality." Isabel smugly replies, "What are my illusions? . . . I try so hard not to have any." But Isabel's retort is comic to the reader who has seen her obviously romantic naiveté. Isabel defines "happiness" as "a swift carriage of a dark night, rattling with four horses over roads that one can't see." She sees Lord Warburton as the hero of a romance and exclaims, "Oh, I do hope they'll make a revolution! . . . I should delight in seeing a revolution." Isabel's naiveté and innocence, juxtaposed with her almost arrogant self-assurance and assumed worldly wisdom, must draw sympathetic smiles from the reader. But Isabel, like Christopher Newman, is herself rather humorless. James describes Isabel gazing "with that solemn stare which sometimes seemed to proclaim her deficient in the sense of comedy."

Isabel thus belongs to the tradition of Emma Woodhouse and Dorothea Brooke. But that tradition appeared long before the nineteenth century. The type of the self-deceived protagonist is perhaps most obvious in the plays of Molière, and Isabel shares many traits with the Molière comic hero.

Molière's Arnolphe and Sganarelle are type comic characters who flout established society and, as Lionel Gossman suggests:

The rejection of society is not, clearly, confined to articles of clothing. . . . Everybody wants an entertaining, witty and sociable wife? Arnolphe and Sganarelle will choose a "bête," and they will value precisely that in her which nobody else seems to admire.

Characters like Harpagon, Alceste, Don Juan, Madame Pernelle, and Orgon refuse to admit that they are members of human society like everybody else, and possess no special sensibility which raises them to the superhuman level. Instead they pretend to themselves that they are special cases, and they use other people as instruments for asserting their "superiority" to the world around them.

> What these characters want above all is *to be distinguished,* but they refuse to adopt the usual method of social advancement and privilege, since this method offers only a *relative* superiority to others, whereas the superiority they desire is *absolute.* . . . They are comic not only because there is a constant contradiction between what they are and what they affect to be, but because their attempt to transcend all social superiorities and to reach an absolute superiority misfires.

The description fits Isabel rather closely. In an early discussion with Madame Merle these comic character traits are evident immediately. Isabel tells Madame Merle that she defines success as "some dream of one's youth come true." And when Madame Merle insists that it never happens, Isabel replies that it has already happened to her. Madame Merle remarks:

> "Ah, if you mean the aspirations of your childhood—that of having a pink sash and a doll that could close her eyes."
> "No, I don't mean that."
> "Or a young man with a fine moustache going down on his knees to you."
> "No, nor that either," Isabel declared with still more emphasis.
> Madame Merle appeared to note this eagerness. "I suspect that's what you do mean. We've all had the young man with the moustache. He's the inevitable young man; he doesn't count. . . ."
> "Why shouldn't he count? There are young men and young men."

Isabel, like the Molière characters, will not admit to being at all like anyone else. *Her* affairs are special. Yet her eagerness to contradict Madame Merle reveals to the reader an aspect of her character of which she, herself, is quite unaware. In the same conversation Madame Merle again undercuts Isabel's pretensions. She suggests that clothes express the person, and Isabel disagrees:

> "To begin with it's not my own choice that I wear them; they're imposed upon me by society."
> "Should you prefer to go without them?" Madame Merle enquired in a tone which virtually terminated the discussion.

Isabel bridles at any suggestion that she is a part of society to which other people belong.

Further, like Arnolphe and Sganarelle who flout society by rejecting women who are socially desirable and courting those who are not, Isabel thrills to the joy of refusing two socially respectable and desirable suitors. After sending Caspar away she "yielded to the satisfaction of having refused two ardent suitors in a fortnight." Isabel claims publicly that she wishes no one would propose to her, but she secretly revels in the attention and would be most disappointed if left to herself. And, like the Molière characters, one of the reasons she finally chooses Gilbert

Osmond is just the fact that no one else appreciates him. Ralph perceives this when he comments, "It was wonderfully characteristic of her that, having invented a fine theory about Gilbert Osmond, she loved him not for what he really possessed, but for his very poverties dressed out as honours."

Isabel exerts much energy in avoiding any commitment which would result in "limitation." She rejects the physical coercion of Goodwood and the social restrictiveness of Warburton. She does not want this kind of relative superiority. Marrying Osmond in the face of widespread opposition, she feels, will assure absolute superiority. Isabel's bad marriage and subsequent suffering, then, are largely the result of her own comic egotism.

Like Christopher Newman, Isabel, in her pride and ignorance, becomes almost demonic toward the end of the book. She constantly assures herself that she is an unimpeachable wife to her malevolent husband, and yet James exposes a satanic streak in her. When she asks Osmond if he would like Warburton to marry Pansy, "she knew exactly the effect on his mind of her question: it would operate as an humiliation. Never mind; he was terribly capable of humiliating *her*." And later she rationalizes to herself that it is her duty to keep her marital unhappiness a secret from Ralph. She calls it a "kindness" to him. But both Ralph and the reader see that Isabel's deception is just a further example of her desire to think well of herself at other people's expense. Ralph, with characteristic selfless good humor, observes:

> As it was, the kindness consisted mainly in trying to make him believe that he had once wounded her greatly and that the event had put him to shame, but that, as she was very generous and he was so ill, she bore him no grudge and even considerately forbore to flaunt her happiness in his face. Ralph smiled to himself, as he lay on his sofa, at this extraordinary form of consideration.

I have, of course, emphasized Isabel's negative qualities at the expense of her more admirable traits. And it must be admitted that she does attain a kind of self-knowledge at the close when she perceives her responsibility for her bad marriage.

The character of Isabel, however, derives in part from the tradition of the self-deceived protagonist and the Molière egotist. If the plot of *The Portrait* were a tragic plot, the flaws in Isabel's character would render her tragic. But the plot of the novel is that of tragicomedy. And Isabel, in her self-exposure and resilient optimism, is a tragicomic heroine.

—RONALD WALLACE, "The Jamesian Character," *Henry James and the Comic Form* (Ann Arbor: University of Michigan Press, 1975), pp. 24–30

PETER JONES

It would be anachronistic to interpret the novel in terms of lectures delivered in 1906, but there are remarks in William James's *Pragmatism* which help us to determine the kind of attitudes to be contrasted with those of Isabel Archer. First, as William James understands it, pragmatism "is a method only"; "the attitude of looking away from first things, principles, 'categories,' supposed necessities; and of looking towards last things, fruits, consequences, facts." Second, "true ideas are those that we can assimilate, validate, corroborate and verify." Third, "purely objective truth . . . is nowhere to be found"; "we break the flux of sensible reality, then, at our will. We create the subjects of our true as well as of our false propositions." Such views, when properly understood, James contended, represented both a less objectionable and a more radical version of the familiar empiricist attitude. In brief, it is an empiricism shorn of its original rationalist elements.

Commenting on his brother's book in 1907, Henry James expressed delight in the apparent discovery that he had "unconsciously pragmatised" all his life. However disingenuous that declaration, it is significant that no thesis is presented or argued for in *The Portrait of a Lady,* no conclusions are drawn from premises, and the few generalizations that occur lack theoretical support; and, of course, if some form of the pragmatic method informed the novel there could be no place for the old empiricist tenets that are found in *Middlemarch.* But even if Henry James agreed with his brother that pragmatism "does not stand for any special results," this does not mean that, in the particular contexts in which the pragmatic method is used, no conclusions of any kind are to be expected. Although Isabel Archer's determinable attitudes and beliefs are so conspicuously mistaken, and the novel is concerned with the consequences of such mistakes, the outlines of an appropriate attitude and approach to life emerge in the presentation of contrasting characters and views. A properly "experimental" attitude towards knowledge will be more concerned with the particular case than with consistency or abstract formulae, and will recognize that different ideas, associations, and desires can attach "to the same formulas." Mrs. Touchett contends that "there are as many points of view in the world as there are people of sense to take them," but if it is impossible, in practice, to take account of them all, Ralph's "hesitations and compunctions" and his "loose-fitting urbanity" which can help one feel "one's relations . . . to others" are less likely to be disastrous prescriptions for action than Isabel's "confidence at once innocent and dogmatic."

The ever-present narrator of *The Portrait of a Lady,* unlike his counterpart in *Middlemarch,* rarely offers interpretations of his own, and the philosophical dimension of the work is not evident in his remarks. Moreover, there is little indication in the leisurely opening chapters of the notions that come to central prominence in the novel—the notions of freedom and independence, and the special role played by ideas.

From the outset, Isabel admits to having "too many theories," and she later concedes that at her marriage she retained "too many ideas." The point to be made concerns not possession of ideas as such, but rather their nature, their sources, and their roles. Although "she really preferred almost any source of information to the printed page," the "foundation" of Isabel's knowledge, through no fault of her own, lay in "the idleness of her grandmother's house," especially in the "books with frontispieces." Her "imagination was by habit ridiculously active" and she often "paid the penalty of . . . seeing without judging." "She carried within herself a great fund of life" but to the extent that the life had been denied the opportunity for outward expression, it had merely further animated her active imagination. Because she thought she knew a great deal of the world she sought for "knowledge that was tinged with the unfamiliar"—even the "unpleasant," according to literature, might be "a source of interest." Isabel's thoughts were "a tangle of vague outlines which had never been corrected by the judgment of people speaking with authority," and she had a theory that "life was worth living" only if one moved "in a realm of light, of natural wisdom, of happy impulse, of inspiration gracefully chronic. It was almost as unnecessary to cultivate doubt of one's self as to cultivate doubt of one's best friend."

Four points can be made here. First, her thoughts had never been "corrected"; Isabel ignored the crucial role to be played by verification. Second, she failed to appeal to those who could speak "with authority," because she believed she could acquire knowledge essentially by herself. Many writers have seen, however, that it is impossible for a man to acquire knowledge by himself alone, because knowledge has an essential social dimension. If we begin by imitating others, we are subsequently taught the rules, conventions, and practices which operate in our society; we have to take a great deal on trust, and we learn who the authorities are, in a given field, whilst we are being taught in that field. Third, Isabel is reluctant to doubt, just as she feels no need to verify. But ideas carry no warrant of truth, and the varied descriptions of our experiences can be interpreted in many ways. It is not surprising that her imagination "played her a great many tricks." Fourth, Isabel wished to celebrate "natural wisdom" and "happy impulse." It will be necessary, later, to comment on what is alleged to be natural.

Isabel was "impatient to live" and in her eagerness usually asked whether things new to her "corresponded with the descriptions in the books" ("it's just like a novel"). As a result, the word "specimen" "played a considerable part in her vocabulary," as when she saw Osmond as "a specimen apart." Specimens belong to kinds, of course, and an over-readiness to classify may lead one to disregard uniqueness and particularity. Isabel held both that in order to "prevent mistakes" one "should begin by getting a general impression of life," and that "if a thing strikes me with a certain intensity I accept it." Traditional empiricists held that intensity or vivacity was the property by which impressions of reality could be separated from ideas conjured up by imagination; impressions were the basic, uninterpreted data of perception, which impinged upon the passively receptive mind. Isabel is always eager for new impressions, but when she tells Henrietta that "one should get as many new ideas as possible," she is told that "they shouldn't interfere with the old ones when the old ones have been the right ones." The view that loyalty to established truths is often the only fruitful principle to follow was a central tenet of pragmatism, at least in William James's version. Ralph was "equally unable to accept or refute" Isabel's "brave theories, as to historic cause and social effect," because of their indeterminacy and the fact that she lacked the experience to ground them. Early on, Isabel held that "the essence of the aristocratic situation" was "to be in a better position for appreciating" others than they were for observing her, a one-sided and detached view that contributed to her lack of interest in the responses of her hearers. Essentially, "the love of knowledge coexisted in her mind with the

finest capacity for ignorance"; she rarely tested her knowledge claims and frequently saw "in the things she looked at a great deal more than was there." She had
"rather a dense little group of ideas" about herself, constantly pictured her career
"to herself by the light of her hopes, her fears, her fancies, her ambitions, her
predilections," and, indeed, "lost herself in a maze of visions." Although it occasionally puzzled her that she had an idea of something which "the actual" failed to
express, she believed she always acted "with reason."

It is significant that none of Isabel's ideas or theories is spelled out in an
articulate fashion; and that is because she herself never thought them out. The
mainly literary source of her ideas and opinions would not have mattered so much
had she sought to establish their nature and their truth in the light of her own
experience and that of others around her. Isabel's most frequently mentioned
theory concerns "freedom" or "independence"—the terms appear almost 100
times in the story—but what the theory amounts to can only be gauged by
reflecting on the nature of her actions.

From the outset, Isabel proclaims her fondness for liberty or independence,
interpreted by others as fondness for her own ways, and by the narrator as a
possible form of solitude. Ralph points out that independence may be understood
"in a moral or in a financial sense" but believes there to be close connections
between the two, and secures a bequest to Isabel so that she may be free to do
what she likes; only later does he realize that the error of his well-meaning interference arises, in part, from his wish to influence her from a distance, without
responsibility for the consequences. Isabel associated her "love of liberty" with her
desire to find out "how to live" for herself, but her essentially "theoretic" notion had
rather more to do with her "scheme of the agreeable for one's self," her reluctance
to be bound by family ties or any other conventions, and her unwillingness to seek
advice from others. An important exchange between Mme. Merle and Isabel
emphasizes what might be called the "atomic" nature of Isabel's ideas, and her
notion of the self. Mme. Merle says:

> When you've lived as long as I you'll see that every human being has his shell
> and that you must take the shell into account. By the shell I mean the whole
> envelope of circumstances. There's no such thing as an isolated man or woman;
> we're each of us made up of some cluster of appurtenances. What shall we
> call our "self"? Where does it begin? where does it end? It overflows into
> everything that belongs to us—and then it flows back again. I know a large part
> of myself is in the clothes I choose to wear. I've a great respect for *things!*
> One's self—for other people—is one's expression of one's self; and one's
> house, one's furniture, one's garments, the books one reads, the company one
> keeps—these things are all expressive.

To this metaphysical speech Isabel replies:

> I think just the other way. I don't know whether I succeed in expressing myself,
> but I know that nothing else expresses me. Nothing that belongs to me is any
> measure of me; everything's on the contrary a limit, a barrier, and a perfectly

arbitrary one. Certainly the clothes which, as you say, I choose to wear, don't express me. . . .

A reader is not required to align himself with either pronouncement, the former view representing an analysis of the self in terms of appearances and relations, and the latter in terms of some unidentified substance. Nevertheless, a reader does well to juxtapose such views with those of Henrietta, who held that persons are "simple and homogeneous organisms," and Ralph, who held that "everything is relative."

Isabel's failure in the present context partly explains her failure to grapple with the pointed questions raised about Osmond's identity. Ironically, Mme. Merle first raises the question, when contrasting Ralph and Osmond, but we later learn of both Ralph's and Warburton's views. Both the Countess Gemini and Goodwood ask "What has he ever done?", and Mme. Merle tells the Countess that he has "done nothing that has had to be undone."

Isabel's refusal to find out what her ideas really are, and her refusal to articulate and thus to share and to test them, manifest her reluctance to share herself. Ralph noticed how she withdrew from intimacy, and that he saw her "only by glimpses." Of course, Isabel held that "if a certain light should dawn she could give herself completely," but this desire for revelation serves to diminish her own efforts towards others. As Isabel begins to sense what might be involved in genuine freedom, she draws back, reminding herself "that there were essential reasons why one's ideal could never become concrete"; it is no surprise that she wonders whether, in view of the constant effort to keep thinking, "it's not a greater happiness to be powerless." The reference to power is important.

Isabel discovered that her newly inherited wealth was a further "acquisition of power," and she found that she enjoyed "the exercise of her power" in refusing Goodwood. Before her marriage she saw Osmond as "her lover, her own"; the subtlest "manly organism she had ever known had become her property." An intellectually immature person may feel greater power over what he merely imagines because he has yet to define the boundaries of the self, and in his own imaginings each man is an absolute master. Isabel gradually discovers that she lacks the power in actuality that she assigned to herself in imagination. For example, on hearing of Warburton's impending marriage, she felt as if she had heard of his death; she is shocked to realize that she had known him "only as a suitor." Although she repulsed all his approaches to her, both before and after her marriage, she could not envisage his life as directed towards others. It may be that the attention given to her by so many admirers only hampered any of her efforts at self-knowledge and, indeed, knowledge of others. Isabel dreads having "to choose and decide," and her characteristic moral reaction is retreat. This is consistent with her liking "better to think of the future, than of the past," since the future could be fashioned in imagination, and with her finding the sweetest liberty, "the liberty to forget." Looking back over her past, Warburton had been "something to be resisted and reasoned with," and Goodwood always "seemed to deprive her of her sense of freedom." Isabel resents Goodwood's visit prior to her marriage precisely because "it implied things she could never assent to—rights, reproaches, remonstrance, rebuke, the expectation of making her change her purpose." In the final scene, Goodwood tells her that she is "perfectly alone," and to some extent this characterizes her attitude, if not her real position, throughout. It is noble, for example, that she tells Ralph, early on: "I don't wish to touch the cup of experience. It's a poisoned drink! I only want to see for myself." "Seeing" here seems to exclude involvement, although not "enjoyment." Before her marriage, Isabel characterized her ambition as being "free to follow out a good feeling," and as she became enmeshed in Osmond's stifling notion of propriety she "pleaded the cause of freedom, of doing as they chose, of not caring for the aspect and denomination of their life."

Like Henrietta, and Ralph, and above all Osmond, although in different ways in each case, Isabel wants to be an observer, a taster, where the notion of tasting is essentially an attitude towards objects, not persons. Some measure of the widening gap between Osmond and Isabel is shown by the fact that he ceases even to regard her as an object, "but only a rather disagreeable incident, of thought." One of Osmond's reasons for remaining quiet, apart from his posture of "not attempting," was a wish to make his life appear "a work of art," and the same desire underlay his attempt to see Isabel when she was "tired and satiated," because her energies and demands would no longer be disturbing and intrusive. Isabel's initial willingness to view Osmond as quiet blinded her to the force of her aunt's belief that "there's nothing *of* him." We are told that "it was wonderfully characteristic of her that, having invented a fine theory about Gilbert Osmond, she loved him not for what he really possessed, but for his very poverties dressed out as honours." Even if it was only half the story to say that "she had really married on a factitious theory"—for, in addition, "a certain ardour took possession of her"—"she had imagined a world of things that had no substance."

When Henrietta rebukes Isabel for her romantic views, she accuses her of being "not enough in contact with reality"; and the remark can be taken to refer not only to Isabel's self-indulgent imaginings, but also to her failure to appreciate her real links with other people, not least via the consequences of her own actions. Even when she reflects upon her tragic mistake, Isabel contends that "the sole source of her mistake had been within herself," and although she does express pity for Mme. Merle, for Osmond's first wife, for Pansy, Ralph, and Goodwood towards the end, there are obvious traces of pride and egoism in her rejection of help. There are other elements, however, to which we must return.

The notion of freedom from constraints of any kind can be linked with the numerous references to what it is, or is thought to be, "natural" to do. Appropriate synonyms for the term vary with the context: "spontaneous," "relaxed," "unselfconscious" would evidently be synonyms on some occasions. Sometimes, "natural" means "expected in the context," and in this sense the notion can embrace habits and conventions—hence Mme. Merle could be natural even while "playing a part." Isabel's wish to "lead a natural life," however, refers to the avoidance of social veneer and artificial custom; a person can become "too perfectly the social animal" and rid himself "of every remnant of that tonic wildness which we may assume to have belonged even to the most amiable persons in the ages before country house life was the fashion." Just as there seemed to be something "professional" and "slightly mechanical" in Mme. Merle's "freshness," so Isabel wondered whether the extremity of Pansy's candor, which seemed so natural, might not be "the perfection of self-consciousness." In the end, Isabel discovers that with Osmond everything was "*pose—pose* so subtly considered that if one were not on the lookout one mistook it for impulse." "His ambition was not to please the world, but to please himself by exciting the world's curiosity and then declining to satisfy it." In spite of, or perhaps because of, her wish "to look at life for herself," Isabel is "ground in the very mill of the conventional," and is deceived by the "ingenuity" of others—a term frequently used to denote cunning, contrivance, or artifice.

The active and passive dimensions of attention are clearly captured in the frequent references to "interest" or to what is found "interesting." I may become interested in *x* by attending to it; on the other hand, *x* may interest me by catching my attention. To possess an interest is to possess a key to overcoming boredom and self-absorption. When characters proclaim an interest, or something to be interesting (the notions are not equivalent), we may infer not only their attention to some state of affairs, but some involvement with it, and a set of beliefs directed to possible action. As we know, Isabel's "mind contained no natural class offering a place to Mr. Osmond—he was a specimen apart"; because of this, so much about him was of interest, "for his meaning was not at all times obvious." The supposition that Mme. Merle was French "made the visitor more interesting to our speculative heroine," and Mrs. Touchett was similarly interesting to Isabel because she was unique to her experience. Pride in her own knowledge led her to believe that what she did not know must be profound or exceptional in some way. Genuine interest in another person enables one to escape from oneself, but it is necessary first to focus one's attention properly; this may be difficult, but failure can lead to disastrous consequences, as the case of Isabel and Osmond shows: ". . . he was poor and lonely and yet somehow he was noble—that was what had interested her and seemed to give her her opportunity."

With few exceptions, for example Mrs. Touchett lightly and Henrietta solemnly, only Isabel talks about duty. Although she often found it disagreeable, she held that we must look for it as much as possible, and take it where we find it. She always gave special weight to promises—"I think a great deal of my promises"—and this explains not only why she emphasizes the solemn promise at her marriage, but also why she was careful not to promise Goodwood anything if he returned in a couple of years, and why her promise to Pansy constituted a sufficient reason for returning to Rome. It might be held that she misconceived the "single sacred act of her life," the marriage promise, and that her final visit to Ralph on his deathbed merited the description rather more, even though she herself was not sure she would come until she came. Isabel's belief that "one must accept one's deeds" is ironically echoed by Osmond's "blasphemous sophistry"—"I think we should accept the consequences of our actions, and what I value most in life is the honour of a thing." Readers may well wonder, with Isabel herself, why she was "so afraid of not doing right"—a phrase echoed at Ralph's death—and recall that she was sharply reminded that refusing is nevertheless a decision, and thus an exercise of power. Isabel thought she envied the "happier lot of men, who are always free to plunge into the healing waters of action," and yet, with rare exceptions, she sought to avoid acting herself. We are told, however, that whenever she was unhappy she "always looked about her—partly from impulse and partly by theory—for some form of positive exertion. She could never rid herself of the sense that unhappiness was a state of disease—a suffering as opposed to doing. To 'do'— it hardly mattered what—would therefore be an escape, perhaps in some degree a remedy." This passage, so reminiscent of *Anna Karenina,* might encourage one to describe Isabel's condition as a *metaphysical sickness.* Suffering "was an active condition," and she "desired occupation"; but she yearned for what she could not achieve. Although we are told that with Osmond and Isabel "the vital principle of the one was a thing of contempt to the other," we must ask what Isabel's vital principle amounted to.

Isabel believed that she and Osmond had been mistaken about each other because she herself had "kept still," "pretending there was less of her than there really was"; yet she also came to see that Osmond's studied "wilful renunciation" was far from being the expression of an "exquisite independence" and indifference—as it might have been for Ralph. On the contrary, Osmond "was unable to live without" society, and "under the guise of caring only for intrinsic values . . . lived exclusively for the world." If Isabel had formulated in her mind principles which found no exemplification in the real world, it is no wonder that she comes to envy Ralph his dying, on the one hand, and on the other hand to yearn for "the joy of irreflective action"; both attitudes are consistent with her tormenting need "to feel that her unhappiness should not have come to her through her own fault"—a need she never satisfied.

It is impossible to overlook the references to fear, dread, and terror—more than fifty in number—which form a crescendo in the last third of the book. Early on, Isabel declares that she is afraid of herself and her mind, of appearing narrow-minded and indiscriminate; and at various times thereafter she is afraid of Goodwood, sex, Mme. Merle, Countess Gemini, and Pansy's wisdom; she is also afraid of several possibilities, such as pursuit by Warburton, Goodwood's arrival, Ralph's death in Rome, and a rupture with Osmond. Her fears have a major source in the dramatic failure of reality to match her imagined ideas of it, and as she begins to grasp the extent of her "innocent ignorance," she fears yet further revelations of errors. But with Isabel fear is not only a criterion of dawning awareness. She claims and yearns to be free, but shrinks from all demands by others, finding even wealth to be a burden, and fearing the freedom wealth brings; above all, she fears action, with its attendant responsibility for consequences and to others. Refusal to act may well preserve, in some sense, pristine ideals; but what are they then worth? Isabel finds herself unable and unwilling to explain her central decision; she cannot explain to Goodwood, Mrs. Touchett, or to Ralph why she has chosen to marry Osmond, although we may certainly infer that his effort to be "as quiet as possible" appealed to her, in contrast to Goodwood's insistence. She explains her decision to herself, however, as we have already seen, by saying that "he was her lover, her own, and that she should be able to be of use to him." Later, however, she looks on such justifications as inappropriate or morally inadequate, and, in overreaction, seems inclined to distrust the roles of intellect completely—like Levin in *Anna Karenina*.

Isabel is a tragi-comic heroine. Osmond acquired her "to figure in his collection of choice objects," and after marriage Isabel comes only to "represent" Osmond himself, as a portrait represents the living model and stands as a two-dimensional token of it. Osmond tells her that they are as united "as the candlestick and the snuffers," and this horrifying simile is underlined by Ralph's parting words: "There's nothing makes us feel so much alive as to see others die. That's the sensation of life—the sense that we remain."

At the outset, and, as it happens, before the novel had been completed, the narrator is made to concede that Isabel "would be an easy victim of scientific criticism," and if one asks what kind of freedom was possible for a girl of her class and background in the 1870s, consideration should be given to the observation that most women "waited, in attitudes more or less gracefully passive, for a man to come that way and furnish them with a destiny. Isabel's originality was that she gave one an impression of having intentions of her own." The opportunities open to her, severely limited in contrast with those open to men, partly explain the vacuity of her ideas. But do any of the characters posses or enact an intelligible notion of freedom? Can any of them be said to be morally responsible? Indeed, does the portrayal of an apparently seamless web of experience, viewed from varying perspectives, yield any implications about what can be treated as knowledge, understanding, or responsible action? There is a gap, of course, between what a reader knows and what the characters are shown to perceive and believe, and the narrator requires a reader to adopt a framework other than that of the characters. In so doing, however, he risks losing a reader's sympathy for those who adopt an essentially egocentric epistemology and ethic; sympathy for Isabel, for example, would be inadequately grounded on a reader's covert self-concern, and must trade, in part, on his residual habits or desires which outlive their original context, and on respect for her real virtues.

Philosophical conclusions about the novel can be stated, if at all, only in a general and relatively uninteresting manner: from a story of the disastrous conse-quences of following untested and self-centered ideas, a reader is expected to conclude that there is an essential social dimension to knowledge and its acquisition, and that morally responsible behavior requires directed thought towards others, based on concern for them and an effort to transcend any natural egoism. Along-side such a view, supported by considerations of the kind discussed in this article, a reader might also conclude that a particular recipe for avoiding such disasters is implied in the novel; and the recipe, which might be called the pragmatic method, urges recognition of the open-endedness of all inquiry, the provisional nature of empirical conclusions, the multiplicity of possibly fruitful viewpoints, the interrelation of our knowledge claims and their fallibility. The absence of detailed support and justification for such tenets, however, has sometimes been alleged to be a major difficulty for philosophical pragmatism, especially since they seem to be compatible with vacillation, indecision, and inaction. Any dissatisfaction with the moral and epistemological ambiguities in *The Portrait of a Lady* is likely to have one major source in the vagueness of the pragmatic method and its central concepts, insofar as that method is shown, or implied to be, a proper method for conducting one's life.

—PETER JONES, "Pragmatism and *The Portrait of a Lady*," *Philosophy and Literature* 5, No. 1 (Spring 1981): 50–60

CRITICAL ESSAYS

Tony Tanner

THE FEARFUL SELF

I

The feeling which Isabel Archer most consistently experiences is fear. She is frightened by Warburton's offer, of Caspar Goodwood's persistence, and Gilbert Osmond's anger; she is frightened of sexual passion, of her unexpected wealth, of her 'freedom'; but beneath all these specific apprehensions there is, she admits, a deeper, radical fear—fear of herself. Seeing that it is a self which can misread Osmond so disastrously and make such a profoundly mistaken choice then, we may say, she has good grounds for her fear. But her fear, her error, and her final resolution are, it seems to me, crucial stages on a psychic journey which forms the very heart of the novel. This journey is the journey of an uncommitted, undefined self which sets out to find the right house to live in and the right partner to live with. A house—because the undefined self needs a defining shape: a partner—because the self can only realise what it is, by seeing itself reflected in the chosen and respected eyes of another; in selecting a partner it is selecting the gaze and regard which will assure it of its own reality and value. Putting it very crudely, Isabel Archer chooses the wrong house and the wrong partner. It is the full nature of this error—and her subsequent actions—that I wish to explore. But first I should like to make it clear that if I tend to treat characters, events and buildings as being 'emblematic' (Quentin Anderson's word), this does not mean that I am insensitive to the more realistic qualities of the novel which are praised, for example, by F. R. Leavis in *The Great Tradition.* I certainly do not wish to suggest that the book is something aridly schematised and drained of the opaque complexity of life in the interests of abstract meanings. The life is there: Isabel remains a hauntingly authentic and elusive character moving through vivid and tangible territories. But James has so selected and arranged his realistic data, and has so saturated it with deeper implications, that Isabel's journey is also an analogue of the journey of the inquiring

From *Critical Quarterly* 7, No. 3 (Autumn 1965): 205–19.

self seeking realisation and identity. Everyone she meets, every house she enters, all are detailed, plausible, recognisably of the world. But they are also significant steps of an inward quest which far transcends the social realism of a young American girl living in late nineteenth century Europe. In this essay I shall be stressing the inner quest more than the outer realism—but of course, either without the other would be an immeasurably poorer thing. To suggest the full significance of Isabel's error I shall be considering some of the characters and then some of the architecture. But first I want to make a general point about the Jamesian world which I can best clarify by introducing a quotation from Kant (not, indeed, suggesting any direct influence, even though Henry James Senior studied Kant fairly thoroughly). Kant asserts that 'in the realm of ends everything has either a value or a worth. What has a value has a substitute which can replace it as its equivalent; but whatever is, on the other hand, exalted above all values, and thus lacks an equivalent . . . has no merely relative value, that is, a price, but rather an inner worth, that is, dignity. Now morality is the condition in accordance with which alone a reasonable being can be an end in himself, because only through morality is it possible to be an autonomous member of the realm of ends. Hence morality, and humanity, in so far as it is capable of morality, can alone possess dignity'. This idea is compactly summarised in his second categorical imperative. 'So act as to treat humanity, whether in thine own person or in that of any other, in every case as an end withal, never as a means whereby.' And this key statement was probably influenced, as Ernst Cassirer has suggested, by Rousseau's maxim: 'Man is too noble a being to serve simply as the instrument for others, and he must not be used for what suits them without consulting also what suits himself. . . . It is never right to harm a human soul for the Advantage of others'.

I have introduced these quotations because I think they offer useful terms with which to outline James's moral universe. Imagine two worlds. One is the world of ends in which everything and everyone has an intrinsic worth and they are all respected for what they are. That is, literally, they are regarded as ends in themselves. This is the moral world. In the other world, everything and everyone is regarded as a means, nothing is considered as having a fixed inherent worth but only what Kant calls a 'value'. This is misleading since we tend to use 'value' to imply 'worth', so let us say 'price' i.e. a market value which may change as appetites change, as opposed to an inner spiritual value, a permanent immutable worth. In this lower world of means, people only look at each other in the light of how they can use people, manipulate them, exploit or coerce them in the interests of some personal desire or appetite, or indeed mutilate and shape them to fit the dictates of a theory or a whim. In this world people see other people only as things or instruments, and they work to appropriate them as suits their own ambition. The world of means is a world of rampant egoism, while the world of ends is the realm of true morality and love. These two worlds are effectively the upper and lower parts of James's moral world. And what happens to Isabel Archer is that while she thinks she is ascending towards the world of ends, she is in fact getting more deeply involved in the world of means. The shocking knowledge she has to confront after her marriage is that she is "a woman who has been made use of" as the Countess Gemini puts it. She who thought herself so free, so independent, a pure disciple of the beautiful, now has to face up to the 'dry staring fact that she had been an applied hung-up tool, as senseless and convenient as mere shaped wood and iron'. She, of all people, finds herself trapped in the world of instruments and things. Seeking a world of disinterested appreciation, she falls into a world of calculating appropriation. How does an error of such magnitude come about?

II

Isabel Archer's character has been amply analysed by many other critics so all I want to do is stress that from the outset her approach to life is very romantic, idealistic, and theoretic. 'Isabel Archer was a young person of many theories; her imagination was remarkably active' as James tells us clearly enough. And Henrietta Stackpole is certainly correct when she says to Isabel: "The peril for you is that you live too much in the world of your own dreams". What these dreams consist of we know right from the start: 'she spent half her time in thinking of beauty and bravery and magnanimity; she had a fixed determination to regard the world as a place of brightness, of free expansion, of irresistible action . . . she was always planning out her development, desiring her perfection, observing her progress'. Thus, she views the world as a benevolent sphere which will be plastic to her theories of 'free expansion' and 'irresistible action'. She seems unprepared for any harsh encounter with all that indifferent otherness which is not the self, which is not amenable to the self, and which may well prove cruel and hostile to the self. More dangerously, it is hard to see how she intends to put her theories of self-development into practice. What will that expansion and action consist of? As we soon realise, her most characteristic response in the real world is one of refusal and rejection. Like many another character in American fiction much of her energy goes into avoiding any commitment which might serve to define and arrest her. She is generally in favour of 'the free exploration of life' and yet she shrinks from any of the solid offers that life holds forth. Caspar Goodwood suggests oppression, coercion and constraint on the plain physical level. Lord Warburton with his complex social relations and obligations suggests immobilisation on the social level. If she rejects the first out of a distinct disinclination to enter a firm physical embrace, she rejects the second on 'theoretic' grounds because what he offers does not tally with her vague notions of indefinite expansion. So we may say, summing up, that she rejects the physical and the social in her theoretic pursuit of freedom, knowledge, and self-realisation. Why, then, does she go on to accept Osmond? As she realises, 'The world lay before her—she could do whatever she chose'—the Miltonic echo is deliberate, it recurs again. And out of the whole world to choose Osmond! Notice that she is the only character in the book who is remotely taken in by this 'sterile dilettante' as Ralph so cogently calls him. Why? When we first see her she is reading a history of German thought; that is to say, drinking from the very source of

American transcendentalism. And when, later, she imagines her future married life with Osmond, she feels assured of 'a future at a high level of consciousness of the beautiful'. This implies a sort of romantic Platonism which she might well have found in her youthful reading. She wants to exist at the heights of sheer communion with ideal beauty. As opposed, we may say, to involving herself with the lower levels of un-ideal actuality, From the start she tests things and people by whether they please her 'sublime soul'; and when she receives her fortune, the vast amount of money gives her 'to her imagination, a certain ideal beauty'. Isabel's instinct for the actual is as curtailed as her longing for the ideal is exaggerated. She rejects the sexual and social life. In marrying Osmond she thinks she is embracing the ideal. She idealises herself, her motives for marrying, her ambitions, and Osmond himself. It is all pathetically wrong. But as Mrs. Touchett shrewdly says: "there's nothing in life to prevent her marrying Mr. Osmond if only she looks at him in a certain way". Looking at him in her own way—romantically, theoretically (she 'invented a fine theory about Gilbert Osmond'), consulting her yearning for a life lived on the ideal level—Osmond seems perfectly suited to Isabel's needs.

Among other things, then, her mistake is the result of a radical failure of vision: idealising too much, she has perceived all too little. But more than that, Osmond is exactly what a large part of Isabel wants. He seems to offer release from the troubling life of turbulent passions; he seems to offer a life dedicated to the appreciation of ideal beauty. As we well know, Osmond merely regards Isabel as worthy 'to figure in his collection of choice objects'; but consider how Isabel feels about herself just before her marriage and at the height of her confidence in herself: 'she walked in no small shimmering splendour. She only felt older—ever so much, and as if she were "worth more" for it, like some curious piece in an antiquary's collection'. And she enjoys this feeling. It is hard to resist the conclusion that a part of her—the theorising, idealising part—is quite prepared to be placed in Osmond's collection. The lady is half willing to be turned into a portrait. And, given her temperament, there is much to be said for becoming a work of art. It offers a reprieve from the disturbing ordeals awaiting the self in the mire of the actual. Osmond is a student of the 'exquisite' and we discover how cruel and sterile that can be. But in her own way so is Isabel. She speaks honest words about their marriage: 'They had attempted only one thing, but that one thing was to have been exquisite'. In some ways Osmond is as much a collaborator as a deceiver.

Although there are hints of the proper villain about Osmond (James perhaps goes a little too far by revealing that Osmond's favourite author is Machiavelli), he is in fact a curiously hollow, insubstantial man: "no career, no name, no position, no fortune, no past, no future, no anything" as Madame Merle says. Perhaps this apparent lightness, this seemingly empty detachment from the world is more attractive to Isabel than the solid identity, the heavy actuality of Goodwood and Warburton. Certainly his claim that he has renounced passional life and ordinary human attachments to pursue his high-minded study, his 'taste', echoes something in Isabel. The paradox, of course, as Ralph sees, is 'that under the guise of caring only for intrinsic values Osmond lived exclusively for the world. Far from being its master as he pretended to be, he was its very humble servant, and the degree of its attention was his only measure of success'. He pretends to be a devotee of the ideal, to have renounced the base world. This is what draws Isabel. But to care so totally and uncritically for forms, taste, convention ("I'm convention itself" he revealingly admits) is to be absolutely enslaved to mere appearances, never questioning essences or the intrinsic worth of things. This, precisely, makes him a dedicated inhabitant of the world of means. He has renounced the lived life of instinct and action not, like Ralph, the better to appreciate its intrinsic values, but in order to give himself over entirely to calculated surface effects. How far he will take this is of course revealed by what he does to his daughter Pansy. It is the same thing as what he wants to do to Isabel—to turn her into a reflector of himself, utterly devoid of any spontaneous life of her own. Isabel of course, having stronger and richer stuff in her, can resist. But Pansy shows the process all but complete. All her natural vitality and spontaneity have been quietly suffocated to be replaced by a perfected puppet-like behaviour which does not *express* Pansy's own inner life, but simply *reflects* Osmond's taste. Such a total appropriation of another person's life for egotistical ends is of course the cardinal Jamesian sin. But there is something in Isabel herself which is not so remote from Osmond's disposition. At one point we read that she was 'interested' (a neutral word) to watch Osmond 'playing theoretic tricks on the delicate organism of his daughter'. She should be interested, for she has spent her whole life playing theoretic tricks on her own organism. Osmond is an egotist, but so, we are told, is Isabel: he is cold and dry, but so is she: he pays excessive attention to appearances rather than realities, and up to a point so does she (I will return to this): he prefers art to life, and so does she: he has more theories than feelings, more ideals than instincts, and so does she. He is a collector of things, and she offers herself up to him as a fine finished object. Isabel accepting Osmond's proposal of marriage is the uncertain self thinking it is embracing the very image of what it *seeks* to become. Her later shock and revulsion is the self discovering the true worthlessness of what it *might* have become. Osmond is Isabel's anti-self. This is why, I think, James made Osmond American when he might well have made him a cynical European ensnaring American gullibility. He is American because Isabel is American. She of course has qualities which differentiate her sharply from Osmond. But she also has tendencies which draw her straight to him. He is an actualisation, a projection, of some of the mixed potentialities and aspirations of her questing, uncommitted self. He is part of her self writ large, and when she learns to read that writing properly (she actually refers to not having 'read him right'), she is not unnaturally appalled.

I must here say a little about the other American 'parasite' and plotter, Madame Merle. As Osmond is 'convention itself' so she is 'the great round world itself'. She is totally devoted to the world of things—she thinks of it in terms of 'spoils'—and she has subjected the unruliness of authentic nature to the surface perfection of contrived manner. Isabel is not so blind as not to be able to detect her occasional cruelty, her subtle dishonesty, the sense she gives of 'values gone wrong'. But unlike Osmond, there is something pathetic about her, and something which also offers a warning to Isabel. For clearly Madame Merle was, like Isabel, first used and then abused by Osmond, and she has not gained anything from the world even though she has devoted herself to it. She keeps herself going by 'will', forcing, always, the right mask for the right occasion. But she ends up utterly dried up, unable to cry: "you've dried up my soul" she says to Osmond (it is worth recalling here that no less a writer than Shakespeare habitually depicted evil as a state of dessication, a complete lack of the very sap and tears of life). Perhaps the saddest cry in the whole novel is Madame Merle's lament: "Have I been so vile for nothing?" It at least attests to a vestigial moral sense which she has deliberately subverted for the world's ends, only to see no gains. She has been a disciple of appearances and indeed has mastered the art, but she is rewarded by being banished to America (apparently the worst fate James could conceive of for an erring character). She is a sadder case than Osmond because she knows that she is doing bad things to Isabel. Her effects are as calculated as Osmond's but at least she winces at perpetrating them. She is an almost tragic example of the scant rewards and plentiful shames awaiting those who live only for 'the world'. And it is Madame Merle who gives perhaps the most succinct expression of living in the world of means to be found in the whole book. "I don't pretend to know what people are for" she says, "I only know what I can do with them". She exactly fits Kant's (and Rousseau's) definition of the immoral world. She sees people as instruments but has no sense of their intrinsic worth: means to her hand, not ends in themselves.

In the world of Osmond and Madame Merle, self-seeking and simulation go together. They have to calculate effects: what *is*, is neglected; what *seems* is paramount. Now Isabel herself is a partial devotee of appearances. I will quote a few references to this. She has 'an unquenchable desire to please' and 'an unquenchable desire to think well of herself': thus she is 'very liable to the sin of self-esteem'. More subtly, we read of 'her desire to *look* very well and to *be* if possible even better'. A similar crucial distinction is made later: Isabel's chief dread 'was that she should *appear* narrow-minded; what she feared next afterwards was that she should really *be* so'. (My italics in both cases.) These fine hints reveal a problem of great importance for the novitiate self: which will receive more attention—appearance, or essence? For much of the early part of her travels Isabel falls into the subtle and understandable error of devoting herself to appearances. She wishes to emulate Madame Merle. She contrives to appear to Osmond as she thinks he wants her to appear; like a fine finished work of art which re-echoes and reflects his ideas and taste. In this sense Osmond *is* a man deceived, and Isabel is right to realise that she did mislead him by appearing to be what in fact she was not. That is why Isabel has a true instinct when she says she is afraid of her self. Realising the depths of her error with regard to Osmond is also to realise that she does not know what her self is, nor what it may do. (After all there is Madame Merle, a terrible example of how the self may mutilate the self from a sense of misplaced devotion and ambition.) And indeed this is the crucial difficulty for the self. Only by engaging itself in a situation, projecting itself into the world of things and appearances, can the self realise the self (i.e. transform latent potentialities into visible realities). But once in that situation, it may find that it has chosen a position, a role, which falsifies the self. We don't know what is in us until we commit ourselves in a certain direction: then we may find that the commitment is utterly wrong. Thus all choice may turn out to be error and in this way the self may ruin the self. Certainly Isabel exacerbates her chances of choosing wrong by coldly consulting her theories, her imaginative ideals, her book-fed romanticisms; and that wrong choice does seem to threaten years to come of waste and disappointment. Seen thus, Isabel's difficulty, her error, her fate, form a journey on which we must all, in our different ways, go. For it is only through choice and commitment that we can find out what we are. In this sense error is also discovery. Isabel has to close with Osmond in order to arrive at a deeper knowledge of her self, of her distorted values, of her egotism, and of the real pain and cruelty of life. By marrying Osmond she suffers in good earnest, but she thus earns the right to see the ghost of Gardencourt. Her consolation—and it is the supreme one in James—is truer vision.

III

To bring out more clearly Isabel's journey as the journey of the developing but all-too-often erring self, I now want to move from the characters she meets to the buildings and settings she moves through. And first I must quote from a crucial exchange between Isabel and Madame Merle: it comes near the end of chapter nineteen and is really central to the whole book. Talking of an earlier suitor Isabel says: "I don't care anything about his house" and Madame Merle replies: "That's very crude of you. When you've lived as long as I you'll see that every human being has his shell and that you must take the shell into account. By the shell I mean the whole envelope of circumstances. There's no such thing as an isolated man or woman; we're each of us made up of some cluster of appurtenances. What shall we call our 'self'? Where does it begin? where does it end? It overflows into everything that belongs to us—and then it flows back again. I know a large part of myself is in the clothes I choose to wear. I've a great respect for *things!* One's self—for other people—is one's expression of one's self; and one's house, one's furniture, one's garments, the books one reads, the company one keeps—these things are all expressive".

Now this idea that the self is only the self that we consciously create and play at being, the self that we visibly express and project, is still being explored by existential psychologists like Sartre (for instance in *Being and Nothingness* where he discusses the waiter 'playing at being a waiter ... the waiter in the cafe plays with his condition in order to *realize* it'), and by such imaginative sociologists as Erving Goffman (his brilliant book *The Presentation of Self in Everyday Life* is very relevant here). So Madame Merle's attitude expresses a deep truth about our society. She has gone the whole way. She is concerned only with the agents of expression—things, clothes, appearances, appurtenances. She reconstructs a false self to show the world. She is what she dresses to be. This is extreme: it entails the death of the soul and the ultimate disappearance of the individual inner self. As Isabel says to herself, it is difficult to imagine Madame Merle 'in any detachment or privacy, she existed only in relations . . . one might wonder what commerce she could possibly hold with her own spirit'. She is rather like Lord Mellifont in "The Private Life" who disappears when he is on his own. If you care only for appearances, you exist only when there are people to look at you.

However, in this key conversation, Isabel's answer to Madame Merle is also extreme. She says: "I know that nothing else expresses me. Nothing that belongs to me is any measure of me; everything's on the contrary a limit, a barrier, and a perfectly arbitrary one. . . . My clothes may express the dressmaker, but they don't express me. To begin with it's not my own choice that I wear them; they're imposed upon me by society". To which Madame Merle wryly answers: "Should you prefer to go without them?"

Emersonian

This is a classic formulation of a basic American attitude. Lionel Trilling once noted that there is something in the American temperament which wishes to resist all conditioning, all actual society, and aspires to a life which will permit the spirit to make its own terms. 'Somewhere in our mental constitution is the demand for life as pure spirit'. (See his essay "William Dean Howells" in *The Opposing Self*.) Emerson's 'Self-Reliance', Thoreau by Walden Pond, Whitman celebrating the self—these, of course, are the classic types for the American imagination. They certainly did believe there was such a thing as the 'isolated' self, and welcomed the fact. And characters like Bartleby and Huck Finn and Augie March reveal the ineradicable suspicion of all conditioning forces, all actual fixed social situations. They refuse, opt out, move on. Like Isabel they see barriers and limits everywhere, and much of their energy goes into avoiding the shaping pressures (and appurtenances) of society. Isabel's retort is, thus, in a great American tradition. And up to a point she is right. Things and appurtenances are not identical with the self, as Osmond and Madame Merle make them. We are not what we wear. But to see everything in the actual world as sheer barrier, hindrance, and limit is also dangerous. For without any limits the self can never take on any contours, cannot become something real. The pure spirit of the self has to involve itself with the material world of things and society in order to work out an identity for itself, indeed in order to realise itself. To that extent the self must dress itself and must choose its clothes. In laying the responsibility for her clothes (i.e. her appearance, her situation etc.) on society and calling it an arbitrary imposition, Isabel is being dangerously irresponsible. For it is her error in thinking that life can be lived as pure spirit in contempt of things that leads her to mistake Osmond's attitude. The ironic result is that she puts herself in the power of a man who wants to treat *her* as a thing. James's insight here is profound. For there is indeed a dangerously close connection between an idealistic *rejection* of 'things' and an idealising *of* 'things'. This is why Osmond is such a telling figure. In the appearance of living for the spirit in disregard of the material, he has in fact simply spiritualised the material. And James must surely have been one of the first to see into this particularly modern malaise which other American critics have mentioned in discussing modern society; namely, the confusion of the spiritual and material realms, the spiritualising of things. James knew that things and surroundings (the shell) *were* important: there was a way of being among things which manifested the quality of the self, which enabled it to realise itself. But of course there was also a way of being among things which menaced and could destroy the self. Isabel Archer's journey is hazardous but representative: and her error no less than human.

We first see Isabel—as we last see her—in a garden. This is always an important setting in James (usually indicating a place of meditation and appreciation). Gardens are certainly important in this book. At the start of her European journey Isabel regards her inner world as a garden and indeed many of her happiest moments are spent in them. She is happiest, in particular, at Gardencourt, and the very name points to the fact that this is the locale in the book which most exudes a mood of mellow reciprocity between the civilised and the natural. But Isabel is far from appreciating it at the start of her adventures. She sees it only as romantic and picturesque. It is only much later that she appreciates that it is something more real and indeed more sacred than that. After this opening glimpse James takes us back to the house in Albany, New England, where Isabel started on her travels. The most important of many suggestive details about this house is the 'condemned door', the entrance which 'was secured by bolts which a particularly slender little girl found it impossible to slide'. It is to be Isabel's later fate again to be locked in. Also, the windows are covered, but 'she had no wish to look out, for this would have interfered with her theory that there was a strange, unseen place on the other side—a place which became to the child's imagination, according to different moods, a region of delight or terror'. This of course expresses Isabel's whole attitude to life: her theories and imagined versions of reality are generated behind closed doors and covered windows. Instead of venturing forth she sits poring over books. One more detail is particularly prophetic: she 'had the whole house to choose from, and the room she had selected was the most depressed of its scenes'. James often used the metaphor 'the house of life' and indeed, of its many rooms, Isabel is yet to choose the darkest and most imprisoning.

If you see Isabel's quest as being at least in part a search for the right house then her reactions to Warburton and Osmond become even more revealing. When she rejects Warburton after visiting his house, Lockleigh, she puts her rejection in this way: she says she is unable "to think of your home ... as the settled seat of my existence". As though the main thing about him was the fact that he doesn't have what she regards as the right house. Osmond's house is brilliantly described. First of all, it is on a hill-top, the best place for a person who wants to put the claims of the base world behind and live a life of ideal appreciation and detached observation. Clearly Isabel is attracted to this degree of rarefied removal. But we note that in the first, perfectly plausible, topographical description, the front of the house is deceptive. 'It was the mask, not the face of the house. It had heavy lids, but no eyes; the house in reality looked another way....' This, I need hardly point out, is entirely true of its owner. Even the windows bespeak Osmond: their function seemed less to offer communication with the world than to defy the world to look in'. Isabel's approach to this key dwelling is laced with subtle portent, and I must quote at some length here. 'The companions drove out of the Roman Gate ... and wound between high-walled lanes into which the wealth of blossoming orchards overdrooped and flung a fragrance, until they reached the small suburban piazza, of crooked shape, where the long brown wall of the villa occupied by Mr. Osmond formed a principle, or at least very imposing, object'. They drive into the courtyard. 'There was something grave and strong in the place; it looked somehow as if, once you were in, you would need an act of energy to get out. For Isabel, however, there was of course as yet no thought of getting out, but only of advancing'. The whole drive provides a compressed analogue for Isabel's venture into life so far. The blooming promising beginning, the flung fragrance (Touchett's unlooked-for bequest perhaps), then the crooked square, the preventing wall, and the enclosing courtyard—the whole passage subtly prepares us for what becomes explicit only much later when Isabel realises that 'she had taken all the first steps in the purest confidence, and then she had suddenly found the infinite vistas of a multiplied life to be a dark, narrow alley with a dead wall at the end'. And note the geography of the following image. 'Instead of leading to the high places of happiness, from which the world could seem to lie below one, so that one could look down with a sense of exaltation and advantage, and judge and choose and pity, it led rather downward and earthward, into the realms of restriction and depression where the sound of other lives, easier and freer, was heard as from above, and where it served to deepen the feeling of failure'. Isabel thinks Osmond lives on the heights of meditation and free appreciation, but really he dwells in the depths of calculation and constricting appropriation. Her life seemed to lead up to the world of ends; instead she was plunging down into the world of means. Osmond's palace of art turns out to be 'the house of darkness, the house of dumbness, the house of suffocation'. But it was the house she chose. James knits his imagery together in the famous description of Isabel's reaction when Osmond proposes. She feels 'a pang that suggested to her somehow the slipping of a fine bolt—backward, forward, she couldn't have said which'. Is she about to be released or immured? In her most testing moment she is unable to distinguish what presages liberation and expansion, and what threatens detainment and constriction. Her radical confusion is all there in the image.

I will not here describe the many galleries and museums and other houses and rooms Isabel passes through, but all repay careful study. For in this book all the architecture means something of specific importance to Isabel, as of course it must to the self seeking both freedom *and* form. Pansy's convent, for instance, has all the appearance of a prison to Isabel's clearer vision. On the other hand, some architecture can offer consolation. For example there is a beautiful passage describing a ride she takes in Rome—'the place where people had suffered'—some time after her discovery of the truth about Osmond. 'She had long before taken old Rome into her confidence, for in a world of ruins the ruin of her happiness seemed a less unnatural catastrophe. She rested her weariness upon things that had crumbled for centuries and yet were still upright; she dropped her secret sadness into the silence of lonely places'. It is a most moving description of the bruised and erring spirit absorbing strengthening reminders and consoling clues from the marred but splendid debris of human habitations of the past. And one of the reasons why Isabel returns to Rome at the end, renouncing the refuge of Gardencourt which she now does appreciate as sacred, is that the self has to return to the place where it made its most defining, if mistaken, choice. That is where the work of re-habilitation and re-education must go on. It is where knowledge is earned. I think this is why, in the last scene of the book, we see Isabel running from the darkening garden of meditation back into the well-lit house of life. But before exploring that decision I want to discuss the significance of Ralph.

IV

Ralph is of course a recurring Jamesian figure—the subtly debarred spectator who enjoys everything in imagination and nothing in action. Thus Ralph has 'the imagination of loving' but has 'forbidden himself the riot of expression'. All his happiness consists of 'the sweet-tasting property of the observed thing in itself'. To appreciate the 'thing in itself' is precisely to be an inhabitant of the world of ends. Ralph is wise, he is dying: 'restricted to mere spectatorship at the game of life', banned from participation, addicted to appreciation. A true Jamesian artist figure. Suitably, he is most often seen sitting in gardens. On one occasion in particular the contrast between 'house' and 'garden' is used to good effect. This is when Ralph tells Isabel the real truth about Osmond. She, with her theories, rejects his visions— and leaves the garden. She ends the conversation 'by turning away and walking back to the house'. But Ralph cannot follow her: it is too cold for him in the house, he is too susceptible to 'the lurking chill of the high-walled court'. It does not seem to me excessive to see Ralph as the artist-meditator, who cannot function in the house of life but who indulges his imagination and speculation in the garden. He sits; he does not act. He is content to watch and appreciate Isabel; he has no thought of dominating or manipulating her. In his own way he is also an aesthete, someone who stands back and relishes the beautiful. But where Osmond is a false aesthete, Ralph has the true artistic instincts. Osmond wants to turn Isabel into a work of art (we see her at his home 'framed in the gilded doorway' already adjusting to her status as portrait); Ralph appreciates her living qualities artistically. Osmond hates Ralph because he is 'an apostle of freedom'. But as Isabel comes to see, Ralph is more intelligent, more just, better. Not egotistic, as Osmond always is. This leads up to the deathbed scene. Isabel is back at Gardencourt, happy at least that she is no longer having to act and falsify. At Gardencourt she can be her self, her true self. And, dying, Ralph comforts her: "But love remains". He tells her she has been adored and her response is revealingly simple. "Oh my brother". In Osmond Isabel thought she recognised a soul mate. She was very wrong. At last, having suffered, she realises who is the true image of what her self wants to be—Ralph. "Oh my brother". Having seen through the false aesthetic approach to life, she now appreciates the true artistic attitude: a vision based on love, on generosity, on respect for things in themselves and a gift of unselfish appreciation.

In taking the measure of Osmond, Isabel has started to move towards Ralph's point of view. The great chapter, forty-two, when she takes stock, is really the beginning of her deeper knowledge and clearer vision. She is starting to read things properly, as Ralph does. And with this new access of vision, Isabel becomes less active externally and more active internally. She has started on what James later called 'the subjective adventure': the adventure of trying to understand, to sound out depths, to appreciate qualities, to transcend the importunities of the ego. By the end of the book Isabel Archer has started to become a Jamesian artist.

Just before the end we see her in the garden at Gardencourt: this time pensive and quiet, much closer to a knowledge of true values than when we saw her stride so confidently on to that lawn at the start. It is now twilight: she is sitting on a bench alone. This stance, this setting, becomes a dominant one in James's later work—not only in the last great story "The Bench of Desolation" but in such works as *The Ambassadors* as well as in many stories like "Crapy Cornelia" and "Mora Montravers". In that last story, for instance, we see the self-effacing Traffle, excluded, estranged, sitting staring at the approaching evening with only one consolation. As the night comes down on him he has, for company, his Jamesian mind: 'exquisite, occult, dangerous and sacred, to which everything ministered and which nothing could take away'. Clearly James had a recurring vision of a person who has somehow failed to realise him (or her) self in the physical world, who has renounced all active participation, and who withdraws into sedentary isolation consoling himself with the fruits of a finer, if sadder, consciousness. Isabel, we feel, is drawing towards her truer role as she sits in the darkening garden. But she is interrupted by Caspar Goodwood, who comes to disturb her on her bench in the garden: she cannot yet enjoy Ralph's invalid immunity from the challenge and threat of engagement. Goodwood kisses her, and in a curious cluster of images James implies that she is both wrecked and then freed. Goodwood brings a possessive lightning, 'but when darkness returned she was free'. I am not fully certain of James's intention here, but the effect is this. For a long time she has wondered if her true fate, the true realisation of her self, should not have been with Goodwood. Now for the first time she is subjected to the full force of his sexual claims. It is a shattering experience, but it is also a release. She was not made to go that way. There is no going back to the simple level of life he represents. He tries to prevent her from returning to Rome where, as he says, she has to 'play a part' and maintain a false 'form': but it is precisely this that she must, at this stage, do. She runs back to the house: 'there were lights in the window of the house; they shone far across the lawn'. She reaches the door. 'Here only she paused. She looked all about her; she listened a little; then she put her hand on the latch. She had not known where to turn; but she knew now. There was a very straight path'. James has annoyed readers by not saying what that path is. But I think the wonderful suggestivity of this last scene tells us all we need. The last pause and lingering look surely imply that she is reluctant to leave the garden—a refuge and a place of meditation. But she cannot opt out of her fate so easily, just as even more she cannot return to American innocence and physical simplicity with Goodwood. She chose her room in the house of life and she must return to it. She must return to the chill and ruins of Rome: for the self cannot back out of a mistaken course but only push through and move beyond. But she takes back with her a new vision, a deeper understanding, a capacity for modest un-egotistical contemplation which all promise a richer future—a future in which she will come to a true realisation of what her real self is. It is beside the point to ask whether she will divorce Osmond. When she has attained her new vision, he simply shrinks into insignificance, just as Madame Merle melts away to America. We do not even hear his voice for the last seventy pages or so of the book, and by the end of the book we feel that Isabel has attained the most important kind of freedom, an internal one. She is liberated from her twisted vision and her confused values. She can see through all false appearances. She returns to Italy, to the 'ruins' she herself was partly responsible for. But she will not, we feel, ever again be subor-dinate to the deceptions and calculations of a worldling like Osmond. Even if she does not break out of the house and kick over the traces, and even if she never again indulges in any more passions, her future will be quite other. For her way of looking has changed. Now I think one might fairly suggest that James, in fact, could not see exactly what sort of future such a person might have, how she might take up her place again in the social scene. We can admire Isabel's fine stoicism and admit at the same time that it is hard to visualise the details of her future. And this, I think, is because James is already feeling the necessary connection between the artistic observation of life *and* the renunciation of active participation in it. As Isabel becomes more the artist, in her mind, so she will withdraw from social involvement, if not physically then at least psychologically. If she never returns to sit in the garden of Gardencourt, then we may be sure she will spend many later years reposing in the garden of her mind. With James's later artist figures or observers, the attempt at any active participation is all but abandoned from the start. Hyacinth Robinson finds no satisfying role or niche for himself in society and shoots himself. Lambert Strether develops a new complex comprehensiveness of vision and appreciation, but to retain it, it is essential that he must not get 'anything for myself'—no spoils, no physical relationships. The narrator of *The Sacred Fount* is the conscience of society, at the cost of never enjoying its actual embrace. There are other such figures, but none perhaps so humanly comprehensible as Isabel Archer, in whom we can see the erring self emerging into the incipient artist. With later characters the divorce between action and observation is almost accepted as inevitable from the start. It would seem that James, in his own way, came to share Goethe's reflection that 'the acting man is always without conscience; no one has conscience but the observing man'. If nothing else, *The Portrait of a Lady* shows us the birth of a conscience out of the spoiling of a life.

Annette Niemtzow

MARRIAGE AND THE NEW WOMAN IN *THE PORTRAIT OF A LADY*

The questions of marriage, his father's questions, were urgent within the domestic circle in which the novelist Henry James was raised. If *The Portrait of a Lady* mocks the transcendental innocence in which his father revelled,[1] still, the overall pattern of the book, in which Isabel Archer chooses to return to her dismal marriage, reflects ideas about the relationship between husband and wife, akin to those which Henry James, Sr. espoused. The most concise presentation of the father's views appeared first in a series of debates, which began in 1852 in the New York *Tribune,* between himself, Horace Greeley, and the inveterate reformer, Stephen Pearl Andrews; and then appeared again in a series of papers on marriage which were published in the *Atlantic Monthly* in 1870.[2]

In the second *Atlantic* article, entitled "Is Marriage Holy?" the elder James posits a hypothetical situation (the reverse occurs in *The Portrait*) in which a wife has offended her marriage vows. What is the husband to do? His answer comes fast: "Pray tell me then, my reader, what business it is of yours and mine, that any man's wife in the community, or any woman's husband, has either veritably or conjecturally committed adultery, and should be legally convicted or legally absolved of that unrighteousness. What social right has any man or woman to thrust the evidence of a transaction so essentially private, personal, and irremediable up to the light of day?"[3] Or, as he states the case more dramatically: "Thus, to keep to the case supposed, when the civil magistrate says to me, 'Your wife has violated the conjugal bond, and so exposed herself to condign punishment at my hands,' I shut my ears to his invitation. I dare not listen to its solicitations. The awful voice of God within me forbids me to do so, compels me rather to say to him, 'Get thee behind me, Satan!' "[4] We, as readers, stand puzzled. Was this famous iconoclast inveighing vigorously against divorce?

Not that Henry James, Sr. was opposed to divorce as theory. In his well-known exchange with Greeley and Andrews, he had pleaded effectively to the contrary: "I have invariably aimed to advance the honor of marriage by seeking to

From *American Literature* 47, No. 3 (November 1975): 377–95.

free it from certain purely arbitrary and conventional obstructions in reference to divorce. For example, I have always argued against Mr. Greeley that it was not essential to the honor of marriage that two persons should be compelled to live together, when they held the reciprocal relation of dog and cat, and that in the state of things divorce might profitably intervene, provided the parties guaranteed the State against the charge of their offspring."[5] And yet, Andrews himself offered the most precise, if harsh, judgment when he declared James was "of the class of purely ideal reformers,"[6] one of a "good many persons transcendentally inclined, . . . whose views of prospective human improvement take no broader and more practical shape than that of *spiritualizing* whatsoever things, however stupid, which happen now to exist among us."[7]

James favored divorce, in the end, for the same reasons he favored the elimination of all legalism. The abolishment of contracts was supposed to effect a recognition of the original spiritual state inherent in marriage, but too often obscured by its laws. Marriage laws were, for him, like many social laws, concrete articulations of human instincts. To change them would bring about only spiritual improvement, not practical change (James, of course, would never have acknowledged the distinction). Convinced as he was that "constancy would speedily avouch itself as the *law* of the conjugal relations, in absence of all legislation to enforce it,"[8] he never suspected that a man or woman might choose divorce, given it as an option.

And so, when faced with a specific case of domestic discord or adultery, as in his imagined case or in the Beecher-Tilton scandal,[9] James responded with a brisk "Get thee behind me, Satan!" Divorce remained, to his thinking, only a private, ethical dilemma. As he stated the question for his couple in "Is Marriage Holy?": "my sole debate with myself is, whether I shall make my private grief a matter of public concern, and so condemn my wife to open and notorious shame."[10] His solution was clear. He dreaded that divorce too be reduced to sets of laws, rather than be treated as an individual moral problem: "I cannot imagine, for example, that any man or woman whose own bosom is the abode of chaste love could ever be tempted by any selfish reward to fasten a stigma of unchastity upon anybody else."[11]

His then was a complex position on divorce, surrounded more by metaphysics than by mores, for always, the elder James proved more a Swedenborgian than a Fourierist, more a spiritual theologian than a social reformer. For him, marriage remained part of a universal allegory, as he demanded ample spirituality of even its conventional form: "For I cannot help regarding the marriage of man and woman as a crude earthly type or symbol of a profounder marriage which, in invisible depths of being, is taking place between the public and private life of man, or the sphere of his natural instinct and that of his spiritual culture. . . ."[12] Within such an infinitely entangled view of marriage and personal morality, it is no wonder that the senior James decreed marriage, once undertaken, a private, not public, concern. Although he had theorized that divorce might be an attractive means to end marital laws in his early discussions, he recognized that divorce created another nexus of legal complications. As such, it appeared to him as a reckless surrender of personal commitments. This he reluctantly suggested when dealing with a particular case in his later *Atlantic Monthly* essay.

Although it was written ten years after the father's work, the younger James's novel remains curiously sensitive to the position his father expounded on the question of the ethical status of divorce. In a letter to William James, March 8, 1870, James himself had commented favorably on the elder James's testament to the horror of legalistic divorce and the inviolability of the institution of marriage. "Among the things I have recently read is Father's Marriage paper in the Atlantic—with great enjoyment of its manner and approval of its matter."[13] It is this same approval that seems to guide the last hundred pages of his novel, in which the narrator's approval of Isabel's decisions echoes the father's position.

As we recall, after her fatal glimpse of Madame Merle and Osmond together, Isabel's moral earnestness forces her still to reconsider her visits to Ralph Touchett, her beloved cousin, because of her husband's opposition:

> I have already had reason to say that Isabel knew her husband to be displeased by the continuance of Ralph's visit to Rome. That knowledge was very present to her as she went to her cousin's hotel the day after she had invited Lord Warburton to give a tangible proof of his sincerity; and at this moment, as at others, she had a sufficient perception of the sources of Osmond's opposition. He wished her to have no freedom of mind, and he knew perfectly well that Ralph was an apostle of freedom. It was just because he was this, Isabel said to herself, that it was a refreshment to go and see him. It will be perceived that she partook of this refreshment in spite of her husband's aversion to it, that is partook of it, as she flattered herself, discreetly. She had not as yet undertaken to act in direct opposition to his wishes; he was her appointed and inscribed master; she gazed at moments with a sort of incredulous blankness at this fact. It weighed upon her imagination, however; constantly present to her mind were all the traditional decencies and sanctities of marriage. The idea of violating them filled her with shame as well as with dread, for on giving herself away she had lost sight of this contingency in the perfect belief that her husband's intentions were as generous as her own. She seemed to see, nonetheless, the rapid approach of the day when she would have to take back something she had solemnly bestown. Such a ceremony would be odious and monstrous; she tried to shut her eyes to it meanwhile. Osmond would do nothing to help it by beginning first; he would put that burden upon her to the end.[14]

Isabel is thinking of disobedience or divorce—we cannot be sure which, though either would be morally culpable—and before her rise "the decencies and sanctities of marriage." "Shame" and "dread" overwhelm her; and while she wants to shut her eyes, she is forced to face the ethical questions of marriage. The woman who once flaunted, "I don't want to begin life by marrying. There are other things a woman can do," is transformed into the custodian of domestic organization. Despite her unconventional visits to Ralph, her path to renunciation is straight.

While Isabel never forsakes her belief in freedom, she surrenders it to an ethic understandable only to a world that appreciated and bowed to the elder James's work:

> "Yes, I'm wretched," she said very mildly. She hated to hear herself say it; she tried to say it as judicially as possible.
>
> "What does he do to you?" Henrietta asked, frowning as if she were enquiring into the operations of a quack doctor.
>
> "He does nothing. But he doesn't like me."
>
> "He's very hard to please!" cried Miss Stackpole. "Why don't you leave him?"
>
> "I can't change that way," Isabel said. (p. 449)

Although Henrietta Stackpole, James's spectre of the new woman, sees divorce as a possibility, Isabel differs from her friend, who is public, while she, Isabel remains essentially private:

> "I don't know whether I'm too proud. But I can't publish my mistake. I don't think that's decent. I'd much rather die."
>
> "You won't think so always," said Henrietta.
>
> "I don't know what great unhappiness might bring me to; but it seems to me I shall always be ashamed. One must accept one's deeds. I married him before all the world; I was perfectly free; it was impossible to do anything more deliberate. One can't change that way," Isabel repeated.
>
> "You *have* changed, in spite of the impossibility. I hope you don't mean to say you like him."
>
> "Isabel debated. "No, I don't like him. I can tell you, because I'm weary of my secret. But that's enough; I can't announce it on the rooftops." (p. 449)

It is her sense of privacy that forces her to reject divorce as a possibility. Because she passionately believes in her freedom to choose, she also believes, as the elder James did, that she alone is accountable for her choices. Her final acceptance of her oppressive condition is predicated on her sense that a woman accepts public responsibilities to the marriage institution itself when she becomes a wife. As she says to Henrietta and again to Ralph, her creed is simple: "If I were afraid of my husband that would be simply my duty. That's what women are expected to be" (p. 463). If the tone James gives her is understandably bitter, ironic about the female condition, he unceasingly pushes her into an eternal pit in the name of salvation and blesses her with the title lady, in reward for her moral sacrifice. In a way acceptable to his father and coincidentally to American society at large, James creates a character too moral to flee what is abhorrent and smothering.

In American society of the 1870's, no woman could blithely walk out the door of her marriage, despite Henrietta's invitation to do so. As Matthiessen reminded us, "Our age no longer feels as he—and she—did about the strictness of the marriage vow."[15] But they did, and *The Portrait of a Lady* is a book largely about the seriousness of this vow. Isabel makes this clear time and time again: "What he thought of her she knew, what he was capable of saying to her she had felt; that they were married, for all that, and marriage meant that a woman should cleave to the man with whom, uttering tremendous vows, she had stood at the altar. She sank down on her sofa at last and buried her head in a pile of pillows" (p. 496).

As Isabel buries her head, James plays a wonderful literary trick on her. He places before her—magically—the Countess Gemini, whose name suggests her false position. The Countess's person is transformed into an apparition of Isabel's own fears about what she herself may become. What James has done is to unite objective physical reality with Isabel's psychological state, as Isabel becomes aware of her sister-in-law's presence: "When she raised her head again the Countess Gemini hovered before her" (p. 496). The word "hovered," added by James in his focused revision, captures the dream level on which the Countess's appearance affects Isabel. She arrives as a physical being, but presides as a spirit conjured up by Isabel's mind: a concrete representation of Isabel's fear of being an adulteress. Like her predecessor, Hester Prynne, Isabel, burdened with strong moral sensibilities, is capable of placing the visibilia of adultery on her own chest, if society is too corrupt or derelict to punish her. She is, as the Countess retorts, "a woman with such a beastly pure mind" (p. 497); this fact not only blinds her to the affair which had existed between Osmond and Madame Merle, but also cuts her off from fleeing the cloistered fortress in which Osmond holds her.

To take this argument one step further is to realize that the charge often levelled at James's heroine, that she suffers from a near psychotic fear of sexuality, is hopelessly misplaced. One critic, William Bysshe Stein, for instance, denounces Isabel as a "fleshless robot, a contemptuous prig who flaunts her impotent femininity in the guise of innocence." He finds her "oblivious to the force of nature, the vis inertiae with which the female had long controlled the world. Instead, like the men, she was obsessed with the abstractions of independence and freedom."[16] To him, Isabel's repression is proof of her sickness. But Stein is suffering from historical parochialism as well as from an odd, if not untypical, fantasy about women's sexuality. To Henry James (who was not, after all, Henry Adams), Isabel was a delightful, albeit difficult, rebel. *The Portrait of a Lady* is not "James's treatment of the stagnant emotions of the Victorian female";[17] rather, it is a study of how a woman is to behave if she is to be a "lady." While the novel begins as a study of a single woman, searching for options other than marriage, who must control her sexuality because it could shatter her and society's notion of what is "decent," it ends as a study of the same woman, now married, who continues to control her sexuality because it threatens her respectability, morality, and marriage. When Isabel asserts, "I don't want to begin life by marrying," she is adventurous, not frigid.

For instance, what of Isabel and Caspar Goodwood? Isabel, as we see her, is both fearful of and attracted to him. Her encounters with him are always anxious because she is aware of his insistent physical presence. To Isabel, "He was the finest young man she had ever seen, was indeed quite a splendid young man; he had inspired her with a sentiment of high, of rare respect. She had never felt equally moved to it by any other person" (p. 41). But more, for her: "He was tall, strong and somewhat stiff; he was also lean and brown. He was not romantically; he was much rather obscurely, handsome; but his physiognomy had an air of requesting your attention, which was rewarded according to the charm you found in blue eyes of remarkable fixedness, the eyes of a complexion other than his own, and a jaw of somewhat angular mould which is supposed to bespeak resolution" (p. 41). Isabel even defends Caspar's physical appearance against the attack of his ally, Henrietta Stackpole:

> "He's dying for a little encouragement. I see his face now, and his earnest absorbed look while I talked. I never saw an ugly man look so handsome."
> "He's very simple-minded," said Isabel. "And he's not so ugly." (pp. 97–98)

The only complaint Isabel offers against Caspar's appearance is that his chin, suggestive of his sexuality, protrudes *too* aggressively, but she is clearly not unaware of his appeal: "She wished him no ounce less of his manhood, but she sometimes thought he would be rather nicer if he looked, for instance, a little differently. His jaw was too strong and set and his figure too straight and stiff" (p. 114). From the opening of *The Portrait,* Isabel complains that the main trouble with Goodwood's attractiveness is that the option it offers, marriage, would end all her hopes for experiment. Again and again, she asserts what she wants; we have no reason to doubt her. Of marriage she says, "There are other things a woman can do" (p. 144); and she offers praise to Henrietta for carving a trail for her weaker sisters: "Henrietta, for Isabel, was chiefly a proof that a woman might suffice for herself and be happy" (p. 56). Yet Isabel is not Henrietta, who functions efficiently, undauntedly as a woman of a new type. (When Ralph Touchett tries to push Isabel into that mould, she answers him curtly, "Women are not like men," p. 144.) And yet she is not the traditional woman either. Isabel Archer seeks a life of her own; ultimately she finds that her own requisite is that it not be shocking.

It is in her interview with Goodwood in her hotel room that Isabel's image of herself as a woman open to all possibilities starts to waver because of the challenge he presents. For him, Isabel has only one definition; she is to be his wife. Threatened, she feels compelled to assert her right to independence in a confrontation with a man who appears to her "naturally plated and steeled, armed essentially for aggression" (p. 148). Still, he presses her, until despite herself, she must admit that she was thinking of him when she refused Warburton:

> "You do me very little justice—after my telling you what I told you just now. I'm sorry I told you—since it matters so little to you."
> "Ah," cried the young man, "if you were thinking of *me* when you did it!" And then he paused with the fear that she might contradict so happy a thought. (p. 152)

Not only does Isabel not contradict him; she admits that he is right, "I was thinking of you a little." She refuses him, of course, but her explanation is crucial: "I don't wish to be a mere sheep in the flock; I wish to choose my own fate and know something of human affairs beyond what other people think it compatible with propriety to tell me" (p. 154). Isabel explains that she seeks possibilities in life that Goodwood would end; and yet, she leaves the door open to the future, because she is attracted to him: "They stood so for a moment, looking at each other, united by a hand-clasp *which was not merely passive on her side*" (p. 155; italics mine).

Is there any wonder that Isabel breaks down, trembling, at the end of the interview? Determined to be independent, yet aware of her own sexuality, Isabel gets a frightening vision—an unveiling of herself as a "loose woman":

> She had laid her hand on the knob of the door that led into her room, and she waited a moment to see whether her visitor would not take his departure. But he appeared unable to move; there was an immense unwillingness in his attitude and a sore remonstrance in his eyes. "I must leave you now," said Isabel; and she opened the door and passed into the other room.
>
> This apartment was dark, but the darkness was tempered by a vague radiance sent up through the window from the court of the hotel, and Isabel could make out the masses of the furniture, the dim shining of the mirror and the looming of the big four-posted bed. (p. 155)

The darkness here is suggestive of the darkness that Goodwood threatens her with again, in their final meeting; and like the Countess Gemini, who will "hover" before Isabel later as a menacing reminder of adultery, the bed "looms" at her with frightening force. Questions of morality and sexuality are so intertwined in Isabel's mind that her response is never mild. Because she feels her sexuality so strongly, she feels in danger of falling.

Isabel's imagination can, in fact, turn beds into menacing creatures and sisters-in-law into warnings. She possesses an almost obscene—certainly no frigid—imagination, filled with disturbing sexual fantasies. She recalls a day-dream about "drifting": " 'A swift carriage, of a dark night, rattling with four horses over roads that one can't see—that's my idea of happiness' " (p. 158). This "idea of happiness" has its source in French pornographic novels, as Henrietta is only too quick to grasp: " 'Mr. Goodwood certainly didn't teach you to say such things as that—like the heroine of an immoral novel' " (p. 158). And Isabel manages to flee the possibility that she will become such a heroine, as James avoids making his novel "immoral"—in the end.

Isabel Archer marries Osmond because she finds no options other than marriage. With him, she is not made to feel so passionately those emotions which cripple her, which force her to remember her anatomy more than her mind. Unlike Henrietta, soon to be queen of American journalism, Isabel was drifting aimlessly, without a vocation. Osmond and his daughter Pansy give her one, "There was exploration enough in the fact that he was her lover, her own, and that she should be able to be of use to him" (p. 326). Or, "She would launch his boat for him; she would be his providence; it would be his providence. . . . As she looked back at the passion of those full weeks she perceived in it a kind of maternal strain—the happiness of a woman who felt that she was a contributor, that she came with charged hands" (p. 393).

The Portrait of a Lady, then, is a record of the thwarted search a woman makes for a vocation; and of her surrender to marriage for fear that she may rip asunder the mores which are her own. Isabel is a boxed woman, one of a new breed, but one who does not realize—or believe—that sexual freedom is a pre-requisite for other kinds. In her painful marriage, it is of sex, of an affair, that she thinks, to her own shock: "She was not a daughter of the Puritans, but for all that she believed in such a thing as chastity and even as decency. It would appear that Osmond was far from doing anything of the sort; some of his traditions made her push back her skirts. Did all women have lovers? Did they all lie and even the best have their price?" (p. 398). But she cannot—will not—"push back her skirts"; she instead pushes them down.[18] For, to her, the moral laws are set; she must resist her sexuality or run the risk of living in "concubinage." Of this, the younger as well as the elder James approved.

The metaphors of the book (other than the eye imaginary, which has been rightly identified as Emersonian) may also be attributed to suggestions of the elder James, who drew a crucial contrast between private and public worlds. As Richard Chase has reminded us, "The idea of leaving and entering a house, the contrast of different kinds of houses, the question of whether a house is a prison or the scene of liberation and fulfillment—these are the substance of the metaphors in *The Portrait of a Lady*."[19] Ralph and Osmond define that metaphor as each one dwells in privacy and admits guests first to the anteroom prior to admission to the inner apartment. When Caspar Goodwood gives Isabel that famous kiss, they are, of course, out of doors, outside the houses which define the private world in which married life thrives; and the kiss not only challenges her sexuality but her privacy. Isabel opts to respect the notion of a private world, to reenter the door to the house. James captures the tension as she tremulously forms her decision:

> So had she heard of those wrecked and under water following a train of images before they sink. But when darkness returned she was free. She never looked about her; she only darted from the spot. There were lights in the windows of the house; they shone far across the lawn. In an extraordinarily short time—for the distance was considerable—she had moved through the darkness (for she saw nothing) and reached the door. Here only she paused. She looked all about her; she listened a little; then she put her hand on the latch. She had not known where to turn; but she knew now. There was a very straight path. (pp. 542–543)

The setting itself again becomes psychological and reveals the terms of Isabel's struggle—all had been "dark"; Isabel was not "free" as she "put her hand on the latch." For James, these two remarks are not contradictory, for, like Hawthorne, he seems to define freedom as a willful entrance into the flow of conventions which themselves might be incarcerating. Involved in such a landscape, with a morality fixed so that the world outside domestic forms is dark while the forms alone are light, Isabel understandably races to the door for safety. And it is Gardencourt, rather than Osmond's house, to which she returns—for James is drawing analogues between hostile and hospitable houses in the bourgeois environment; he is arguing for a rule of conduct that is unwavering, despite even the most terrible circumstances—as Isabel's are. James forces Isabel, in short, to satisfy the moral code that the elder James prophesied would come if legal marriage contracts were dissolved and she does so "freely" and "consciously," as she must, to be moral.

But the idea that James may be said to dramatize a point of view which regards the social responsibilities of marriage vows as crucial—a point of view which he shared with, indeed, may have derived from, his father—should not alter the readily accessible fact that James was equally a critic of bourgeois marital life. Indeed, the bourgeois and marital life seem linked. In critiques as corrosive and therapeutic as the angriest social indignation spewed out by thinkers of temperaments different from his, such as Chopin and Shaw, James inevitably singled out the acquisitive spirit of the bourgeoisie. But is it accidental that his father too had singled out the evil inherent in this spirit? It is from this domestic source that James derives his criticisms.

James's short stories abound with such criticism; "Rose-Agathe," a story published in 1878, is the most pointed of these tales dealing with marriage. It is a parody of the acquisitive nature of marriage and love; and it offers as the love-sick hero a collector who invites the narrator to catch a glimpse at the darling with whom he is in love:

> In spite of our approach she stood motionless, until my friend went up to her and with a gallant, affectionate movement placed his arm around her waist. Hereupon she gazed at me with a brilliant face and large quiet eyes.
>
> "It is a pity she creaks," said my companion as I was making my bow. And then, as I made it, I perceived with amazement—and amusement—the cause of her creaking. She existed only from the waist upward.[20]

"Rose-Agathe" is a black comedy, drawn with perverse humor to describe a society in which marriage is merchandising and women are mannequins.

Even the good-hearted Christopher Newman of The American, who aimed at nothing but to make money until his thirty-fifth year, does not escape James's charge that he assesses a would-be wife as if he were buying a "fine piece":

> "Well," he said, at last, "I want a great woman. I stick to that. That's one thing I can treat myself to, and if it is to be had I mean to have it. What else have I toiled and struggled for, all these years? I have succeeded, and now what am I to do with my success? To make it perfect, as I see it, there must be a beautiful woman perched on the pile, like a statue on a monument. She must be as good as she is beautiful, and as clever as she is good. I can give my wife a good deal, so I am not afraid to ask a good deal myself. She shall have

everything a woman can desire; I shall not even object to her being too good for me; she may be cleverer and wiser than I can understand, and I shall only be the better pleased. I want to possess, in a word, *the best article in the market."* (Italics mine)[21]

The late novels, often cited as evidence of James's withdrawal into aesthetic isolation, offer such analyses too. In the opening scene of *The Golden Bowl*, Maggie Verver and the Prince explain that the appropriating spirit controls Adam Verver, the American industrialist:

> "You're at any rate a part of his collection," she had explained—"one of those things that can only be got over here. You're a rarity, an object of beauty, an object of price. You're not perhaps absolutely unique, but you're so curious and eminent that there are very few others like you—you belong to a class about which everything's known. You're what they call a *morceau de musee."*
>   "I see. I have the great sign of it," she had risked, "that I cost a lot of money."[22]

The two are right; James is depicting a world of collectors. When Maggie and the Prince have a child themselves, the boy, the Principino too, is treated not as a person but as an object in the family. Like the pathetic child of *What Maisie Knew* (which too indicts a bourgeois mother and father who view their offspring as a possession to be volleyed between them), the Principino serves as a "new link between wife and husband" and even more as a "link between mama and grand-pa."[23] *The Golden Bowl* stands connected closely to James's earlier works which offer critiques of "innocent" men, like Adam Verver, who share in Osmond's penchant for treating people, especially women, as if they were objects.

Gilbert Osmond personifies the collector. To him, Isabel is not only a source of fortune, but a previous object in herself—suitable for a place in his collection. His words to Madame Merle on Isabel (similar to those of Newman) are those of a connoisseur in quest of a precious object:

> "Is she beautiful, clever, rich, splendid, universally intelligent and unprecedentedly virtuous? It's only on those conditions that I care to make her acquaintance. You know I asked you some time ago never to speak to me of a creature who shouldn't correspond to that description. I know plenty of dingy people; I don't want to know any more."
>   "Miss Archer isn't dingy; she's as bright as the morning. She corresponds to your description; it's for that I wish you to know her. She fills all your requirements." (p. 225)

The overabundant adjectives that Osmond unwinds suggest there is an element of caricature in James's attitude toward Osmond's "requirements" for a woman, just as there is in his attitude toward Isabel's dream of a "prince"; but while Isabel's visions are naive, Osmond's are mercantile. He views his daughter too as a precious possession; and James shows us that, as her father-owner, Osmond is intent not to sell her for less than a great fortune. The marriages in *The Portrait of a Lady* are centered in money and are the means by which people seek to advance themselves in society. Osmond himself exemplifies the worst bourgeois spirit—which substitutes bibelots for people; he, in fact, is even willing to accept the overall social view his collector's mentality drives him towards. He says of Lord Warburton:

> "He owns about half England; that's his character," Henrietta remarked. "That's what they call a free country!"
>
> "Ah, he's a great proprietor? Happy man!" said Gilbert Osmond.
>
> "Do you call that happiness—the ownership of wretched human beings?" cried Miss Stackpole. "He owns his tenants and has thousands of them. It's pleasant to own something, but inanimate objects are enough for me. I don't insist on flesh and blood and minds and consciences." (p. 279)

Osmond, however, cannot make such a fine discrimination; and James unhesitatingly castigates him for his values. For James is not what John Leonard has dubbed "an English department avatar because he incarnated a dream of the Genteel Artist, the Writer preserved in formaldehyde."[24] Instead, despite his self-proclaimed conservatism, James was in part a Hyacinth Robinson, trapped between a world of art and a world of politics; and while he tried to exorcise that part of his consciousness, moving more and more into art, more and more into allegory, James never fully lost the moral indignation he had been raised with. He continued to probe and realize facts about the real world.

James, for instance, makes it clear throughout *The Portrait* that Osmond, although an extreme, is no aberrant fortune hunter in a society of pure people. Just as the women in the novel seem to be transformations of each other (Isabel = Mrs. Touchett = Henrietta = Osmond's mother = Pansy), the men too mirror each other, and each reflects a bit of Gilbert Osmond. Osmond, as I have suggested, is pure villain, thriving on a poisonous state of mind which would incapacitate such comparative innocents as Ralph Touchett or Ned Rosier. Yet Ralph allies himself with Gilbert Osmond by his desire to tamper with Isabel and by his faith in money as a means for control. To him—a collector of boxes—Isabel becomes at one moment "a yard of calico" (p. 49); and James explicitly compares him to Osmond, saying that Osmond "consulted his taste in everything—his taste alone perhaps, as a sick man consciously incurable consults at last only his lawyer; but that was what made him so different from every one else. Ralph had something of this same quality, this appearance of thinking that life was a matter of connoisseurship; but in Ralph it was an anomaly, a kind of humorous excrescence, whereas in Mr. Osmond it was the keynote, and everything was in harmony with it" (pp. 244–245). Rosier too is solidly cast in the collector's mold; even his love for Pansy, tender though it seems, is saturated with the acquisitive spirit. He looks to Osmond as a hero: "the fact that Gilbert Osmond had landed his highest prizes during his impecunious season confirmed his most cherished doctrine—the doctrine that a collector may be poor if he only be patient" (p. 338). These men mirror each other, because James is trying to offer a portrait of a society of collectors, like Osmond, and spectators, like Isabel, who between them divide the world into objects and specimens. In such a world—in which the bourgeois household filled with precious objects (including the wedded couple themselves) is the center—there is hardly room for human sympathy.

And yet, how could James, knowing all this, still create a marital prison for Isabel Archer? Committed as he was to a stable world of manners, James could not afford to allow the experimental female to walk away from domesticity. Isabel, as I have suggested, is allowed to "choose" her fate, just as Hester Prynne is allowed to "choose" hers, but she has no options except marriage. *The Portrait of a Lady* opens with the question of whether or not a woman must marry, but moves quickly, conservatively, to the question of whom she will marry. Isabel's alternatives become limited to one of four men. Further, James passionately believed this stable world of manners was essential to the writer of fiction. As we can remind ourselves, he had written of Hawthorne's case: "This moral is that the flower of art blooms only where the soil is deep, that it takes a complex social machinery to set a writer in motion."[25] Conventions which perhaps lacked spirituality were ironically the soil necessary for art.

Still, there is another tendency in *The Portrait;* and this was part of the initial plan for the book: "After Isabel's marriage there are five more installments."[26] From the conception of *The Portrait,* James was insisting on requirements for an open-ended, rather than maritally complete, novel. The ending of *The Portrait* is crucial if we are to understand the complex interaction that James's art has with the social order of his time. If, as I have argued, James's writing was not biographically or personally removed from questions urgent to him, yet critics such as Poirier and Stone are at least partially correct when they assert that James had "confidence in the power of language to make us citizens of the world we crave rather than in the world where we actually live"[27] or that "James, by shifting his values from the world to his own inner world and their own artistic standards, successfully salvaged the writing of fiction—and the need for fiction—for the modern world."[28] By his discovery of equivocal endings, James found a literary solution which created possibilities of freedom for himself as an artist, as well as the possibilities of freedom for the women he admired, even if their actions might be dangerous to his world. In *The Portrait of a Lady,* for example (as in *The Bostonians* or in *The Golden Bowl*) the final scene refuses to be final; it reserves for James as for us the possibility, on one hand, of believing that the heroine has no future (that she is trapped by social history, i.e., marriage) and, on the other, of believing that she has a future (that she may flee society, i.e., marriage). It was James's discovery of the open-ended novel that shocked his contemporaries reviewing *The Portrait* who saw in it a prediction of adultery between Isabel and Caspar; they were not far wrong. For James had through art moved us from the marriage novel to the verge of the divorce novel. His scorn for the happy ending, the marital ending, was an aesthetic commitment, to be sure, but was an aesthetic commitment in consonance with newly visible nineteenth-century social reality and with James's quiet, albeit anti-social and critical, sympathies.

James's fights over the "marriage ending" were not unique to *The Portrait*. Before and after writing the novel, James squabbled over his refusal to capitulate to conventional finales. When he serialized *The American* in the *Atlantic Monthly*, William Dean Howells argued that Newman should marry his aristocratic lady, and James retorted, "They would have been an impossible couple. . . . I should have felt as if I were throwing a rather vulgar sop to readers who don't really know the world."[29] The debate on *Guy Domville*'s ending was more lengthy, with backers who felt that they could not buy a play without a happy ending. James was adamant, saying that returning his priest hero to the monastery was "the only ending I have ever dreamed of giving the play."[30]

Withdrawing his heroes (heroines too) from marriage may have been James's aesthetic retreat from society: "The obvious criticism of course will be that it is not finished—that I have not seen the heroine to the end of her situation, but I have left her *en l'air*. This is both true and false. The whole of anything is never told; you can only take what groups together. What I have done has that unity—it groups together. It is complete in itself—and the rest may be taken up or not, later."[31] But it involved a social position as well. What James is challenging is his contemporaries' belief in marriage as an apocalypse; he assaults the conventional temporal paradigms to which these beliefs had forced the novel to give consent. Following the Austen tradition, marriage ended time, and the novel had committed itself to reducing reality to a paced and defined human plot. To use Kermode's terminology, the plot of life was seen as "tock-tock";[32] and in most novels, birth was "tick," marriage, the inevitable and final "tock." In such an ordered world (and in such ordered novels), the interval in between was precisely that—an interval, a period charged with anticipation and existing only for the sake of the ending. The marital apocalypse, like any apocalypse, was expected to reorder time, structure its random flow and provide it with meaning. But this is, as we moderns know, a lie—a dream of social order and rigidity, of easy answers. James, however,—and this perhaps is a too long neglected fact of what constitutes his major vision—exploded that lie and the novel with it. *The Portrait* makes clear what other writers ignored, that often marriage created rather than solved problems; as we learn daily, even if the princess marries the prince, the grimmest possibilities remain. What *The Portrait* offers, then, is an adjustment that is contradictorily and simultaneously a move to realism and, in Poirier's phrase, a move to the world elsewhere. While James's book, written, on one hand, by a member of the James family, tames the experimental woman[33] and restricts her physical options for her psychic salvation; on the other, it is James himself who proves bolder than he permits his heroine to be. Isabel thinks of herself as an adventurer, asserting her belief in free will, in the Emersonian system, but she emerges before us as a voice shouting "I want to live," rather than "I am living"; to her, the present seems merely a promise of the future, and despite her assertion that she does not want to begin life by marrying—by her sense of time—she is tacitly consenting to the premise of the marital ending. James, on the other hand—through the implication of his endings—was insisting on the pregnant interval between "tick" and "tock." What he wrote was, to adapt the Kermode language, "tick-tock."

The Portrait of a Lady exploded the domestic novel, converted it into the more fluid form open to the modern novel, made way, in effect, for Joyce and Stein. If James was no modern in being unable to conceive that there might be other options open to Isabel (Quentin Anderson has suggested, for instance, that she might have become an artist), *The Portrait of a Lady* still offered something new to the novel. Indeed, its strength, rather than its failing (as Anderson—and we too— would have it) may curiously reside in James's narrow, conventional vision of women. For his limited vision was not simple; if he wanted to trap Isabel, he wanted as well to free her. It is the tension in the novel, which comes from the struggle between his (and her) desire for confinement and his (her) move to freedom that creates the explosive architecture of *The Portrait*. It might be said too, that the new woman led James on a new path to modernism, as he unsystematically made the marriage novel—like the marrying world about him—burst its mold to tell her tale.

NOTES

[1] See, for example, Donald Stone, *Novelists in a Changing World* (Cambridge, Mass., 1972), pp. 219–220.

[2] The works referred to are Stephen Pearl Andrews, Horace Greeley, and Henry James, Sr., *Love, Marriage, and Divorce, and the Sovereignty of the Individual* (Boston, 1883) and Henry James, Sr., "The Woman Thou Gavest with Me," *Atlantic Monthly*, XXV (Jan., 1870), 66–72; "Is Marriage Holy?" *Atlantic Monthly*, XXV (March, 1870); and "The Logic of Marriage and Murder," *Atlantic Monthly*, XXV (June, 1870).

[3] Henry James, Sr., "Is Marriage Holy?" p. 366.

[4] Ibid., p. 362.

[5] Henry James, Sr.'s letter "To the Editor of the New York *Observer*, printed in the New York *Tribune* on November 13, 1852, included in the Andrews, Greeley, and James volume, *Love, Marriage, and Divorce, and the Sovereignty of the Individual*, p. 24.

[6] Ibid., p. 10.

[7] Ibid., p. 74.

[8] Ibid.

[9] James alluded directly to the scandal between the famous minister Henry Ward Beecher and Elizabeth Richards Tilton in the December, 1872, letter which he wrote to one "H.Y.R." "H.Y.R." obliged by writing to Andrews and sending James's letter; Andrews printed both letters in *Woodhull & Claflin's Weekly*, the same publication which had announced Beecher's sexual promiscuity with his parishioner. These later papers are included in the 1883 edition of *Love, Marriage, and Divorce, and the Sovereignty of the Individual*. While the *Atlantic* papers appear a bit too early to connect themselves directly to the published scandal, the Beecher-Tilton affair was hearsay in New York prior to Mrs. Tilton's disclosure (July, 1870) to her husband of her adultery. It may be that "Is Marriage Holy?" anticipates the public notice of the affair.

[10] Henry James, Sr., "Is Marriage Holy?" p. 362.

[11] Ibid., p. 366.

[12] Henry James, Sr., "The Woman Thou Gavest with Me," p. 71.

[13] Percy Lubbock, ed., *Henry James, Letters* (New York, 1955), I, 27.

[14] Henry James, *The Portrait of a Lady*, ed. R. P. Blackmur (New York, 1961), p. 256. Hereafter all references to *The Portrait* will cite this edition and will appear in the text.

[15] F. O. Matthiessen, *Henry James: The Major Phase* (New York, 1947), p. 182.

[16] William Bysshe Stein, *"The Portrait of a Lady: Vis Inertiae,"* *Western Humanities Review*, XIII (Spring, 1959), 177.

[17] Ibid., p. 181.

[18] It may be that "pushing back her skirts" means "pushing them down." At any rate, Isabel's intentions are the same. She chooses chastity. I am grateful to Professor Edwin Cady of the journal *American Literature* for this second reading.

[19] Richard Chase, *The American Novel and Its Tradition* (Garden City, N.Y., 1957), p. 121.

[20] Henry James, "Rose-Agathe," *The Complete Tales of Henry James* (London, 1962), p. 140.

[21] Henry James, *The American,* ed. R. P. Blackmur (New York, 1960), p. 51.

[22] Henry James, *The Golden Bowl* (New York, 1963), p. 23.

[23] Ibid., p. 115.

[24] John Leonard, "Review of Leon Edel's *Henry James: The Master,"* New York Times (Feb. 14, 1972), p. 27.

[25] Henry James, *Hawthorne* (Ithaca, N.Y., 1956), p. 2.

[26] Henry James, *The Notebooks of Henry James,* ed. F. O. Matthiessen and Kenneth Murdock (New York, 1947), p. 15. Entry of March 18, 1879.

[27] Richard Poirier, *A World Elsewhere* (New York, 1968), p. 210.

[28] Donald Stone, p. 337.

[29] Quoted in Leon Edel, *Henry James: The Treacherous Years* (Philadelphia, 1969), p. 23.

[30] Ibid.

[31] *The Notebooks of Henry James,* p. 18.

[32] See discussion in Frank Kermode, *The Sense of an Ending* (New York, 1968), pp. 43–46.

[33] For Henry James, Sr.'s hostile attack on feminist women, see "Woman and the Women's Movement," *Putnam's Monthly Magazine,* I (1853), 279–288.

Nina Baym

REVISION AND THEMATIC CHANGE IN *THE PORTRAIT OF A LADY*

When Henry James revised *The Portrait of a Lady* for the New York Edition he made thousands of changes in the wording of the text.[1] The revised version is stylistically and thematically closer to his later interests than the early one had been. Its writing is more complex, mannered, and metaphorical. It is thematically less timely and realistic, for its main concern is the private consciousness. In the 1908 version, Isabel Archer's inner life is the center of the character and of the novel's reality. In the early version the inner life is only one aspect of character, which is defined by behavior in a social context.

Owing to the prestige of the New York Edition, the novel of 1881 has largely been ignored by readers and critics, with a resulting loss in our sense of the early James as opposed to the later. In particular we do not see how topical and timely *The Portrait of a Lady* was. The 1881 novel was one of an increasing number of works about "the woman question." The heroine, an appealing young American, wants to live an independent and meaningful life; but she is thwarted. Unlike many works of the period on this theme, *The Portrait* did not depict Isabel's desire as unnatural and misguidedly unfeminine, nor did it employ the standard formula of saving her from this delusion by love and marriage. On the contrary, the novel sympathized with her aim to the point of calling both love and marriage into question. Moreover, it judged Isabel as limited by those inner qualities that, together with external obstacles, prevented her from pursuing and realizing her wish.

The changes of 1908, transforming the story into a drama of consciousness, overlaid and in places obliterated the coherence of the 1881 version. Omissions and additions altered all the characters significantly.[2] Finally, James wrote a preface for the new work which announced that the story centered in the heroine's consciousness and that its action was the development of her perception and awareness. The preface instructed the reader in how to interpret, what to admire, and what to deplore in the work. This preface is significant because it has largely controlled the critical readings of *The Portrait*. Since its interpretation works for

From *Modern Fiction Studies* 22, No. 2 (Summer 1976): 183–88, 190–200.

1908 but not so well for 1881, readers turning to the early version with the preface in mind naturally find an imperfect approximation of the revision. In case after case, passages which figure importantly in criticism of *The Portrait* occur in 1908 only. Strong arguments for Isabel's spiritual transcendence, and equally strong arguments for her hypocritical egotism, derive from that text.[3] But the version of 1881 is a different work. Early James was a masterful writer with his own interests. Once recovered, the 1881 story with its topical focus on the "new woman" and its skillful use of fictional formulae, may prove to be just as interesting as the version of 1908.

The most extensive revisions concern Isabel Archer. She appears on almost every page of the book, and virtually every page about her undergoes change. Although some of these are only excisions or substitutions of single words, the cumulative effect is considerable. The chief intent of these changes is to endow her with the acute, subtle consciousness required for a late James work, which the early Isabel lacks. At the same time that James gives her a rich mental life in 1908, he effaces the original main quality of her character, emotional responsiveness. Her intellectual agility is greatly extended at the expense of her emotional nature.

From this basic change, others follow. Early Isabel is trapped by her simplicity; late Isabel must be the dupe of her subtlety. Victimized by an appeal to her highest faculties, she is less a fool than a saint. There is a corresponding change of tone to treat this more remarkable being. For example, "brilliant and noble" in 1881 becomes "high and splendid . . . and yet oh so radiantly gentle!" in 1908, while "a bright spirit" is rewritten as "a 'lustre' beyond any recorded losing or rediscovering" (Ch. 37).[4] As Isabel is exalted, other characters are degraded. Madame Merle and Osmond are thoroughly blackened, and many supporting figures are flattened and undercut by exaggerated comic treatment. The change in the two villains enhances the pathos in the situation of the trapped sensibility—Isabel Archer as redrawn is much more like Milly Theale than like the original Isabel Archer—while the minor characters lose their function as independent centers of judgment and awareness in the novel. When he is through, James has left nothing solid for the reader except the boundless imagination of Isabel. But in 1881 a limited imagination is her greatest shortcoming.

In 1881, Isabel is an intelligent, sensitive, perceptive, idealistic girl with a ready interest in life. Her imagination, however, is conventionally romantic (like that of many other heroines of fiction), the natural expression of a youthful spirit limited in education and experience. Unfortunately, this imaginativeness is mistaken by Isabel and those who surround her as some sort of brilliance. Isabel's overestimation of herself is a fault, but her real wish to be morally and spiritually fine is extremely attractive. Endowing her with a real, rather than a fancied, imaginative superiority in 1908, James takes away the aspiring quality of her character which is so endearing. Making her live intensely in her mind rather than her feelings, he deprives her of some of the appealing spontaneity, vivacity, and activity in the 1881 character.

Let us note some of the changes which make her more observant and less active, more intellectual and less emotional. In Chapter 2, "quick" perception becomes "clear," "startled" eyes merely "widen," and "brilliant" eyes are toned down to "lighted." In Chapter 3, Isabel finds the rainy springtime "a questionable improvement" over winter; this is sophisticated in 1908 to "an appeal—and it seemed a cynical, insincere appeal—to patience," just as "the incongruities of the season" become "cosmic treacheries." "Fresh impressions" of her "entertaining" Aunt Lydia become "a matter of high but easy irony, or comedy," which "so held" her, and Mrs. Touchett's "deeply interesting" conversation changes to "food for deep reflexion." Vague impulses of feeling are replaced by more precise thoughts, and ordinary ideas become more intense and extravagant.

This process continues even in indirect changes like the alteration of Isabel's wish not to "take a nap" in 1881 to a disinclination for "dozing forgetfulness" in 1908. Taking a nap is a simple physical action; dozing forgetfulness shows that for Isabel sleep means a sacrifice of intellectual activity. In the same chapter (Ch. 4) Isabel's "heart" is changed to her "soul" and her having "gone so far as to forgive" becomes "committed the conscious solecism of forgiving." Similarly, "a certain feeling of embarrassment" becomes "a new sense of complications." The emotion of uneasiness is regularly replaced in 1908 by this sense of complication; another example occurs in Chapter 27 when Lord Warburton's appearance in the first version "made her vaguely uneasy" but in 1908 "affected her as a complication of the wrong sort—she liked so complications of the right." In Chapter 6, James removes the characterizing word "impulsively," and revises "absorbing happiness" to "fine, full consciousness" and "artless" to "prompt." In Chapter 9, he replaces "coquetry" with "the calculation of her effect" and in Chapter 11 "a fine freedom of composition" with "a free play of intelligence." James is recreating the heroine as a person who is continually "reading" her environment and is consequently less active in it.

James brings this out clearly in changing her responses toward her suitors from feeling and impulse to reflection and analysis. She judges their offers in 1908 according to whether life with them will support imaginative freedom. Visions of a "completed life" with Lord Warburton in 1881 change to "completed consciousness" in 1908; instead of possibly being "an incumbrance" Lord Warburton may represent "a complication of every hour"; an offer that "failed to correspond to any vision of happiness" in 1881 "failed to support any enlightened prejudice in favour of the free exploration of life" in 1908; and "elements that would displease her" became "narrowing elements . . . a stupefying anodyne" (Ch. 12). As for Caspar Goodwood, his "limitations" became "impediments to the finer respiration" (Ch. 21). Isabel in 1881 is much more ordinary, so to speak, in that she wants happiness and pleasure from a relationship with a man; in 1908, her requirements are more ascetic and aesthetic.

James also rewrote passages describing her responses to Europe. Her "impressions" change to a "fulness" of "response" and her "feelings" of Rome predictably become her "consciousness" of the city. St. Peter's is no longer just a "church" to her, but "the greatest of human temples" (Ch. 27). In this context, the image of Osmond on his hilltop (Ch. 26) which "happened to take her fancy particularly" in

1881 is revised in 1908 to "put on for her a particular harmony with other supposed and divined things, histories within histories." Isabel's awareness replaces her faculty of feeling in 1908; she responds with her mind rather than her emotions. In 1881 Isabel's emotions, besides being quick, are also rather imprecise. The 1908 responses are more intellectual and also more specific. But imprecision in 1881 is not a stylistic fault; it conveys an important aspect of Isabel's character. She respects herself partly as a person of sensibility, and rightly so, but the vagueness of her feelings leads directly to many of her mistakes. (James tells us all this in the long analytic passages of Chapter 6, but much of what he says no longer seems applicable in 1908.) Because she values her feelings she permits, even encourages, them to guide her. But good and true feelings can be as treacherous as bad ones. This point is important for the theme of *The Portrait* in 1881 and for James's handling of Isabel in love. Love is necessarily quite different in the two versions. In 1881 James makes Isabel genuinely in love with Osmond, shows that this real feeling is untrustworthy, and demonstrates thereby how the desire for independence can be subverted by true love.

In 1908, love is complicated by the heroine's self-awareness. She is not a character likely to get swept away on a wave of feeling. The question of her attraction to Osmond is a major interpretive problem in the 1908 version. One example will demonstrate the nature of James's changes. In 1881, when Osmond declares his love, Isabel feels dread. "What made her dread great was precisely the force which, as it would seem, ought to have banished all dread—the consciousness of what was in her own heart. It was terrible to have to surrender herself to that" (Ch. 29). Here is a conventional maidenly response to the first sensation of sexual passion. The feeling is there and though she will eventually surrender to it, it frightens her as it should frighten a pure and decorous Victorian girl. But in 1908, James attributes her dread to "the sense of something within herself, deep down, that she supposed to be inspired and trustful passion. It was there like a large sum stored in a bank—which there was a terror in having to begin to spend. If she touched it, it would all come out."

This major change adds much that was not there, even implicitly, in 1881. Dozens of critical essays have quoted the "money in the bank" metaphor to impute corrupt or at least disagreeable qualities to Isabel. That she thinks of her feelings as hoarded money, and of love as disbursement, clearly puts obstacles in the way of reading the character as purely admirable and generous. For our purposes, the phrasing "which she supposed to be inspired and trustful passion" is especially baffling. Does James mean that love founded on misperception is not really love, and that therefore Isabel does not love Osmond? Or that she has mistaken not Osmond but her own feelings toward him, and feels not love but some other, more devious, emotion? The cagey phrasing of the revision has opened the door to many theories, some of great sensitivity and perception, about Isabel's feelings. But her feelings in 1881 present no difficulties and require no theories.

The change of Isabel's sphere from emotional to intellectual has reverberations for other aspects of the book. How can so acute and subtle a mind be so seriously wrong about her surroundings? It is easy to comprehend how the Isabel of 1881 might be taken in. But for Isabel in 1908, as for late James characters in general, only a profound, complete, accomplished conspiracy in the outer world can keep her from seeing what is there. This is the reason why, in the revision, Madame Merle and Osmond lose such good qualities as they possess in the original, and are turned into wholly devious and shallow people. Their modicum of natural warmth and their substantial capacities disappear; both become mere swindlers. ....

Even though Isabel is a simple character in 1881, the fact that Madame Merle and Osmond are better people means that in an important way she is less taken in by them than is the revised character. Some of the good things that the early Isabel perceives in them are really there. But the finer intelligence of 1908 demands a finer trap, and Merle and Osmond must put on a better show. This requires that they become more complete performers. Because the revisions to this effect deprive them of substance and transform them into empty shells, the heroine of 1908, even though she is so subtle, is paradoxically much more superficial and dense than the Isabel of 1881. She is certainly a worse judge of people, and since she is alone in 1908 in her uncritical evaluation of this pair, she is more stiff and self-righteous in her mistake. This peculiar combination has not struck all readers as attractive, and has given many students of the revised novel a good deal of trouble. This trouble exists to a much smaller degree, if at all, in the early version.

Besides making Osmond and Madame Merle more vicious, James touches almost all the other characters to reduce them as independent centers of value and judgment. It is as though the younger James had cared for all his characters and tried to give them an illusion of life and depth, while in 1908 only Isabel was real to him. The one character who is not played down is Ralph, in whom James brings out the victimized but transcendent consciousness more than in 1881. Ralph's affinity with Isabel is more pronounced in 1908 than his curiosity or affection. In 1881, his intervention in her life is largely a substitute for an undeclarable love, while in 1908 Isabel is more like an alter ego. He cannot realize his dreams, but possibly she will do it for him. The great moment of the 1908 novel is his death scene—much sentimentalized in the rewriting—when for an instant he and Isabel look at the truth together. This is the union of two consciousnesses. The development of Ralph in 1908 heightens the consciousness theme, and since Ralph's view of Isabel is so uncritical, it also supports the adulatory approach to her character. ....

The most important set of changes of this kind result in the systematic vulgarization of Henrietta Stackpole in the 1908 version. Her friend, Bantling, a comic character from the first, becomes sillier in 1908, a change less important in itself than for the way it reflects on her. He is her companion, after all, and to the extent that he is more vulgar, so is she. The relationship is crudely treated: "frank allies" in 1881, they are "groping celibates" in 1908 (Ch. 20). Dozens of revisions make Henrietta harsher, more unpleasant, and more stupid. This is important, because Isabel thinks of her in both versions as an "example of useful activity" and takes her for "a model" (Ch. 6). In 1881 Isabel is partly measured by her inability to emulate her model; but in 1908 the character is so belittled that the idea of Henrietta as a model is simply absurd. For one thing, James adopts a newly patronizing tone toward her journalistic talents and writings, satirizing aspects of the character which were more respectfully treated in 1881. Though very much a "journalist" and hence not very profound in 1881, she is nevertheless highly talented and thoroughly professional. Quite possibly in later years James became more conservative on such issues as woman's equality, but more likely his growing absorption with the inner life made a character who was engrossed in the world of work and action appear inconsequential.

In Chapter 10, her first appearance, Henrietta is no longer "decidedly pretty" but only "delicately . . . fair." James removes the approving phrases "very well dressed" and "scrupulously, fastidiously neat," substituting for the latter phrase "crisp and new and comprehensive as a first issue before the folding." In 1881 she "carried not an ink-stain" while in 1908 she "had probably no misprint." The point of the 1881 description is to demonstrate that Henrietta is not a stereotyped female journalist, unsexed and unkempt. She is pretty, decorous, and ladylike. The later images stress her modernity and brashness, turning her into a different cliché—the tough, efficient career girl. Removing the element of softness and personal understatement from Henrietta's character, James makes her loud, over-bearing, and obnoxious.

The process extends to very fine details. An 1881 image of her eyes as large polished buttons (Ch. 10) expands in 1908 to "buttons that might have fixed the elastic loops of some tense receptacle," introducing tension into a previously serene character. The originally "brave" Henrietta "went into cages" and "flourished lashes, like a spangled lion-tamer" in revision. The spangles are out of keeping with her earlier sartorial decorum, and the flourished lashes bring a new image of aggressiveness to the depiction. When he changes "Miss Stackpole's brilliant eyes expanded still further" to "ocular surfaces" which "unwinkingly caught the sun," he is certainly making her more machine-like, and when Ralph's comment that she is "decidedly fragrant" is altered to "Henrietta, however, does smell of the Future—it almost knocks one down!" an image of subtlety is replaced by its opposite. Matthiessen notes some of these changes approvingly, pointing out how James has "brightened every inch" of his portrait; but it is precisely the brightening operation that cheapens the character.

It is odd to read in James's preface to the New York Edition the author's apology for Henrietta—as exemplifying "in her superabundance not an element of my plan, but only an excess of my zeal. . . . Henrietta must have been at that time a part of my wonderful notion of the lively"—when one is aware that much of the liveliness was in fact put into the treatment by the revisions. When Henrietta comes to Rome after Isabel has married, we read originally that "her eye had lost none of its serenity" but in the revision that "her remarkably open eyes, lighted like great glazed railway-stations, had put up no shutters" (Ch. 47). And the final sentences of the book, which have her "shining" at Caspar Goodwood with "cheap comfort," were also added in 1908.

These revisions are thematically crucial; as I have suggested, Henrietta is originally presented as a partial touchstone for Isabel. In 1881 the two women are more like one another than in 1908, and their stories are both germane to the issue of women's independence. As some critics have observed with surprise, Henrietta is the one character in the novel to achieve a successful and meaningful life. Moreover, she advances many of the most perceptive comments about Isabel, which are constantly being utilized by critics even as they belittle the speaker of them. Henrietta exemplifies a realized independence; she suggests what the "new woman" has and what she lacks, what she gains and what she sacrifices. Finally, she shows clearly by contrast that Isabel is not a new woman despite the goals she sets for herself. The contrast between Henrietta's sense and Isabel's sensibility recalls Jane Austen, and although Henrietta never has importance in the novel comparable to Isabel's, their stories are balanced to a certain extent. She is not merely a *ficelle* in 1881, but has an independent function.

It is hardly surprising that twenty-seven busy years after he wrote *The Portrait* James would be unable to reproduce the context from which the work had originally been created. One never steps twice into the same river, and no changing artist can write the same work twice. We can recapture the context of *The Portrait of a Lady* in 1881 to some extent ourselves by so simple a historical exercise as reading the serialization in the *Atlantic Monthly* from November 1880 through December 1881, amidst many fictional and essayistic treatments of the new American girl. "What is this curious product of today, the American girl or woman?" began Kate Gannett Wells in an essay entitled "The Transitional American Woman," which appeared in December 1881 along with the second installment of *The Portrait*. "Does the heroine of any American novel fitly stand as a type of what she is? And, furthermore, is it possible for any novel, within the next fifty years, truly to depict her as a finality, when she is still emerging from new conditions in a comparatively old civilization, when she does not yet understand herself, and when her actions are often the awkward results of motives, complex in their character, unconsciously [sic] to herself?"[5]

To this contemporary question James's story at once seems to offer a response. A certain fictional formula, too, had already developed for the new American girl; indeed it seems to have developed simultaneously with the obvious and widespread change in feminine aspirations epitomized by (though by no means confined to) the woman's movement. The formula was both a conservative answer to, and a literary exploitation of, the new woman's situation—a modern version of the essential feminine fable, the rescue story. An intelligent and attractive young girl, who is independent and wishes to remain so, is "rescued" from this false conception of an appropriate feminine life, by love and marriage. When she falls in love, the natural impulses denied by her desire for independence assert themselves. She finds independence incompatible with a woman's way of living. But this is a happy discovery, for the traditional feminine life fulfills her, and she learns the error of her earlier aspirations. An interesting example of the formula appeared concurrently with *The Portrait* in the *Atlantic Monthly* from June through November of 1881. This was William D. Howell's brief novel, *Dr. Breen's Practice*. In this rather weak story, the heroine is a young doctor who gives up her career after her first patient because she becomes conscious of her psychological unfitness for professional pressure and responsibility. As the wife of a mill owner she will use her traditional medical training in an acceptable feminine way by tending the children of the workers.

This "marriage versus independence" formula is now the most common plot in stories about women.[6] James's use of it can be traced from *Washington Square*, a beautiful and bitter little work which immediately preceded *The Portrait* in composition (and has much in common with it), on to *The Bostonians* in 1886 and *The Tragic Muse* in 1890. It can be associated only with his early phase, when his fiction often dealt with current social material. That the original *Portrait* is controlled by the dynamics of the formula can be seen in the first few chapters, which introduce Isabel amidst conversation about Lord Warburton's need to marry an interesting woman and define her mainly by her fondness for her independence.[7] A reader following the story for the first time would certainly expect Isabel eventually to be brought back into her proper sphere by happy love and see the plot propelled by the question of which suitor could succeed in effecting her rescue. But, as she resists the offers of lovers who believe that they are giving her great opportunities, the embattled Isabel becomes increasingly sympathetic, and when she is finally "saved" from her independence, the event is no rescue but a capture. That is, James uses the popular formula while rejecting its assumptions, so that his form and theme reach beyond formulaic simplification.

Since both Warburton and Goodwood are highly eligible as husbands, the reader may feel that Isabel's solution would have been a different marriage rather than none at all. Critics have mostly believed that Isabel ought to have married and take her severely to task for failing to fall in love with one or the other, dividing into camps according to whom they favor. But the formula proposes love as invariably saving by making young women invariably love wisely, and this is one falsehood James is exposing. Moreover, to assume that Isabel ought to marry because she is female is to beg one of the major questions raised by her story—and, indeed, by the stories of all the other women in *The Portrait*, Henrietta excepted. Many of the critics have just the attitude that disturbs Isabel in her suitors: the presumption that because an offer has been made, she is obligated to accept it or to have an excellent reason for turning it down. Neither Warburton nor Goodwood can accept the idea that she refuses them because she is unwilling to accept any mode of existence that is not self-expressive. But this is Isabel's good transcendental reason (as Quentin Anderson and others have stressed)—this and the unimpeachable emotional truth that she doesn't love either of them.

Warburton "had conceived the design of drawing her into the system in which he lived and moved. A certain instinct, not imperious, but persuasive, told her to resist—it murmured to her that virtually she had a system and an orbit of her own" (Ch. 12). It does not matter that the forms of Goodwood's and Warburton's lives are good, and that a woman might live happily and usefully within them. They require the woman to be a satellite in someone else's solar system, and Isabel claims the right to be her own sun. If we define her by membership in the human race rather than the female sex, her claim is admirable. This is how James regards her. He shows it clearly by the fact that Isabel's rejection of Lord Warburton leads Ralph directly to his decision to give her money. The rejection convinces Ralph that her wish for independence is serious and that she is worthy of achieving it. Her wish is thus treated with great respect, not in the least as an aberration.

Ralph is also convinced—wrongly, as it turns out—that a woman could not be strong enough to refuse Lord Warburton unless she had an alternate vision of an independent life. But here Isabel's femaleness does play an important part—brought up female, she has no idea what she might "do" to be independent. The word does not translate into action. This is a terrible limitation, and although James traces its awful consequences, he does not blame her for it. The actual condition of feminine independence, rare as it is, comes about (as Henrietta's story demonstrates) less by choice than necessity, is expressed in unremitting commitment and hard work, and requires fortitude and ability in unusual degree. For these tough requirements Isabel is unfitted by her protected and insulated background, by her lack of training and discipline, and by a "romantic" temperament encouraged by her circumstances.

Here is a subtlety in James's consideration of the theme: modern as it seems, the desire for independence in a young woman may well represent an old-fashioned feminine ignorance of the real world. Consequently, Ralph's gift is no boon to Isabel, and the covert bequest deprives her of one option she has hitherto successfully employed in threatening situations: the choice of turning it down. The fortune imposes on her a necessity to act for which she is hopelessly unprepared. It is no wonder that her first reactions are depression and restlessness and that, startled into premature action, she becomes conventional and traditional.

Basically, she wants to get rid of the fortune and escape the burdens it imposes on her. Because of this special need she is vulnerable to Osmond in a way that she would not have been were she poor (quite apart from the fact that, then, he would not have been interested in her). Older and wiser than she, he will know how to use the money. His apparent lifelong resistance to commitment corresponds to a negative idea of freedom which now, under the pressure of Isabel's need, transforms itself into a positive goal. Because Osmond is less obviously a product of environment than Goodwood and Warburton, Isabel thinks him more free. More important, no clear shape defines itself for the existence of Osmond's putative wife, and therefore Isabel imagines that as Mrs. Osmond she can shape her own life. Although running from independence by reverting to the traditional pattern of love and marriage, Isabel does so in a way that permits her the illusion that she is still seeking freedom. Thus, though the cage she runs into is much smaller than she anticipated, there is no denying that her first free action was to put herself into it. James's point is not that the desire to be independent is dangerous in itself, but that such a desire when its substance is all romantic is no different from any other romantic dream, and will meet the same defeat in real life.

Yet surely he could have established this point without making Osmond and Merle so treacherous. The melodrama of Isabel's later situation certainly detracts from the novel's social realism, and makes her story more specialized, less universal, than it appeared at first. But there is a reason for the many ugly interactions and dreadful revelations of the last third of the book. They push Isabel to the inevitable point of leaving Osmond. This eventuality is much on her mind. As a conventional woman with no more idea than before of how she might live independently, Isabel shrinks from the possibility but cannot see how it can finally be avoided. "She seemed to see, however, the rapid approach of the day when she should have to take back something that she had solemnly given. Such a ceremony would be odious and monstrous; she tried to shut her eyes to it meanwhile" (Ch. 45). The later events in the book force her to defy Osmond, and she increasingly realizes the groundlessness of all the reasons she can advance to stay with him. The conspiracy against her is necessary for the plot line because her learning of it destroys her last illusion—that she had married Osmond with her eyes open. Since Isabel did not freely choose him but was manipulated into the marriage, she is absolved from the moral obligation to suffer the results of her own decision. Therefore, if she remains with Osmond, it will be for the same kinds of reasons that originally drew her to him—his promise of an escape from independence and its implications.

Thus the question of whether Isabel will leave Osmond, which propels the story in the last third of the novel, continues the theme of female independence beyond Isabel's marriage. Because James has not followed the popular formula into its apotheosis of love and marriage, he is logically pushed to consider the aftermath of a bad union. Though not part of the formula—which did not and is only now beginning to accept divorce as part of the texture of human social life—the issue of divorce was from the beginning implicated in questions of female independence and had been debated as a separate question since at least the late 1830's. Henry James, Sr., had taken part in an exchange of letters about it in the *Tribune* and declared himself in favor of "freely legitimating divorce, within the limits of a complete guarantee to society against the support of offspring."[8] Thus it is by no means true that only vulgar or profligate people were associated with the cause of liberalizing the divorce laws.

The senior James's remark also explains why Isabel, having been given a child, was made to lose it. As Goodwood says, in his passionate exhortation, "What have you to care about? You have no children; that perhaps would be an obstacle. As it is you've nothing to consider" (Ch. 55). So even this matter is plotted to give Isabel free rein to leave Osmond. And if Isabel cannot bring herself to the modern American solution of divorce—it is so advanced by Henrietta—she can certainly simply separate from Osmond. Obviously, separation carries no social stricture in the world of the novel. Mrs. Touchett is an apostle of propriety, but lives apart from her husband for no reason except that she prefers to. In fact James is not writing about the abstract right or wrong of divorce, and this judgment does not control his plotting. He is considering what a certain kind of character would do in given circumstances. He concludes that Isabel would come very close to breaking with Osmond, but would recoil at the last.

The agent of recoil is Caspar Goodwood, but we must remember that Isabel's alternatives are not all subsumed in the choice between him and Osmond. She has still the alternative of going her own way, but in fact is less able than before to translate this idea into action. If, as a "free" woman, her greatest independent gesture had been to walk alone from Euston Station to her hotel (Ch. 31), she realizes when she returns to London that even this motion is beyond her now. "She remembered how she walked away from Euston, in the winter dusk, in the crowded streets, five years before. She could not have done that to-day, and the incident came before her as the deed of another person" (Ch. 53).

In contrast, James gives us Henrietta, crossing continents and oceans without flutter. In Henrietta, too, we have evidence that James does not want to say that independence is metaphysically incompatible with love and marriage. Despite the rather cynical portrayal of love and marriage in most of his fiction, he does not go so far as this in *The Portrait*. The independent spirits in the book—Henrietta and Bantling—fall in love and plan to marry, and this is presented as a happy event. Isabel's disappointment in her friend for showing such weakness is only an extension of her own disillusionment. James's idea, however, seems almost to be that the real possibilities of love and marriage are to be experienced only by those who do not depend on them to give life meaning.

James sympathizes with Isabel's ideals, deplores the external obstacles that thwart them, and still objectively shows how much the obstacles are internal, in Isabel's inadequate preparation for and understanding of the life she thinks she has chosen. He also appears to suggest that those whose romantic idealism may most attract them to this "modern" goal may be the least fitted to achieve it because romantic idealism is other-worldly. His own attraction to the romantic idealist as a type enabled him to bind all this into a single structure with an appropriate tone.

The text of 1908 is not sufficiently revised to transform the work into a late James piece, but is enough changed to cloud the original dynamics of the story. It is a baffling and problematical work, much more so than the text of 1881. The changes created many of the problems. They override the social theme of the work and partly erase it. The matrix of values which radiates out from "independence" in 1881 centers in "awareness" in 1908, with attendant dislocations of emphasis. Awareness in 1881 is a means toward the end of an independent life; in 1908 the independent life is attained only in awareness—the two things are almost identical. The only possible independence is the independence of perfect enlightenment. Consequently, Isabel is no longer perceived as having failed, and, not having failed, she has no limitations or shortcomings of thematic consequence.

NOTES

[1] *The Portrait of a Lady* was originally serialized in twelve installments in *Macmillan's Magazine* beginning in October 1880 and in the *Atlantic Monthly* beginning one month later. First editions were separately published in England and America in 1881. The first edition shows a few hundred minor revisions in wording from the serialized version. The New York Edition, a selection of James's writing, appeared from 1907 to 1909, the extensively reworded text of *The Portrait* being published in 1908.

[2] The two chief studies of the revisions are F. O. Matthiessen, "The Painter's Sponge and Varnish Bottle,"

in *Henry James: The Major Phase* (New York: Oxford University Press, 1944), pp. 152–86, and Sydney J. Krause, "James's Revisions of the Style of *The Portrait of a Lady*," *American Literature*, 30 (1958), 67–88. Both concentrate primarily on craft, and consider theme only to argue that the revisions clarify or intensify aspects of the 1881 version.

[3] Every major study of Henry James considers *The Portrait* at some length, and it is also treated in many general studies of the American novel. It has spawned innumerable special critical studies as well. In general studies it often appears as an example of James's "international theme" or of his theme of innocence versus experience. Extended studies tend to provide psychological analysis and moral judgment of Isabel. Until recently, the overwhelming majority of such studies saw her in wholly favorable terms: critics like Dorothy Van Ghent, Dorothea Krook, William Gass, S. Gorley Putt, R. P. Blackmur, Richard Poirier, and Philip Weinstein (to name but a few) feel that she is trapped by excess of virtue and that she grows morally in response to what happens to her. A new critical line, found more often in short studies than book-length treatments, has been antagonistic toward her, stressing her self-righteousness, ignorance, and conceit, or her sexual coldness, inhibition, and general fear of life—Tony Tanner, R. W. Stallman, and William Bysshe Stein, for example. Still others mediate between these views, finding virtue and limitation in the character: writings on James by Oscar Cargill, Leon Edel, Richard Chase, and Charles Samuels are representative of this class.

[4] I follow the New York Edition for the 1908 text, and the American edition of 1881 (Boston and New York: Houghton Mifflin Company) for the early version. To make quotations useful for owners of various other texts, I cite chapter rather than page number in my discussion.

[5] *Atlantic Monthly*, 46 (1880), 817.

[6] The story appears often in a negative version these days, where the misery and wretchedness of successful, independent woman displays, by contrast, the superiority of traditional patterns.

[7] The relation of Isabel's story to the woman's movement has scarcely been noticed, even by recent feminist criticism, with the important exception of Donald D. Stone's "Victorian Feminism and the Nineteenth-Century Novel," *Women's Studies*, 1 (1972), 65–91. Critics like Christoff Wegelin, who see her as a formulaic representation of the American girl, fail to make a connection between the actual situation of that type, and the growing demand for equal rights. William Veeder, in *Henry James: The Lessons of the Master* (Chicago: University of Chicago Press, 1975), pp. 151–72 passim, discusses Isabel's characterization in relation to the Woman Question; he rightly observes that despite her emancipation, Isabel is "a representative Victorian woman" (p. 165). His discussion of the Question, and its treatment in other fiction and poetry, is alarmingly haphazard, however.

[8] Henry James, Horace Greeley, and Stephen Pearl Andrews, *Love, Marriage and Divorce, and the Sovereignty of the Individual* (New York: Stringer and Townsend, 1853), p. 40. Reprinted in 1972 by Source Book Press, New York.

Zephyra Porat

TRANSCENDENTAL IDEALISM AND TRAGIC REALISM IN *THE PORTRAIT OF A LADY*

> Let us sit apart as the gods, talking from peak to peak.
> —Emerson, "Manners"

I

Never was there a story about love that is less a love story, Henry James says of Hawthorne's *The Scarlet Letter*.[1] As loveless seems *The Portrait of a Lady,* Isabel and Ralph make conversation, not love. At Gardencourt and at Rome ladies and gentlemen discuss dispassionately the mysteries of freedom and fate, nature and art, personal identity and social mask. Women whisper about the metaphysics of the self and the composition of a real personality. Yet never were self-conscious people less aware of the realities lurking in the depths of their character. Strangely cold seem the art galleries where Isabel plays platonic games of intellect and imagination with Ralph and Osmond. Hardly natural seems Ralph's taboo on all love but the "imagination of loving." Preceding Osmond in playing snuffers to her candle, her loving cousin contemplates an image of Isabel as sinister as the portrait of the Duchess in Browning's poem. To Ralph as to Osmond, she is rather a work of art than a woman of flesh and blood, an inanimate object, a picture, a statue, a cathedral, a polygon—rather than a person.[2]

Neither English nor American writers explore the depths of passionate experience, James remarks in *Hawthorne* and in *French Poets and Novelists*.[3] But the American suffers most from this deprivation. He is imprisoned in a lonely chamber of dreamy contemplation and can "never break through its viewless bolts and bars," because—haunted by his Puritan ancestors—he shares their mistrust of the vulgar world outside. "Half a poet, half a critic, and all a spectator," his is "a portrait of a man ... whose passions are slender, whose imagination is active, whose happiness lies not in doing but in perceiving."[4] By nature, Hawthorne craved intimacy with the

From *Hebrew University Studies in Literature* 5, No. 1 (Spring 1977): 67–101.

outer world of human action and passion. But a "strong and deep Puritan con-science," of which he was but half conscious, and which had filtered into his character through a long succession of generations, had contaminated him with "constant mistrust and suspicion of the society that surrounded him." "This constant exteriority," which characterizes "the national consciousness" collectively—marks Hawthorne's writings with a "serious defect":

> It is the work of an outsider, of a stranger, of a man who remains to the end a mere spectator (something less even than an observer), and always lacks the final initiation . . .[5]

In the nineteenth century, the American's "constant exteriority" was the badge of "Transcendentalism," not "Puritanism." But "the Transcendentalist *par excel-lence,*"[6]—as James describes Ralph Waldo Emerson,—was "not in least a secu-lariser, but in his own subtle insinuating way a sanctifier." "A fruit of a long Puritan stem," his "American Scholar" was but the old stranger and spectator under a new name.

> There is much that makes us smile, today, in the commotion produced by his secession from the . . . pulpit . . . there is even a sort of drollery in the spectacle of a body of people among whom the author of The American Scholar and of the Address . . . at the Harvard divinity college passed for profane, and who failed to see that he only gave his plea for the spiritual life the advantage of a brilliant expression.[7]

In the name of godlike heroism, the idealistic Emerson withdrew from the world with the same mistrust his grandparents had displayed in the name of godly holi-ness. To be sure, his Christian idealism had been "gently raked and refreshed by an imported culture." Influenced by the apostles of passion Goethe and George Sand, he enjoined his disciples to live with their doors open to all experience. The result was a strange blend of Romantic expansion and Puritan exclusion, which James illustrates by citing Margaret Fuller's *Journal:*

> In the evening, a conversation on Impulse . . . I defended nature, as I always do—the spirit ascending through, not superseding, nature. But in the scale of Sense, Intellect, Spirit, I advocated the claims of the Intellect.

Of their "Romanticism on Puritan ground," all that remained in practice was "a Puritan carnival," James notes in "Emerson." Judging from their life at Brook Farm, what these "passionless pilgrims" wanted was innocence, not experience, immunity from, not intimacy with, the outer world. Wordsworth's "plain living and high *thinking,*" was their ideal, not George Sand's licentious living and deep feeling. From the moral games played by these "innocent youths and maidens," all "irregularities" were conspicuous by their absence. To a visitor from abroad, their "Spirit of conformity" is far more marked than "their *dérèglements,*" their fascination with the "inner landscape of the soul" far more pronounced than any awareness of the "outer life" of the body.[8]

Years before William James attacked Emerson's idealism in *Principles of Psychology* (1890) and *Pragmatism* (1907), Henry James challenged Emerson's "provincial" psychology in terms and images that his elder brother was to echo almost verbatim.[9] Rejecting Emerson's division of the Self into I and Not-Me, and his declaration that the Subject alone is real,[10] James proposed instead to distinguish between a Collector and his Collection who lead intimately related, equally real, though conflicting lives. The "collection" of objects, people, and opinions the outer self gathers in his "worldly" or "European" exile, form the material that the Collector re-collects in his "Unworldly" or "American" kingdom. The outer self, who interacts with others in a field of experience where one man's action is another man's feeling, is the only self a dramatic artist can portray, the only self a pragmatic psychologist can examine.[11]

When *Pragmatism* appeared, Henry James greeted it in a witty letter to his brother: "I was lost in wonder at the extent to which all my life I have (like M. Jourdain) unconsciously pragmatized." In the same vein he greeted *A Pluralistic Universe:*

> It may sustain and inspire you a little to know that I'm *with* you, all along the line—and can conceive of no sense in any philosophy that is not yours! As an artist and a "creator" I can catch on, hold on, to pragmatism and can work in the light of it and apply it...[12]

Indeed from *Hawthorne, French Poets*, and *Roderick Hudson* (1868) to "Emerson" and *The Golden Bowl,* through *The Bostonians* and *The Tragic Muse,* James praises European realists who never leave their character "shivering for its fleshly envelope" (of material, social and cultural circumstances)[13] and parodies transcendental idealists who always do. He might indeed wonder at the extent to which all his life he had pragmatized, or dramatized in an effort to exorcise the ghost of his American heritage which kept the gate to communion with outer life barred and bolted. But in no single work does Emerson's ghost hover quite so actively over the entire action, as in the *Portrait* of an Emersonian lady, adopted into the house of Touchett, and driven by the family ghost to the position of "a disembodied spirit imprisoned in the haunted chamber" of "her own contemplation."[14]

Like Ralph Waldo Emerson, Ralph Touchett withdraws with one hand the cup of experience he offers Isabel with the other. "You want to drain the cup of experience," he says. "No, I don't wish to touch the cup of experience. It's a poisoned drink! I only want to see for myself." And he praises her preference for the role of detached spectatorship, like Emerson calling her old fear of passion, heroism, and the old exteriority, liberty. The Puritanic fears concealed and indulged by Ralph's and Isabel's transcendental euphemisms cannot be exhibited without tracing the tragedy of their flight from passionate experience. But James's view of women who flee from the pain of feeling to philosophies of self-reliance can be illustrated by his portrait of an obscure daughter of the Age of Reason, Madame de Sabran. Afraid of her strong feelings for a man she addresses in her letters as a friend, she consoles herself with Stoic and Epicurean theories of self-sufficiency.

Viewed from these philosophical heights, "objects grew so small to my imagination that you also seemed no more to me than a worm, and I was indignant that so little an animal could do me so much harm." But, James notes, she "hardly pretends to deceive herself," and calls her fear fear, her other-defiant philosophy an illusion and a cheat. "You have no idea what I have suffered," she confesses, "and I am so frightened . . . that there is nothing I wouldn't do to recover my reason":

> She was afraid of the deeper currents of life, and she thought that when one felt one's feet touching bottom it was the part of wisdom to stand still. 'I don't rejoice as you do in the discovery of *truth*. I am afraid it will hurt me . . . It makes one shudder to see how little we know ourselves. Is it a good?—is it evil? . . . I believe that illusion is the truth . . . Happily every individual has a common interest in being cheated.'[15]

Like Madame de Sabran, Ralph and Isabel are afraid of knowing the truth about themselves, the truth that they are vulnerable to the pain of passionate involvement with others. For Isabel as for Madame de Sabran, "imagination was the deepest depths of her imbroglio."[16] But both Isabel and Ralph lack the honesty to admit they have a common interest in being cheated because, like Emerson, they call fear of others—heroism. Isabel deludes herself that a heroic woman must "suffice unto herself and be happy." Ralph deludes himself that a philosopher is like a postage stamp without gum (p. 14)—untouched subjectively by whatever touches his "person" objectively: "it appeared to him it was not himself in the least he was taking care of, but an uninteresting and uninterested person with whom he had nothing in common" (p. 39).

Blind to the deeper motives for his "crazy illusions" and her "sweet delusion," they make a philosophical virtue of psychological necessity, a religion of ignoring the others who hurt them, their own person included. Translated from his theory to her practice, self-reliant other-defiance nips their own love in the bud, conceals their warm, out-going nature behind a "fine ivory surface . . . opposed to possibilities of penetration" (p. 38), precludes communication and arrests initiation into self-knowledge. In the tragedy caused by their American (Emersonian) mask, James questions Emerson's faith in the reality and force of character, and in the triumph of individual personality over the collective persona society seeks to impose.[17]

II

In the Preface to the *Portrait,* James describes Isabel as a presumptuous young lady "affronting her destiny," yet "bent upon her fate" (x, xi). What destiny she affronts and what fate she pursues are questions dramatized not only in her central action, but in the supporting stories of Lydia Touchett, Pansy Osmond, Serena Merle, Amy Gemini and Henrietta Stackpole. All the ladies experience a conflict between their nature and their mask, their feminine personality and their social persona, their innate inclinations and their acquired taste. The fate they all face, whether defiantly or submissively, is the conventional "position of woman" (p. 451), as dictated by the conventional taste of men. A woman in search of a respectable position or dazzling persona must meet the requirements of a fastidious (transcendental-idealistic)[18] imagination. For connoisseurs like Ralph or Osmond, women are pleasing only when "superior," "clever," "self-possessed." With comic humility, Henrietta confesses "herself human and feminine" (beneath her mask of literary lady), laughs at the look of things, and exchanges the glory of appearing a "light keen flame, a disembodied voice," for the privilege of sharing "personal susceptibilities and common passions" with Mr. Bantling (pp. 282, 567). With Falstaff-like shamelessness, the irrepressible Amy "whose folly has the irrepressibility of genius" (p. 449), does not care about reasons (p. 257), grits her teeth at her brother's icy intellect (pp. 453–455), and gives her heart away with licentious generosity (p. 449). For Amy and Henrietta who scorn it, transcendental taste entails no tragic sacrifice of their passionate nature (pp. 260–282).

But Isabel, Lydia Touchett, Serena Merle and Pansy Osmond are "deficient in the sense of comedy" (p. 245) concerning their position. Woven into the texture of their character with threads of pride, ambition and gravity, their conventional persona becomes a prison to which their ego is both lock and key. Unable to smile with Emerson's "beautiful irony"[19] at the tricks idealist taste plays with their natural mission (p. 260), each experiences "the surrender of a personality, the authority of the Church" (p. 555), whether the Catholic Church of Rome or the Transcendental (Unitarian) Temple of Boston.[20] Masked in masculine honor to please men who fear her larger feminine qualities,[21] each woman passively or actively pursues her fate by denying her natural destiny. To please an American gentleman, a lady's passionate nature must not be too large. Ralph sees Isabel as a "real little passionate force to watch at play" (p. 63). Osmond confesses: "I prefer women like books— very good and not too long" (p. 230). In Transcendental Boston, as in Catholic Rome, men's taste in Women is still conservative.[22] The ideal woman is modelled after the Cimabue Madonna or the Correggio Madonna, not after the Venus de Medici (pp. 210, 458). Her right worship is metaphysical adoration, not physical love (p. 578). Classified under the exclusive headings of cats or madonnas by French realists and American idealists alike,[23] few women can confess themselves "human and feminine" (p. 567). Too proud to "be easy, natural and nasty" as Amy advises (p. 547), or too ashamed to confess she has "common passions" as Henrietta urges, Isabel masks her feline femininity in "the cloudy envelope of a goddess" (p. 35) and Serena Merle hers in the mask of a Juno, or worse, of an Aristides the Just (pp. 175, 251).

In vain Henrietta, speaking for Henry James (Preface xv, xvii), warns Isabel and Ralph against excluding her passionate nature and personal contacts from their dreamy image of her character. In vain she denounces as "dangerous," "selfish" and "heartless" their common tendency to call only her "inner self" important and to dismiss as "vulgar" her so-called "outer life," in "the toiling, striving, suffering, I may even say sinning, world that surrounds" her. By this she does not mean Isabel to become a "grossly sensual" cat. She simply means that Isabel's introverted soul is "not enough in contact with reality . . . Whatever life you lead you must put your soul in it" (pp. 216–217), and not stay fastidiously out of it in the position of a spectator and a stranger. In vain Henrietta warns Ralph against absorbing Isabel into the world of *his* dreams and ignoring *her* reality, which happens to be other than his own. "I'm not talking about imaginary characters; I'm talking about Isabel. Isabel's intensely real." Finding Isabel "fearfully changed," and suspecting Ralph's influence, Henrietta reminds him that if he were really in love with "Another," as he claims, he would respect her otherness and not love in her his own image. "You're in love with yourself, that's the Other!" she accuses him (p. 119).

Ralph pretends he has no intention of acting on Isabel (p. 120), or of shaping her in the image of his dreams. All he wants, he claims, is to leave her alone and to watch her develop her many-sided nature. He even expressly criticizes her dangerous tendency to transfer her center of consciousness to "the organ of pure reason" (p. 100), as she calls it. "Don't question your conscience so much," he advises her. "You've too much power of thought—above all too much conscience" (p. 222). But deep down, Ralph wants to have Isabel in his power (p. 145), to meet the requirements of *his* imagination by giving her the power to meet *hers* (pp. 183–186), to fill her purse with his money, her sails with his wind, her mind with his suggestions (p. 223). He wants to see his ideas embodied in her actions (p. 41). He doesn't want to marry her body; it's her soul, her imagination he wants to use. Or, as James permits him to put it in an awkwardly mixed metaphor (in reply to her question "Are *you* thinking of proposing to me?"):

> By no means. . . . that would be fatal; I should kill the goose that supplies me with the material of my inimitable omelettes. I use that animal as the symbol of my insane illusions. (p. 149)

Emulating Emerson's Prospero-like artist for whom all the world's a stage for self-dramatization, Ralph half consciously carries his art into Isabel's nature and destroys its separate, other existence.[24] In an early short story, "The Madonna of the Future," James parodies an idealist artist as saying "to nature in the form of a beautiful woman, 'you are all wrong, here let me show you how.' "[25] In the *Portrait* (of Isabel as a Madonna), the parody is more subtle. Let me show you how to develop your own character, is all Ralph says to Isabel. But she senses that from *his* plan for her development, *her* feminine nature has been omitted.

Yet Isabel is rather flattered than frightened by the masculine persona Ralph tries to fasten on her. She never prided herself on being like other women. She had always taken pride in having a "finer mind" than most women and did not argue with people who "treated her as if she were rather superior; . . . for it seemed to her often that her mind moved more quickly than theirs" (34, 49–53). While "most women . . . waited in attitudes more or less gracefully passive for a man to come that way and furnish them with a destiny," as Ralph puts it (p. 63), Isabel "spent half her time in thinking of beauty and bravery and magnanimity" (p. 51). Among her "collection of views on the subject of marriage . . . was a conviction of the vulgarity of thinking too much about it." In Henrietta she admired the "light keen flame, a disembodied voice, the living proof that a woman might suffice to herself and be happy." When Henrietta turns out to be a sentient being, Isabel is bitterly disappointed. "There was a kind of want of originality in her marrying . . . even a kind of stupidity" (pp. 53, 567).

It never occurs to Isabel that, in her ideal of disembodiment, there is a similar "want of originality." The notion of feminine inferiority is very "old-fashioned," James remarks in "Balzac"; and the ideal of little (if not disembodied) women, shared by Ralph and Osmond, is convention incarnate. A more original view of femininity (in men or in women) would value feminine sensibility still more than "faculties of quite another order—faculties of a masculine stamp," such as "the solid sense, the constant reason, the moderation, the copious knowledge." In "Sainte-Beuve," James admires the French critic because of his "feminine fineness of perception." Anything but old-fashioned, James praises him for being "more than feminine . . . positively feline":

> He had the organization of a nervous woman . . . there is something feminine in his tact, his penetration, his subtlety and pliability, his rapidity of transition, his magical divinations, his sympathies and antipathies, his marvelous art of insinuation, of expressing himself by fine touches.[26]

But neither Ralph nor Osmond nor Isabel admire her feminine genius, her pliability, her nervous divinations. Their conventional taste prefers "males in petticoats," or women masked in "masculine honour."[27] Only Madame Merle recognizes the tragic mistake she made in exchanging her feminine genius, her sympathies and antipathies, for a "false position." To her the traditional persona of a lily is "horrid," not honourable. She repressed her original personality "for nothing" (pp. 199, 525). If to be conventional is to crawl—as you Americans say—then women can't help crawling, she confesses to Isabel.

> We're mere parasites, crawling over the surface . . . a woman, it seems to me, has no natural place anywhere; wherever she finds herself she has to remain on the surface and, more or less, to crawl. (p. 196)

Bred on Emerson's "Climb they must, or crawl!"[28] Isabel is shocked. She will never crawl in search of a persona. She will never conform to convention. Madame Merle agrees:

> You protest, my dear? you're horrified? you declare you'll never crawl? It's very true that I don't see you crawling; you stand more upright than a good many poor creatures. . . . I want to see what life makes of you . . . it can't spoil you. It may pull you about horribly, but I defy it to break you up. (pp. 188, 196)

But her resolution to remain upright (and unfeminine) is conventionally American, not heroically original. The "military attitude of soul," which her friend observes in her, conforms to the Emersonian pattern of "warlike" heroism, even as Emerson's heroic American scholar, carrying his cross, conforms to the pattern of the Christian soldier. When Isabel greets her suitors "not so much smoothing her hair as girding her spirit" (p. 152); when she receives Madame Merle's assurance "as a young soldier . . . might receive a pat on the shoulder from his colonel" (p. 188); she reminds the reader of Emerson's hero who, to all worldly temptations "assumes a warlike attitude, and affirms his ability to cope single handed with the infinite army of enemies."[29]

Quite conventionally, Isabel fears the tipsy mirth and dissoluteness of Osmond's irrepressible sister. Like the Touchetts, Isabel disapproves of Amy not because she betrayed her husband in taking a lover, but because she betrayed her own character in taking too many. Like Mr. Osmond, Isabel is appalled by his sister not because she has a heart, but because she hasn't—that is because she has scattered it about haphazardly in small unconnected pieces without any unifying principle to lend her character the coherence, the centrality, the tyrannical unity of mind Emerson requires. It isn't that Amy tells fibs, as Madame Merle insinuates, but that her "silly sincerity" lacks a center of reference, a spiritual principle, a soul. "A woman to whom the truth should be habitually sacred" (p. 281), Isabel believes with Emerson and Osmond, is one who is true to herself, to her "better self" (p. 224), that is. Truth of character is singleness of purpose, unity of will, "a centered mind," in a word, integrity.[30]

To be true, centered, self-collected—not scattered, dispersed, fragmented like Amy—"one ought to choose something very deliberately, and be faithful to that," Isabel believes (p. 264). Like Emerson she regards "infidelity" to her own choice or her own promise, as "a capacity for pollution," an impurity from which she draws back her skirts in horror (p. 433).

Of course Amy cannot understand her ideal of uprightness, integrity or purity. "You've such a beastly pure mind," Amy explodes when Isabel refuses to grasp the information which would excuse her for being unfaithful to her husband. "I never saw a woman with such a pure mind!" (p. 541). Only Madame Merle can appreciate how much Isabel thinks of her promises (p. 314). She alone has a nose for "the aroma of purity which is a pervasive emanation" from a character bred on Puritan soil. "The faintly acrid perfume of the New England temperament," the integrity, "the fine distillation of masculine honour, the formidable strength of will, the depths of purpose that nothing in the world can overcome"[31]—all this reassures Madame Merle that Isabel will make a good stepmother to Pansy, unnatural though such a mission might seem to other women (pp. 268, 276–277). Like Madame Merle, Isabel objects to making a scapegoat of Amy as though she were the only woman with a tendency to wander away from the noble center of her character to the common, dreary, unheroic, dispersed circumference. Even Isabel has "a roving disposition" (p. 264), a curiosity, an unreliable tendency to try something new every day, a bold and ungraceful inclination to roam around the world (pp. 306ff.). She scorns and fears her own roving femininity much more than Amy's, whom she "would as soon have thought of despising . . . as of passing a moral judgment on a grasshopper" (p. 449). What Isabel fears most is feeling "her faculties, her energy, her passion . . . dispersed" (p. 538).

Hence, unlike Amy, she sees no horrors in Osmond's "curtains and crucifixes" (p. 255). Like Emerson's heroes, she would rather "live with divine unity" than "weave...a spotted life of shreds and patches."[32] She is neither offended nor frightened by Osmond's scorn for her travels or by his sinister admission: "I don't want to see you on your travels ... I should like to see you when you're tired and satiated." Envying the immutability of paintings and the quiet peace of statues, she is rather pleased than perturbed when Osmond tells her he wants to make her life a work of art, a portrait of "the most important woman in the world" (pp. 307ff., 303, 568–569).

Amy, echoing Henry James, calls her resistance to impurity in feminine nature—her own, or Madame Merle's, or Amy's—"the finest capacity for ignorance" (p. 199). But Isabel takes pride in pursuing the noble ideal despite the sordid facts. If Madame Merle the real woman doesn't match that ideal—so much the worse for Madame Merle. If behind her perfect mask Isabel catches glimpses of cynicism or cruelty or degeneracy, "there were evidently things in the world of which it was not advantageous to hear."[33] Of course the *tabula rasa* of her pure soul must be inscribed with a text which reveals her character. But she prefers the tiny edifying text inscribed in Pansy's innocent character by her father and the nuns, to the spotted, blotted illegible text written on the more experienced Amy and Madame Merle by a "wide variety of hands" (p. 279).

III

Before Isabel inherits the fortune which fits her for the part of Pansy's kind stepmother, Madame Merle tries to correct her innocent self-ignorance and to share with her the lesson she learned from bitter experience. She too had exchanged a life of self-giving sensibility for a self-possessed "corselet of silver" and the honour it bestows. But after discarding the "shell" or the "garment" of her outer life, she discovered that the garment was her self, and the shell her soul. Only to Osmond can she make a full confession of her tragic discovery. After I've lost you and my child, she complains, how can you tell me my soul is immortal and cannot be destroyed by any outer loss?

> I don't believe at all that it's an immortal principle. I believe it can perfectly be destroyed. That's what has happened to mine, which was a very good one to start with ... You've not only dried up my tears; you've dried up my soul. (p. 522)

To Isabel, Madame Merle must put the lesson more discreetly. When Isabel preaches to her the Emersonian lesson of transferring the seat of her consciousness to her subjective accidents, her "memories, graces, talents—," she interrupts bitterly: "What have my talents brought me? Nothing but the need of using them." Take away my "outer life," my personal contacts, even my property, and "the best part's gone, and gone for nothing" (p. 199). You say, in your Emersonian innocence, that the best part of one remains. But one cannot, as Emerson advocates, leave one's outer life like Joseph his coat in the hands of the harlot and flee,[34] not without sacrificing one's self along with it:

> When you've lived as long as I you'll see that every human being has his shell and that you must take the shell into account . . . What shall we call our "self"? Where does it begin? Where does it end? It overflows into everything that belongs to us—and then it flows back again. (p. 200)

Like Emerson, Isabel believes that "a cultivated man becomes ashamed of his property, ashamed of what he has, out of a new respect for his being."[35] But Madame Merle believes, like Henry and William James, that being is having, that no real personality can be left "shivering for its fleshly envelope" of material, social and spiritual possessions:[36]

> There's no such thing as an isolated man or woman; we're each of us made up of some cluster of appurtenances . . . I know a large part of myself is in the clothes I choose to wear. I've a great respect for things! . . . one's house, one's furniture, one's garments, the books one reads, the company one keeps. (p. 201)

Madame Merle knows that the tragedy of misplaced identity is only for her, not for Isabel. "The horrible mistake . . . of a real treasure supposed to be false and hollow,"[37] is a tragedy only for a woman who discovers it, only for a mother who discovers that in throwing away her child (her shell), she has thrown away her pearl for a false position. But Isabel will never "turn herself inside out." For her the truth will never "change sides."[38] The more painfully real her outer circumstances will become, the more she will deny their reality and their power to bend or break her real (ideal) self. If Madame Merle frightens her by revealing her own wickedness and treachery, Isabel will find a way to say: "Poor, poor Madame Merle!" Life can touch but cannot hurt a woman determined that "if she was to be unhappy, it should not be a fault of her own," and resolved to prevent the "objective" misery she does not deny from making her surrender to it "subjectively." Self-blinded by Emerson's conviction that "sin seen from the thought . . . has an objective existence but no subjective,"[39] Isabel is both driven to sacrifice her nature, and protected from suffering "inwardly" by the same idealistic error.

In the same scene that Madame Merle howls "like a wolf" (p. 522) at the sacrifice Osmond demands both of her and Isabel, Isabel escapes to nature where she discovers, beneath the "veil" of her personal sadness, an impersonal reality which makes her sorrow seem small, ridiculous, merely objective:

> She dropped her secret sadness into the silence of lonely places, where its very modern quality detached itself and grew objective, so that as she sat in a sun-warmed angle . . . she could almost smile at it and think of its smallness . . . [she] gazed through the veil of her personal sadness at the splendid

sadness of the scene . . . where the cloud-shadows had the lightness of a blush. (pp. 518–519)

Behind her heroic persona, Isabel's nature rebels against the man who hates her larger qualities and admires her for repressing them. The more rigid the persona, as Jung would put it, the more clamorous and unruly its compensating opposite, the repressed anima.[40] Yet the more defiant her woman's nature becomes, the more frightened Isabel becomes of herself (p. 503) and the stronger does her resisting persona become. The conflict between her masculine conscience (animus) and her feminine nature (anima) explodes when Osmond demands that she sacrifice Pansy's love, and when she suspects for the first time the secret intimacy between her husband and her friend. As in "George Sand," so in the *Portrait,* James describes a rebellious feminine will to live, expand, respond, clashing with a masculine principle of order, virtue, respectability.[41] Consciously Isabel denies both the rebellion and the feminine passions which provoke it. Unlike Madame Merle who initially denied but later recognized she was jealous of Isabel, Isabel denies any such unheroic passion. "Jealous of her—jealous of her and Gilbert? The idea just then suggested no near reality" (pp. 404–405). But from the depths of nature, the angry and jealous woman in Isabel takes revenge on both her friend and her husband with a force that asserts itself in contradiction to propriety and usage. The feminine "element of insubordination and disorder" (of which Gilbert accuses her and which she denies) clashes with the "official" element, the respectable, conservative, exclusive strain. The passionate democrat rises up against the conservative Christian, the military will, the aristocratic taste, the philosophizing mind and the ascetic imagination.[42]

Commenting on an observation Sainte-Beuve made when he freed himself from Christian mythology, James writes that the Frenchman was wrong to fear his Christian morality had killed his feminine sensibilities. "The heart can hardly be said to die . . . It changes its forms of manifesting itself, but there is always a savor of it in the conduct."[43] Similarly, Isabel's heart has only been sublimated into "an imagination of the heart" by her Emersonian, i.e. Christian code. "Oh the imagination of women," Osmond sighs when Madame Merle pleads passionately the cause of the soul she blames him for destroying. Little did he know how Isabel's imagination joins Madame Merle's in celebrating as divine her expanding, life-giving power of love, and denouncing as diabolical his contracting, sterilizing power of tradition, taste and intellect.

At midnight, crossing the threshold of consciousness veiled in her archetypal images: Ocean, Mother, Earth and Moon,[44] Isabel's anima fumes at the man who did not play his archetypal role of her son and lover. She had imagined him waiting for her as

for the tide, looking seaward, yet not putting to sea . . . She would launch his boat for him; she would be his providence . . . As she looked back at the passion of those full weeks she perceived in it a kind of maternal strain . . .

But his icy egoism was rather "a serpent in a bank of flowers," his fastidious taste "a faculty for making everything wither," his intellect "an evil eye," and "his presence . . . a blight" (pp. 424–433). She, the fecund earth, had projected her own shadow onto him, the "dead moon" as Sainte-Beuve describes his murderous mind:

> She had seen only half his nature then, as one saw the disk of the moon when it was partly masked by the shadow of the earth. She saw the full moon now—she saw the whole man. (p. 426)

The more rebellious her anima, or the heavier her heart, or the more blasted the circle of her once centered mind, the more Isabel's heroic persona yearns for Ralph's help in resisting her self. While Osmond treats women's passions with provoking disgust, Ralph soothingly smiles at them and pushes them away from the threatened center of her consciousness. Reinforced by his disinterested humour, her reason can banish the shadows of hatred, shame, revenge, jealousy, anger which "were not an emanation from her own mind" (p. 425), as she tries to believe. "Formerly, when heavy hearted, she had been able . . . to transfer the seat of consciousness to the organ of pure reason." Now without Ralph's help she cannot tell herself her feelings are not her self. It is not for self-knowledge or expanding experience that Isabel appeals to him, but for the "sort of assistance—aid to innocent ignorance" that Amy Gemini refuses to render. Ralph will reinforce Isabel's "beastly pure mind" even when she uses it to conceal from him the knowledge he craves:

> It seemed to her an act of devotion to conceal her misery from him. She concealed it elaborately, she was perpetually, in their talk, hanging out screens . . . Ralph smiled to himself . . . She didn't want him to have the pain of knowing she was unhappy . . . and it didn't matter that such knowledge would rather have righted him. (p. 435)

I V

Wondering who made Isabel's mechanically smiling mask, who transformed her into another person, who made her reflect and represent him, Ralph can only answer: Osmond. But James has informed the reader that many "others" wrought Isabel's "mystic conversion into the stuff of drama" (pp. xiii–xvii), or that the train of her dress was held up by many pages (p. 308). Her mystic smile emulates Madame Merle's; her ironic indifference, Ralph's; her eccentric originality, Lydia Touchett's; her innocence, Pansy's. Further back in the "grey American dawn of the situation" (p. 281) she has been infected with the constant exteriority which makes her relate as an outsider, a spectator to her own "outer" experiences. Of all this she is conscious, except for the lack of originality. What neither she nor Ralph recognize is the conventional fear of others underlying her indifference, her eccentricity, her isolation.

Oblivious both to the fear and to the ghosts who breed it, Isabel denies that self-reliance is other-defiance. Osmond's self-respect does not cause him to disrespect others, she believes. But from the self-portraits James permits Osmond to draw, the reader knows Osmond has no respect for others, as Ralph insists (p. 345). Like Emerson's "Transcendentalist," Osmond degrades others into his reflectors,[45] his mirror, his lamp, his silver plate; music for his words, and a lock to polish up the rusty key of his mind (pp. 258, 350–351). To him, saying *we* is synonymous with saying *I*. "*We, we,* Mrs. Osmond, is all I know," he tells Isabel when she "disobeys him" (p. 537). I speak for my wife and she speaks for me, he taunts Caspar, adding: you ought to get married—it's like talking to yourself (pp. 507–509). Nor does Osmond conceal his disrespect for the otherness of others. He confesses he envies the Emperor of Russia and the Pope of Rome the consideration they enjoy (p. 265). Like Emerson he claims his envy is harmless. I don't want to destroy others, "I only want to *be* them" (p. 301), as James permits him to put it in a brilliant parody of Emerson's declaration: "He who is good has no kind of envy . . . he wished that all things should be as much as possible like himself."[46] Lest the parody be lost on the reader, James has Henrietta point out that such envy is evil, that by becoming others, one destroys them, treating "flesh and blood minds and consciences" as though they were "inanimate objects" (p. 350).

Two years of marriage reveal to Isabel that Osmond indeed has no respect for her subjectivity save as a reflection of his, and no respect for her intellect save as a reiteration of his. Yet Ralph and Isabel suffer from the same envious disrespect for others, and it only makes matters worse that in them it is only a mask, "a humorous excrescence," while in Osmond it is the whole man (p. 262). To describe Isabel's disrespectful attitude to others, James borrows a metaphor Emerson uses in "The Transcendentalist" to describe how an idealist is to degrade "men and all other natures" into "better or worse reflectors" of his own mind:

> He does not respect [them] . . . but hears, as at a vast distance, what they say, as if his consciousness would speak to him through a pantomimic scene.[47]

Like Emerson's idealist, Isabel finds herself "as diverted as a child at a pantomime" (p. 54) not only on her first visit to Europe as a child, but also when, as a young woman, she watches Osmond and Madame Merle converse "as if she had been at a play" and they "might have been distinguished performers figuring for a charity" (p. 247). To her as to Emerson's Prospero-like poet,[48] all the world's a stage for self-reflection and dramatization:

> "She was constantly picturing [her career] to herself by the light of her hopes, her fears, her fancies, her ambitions, her predilections, . . . [it] reflected these subjective accidents in a manner sufficiently dramatic." (p. 223)

Ralph's ideal of friendship, like Isabel's, is determined by Emersonian other-defiance. Use us as spectators, then lose us.[49] Let us adore you in silence, see yourself through our eyes, but don't listen to what we say. His advice echoes the pantomimic attitude to others James describes elsewhere, in explaining why Americans find themselves barred and bolted out of the 'friendliest initiations.' If you take Emerson's advice, and treat Europeans collectively as "the most expensive plaything" whose high cost adds to your amusement, then you will get nothing out of your "frolic intercourse" with them.[50] In the *Portrait* Ralph learns the same bitter lesson. Teaching Isabel to "play the game of life," he will see nothing but her frolic smile, and have only a frolic intercourse with her. Wondering why she rejected Warburton, and praising her for it, he says:

> You've grand ideas—you've a high standard in such matters. I ought at least to bring in a band of music or a company of mountebanks. . . . there will be plenty of spectators! We shall hang on the rest of your career. . . . I'm extremely fond of the unexpected, and now that you've kept the game in your hands I depend on your giving us some grand example of it. (pp. 146, 149)

Isabel did not consciously play games with Warburton (pp. 81, 111), nor is she amused when Ralph plays the mountebank with her. "She accused him of an odious want of seriousness, of laughing at all things beginning with himself . . . 'I don't think you care for anything.'" His irony, "the mask of a mind that greatly enjoyed its independence," frustrates her. She is annoyed that he keeps a band of music playing in his ante-room and gives it "orders to play without stopping."

To "punish" him for his "half-hospitality" (p. 60), Isabel keeps him out of her ante-chamber with the same mask he uses to keep her out of his. She will be as amused and amusing as Americans expect others to be:

> her cousin amused himself with calling her Columbia . . . dressed on the lines of the prevailing fashion, in the folds of the national banner . . . She would be as American as it pleased him to regard her, and if he chose to laugh at her she would give him plenty of occupation. (p. 61)

Warburton was not amused by her American "feathers and warpaint," the mask of the isolated Indian Emerson exalts in "Experience," and James mourns in *Hawthorne*.[51] He denounced Isabel's frivolous exteriority in almost the very words that she had reproached Ralph's:

> You judge only from the outside—you don't care . . . You only care to amuse yourself . . . I don't mean of course that you amuse yourself with trifles. You select grand materials; the foibles, the afflictions of human nature, the peculiarities of nations! (pp. 70, 81)

When Isabel (unintentionally) amuses herself with Warburton, Ralph is amused. But when she deliberately plays the same game with him, his personality protests against the persona he himself enjoins her to wear:

> What's the use of being your cousin if I can't have a few privileges? What's the use of adoring you without hope of reward if I can't have a few compensations? What's the use of being . . . restricted to mere spectatorship at the game

of life if I really can't see the show when I've paid so much for my ticket? (p. 148)

The tragic irony is transparent: Ralph purchases exactly what he paid for—mere spectatorship at the game of her life. Spectators can't see, James wrote in *Hawthorne*. "For a stranger to cease to be a stranger he must stand ready, as the French say, to pay with his person." As "this was an obligation Hawthorne was indisposed to incur," he was self-condemned to remain "an outsider," "a stranger," "a mere spectator (something less even than an observer)."[52] For the privilege of penetrating Isabel's personality, Ralph would have had to reciprocate by dropping the mask which, like his father, he "opposed to possibilities of penetration" (p. 38). But such reciprocal penetration would violate the rules of the American game they play, a game in which—as James observes in the Preface to *The Reverberator*—the players preserve their "immunity," their "security," and their "irremediable innocence" (or ignorance), by refusing all reciprocity, all give and take.[53]

How can you commune with another's "inner life" if you resist what you call "the humiliation of change?," Henrietta asks Isabel. Mutually transforming intimacy is the only key to the mystery.

V

In a cryptic passage, Henrietta says that Mr. Bantling "isn't a bad pun—or even a high flight of American humour" (p. 566). The pun might refer to Emerson's advice, in the motto to "Self-Reliance": "Cast the bantling on the rocks;" or to his observation, in *The Conduct of Life,* that every man is imprisoned by "the bantling he is known to fondle."[54] The bantling Americans are seen by Mr. Bantling as fondling, the illusion which binds them to the rock of their fate, is their exaggeration of the claims of intellect, and their devaluation of the claims of passion. Americans, he believes, are "too infatuated with mere brainpower." Having no such bantling to inspire him with fear of passionate intimacy, he finds "neither difficulty nor dread" in his "prompt commerce with Miss Stackpole." Another bad pun, indirectly associated with Mr. Bantling, explains the good humor with which he responds to Ralph's "strong comedy on the subject of the all-judging one and her British backer" (p. 280). Presumably Ralph laughed at him, as he later laughs at Warburton, for entertaining a love less Platonic than might be desired. The point of Bantling's comedy, as contrasted with Isabel's and Ralph's tragedy, is that there is something "Plutonic" about "Platonic" love (pp. 396–397).

"It is almost dangerous," Emerson writes in "Friendship," to "Crush the sweet poison of the misused wine of the affections."[55] "The more information one has about one's dangers the better," Isabel repeats not quite by rote. Ralph corrects her mistake: "I don't agree to that—it may make them dangers":

We know too much about people in these days; we hear too much. Our ears, our minds, our mouths, are stuffed with personalities. Don't mind anything

anyone tells you about anyone else. Judge everyone and everything by yourself. (pp. 250–251)

Paraphrased in his brief sermon are several Emersonian warnings against
mistaking for realities our passionate attachment to persons.[56] Like Plato Emerson
represents personal relations as merely the first step on a ladder leading eventually
to the highest love of all, love of Beauty, Goodness, Truth. Personal relations are
always painful. Hence "we need not fear that we can lose anything by the progress
of the soul," from the lowest love to the highest:

> It is strange how painful is the actual world, —the painful kingdom of time and
> place . . . There are moments when the affections rule and absorb the man,
> and make his happiness dependent on a person or persons . . . [But] the mind
> is presently seen again . . . and the warm loves and fears that swept over us as
> clouds, must lose their finite character.[57]

When Ralph first warned her against falling from heaven to earth at the toss of
Osmond's faded rosebud, Isabel reacted Warburton's way: she did not understand
what he meant by heavenly or Platonic love beyond persons and passionate personal relations:

> You talk about one's soaring and sailing, but if one marries at all one touches
> the earth. One has human feelings and needs, one has a heart in one's bosom,
> and one must marry a particular individual. (p. 347)

But when the love they discover too late becomes too painfully personal,
Isabel retreats to Ralph's Platonic refuge, and bids their poor love goodbye. Unlike
Gilbert Osmond and Serena Merle, Isabel and Ralph never get sufficiently dis-
Americanized to find more sweetness than poison in transforming communion with
one another. In the first description of their intimacy, James portrays the real lovers
as "knowing each other well and each on the whole willing to accept the satisfaction
of knowing as compensation for the inconvenience—whatever it might be—of
being known" (p. 241). But to Isabel and Ralph, the "pain of knowing" and being
known seems greater than the compensation. As they sip the wine of love with
taste tainted by Emersonian fears, their anxious persona spits out the sweetness
along with the poison "whatever it might be." To them as to all hopelessly innocent
Americans, the gates of communion are barred and bolted by "the statue of
Buddha" (p. 71) as Ralph mistakenly calls Warburton's English mask, but as James
correctly calls Emerson's. Both prefer the "amoindrissement of eccentricity," and
nirvana, to the "enrichments of consciousness" and the "testimony of pain."[58]

VI

Supremely together for the first and last time, both Isabel and Ralph momentarily drop their masks and confess that they have been everything to one another.
But both crave a "truth that is not all anguish," and a love that is not all pain. Instead

of rejoicing in her discovery that all she has is his, Ralph again urges Isabel not to mind others—not only when the other is the husband who hates her, but even when he happens to be the cousin who adores her. When she feels a passionate need to "let her sorrow possess her," and to melt "together into this present pain," all he can say is "Don't mind people . . . I think I'm glad to leave people." When she asks him, "Is it true—is it true? . . . that all I have is yours," he turns away his head and then replies, "Ah, don't speak of that—that was not happy" (pp. 575–576). Reminded by his Emersonian words that heroines are always happy and never surrender to pain, not even to the painful truth of love, she responds:

> Here on my knees, with you dying in my arms, I'm happier than I've been for a long time. And I want you to be happy—not to think of anything sad; only to feel that I'm near you and I love you. Why should there be pain? In such hours as this what have we to do with pain? That's not the deepest thing; there's something deeper. (p. 577)

Like Emerson, Ralph does not deny that unhappiness reigns in the "painful kingdom of time and place," where our happiness depends "on a person or persons." But like him he escapes to a kingdom beyond time ("I have all eternity to rest"—p. 575), a kingdom where love remains though lovers go, where—as Emerson teaches in "Plato,"—"I neither am going nor coming; nor art thou, thou; nor are others, others; nor am I, I":[59]

> You won't lose me—you'll keep me. Keep me in your heart; I shall be nearer to you than I've ever been. . . . You said just now that pain's not the deepest thing. No—no. But it's very deep. . . . It passes after all; it's passing now. But love remains. (pp. 576–578)

Though "incapable of the muscular play of a smile" (p. 575), Ralph still displays the scaffold humor which takes Emerson's fancy in the heroic class. Reflecting his own "strange tranquillity" (p. 574), Isabel parts from him with "Oh Ralph, I'm very happy now" (p. 578). His heroism has "the cathartic virtue" Emerson promises. "She [is] not afraid" to greet his ghost, nor terrified to see his corpse. With Ralph's Platonic "perception of incongruities" she seems to lift the merely personal "veil from the face of the dead" and finds that beauty which guarantees that "the soul will not know either deformity or pain."[60] To her persona Ralph's corpse "was fairer than Ralph had ever been in life," and his burial is gilded by "the beauty of the day, the splendour of nature, the sweetness of the old English churchyard" (pp. 578–580).

VII

Like Emerson, Lydia Touchett seeks consolation for the loss of her son in the reflection that "it was her son's death, not her own" (p. 581).[61] Isabel pities her tragically inexpressive mask, and wonders if she resembles "more a queen regent or the matron of a jail" (pp. 569, 571). Equally tragic seems Isabel's Emersonian armour. "The testimony of pain" she pities her aunt for renouncing, teaches her nothing but her own appetite for renunciation. Protected and imprisoned by the "curse of the Indian"[62] whom nothing can touch, Isabel wages her last victorious battle with the persistent lover who threatens her centered mind (or cage) with dissolution, and her imprisoned heart with the rapture of release. Her persona more frightened by the hot wind of Caspar's real love than by the sweet air of Ralph's Platonic adoration or even the icy air of Osmond's Plutonic hatred (p. 589), Isabel's character is the final answer to the question which puzzles Caspar and many readers, "Why should you go back?" (p. 589).

Isabel's return to Osmond and Pansy "is weighted with the moral that salvation lies in being able . . . to turn on one's will like a screw,"[63] while damnation lies in a self-reliant will stronger than any urge to turn. "You don't know where to turn. You can't turn anywhere . . . Turn straight to *me*," Caspar pleads (p. 589). But the irresistible pressure of his love and the overwhelming response of her own feelings reveal to Isabel that "no man can violate his own nature,"[64] even when it isn't his nature at all, but a conventional mask. In a love scene which is less a consummation than a renunciation, Caspar succeeds only in revealing to Isabel that no natural interests and drives, no material social or sensuous appetites bind her to her fate. Only loyalty to a moral ideal implanted in her imagination almost at birth, only a dream of self-possession reinforced by terror of transforming possession by others make her prefer conventional other-defiance with Osmond, to the rebellious other-reliance Caspar forces upon her with a passion momentarily too strong to resist.

"To get away from *you!*" is the only answer she can offer (p. 589). She can think of nothing more dangerous than his aggressive reality. The more he touches her, the more he presses upon her the hard fact of his physical presence, the more he forces her to be loved as well as to love, to take as well as to give, the more she will resist the threat by questioning the reality of his pressure and her response. The more real the presence of passionate love, the less real it seems to her resisting persona. The harder the facts of his manhood, the harder her impenetrable shell. The more passionate her 'objective' circumstances, the less passionate her 'subjective' response.

For a moment Isabel drops her "military attitude of soul" and surrenders to the rapture of a love she has never felt before. The moment she stops making Emersonian war, and lets Caspar make romantic love, his pressure seems a redeeming release, not a violent threat:

> The world, in truth, had never seemed so large; it seemed to open out, all round her, to take the form of a mighty sea, where she floated in fathomless waters. She had wanted help, and here was help; it had come in a rushing torrent. . . . she believed just then that to let him take her in his arms would be the next best thing to her dying. This belief, for a moment, was a kind of rapture . . . (p. 590)

But when she lets Caspar take her in his arms, and kiss her, the burning reality of "the act of possession" arouses her old American fears and resistances. From the very depths of an overwhelming emotional turmoil, she clutches at the idealistic metaphysics which explain its reality away: all "was but a subjective fact, as the metaphysicians say; the confusion, the noise of waters, all the rest of it, were in her own swimming head" (p. 591). For a moment he had "forced open her set teeth" and "lifted her off her feet." But feeling herself "sink and sink . . . she seemed to beat with her feet, in order to catch herself" (pp. 589–590).

To her restored persona, the very help he offers has the "taste . . . of something potent, acrid, and strange" (p. 589). Taken for an aggressive act of possession, his kiss releases the drawn bow of her resistances and drives her with the "swift keen movement of a feathered arrow,"[65] straight back to the fate from which he struggled to save her:

> His kiss was like white lightning, a flash that spread, and spread again, and stayed; and it was extraordinarily as if, while she took it, she felt each thing in his hard manhood that had least pleased her, each aggressive fact of his face, his figure, his presence, justified of its intense identity and made one with this act of possession. . . . But when darkness returned she was free. She never looked about her . . . She only darted from the spot. . . . She had not known where to turn; but she knew now. There was a very straight path. (p. 591)

Gripped by a force stronger than either he or she can exert, Isabel turns back to her husband's anaesthetic prison where, like "two of the saints in the great picture in the convent chapel," they could "turn their painted heads and shake them at each other" Platonically ever after. Isabel calls her flight from intimacy, freedom. But if flight from light, from facts, from her own larger nature be freedom—what is fate? Caspar calls her sacrifice a horror, a funeral, an atrocity. So it is, but so it was predestined to be by the only dazzling persona a woman could wear in "the heroic age of New England life."[66] James gives the impression of having known few kinds of women intimately, but he has evidently known intimately Isabel Archer's idealistic type. We see the process of her history; we see how it marches from step to step to its self-sacrificing termination, and we see that it could not have been otherwise. It is a case of the ascetic passion for noble martyrdom, for self-possession's highest and most difficult demands; of an intense and complex imagination haunted and sublimated almost in the germ; and finding dangers and humiliations in the most unlikely places. It is a case of Emersonian self-reliance and other-defiance being pressed back upon itself with a force which makes the self-denial Emerson wished to avert inevitable.

NOTES

[1] Henry James, *Nathaniel Hawthorne*, in *The Shock of Recognition*, E. Wilson, ed. (New York, 1955), vol. 1, p. 511.

[2] Henry James, *The Portrait of a Lady* (Penguin Books, 1968), pp. 41, 307ff., 300, 304, 63, 150, 505.

[3] Henry James, "Alfred de Musset," "George Sand," *French Poets and Novelists*, L. Edel, ed. (New York, 1964), pp. 20ff., 171ff.

[4] James, *Hawthorne*, pp. 467, 488–489, 498–505, 541–543.

[5] Ibid., pp. 541–543.

[6] Ibid., pp. 490–491.

[7] James, "Emerson," *The James Family*, F. O. Matthiessen, ed. (New York, 1948), pp. 440–441, 449.

[8] James, *Hawthorne*, pp. 494–495, 488ff., 446ff.; "Emerson," *James Family*, p. 449.

[9] William James, *Principles of Psychology* (New York, 1918), vol. i, p. 291: ". . . a man's self is the total of all that he can call his, not only his body and his psychic powers, but his clothes and his house, his wife and children, his ancestors and friends, his reputation and works, his land and horses, and yacht and bank-account." cf. *Portrait*, pp. 200ff. and 9–10.

[10] Emerson, "Nature," "History," "Experience," "The Transcendentalist."

[11] James, "Preface to *The Princess Casamassima,*" *The Art of the Novel*, R. P. Blackmur, ed. (London, 1962), pp. 64–65; *The Tragic Muse* (New York, 1961), pp. 186, 196, 310; "Emerson," *James Family*, p. 449.

[12] Cited by Matthiessen, *James Family*, pp. 343–344.

[13] James, "Honoré de Balzac," *French Poets*, p. 97.

[14] James, *Hawthorne*, pp. 527–528.

[15] James, "Madame de Sabran," *French Poets*, pp. 296–297.

[16] James, "Preface to *The Princess Casamassima,*" *Art of the Novel*, p. 70.

[17] James, "Emerson," *James Family*, p. 442; *Hawthorne*, p. 490.

[18] Emerson, "The Transcendentalist," *Complete Essays and Other Writings* (Random House, 1950), p. 97; James, "Emerson," *James Family*, p. 449. Both use "fastidious" as synonymous with "transcendental."

[19] James, *Hawthorne*, p. 490.

[20] James, "Emerson," *James Family*, p. 443; *Portrait*, p. 432.

[21] *The Notebooks of Henry James*, F. O. Matthiessen and K. B. Murdock, ed. (New York, 1961), p. 15; James, "Turgenieff," *French Poets*, p. 230.

[22] James, *Hawthorne*, p. 487, cf. "Emerson," *James Family*, p. 445.

[23] James, "Balzac," *French Poets*, pp. 109ff.; "The Madonna of the Future," *The Complete Tales of Henry James*, L. Edel, ed. (London, 1962), vol. iii; *Portrait*, pp. 210, 457ff., 470.

[24] Emerson, "Nature," *Complete Essays*, pp. 29–30; "Art," *Emerson's Essays*, (London, New York, 1967), p. 210; James, *Portrait*, p. 120.

[25] James, "Madonna of the Future," *Tales*, vol. iii, p. 21.

[26] James, "Sainte-Beuve," *French Poets*, pp. 320–323. cf. "George Sand," pp. 160–161.

[27] James, *Roderick Hudson* (Penguin, 1929), p. 300; "Turgenieff," *French Poets*, p. 230.

[28] Emerson, "Politics," *Emerson's Essays*, pp. 321–322.

[29] Emerson, "Heroism," Ibid., pp. 140–141.

[30] Emerson, "Character," Ibid., p. 258; "Self-Reliance," p. 47; "Poet," p. 213.

[31] James, "Turgenieff," *French Poets*, pp. 230–231.

[32] Emerson, "Over-Soul," *Emerson's Essays*, p. 166.

[33] James, "Preface to *The Reverberator*," *Art of the Novel*, pp. 190–191.

[34] Emerson, "Self-Reliance," *Emerson's Essays*, p. 37.

[35] Ibid., p. 55.

[36] William James, *Principles of Psychology*, vol. i, p. 291; Henry James, "Honoré de Balzac," *French Poets*, p. 97.

[37] James, "Preface to *The Author of Beltraffio*," p. 238; cf. *Hawthorne*, p. 467.

[38] James, *The Bostonians*, *The American Novels and Stories of Henry James*, F. O. Matthiessen, ed. (New York, 1956), pp. 696–699.

[39] Emerson, "Experience," *Emerson's Essays*, p. 248.

[40] Unlike Jung, James believes women have anima-problems too, when they repress their femininity and overdevelop their masculine qualities. Jung, *Two Essays on Analytical Psychology*, R. Hull, trans. (New York, 1956), pp. 202–210; *Man and His Symbols*, C. G. Jung, ed. (New York, 1968), pp. 115ff., 186ff.; Emma Jung, *Animus and Anima*, H. Nagel, trans. (New York, 1969).

[41] James, "George Sand," *French Poets*, pp. 151–153, 160–161.

[42] Ibid.

[43] Emerson, "The Transcendentalist," *Complete Essays*, p. 89.

[44] cf. Maud Bodkin, *Archetypal Patterns in Poetry* (New York, 1958), pp. 148ff.; Robert Graves, *The White Goddess* (London, 1962); M. Eliade, *The Sacred and the Profane* (New York, 1961), pp. 138ff.

[45] Emerson, "The Transcendentalist," *Complete Essays,* p. 69.

[46] "Plato," Ibid., pp. 477, 480.

[47] "The Transcendentalist," Ibid., p. 89.

[48] See note 24.

[49] Emerson, "Friendship," *Emerson's Essays,* pp. 123–124.

[50] Emerson, "Culture," *Complete Essays,* p. 726; James, "Preface to *The Reverberator,*" *Art of the Novel,* pp. 188–191.

[51] James, *Portrait,* pp. 70, 492; *Hawthorne,* pp. 440, 500–501; cf. "Experience," *Emerson's Essays,* pp. 230–231: "The Indian who was laid under a curse, that the wind should not blow on him, nor fire burn him, is a type of us all. The dearest events are summer rain, and we the Para coats that shed every drop."

[52] James, *Hawthorne,* pp. 541–543.

[53] James, "Preface to *The Reverberator,*" *Art of the Novel,* pp. 189–190.

[54] Emerson, "Self-Reliance," *Emerson's Essays,* p. 29; "Culture," *The Conduct of Life, The Complete Works of Ralph Waldo Emerson* (Boston, New York, 1904), vol. vi, p. 137.

[55] Emerson, "Friendship," *Emerson's Essays,* p. 112.

[56] "Friendship," "Love," "Illusions," "Plato," "The Transcendentalist." In "Emerson" James notes "the curiously generalized way, as if with an implicit protest against personalities, in which his intercourse . . . with friends was conducted": *James Family,* p. 445.

[57] Emerson, "Love," *Emerson's Essays,* p. 99.

[58] James, *Roderick Hudson,* p. 265; "Emerson," *James Family,* p. 449; *Portrait,* p. 571.

[59] Emerson, "Plato," *Complete Essays,* p. 477.

[60] Emerson, "Heroism," *Emerson's Essays,* p. 144; "Spiritual Laws," p. 77.

[61] "Experience," Ibid., pp. 230–231.

[62] Ibid.

[63] James, "Turgenieff," *French Poets,* p. 241.

[64] Emerson, "Self-Reliance," *Emerson's Essays,* p. 37.

[65] James, "Turgenieff," *French Poets,* pp. 225–226.

[66] James, *The Bostonians,* p. 552.

Jonathan Freedman

JAMES, PATER, AND THE DREAMING OF AESTHETICISM

Ralph, Isabel, James: The Ubiquity of Aestheticism

As virtually all critics of the novel have noted, there are numerous troubling similarities between Isabel's benefactor and her bane, and their common connoisseurship is at the center of them. R. P. Blackmur puts the matter with his customary suavity when he writes that "everyone tampers with Isabel, and it is hard to say whether her cousin Ralph Touchett, who had arranged the bequest, or the Prince, Gilbert Osmond, who marries her because of it, tampers the more deeply."[1] The link between the two inheres in more than just their common "tampering," however: it extends to the very perceptual systems that underlie such acts. Gilbert views Isabel, as he views everyone in his narrow world, as an objet d'art, a potential "figure in his collection of choice objects."[2] Osmond's particular form of what we might call the aestheticizing vision is marked both by the distance of the contemplative observer, coolly evaluating the people he encounters with an assumed—if fraudulent—disinterestedness, and by the ruthlessness with which he seeks to make them into testimonies to his taste. Such a vision carries with it an implicit notion of both self and other. In Gilbert's form of vision, the self is understood to be a smug, observing entity, a private and self-satisfied "point of view," while all others are treated as objects of this contemplative vision, to be either appreciated or rejected but always transformed into signs of the supreme taste of the observer. Gilbert's aestheticizing vision, in other words, might also be said to be a reifying vision. Despite the nobility of his rhetoric, Osmond perceives all the others he encounters as detached, deadened objects of his purely passive perception, and seeks to make those who refuse to be so into such beautiful objects.[3] And when Ralph first meets Isabel, he first resists, and then succumbs to a similar impulse:

> If his cousin were to be nothing more than an entertainment to him, Ralph was conscious that she was an entertainment of a high order. "A character

From *Professions of Taste: Henry James, British Aestheticism, and Commodity Culture* (Stanford: Stanford University Press, 1990), pp. 153–66.

like that," he said to himself, ... "is the finest thing in nature. It's finer than the finest work of art—than a Greek bas-relief, than a great Titian, than a Gothic cathedral. It's very pleasant to be so well treated where one had least looked for it. I had never been more blue, more bored, than for a week before she came; I had never expected less that something agreeable would happen. Suddenly, I receive a Titian, by the post, to hang on my wall—a Greek bas-relief to stick over my chimney piece. The key of a beautiful edifice is thrust into my hand, and I am told to walk in and admire." (254)

At first, Ralph sees Isabel as a character of pure "nature" who possesses a vital energy of her own, whose "play" transcends that of any work of art. Isabel transcends all the mental structures Ralph erects to define her, all the images he conjures up to describe her. But he is not able to sustain this vision of Isabel for long. Soon, he subtly but unmistakably metamorphoses her into that which he had previously claimed she transcended—a work of art. By so doing, he begins inadvertently to show Osmondian characteristics. Having defined the mystery that is Isabel as a painting or bas-relief, he attempts imaginatively to collect her. For after he has mentally transformed Isabel into a particularly beautiful but nevertheless static portrait of a lady, the next logical step is to hang her on the wall of his mental portrait gallery. To translate from the novel's metaphorical language back into the grammar of its plot: Ralph endows Isabel with a fortune (much as one would endow an art museum) in order to continue to contemplate her—to "gratif[y] my imagination" (382).

I mention these well-known passages not to inculpate Ralph, but rather to suggest how unwittingly he falls into Gilbert's aestheticizing vision. This judgment must be calibrated rather delicately, for many critics fall into the traps of wholly idealizing Ralph (as we are clearly meant to do, up to a certain point) or condemning him (as we are also meant to do, but again only up to a certain point). Neither approval nor condemnation, however, does justice to the tragic machine James creates out of the inevitability and the insidiousness of the process of aestheticization. Such acts are inevitable for Ralph because they are a cognitive necessity. It is impossible for even so subtle a consciousness as Ralph's to tolerate a phenomenon like Isabel, which remains so resolutely resistant to definition. Despite his own desire to do otherwise, Ralph is forced by the very structure of his perception to reify and then aestheticize Isabel, to treat her with the detached but appreciative vision of the discerning connoisseur. The novel clearly demonstrates the negative consequences of such an aestheticizing vision—even so generous a vision as one that compares Isabel to a Titian. Ralph thinks he can respond to Isabel as he would to a work of art, with energetic detachment and consummate disinterestedness. But he is forced to discover that this is impossible, for she is neither a painting nor a bas-relief but only an extremely naive human being—prey, like all humans, to making ill-considered decisions. Isabel challenges his disinterestedness by doing what paintings cannot: by growing and changing along the idiosyncratic lines of her own character. And—in one of the bitterest ironies of this endlessly ironic book—she will exercise this freedom by marrying the one man who attempts what Ralph only imagines: to turn her into a beautiful but static and immobile work of art.

For Isabel suffers precisely the same kind of aestheticist contagion as Ralph. She, too, shares a good many of the more problematic qualities of Osmond's aestheticism, albeit in a more benign shape, and it is precisely these qualities that cause her to fall under his control. Isabel's aestheticism is signaled by James through the application of much of the characteristic language of the British aesthetic movement to his descriptions of Isabel, particularly those early in the novel. Indeed, James runs through most of the famous, if not notorious, catchphrases of the Conclusion to *The Renaissance* in depicting her. We learn that Isabel possesses a "delicate . . . flame-like spirit"; that she responds to Lord Warburton with a "quickened consciousness"; that she enjoys a number of aesthetic "pulsations" in St. Peter's; and, late in the novel, that she muses over the "infinite vista of a multiplied life" with which she first encountered Osmond (242, 257, 485, 629). To a certain extent, James employs this language to describe the eagerness with which the young Isabel partakes of the Paterian endeavor of "drain[ing] the cup of experience," a propensity Osmond appeals to in his protracted seduction: "Go everywhere," he said at last, in a low, kind voice, "do everything; get everything out of life" (345, 508). But as in the case of Ralph, Isabel's aestheticism is more deeply ingrained, and more ultimately problematic, than it appears at first glance. Isabel possesses an aestheticizing vision of her own and, as with Ralph, this vision is understood as something of a cognitive necessity. For when Isabel first meets Osmond, her reaction to him, as was Ralph's to her, is one of utter confusion:

> His pictures, his carvings and tapestries were interesting; but after a while Isabel became conscious that the owner was more interesting still. He resembled no one she had ever seen; most of the people she knew might be divided into groups of half a dozen specimens. There were one or two exceptions to this; she could think for instance of no group that would contain her Aunt Lydia. There were other people who were, relatively speaking, original—original, as one might say, by courtesy—such as Mr. Goodwood, as her cousin Ralph, as Henrietta Stackpole, as Lord Warburton, as Madame Merle. But in essentials, when one came to look at them, these individuals belonged to types which were already present to her mind. Her mind contained no class which offered a natural place to Mr. Osmond—he was a specimen apart. (458–59)

As in the case of Ralph, Isabel's cognitive difficulties are caused by Osmond's failure to conform to any of her preexisting mental categories. But Isabel's mistakes are even more extensive. What Isabel fails to realize is that Gilbert's ambiguousness is a result of his limitations, not a sign of the subtlety or fineness of his character. She cannot see that her failure to place Osmond is utterly appropriate: that, having no positive qualities of his own, he can only be defined in terms of negation. This is how virtually every character in the book defines Gilbert. Madame Merle introduces him to Isabel in the language of negation: "No career, no name, no position, no fortune, no past, no future, no anything" (393). After meeting Osmond for the first time in Rome, Ralph identifies him to Warburton by name. "What is he besides?" Warburton asks. "Nothing at all," Ralph replies (495). Gilbert himself proposes to Isabel with a declaration that, like all of Gilbert's statements, is at once literally true and deeply false: "I have neither fortune, nor fame, nor extrinsic advantages of any kind. So I offer nothing" (509–10).

Isabel commits the error of mistaking Gilbert's passivity for mystery, his fastidiousness for subtlety, his indifference for reserve. And she responds to the mystery of his poverty in the same way as Ralph responded to that of her plenitude: by mentally transforming him into a work of art that could meet the requirements of her imagination. This process, again like the one Ralph undertakes with her, reaches a climax in a moment of mental *ekphrasis,* a moment at which she imagines Osmond as a finely drawn "picture":

> She had carried away an image from her visit to his hill-top which her subsequent knowledge of him did nothing to efface and which happened to take her fancy particularly—the image of a quiet, clever, sensitive, distinguished man, strolling on a moss-grown terrace above the sweet Val d'Arno, and holding by the hand a little girl whose sympathetic docility gave a new aspect to childhood. The picture was not brilliant, but she liked its lowness of tone, and the atmosphere of summer twilight that pervaded it. (476)

Indeed, there is even a greater portion of aestheticism in Isabel's response to her mental picture than in Ralph's to his. She explicitly adopts the attitude he unconsciously falls into, that of the connoisseur, for she stands back from her image of Osmond to nod her approval of its "lowness of tone" and the "atmosphere of summer twilight that pervaded it." Her subsequent actions extend this incipient Osmondism. Having so appreciated her own mental image of this "specimen apart," Isabel proceeds to try to add it to her own collection. Just as the greatest triumph of Gilbert's career as a collector was "discovering . . . a sketch by Correggio on a panel daubed over by some inspired idiot," so Isabel fancies that she alone is capable of identifying the true value of the artwork that is Osmond (463). The result, needless to say, is disastrous. Her unwittingly Osmondian tendency to see Osmond as he sees himself—as a rare and fine work of art—leads to her equally unwitting Osmondian attempt to collect Osmond. By seeking to marry "the man who had the best taste in the world" for what she sees as "an indefinable beauty about him—in his situation, in his mind, in his face," Isabel finds herself transformed into a mere extension of that taste, an object for cultivated appreciation possessing "nothing of her own but her pretty appearance" (631, 632). Seeking to collect a collector, she finds herself collected.

My purpose in stressing these parallels is not merely to inculpate Isabel, but rather to suggest the universality of aestheticism in the novel. Aestheticism of one sort or another is a donnée of *The Portrait of a Lady,* a piece of perceptual equipment James issues each of his characters. In doing so, he suggests how a "sterile dilettante" like Osmond can exert so powerful a force. The plot of the novel is so constructed that Osmond's aestheticism causes Isabel's and Ralph's to rebound against them. We have seen this effect in the way that Osmond's designs on Isabel force Ralph to face the consequences of his own disingenuously disinterested vision of her; Osmond confronts Ralph with a grotesque parody of his own attempt to achieve a detached, aestheticized vision of Isabel and blatantly enacts the appropriating reification delicately implicit in Ralph's perception. We may see it even more clearly in Isabel's marriage, in which Osmond's aestheticism corresponds to her naive aestheticist propensities in just enough ways to trap her irrevocably.

Through the first two-thirds of the book, then, we witness a movement that seeks to include all characters—even (or especially) the most sensitive and richly aware characters—in a form of belief and behavior that is satirized, but not expunged, by Osmond. This movement reaches a climax at the beginning of chapter 37, when we see through the eyes of yet another aesthete, Ned Rosier, Isabel "framed in the gilded doorway . . . the picture of a gracious lady" (570). Ned sees Isabel as Ralph had unconsciously seen her and as Osmond consciously wishes to see her: a static, reified art object. But at this moment, the problematic powers of aestheticism seem to have extended even further. For by reminding us that Isabel has been converted, or has converted herself, into a person whose "function" is to "represent" her husband, James is also reminding us of the affinities between aestheticism and his own representational endeavor (597). For insofar as the novel claims to be a "portrait of a lady"—a detached, objective account of Isabel's experience—it aligns itself with the possibilities it has thoroughly criticized: with the purely disinterested aestheticizing vision of Ralph, and the ironic detachment and masked will to power of Osmond. Indeed, it would seem that Gilbert, not Ralph, would most successfully figure James's own authorial aestheticism, since Ralph's irony is qualified by deep imaginative sympathy and since his stance of disinterested observation is abandoned as early as chapter 22, and since Gilbert, not Ralph, is most intensely interested in transforming Isabel into a representation of himself.

The exploration of the problematic dimension of aestheticism reaches its climax, then, with Rosier's identification of Isabel as a portrait of a lady. At this moment, it appears that all the novel's characters and even its author are somehow implicated in one form or another of Gilbert's malevolent aestheticism, just as Roderick and Rowland were in *Roderick Hudson* and just as all the characters of *The Author of Beltraffio* will be. But this same moment also initiates a countermovement. If in the first two-thirds of the novel James is interested in linking divergent characters to Osmond, in its final part, he attempts to differentiate between them and Gilbert. If the novel suggests that even the most noble, if naive, examples of the aestheticizing vision are fatally flawed, then James's alternatives are clear: either he needs to abandon or alter his fictional project entirely, or he needs to find a way to repurify the aesthetic itself, to demonstrate that perceptual and experiential responses like intense observation and the aestheticizing vision might prove redeemable, if not redemptive. And, needless to say, it is this latter path that he chooses.

Aestheticism and the Gospel of Freedom

We may observe the first step in this process by noting the increasing interest the novel gives to discriminating between Osmond and the other characters. The most spectacular instance of this discrimination is its portrayal of the relation between Osmond and Madame Merle. During the first two-thirds of the novel, we have been asked to note their commonality: we have witnessed their combined interest in acquiring a fortune for Gilbert and a mother for Pansy by marrying Osmond to Isabel. More important, we have encountered the view of the world that can make such plots possible. Madame Merle, like Osmond, perceives herself and all those around her as things to be arranged or manipulated, and is thus able to adjust her own appearances the better to shape the actions of others in order to achieve her ends. But in the last third of the novel we discover that the two can—indeed, must—be distinguished from each other. Gilbert is finally the only character who can fully exemplify the reified self that Madame Merle so eloquently defines. This discovery opens the way to more of the novel's ironies, for, just as Gilbert uses the implicit aestheticism of Isabel Archer against her, so he employs Madame Merle's reified vision of the self to reify Madame Merle herself.

The kinds of identifications and discriminations we are asked to make between these two characters are among the subtlest and most complicated in the novel. To cite but one example, Gilbert and Madame Merle are initially united, but ultimately distinguished, by their concern for appearances. We have seen the deep duplicity of this concern throughout the novel, for we have witnessed the ways they present Mrs. Touchett, Isabel, and society at large with artfully arranged poses: Madame Merle as disinterested friend and "the cleverest woman in the world"; Osmond as devoted father and aloof aesthete who cares nothing for the opinion of the world (759). But as soon as we understand the "horror" (as Madame Merle calls it) these facades are constructed to conceal, we are asked to distinguish between their desires (389). Gilbert's concern for propriety and love of convention is shown to be one small part of his obsessive concern for "the world" and that world's opinion of him. Madame Merle's concern, while superficially similar, is ultimately antithetical to his. Her "worship of appearances" is motivated not by her love of convention or her concern for propriety but rather by her fear of the discovery of her adulterous secret. Further, this divergence between Madame Merle and her former lover provides the grounds for the final break in their relation. For, as the Countess Gemini informs Isabel, Madame Merle's "worship of appearances" became "so intense that even Osmond himself got tired of it" (751). In other words, the very ground on which stands the relation she seeks so desperately to conceal is ultimately destroyed by the tenacity with which she is compelled to conceal it.

Just as we are asked to discriminate between the attitudes of Osmond and Madame Merle toward "the world," we are also asked to differentiate between their values and perceptions throughout the rest of the novel. We are initially inclined to grant Madame Merle a stature that is denied Osmond. For one thing,

Madame Merle is ultimately distinguished from the reifying aestheticism with which she has been associated for much of the novel, and Osmond alone is left to bear its taint. This particular discrimination is suggested in a number of ways throughout the last third of *Portrait,* but one of the more important is made by Isabel herself. Late in the novel, just after her ride on the Campagna, Isabel broods over Madame Merle's role in arranging her marriage, and she remembers "the wonder" of her strong "desire" for the "event." "There were people who had the match-making passion, like the votaries of art for art," Isabel reflects, "but Madame Merle, great artist as she was, was scarcely one of these" (725). This passage, of course, reflects Isabel's increasingly bitter view of Madame Merle; after all, she has just applied "the great historical epithet of *wicked"* to her "false" friend (725). And the identification of Madame Merle as a "great artist" associates art with the sinister manipulation of others. But Isabel's observation reminds us that Madame Merle does indeed seem to be granted some of the less equivocal powers of the artist, and that her qualities are therefore to be distinguished from Osmond's sterile aestheticism. Madame Merle possesses in abundance the positive qualities James habitually associated with the artist—a rich sensibility, a subtlety, a complex and ultimately tragic capacity for deep emotion—along with the admittedly less positive side of the Jamesian artist—the ability to manipulate poses and create surfaces to achieve equivocal ends. As a result of this identification, Madame Merle's stature seems to increase. We are led to view her, along with Isabel, as someone who has been trapped and betrayed by circumstance and convention, and who has therefore been forced to employ even (especially) her most positive qualities for mere manipulation—and failed manipulation at that.

Sympathetic as the novel asks us to be toward Madame Merle, however, we also acknowledge that in the final divergence between her and Osmond it traps her in its own relentlessly ironic logic. She may transcend her own definition of the self as a mere collection of reified qualities, but Gilbert does not, and his amoral aestheticism finally punishes her in a chillingly appropriate manner. If Madame Merle, along with Gilbert, has turned Isabel into a deadened object of her will—in Isabel's own words, into "a dull, un-reverenced tool"—so Madame Merle finally discovers, she too has been used by Osmond as a mere tool, to be discarded when she is no longer useful to him (759). This dimension of their relation becomes clear in their final scene together, in which a cracked cup becomes horrifically emblematic of their relations. Madame Merle's "precious object" is established as a symbol of their relation when Gilbert sunders that relation at the same moment as he discovers "a small crack" in the cup (730). By the end of the scene, when Madame Merle turns again to her own object, it takes on an even more resonant meaning: "After he had left her, Madame Merle went and lifted from the mantel-shelf the attenuated coffee-cup in which he had mentioned the existence of a crack; but she looked at it rather abstractedly. 'Have I been so vile all for nothing?' she murmured to herself" (731).

The scene is delicate and subtle, and, as many critics have noted, it adumbrates the symbolistic later James, the James of *The Golden Bowl.*[4] But it is important to observe that the scene is also savagely satiric, and that its satire here too is again cognate with that of popular satires on aestheticism. The notion of representing human relations in terms of crockery is one which, as we have seen, exercised the moral indignation of the *Punch* satirists from the time of Du Maurier's famous 1880 cartoon on the subject of living up to one's teapot. Here, too, the aesthete's propensity to reify his relations in trivializing terms is imaged by these satiric means. But the calculated whimsy of this early cartoon is replaced in James's text by an unsparing irony: the aesthete not only demonstrates his reifying vision, but also the aesthetic flaws of the object of his contemplation. In doing so, the development of James's satire and that of Du Maurier parallel each other with uncanny accuracy. On May 14, 1881, there appeared in *Punch* a mordant sketch, probably by Du Maurier, entitled *Philistia Defiant,* "in which aestheticism, assisted by a Teapot, is the cause of a division between friends."[5] In the sketch, a Mrs. Vamp invites a friend, Betsinda Grig, to her "High-Art boudoir in South Kensington," in order to appreciate, admire, adore, and ultimately "live up to" a newly acquired antique teapot, with a small crack in it. After a long speech in praise of the teapot, Betsinda replies, "with drawlingly deliberate acerbity, 'It's dreadfully cracked, and horribly ugly; if *that's* what you mean by Unutterably Utter and all the rest of it. And, upon my word, Sara, I think you must be living up—or down—to it, for you seem to get more decidedly cracked and more utterly ugly every day.' "

My point in mentioning this sketch is not to point to a "source" for James's scene, but rather to suggest how in this scene he finds his satirical energies developing along lines parallel to those of Du Maurier. Indeed, James outdoes the increasing acidulousness of Du Maurier's satire. In James's hands, a "deliberate acerbity" works to punish not only the reifying aesthete, but his reified victim as well. It is precisely Madame Merle's own reified vision of the self as a collection of things that is turned against her, for she has become to Gilbert nothing more than the appurtenance she believes the self to be. She is of no more consequence to him than an exquisite cup, to be discarded if and when flaws are discovered in it. And, to complete the irony, we realize in her moment of self-discovery, at her own "murmured" threnody to her love for Gilbert and her lament for what she has done in the name of that love, that Osmond rejects her for precisely the passionate emotion and keen intelligence she displays in her moment of horrified recognition. In short, all the qualities that make her more than a mere object are precisely those that cause Osmond to discard her as one.

The most important discrimination established in the last third of the novel, however, is that between Isabel and Osmond. For as Isabel grasps the flaws of her aestheticizing vision and begins to move beyond this form of apprehension, she progresses into a heightened and purified form of aestheticism—a form of aestheticism superficially similar to, but ultimately distinguishable from, the reifying aestheticism of an Osmond. It's true that Osmondian language tends to be associated with the representation of her own thought processes—as, for example, when she too rejects Madame Merle. The effect of Madame Merle's unexpectedly appearing at Pansy's convent is compared by Isabel to a "sort of reduplication"; this hint of an aestheticizing temper is carried further when Isabel sees Madame Merle's uncertainty "as distinctly as if it had been a picture on the wall" (756–57, 759). Indeed, Isabel might be said to approach Osmondism here—however justifiably— since her action in this scene, like Osmond's throughout the novel, is to withdraw, to retreat into being "silent still—leav[ing] Madame Merle in this unprecedented situation" (759). But Isabel's aestheticizing imagination leads her in a wholly different direction than does Osmond's. In this scene, her refusal directly to confront Madame Merle still grants her an essential otherness, still allows her her own scope of action—grants Madame Merle the opportunity to judge herself, to do "a kind of proud penance" (767).

What is true of Isabel's behavior in this scene is true of her perceptual apparatus as well. As her aestheticizing vision moves beyond the reifying aestheticism so thoroughly implicated in Osmondism, it progresses to a higher form of aestheticism—if "aesthetic" is understood as informed by the original sense of *aesthesis,* as a heightening or perfection of the act of perception. The most extended exercise in such heightened vision is provided in the most famous moment in the novel—the moment James claimed to have been most proud of—Isabel's silent reverie in chapter 42. That chapter is of the utmost importance for our endeavor, for it provides an example of a form of perception structurally different from that we have seen associated with Gilbert throughout the novel and in which we can implicate every other character. Isabel's visions in this scene are important because they are so intense and because they are so personal. Like Osmond's aestheticizing vision, they are fully grounded in the self, but they are ultimately antithetical to Osmond's. Her flickering visions in chapter 42 do not partake of Osmond's narcissistic attempt to force the objects in the world to serve as objects for his detached contemplation. Rather, unlike Osmond, Isabel achieves a moment of her own vision experienced in, of, and for itself; a moment of vision that is fully detached from the world of objects but that helps her to understand the nature of that world. And, I would suggest, the homology between Isabel's vision and that of Paterian *aesthesis* may be seen more clearly when we juxtapose chapter 42 with the Conclusion to *The Renaissance.* Both Pater and James privilege a special moment at which, under conditions of high intensity, "a quickened, multiplied consciousness" comes into powerful visionary being. It is quite true that there are significant dissimilarities between the circumstances under which such an intense vision may come into being and the uses to which it can be put. For James, the "quickened consciousness" is (as it always is for James) attached to high emotional drama, while for Pater such a consciousness is activated through many forms of intense experience—"great passions" including, among others, both the "ecstasy and sorrow of love" and (first among equals) "the poetic passion, the desire of beauty, the love of art for art's sake."[6] But my point here is that for both James and Pater the moment at which consciousness exercises itself in heightened vision is valuable in and of itself—is the ultimate end, the perfect end. Pater's aesthete and James's heroine both achieve a perfect moment of intense vision which, for their authors, is the highest—perhaps the only—consummation possible in a world shadowed over by death and human failure.

This valorization of *aesthesis*, of what James calls in the Preface to the novel "the mere still lucidity" of Isabel's mental vision, suggests one way that the novel recuperates a form of aestheticism.[7] But it is precisely by means of this recuperation that critics have taken James to task for being an aesthete in the negative sense of the word. Here, the achievement of a form of transcendence by means of consciousness and consciousness alone would seem, at the very best, to associate James with a naive form of reification, and at the very worst to identify him as an arrogant connoisseur of consciousness. For this moment seems to define the transcendent self as fundamentally contemplative, passive, inert, to remove that self from any real contact with others, from any possibility of action, indeed, from history itself; it would thus seem to imprison Isabel in the prison house of consciousness as thoroughly as Osmond imprisons her in the Palazzo Roccanera. Isabel, Michael Gilmore writes, "chooses a freedom that is mental rather than experiential, a freedom uncontaminated by sensuous engagement with the world." James, he adds ominously, "makes a similar choice for his art."[8]

James, however, anticipates—and sidesteps—this critique. For there is another moment in the novel at which the aestheticizing vision is deployed, and to ends that are different from either those we see with Osmond or those we see in chapter 42. I am referring to the scene, a few chapters later, of Isabel's lonely ride on the Campagna. For we encounter in this passage yet another variant of the mode of perception Isabel shares with Osmond. As a tourist, as an observing traveler, Isabel would seem to fall into the detached, contemplative mode of Osmond; moreover she seems to perform the Osmondian task of aestheticizing the natural world she encounters, of responding to it as to a work of art:

> The carriage, passing out of the walls of Rome, rolled through narrow lanes, where the wild honeysuckle had begun to tangle itself in the hedges, or waited for her in quiet places where the fields lay near, while she strolled further and further over the flower-freckled turf, or sat on a stone that had once had a use, and gazed through the veil of her personal sadness at the splendid sadness of the scene—at the dense, warm light, the far gradations and soft confusions of colour, the motionless shepherds in lonely attitudes, the hills where the cloud-shadows had the lightness of a blush. (724)

While this exercise of the aestheticizing vision may seem superficially similar to Gilbert's, it is ultimately antithetical to his vision and value system alike. Isabel may sit in Osmond's position of the detached aesthetic observer, viewing the Campagna spread out before her like a painted landscape—all motion arrested, its figures fixed in "lonely attitudes," its colors and gradations displayed in the rich muted colors of an artist's pallette—but she does not seek to detach herself from that scene. For the "profound sympathy" between Isabel's perception and the objects she encounters is repeatedly suggested in this passage, often by verbal repetition or by transfer of qualities from the Campagna to Isabel's life; "the sadness of landscape" reflecting her "sadness of mood," the "lonely attitudes" of the shepherds reflecting her own sense of loneliness and betrayal. As she "rest[s] her weariness upon things that had crumbled for centuries," as she "drop[s] her secret sadness into the silence of lonely places," Isabel comes to recognize the "haunting sense of the continuity of the human lot" (723–24). Having learned from Rome, a "place where people had suffered," of the commonality of her own suffering, she rejoins the human community—not the corrupt community of Roman society that Gilbert and Madame Merle inhabit, but a more fully human community of shared suffering (724). Rather than possessing a reifying vision of landscape as irrevocably other, as alien and mute objects unconnected to human emotions and events and coldly to be appreciated as such, Isabel achieves at this moment a humanizing vision in which her individual "sadness" and the sadness of the scene connect to form an image of commonality and community, not one of alienation and superiority. If in chapter 42 Isabel moves beyond her superficial Paterian aestheticism into the more valuable mode of Paterian *aesthesis,* so here she moves beyond a superficial form of aestheticizing vision into a richer, more meaningful one: one that emphasizes her own embeddedness in historical process, her own participation in the human community—in short, the very "sensuous engagement with the world" whose absence Gilmore decries.

It is this version of the aestheticist vision that provides James with his most deeply treasured, and most arduously won, triumph. For this moment of detached yet meaningful perception provides a way out of the artistic impasse James has created for himself. Isabel's vision provides a more positive model for the stance of the detached author than does Osmond's, one that can lead to a sense of communion, not solipsism; to sympathy, not superiority. James signals this, I think, by the very abstemiousness with which he treats Isabel's dilemma at the end of the novel. If James is like Osmond in enmeshing Isabel in a plot whose goal is to aestheticize her, to transform her into a static, frozen portrait of a lady (the literary equivalent of the murderous aestheticization performed by the Duke in Browning's *My Last Duchess*), he can demonstrate himself to be a non-Osmondian author only by opening up the plot: by refusing the consolation of closure, whether comic, ironic, or tragic. It is in response to this problematic, I am suggesting, that James ends his novel with an interpretive mystery—and one of the most famous cruxes in American literature: the question of Isabel's mysteriously motivated return to Osmond. Certainly, the novel supplies by implication many reasons for this return: her loyalty to Pansy, her affirmation of convention and of social forms, her affirmation of the value of renunciation.[9] But the novel carefully refuses to choose between these various explanations. Further, it ends without giving any further indication of the success or failure of Isabel's course of action, thereby precluding any final judgment of the wisdom or folly of her choice.

It is this narrative silence that provides the final repudiation of the reifying aestheticism associated with Osmond and of the narrative problematics it initiates. James's narrative voice here may be detached, but it is hardly unsympathetic. Indeed, its failure to pass any final judgment on Isabel may be taken as an acknowledgment of James's authorial sympathy rather than as an indication of his ironic distance. For by this silence, James reminds the reader of the values that Osmond's reifying aestheticism ignores: a respect for the fundamentally mysterious otherness of human beings. The mystery with which the novel concludes indicates James's authorial acknowledgment of the otherness of others, for this gesture acknowledges Isabel's ability to transcend any one vision that tries to fix or define her—even the author's own ostensibly omniscient vision. By granting Isabel such resonant ambiguity, in other words, James endows Isabel with the powers Rossetti endows Jenny or—more relevantly—those Isabel grants Madame Merle. For the effect of this conclusion is to enable Isabel to step beyond the narrative frame within which she is enclosed, to move out of the "Portrait of a Lady"; it is—in a phrase James added to Isabel's final vision of Madame Merle in the New York edition—"like suddenly, and rather awfully, seeing a painted picture move."[10]

NOTES

[1] Blackmur, *"The Portrait of a Lady"* in *Studies in Henry James,* ed. Veronica Makowsky (New York: New Directions, 1983), p. 193.

[2] *The Portrait of a Lady,* in William Stafford, ed., *Henry James: Novels, 1881–1886* (New York: Library of America, 1985), p. 501. Subsequent references will occur in the text.

[3] It is at this point that I need to acknowledge my greatest debt to Carolyn Porter, *Seeing and Being: The Plight of the Participant Observer in Emerson, James, Adams, and Faulkner* (Middletown, Conn.: Wesleyan University Press, 1981).

[4] The best explication of it may be found in Laurence Holland, *The Expense of Vision: Essays on the Craft of Henry James* (Princeton, N.J.: Princeton University Press, 1964).

[5] *Punch* 80 (May 14, 1881): 221.

[6] *The Works of Walter Pater,* 8 vols. (London: Macmillan, 1900–1), 1:238, 239.

[7] *Novels and Tales of Henry James,* 26 vols. (The New York Edition) (New York: Charles Scribner's Sons, 1907–9), 3:xxi.

[8] Michael Gilmore, "The Commodity World of *The Portrait of a Lady,*" *New England Quarterly* 59 (1986): 73.

[9] To Gilmore, however, none of these explanations is sufficient; rather, Isabel "spurns the chance of leaving Osmond for the more rarefied liberation of 'motionlessly *seeing*'" (73). This strikes me as perhaps the least credible of possible explanations, since it ignores entirely the possibility that Isabel might be returning as an active participant in her marriage, particularly with respect to Pansy's future—an interesting omission for so strenuously moralizing a critic as Gilmore to make.

[10] *Novels and Tales of Henry James,* 4:375.

Stephanie A. Smith

THE DELICATE ORGANISMS
AND THEORETIC TRICKS
OF HENRY JAMES

In *The Portrait of a Lady,* as the incarcerative reality of her marriage becomes palpable, Isabel Archer Osmond ponders her husband's idealized description of his daughter:

> His tone, however, was that of a man not so much offering an explanation as putting a thing into words—almost into pictures—to see, himself, how it would look.... Isabel gave an extreme attention to this little sketch... It seemed to show her how far her husband's desire to be effective was capable of going—to the point of playing *theoretic tricks on the delicate organism* of his daughter.[1]

Isabel finds Gilbert Osmond's "sketch" of Pansy a "striking example of her husband's genius" (p. 443). Despite having earlier dismissed Osmond's talent as "a genius for upholstery" (p. 324), Isabel sees in this sketch a "heroine of a tragedy" (p. 443), even if Pansy is elsewhere belittled, called a "Dresden-china shepherdess" (p. 301). She is, in fact, a Gothic heroine in a nunnery/prison, with a determined, if fumbling, suitor and a threatening, if benevolent, papa.

James employs yet mocks a Gothic formula in telling Pansy's story, as is noted by the peevish figure of Pansy's suitor, Edward "Ned" Rosier. Rosier is "haunted by the conviction that at picturesque periods young girls had been shut up ... to keep them from their true loves, and then, under the threat of being thrown into convents, had been forced into unholy marriages" (p. 308). James's Gothic-in-miniature seems designed to invoke and deflect Gothicism. Pansy's nunnery is no ghoulish hole but a quiet home, yet she is confined to it. The "mothers" there are hardly sadistic, yet they discipline Pansy, and although Pansy's lover is a pathetic specimen whom James calls "poor Rosier" (p. 312), he is also a "melancholy youth" (p. 371). James's deflation of Gothic images may keep us from taking Pansy's tragedy too seriously, but he does draw a specifically Gothic veil around her. Indeed, Pansy's eventual "sequestration" (p. 462) causes Isabel to view the convent

From *American Literature* 62, No. 4 (December 1990): 583–605.

as "a well-appointed prison . . . which affronted and almost frightened her" (p. 456).

However, what is far more compelling about Pansy's misfortune is that Isabel's story (one a reader is expected—even commanded by James—to take seriously) has a trajectory that eerily parallels her step-daughter's. After all, Isabel is the subject of James's portrait in the same way that Pansy is the subject of Osmond's sketch; she and Pansy are described as "frail vessels,"[2] and both live in Osmond's suffocating atmosphere. Finally, Isabel is, according to James and his critics, a tragic heroine,[3] as Pansy is, at least in Isabel's eyes. Indeed, Isabel's fate is repeatedly linked to Pansy's tale, and thus the Gothic trappings of the child's life begin to shroud her step-mother's.

Pointing to Pansy as a figure for Isabel Archer's fate may appear, at the outset, as extreme as the Gothic itself is lurid, although James did often write in a Gothic strain, as in, for example, *The Turn of the Screw,* "The Altar of the Dead," and "The Jolly Corner," to name a few ghost stories. But traces of Gothicism can be found in most of James's work, even in those pieces which, like *The Portrait of a Lady,* have been read as concerned primarily with social manners. Leslie Fiedler has noted that James was "deeply influenced by Gothic modes"[4] so that even in such a society piece as *Daisy Miller* he uses a Gothic device, the "malaria, the *miasma* which arises from decaying ruins."[5]

Still, James is clear that the Lady, Isabel Archer, and the mock-Gothic maiden, Pansy Osmond, are not wholly congruent. Isabel is not a water-color sketch, but a rich masterpiece, no diminutive "pansy" but the full-blown rose. She is no mere Gothic heroine of the popular run but a tragic woman, a complex "Subject" (p. 8). In Isabel's story there is no corpse in a wall, skeleton in the closet, or a nun bearing the devil's whelp—or is there? What *does* constitute Isabel's tragedy? Might not the hidden truth behind *The Portrait of a Lady* be, after all, the sad, murderous, and decidedly Gothic story of a woman who has borne a fiend's illegitimate child?

I

Leslie Fiedler has described the Gothic as a novel in which, "through a dream landscape, usually called by the name of some actual Italian place, a girl flees in terror and alone amid crumbling castles, antique dungeons and ghosts who are never really ghosts."[6] In Fiedler's view, terror has resulted from an incestuous perversion of Freud's Oedipal drama; the girl, or the son's *anima,* flees the horror of incest.[7] For Fiedler, the paradigmatic Gothic plot tracks how a son's taboo love for a lost mother has made him a sadistic, erotic anti-hero whose fascination results from his Oedipal "breach of the primal taboo," his "offense against the father."[8] The Gothic thus reveals Western cultural anxieties about a "crumbling" of paternal authority, beneath which "lies the maternal blackness, imagined by the gothic writer as a prison, a torture chamber."[9] For Fiedler, "the guilt which underlies the gothic and motivates its plots is the guilt of the revolutionary haunted by the (paternal) past which he has been striving to destroy."[10]

However, as Claire Kahane points out in "The Gothic Mirror," Fiedler's focus on the villain-hero's psyche fails to account for the fascination Gothicism has exerted on women authors, nor does it adequately explain the path many female protagonists take in Gothic novels.[11] Kahane alters Fiedler's synopsis and thus provides a slightly different psychodynamic basis for Gothic agony:

> Within an imprisoning structure . . . a young woman whose mother has died, is compelled to seek out the center of a mystery, while vague and usually sexual threats to her person from some powerful male figure hover on the periphery of her consciousness. Following clues that pull her onward and inward—bloodstains and mysterious sounds—she penetrates the obscure recesses of a vast labyrinthine space and discovers a secret room sealed off by its association with death.[12]

Kahane assumes Nancy Chodorow's revision of Freud,[13] where the girl who flees is more than the shadow-half of a male psyche. For Kahane what lies "locked into the forbidden center of the Gothic" is "the spectral presence of a dead-undead mother, archaic and all-encompassing, a ghost signifying the problematics of femininity which the heroine must confront."[14] Positing a female psyche as the center of Gothic gravity, Kahane shifts away from a strict Freudian reading and suggests that when the girl goes prowling about what Fiedler has described as maternal darkness, what she discovers is that the mother, who is a mirror to her self, is not simply missing; she has been murdered. Or, as Margaret Homans argues in *Bearing the Word,* the fantasy of Freud's Oedipal drama, as a metaphor of Western cultural aesthetics, depends "not merely on the regrettable loss of the mother, but rather on her active and overt murder."[15]

Still, despite Kahane's revision of Fiedler, both critics see a *version* of the maternal as intrinsic to Gothicism. Fiedler's mother may be a "tomb," but it is still access to this sexuality that is behind the horror, while for Kahane Gothic terror lies in an ambivalent search for the mother. Indeed, both Fiedler and Kahane not only focus on a version of the mother to explain Gothicism, but they also both see a ghost when they look for her. Fiedler's ghost-mother is she who took part in an original disregard of the father's primary reproductive claim upon her. Kahane's ghost is that of an archaic, repressed, murdered, pre-Oedipal maternity. And if, as many Gothic stories themselves suggest, this maternal murder is actually a precondition to the plot of the continuing Freudian (strict or post) fantasy Western culture tells itself, then it is no wonder both Fiedler and Kahane see ghosts. As Homans argues, within a Freudian economy the mother must be dead in order for the son to create; otherwise she will lure him to his death. Yet a female poet, being identified with the mother, if not as a mother, obviously cannot abide such a murder. Thus it is hardly surprising that Fiedler, being focused on the male psyche, should see the maternal as a prison/coffin while Kahane, looking for a female psyche, sees a spectral dead/undead mother.[16]

Now while such fantasmic details as castles, bloodstains, mysterious sounds, or even ghostly, Oedipal, or pre-Oedipal mothers do not seem, on the surface, to be integral to *The Portrait of a Lady,* still, to use both Fiedler and Kahane as guides is revealing. After all, both Pansy and Isabel are versions of Kahane's young woman whose mother has died. Isabel's very name recalls other Gothically dark heroines, such as the mysterious orphan Isabel of Herman Melville's *Pierre* or Isabella in Horace Walpole's Gothic romance, *The Castle of Otranto.* Further, James's Isabel is trapped in an imprisoning structure, an Italian castle, Roccanera, Osmond's crumbling "pile ... which smelt of historic deeds, of crime and craft and violence" (p. 307). In fact this paradigmatic architectural imprisoning of a heroine, so basic to almost any description of the Gothic,[17] finds a curious echo in James's 1907 *Preface* to his revised *Portrait.* There, James describes Isabel herself as a "plot of ground" over which he will build "the neat and careful proportioned pile of bricks ... I would build large—in fine, embossed vaults and painted arches ... and yet never let it appear that the chequered pavement, the ground under the reader's feet, fails to stretch, at every point, to the base of the walls" (p. 11). This "literary monument" (p. 11) James builds in the Preface bears an eerie resemblance to Osmond's own pile. Indeed James's references to his novel as "a square and spacious house [that] had to be put up round" a "slim shade" of a girl (p. 8), although specific to Isabel, nevertheless blur later distinctions between which house and which girl, as the pattern of massive house and frail, slight girl is replicated in Pansy.

One might say that Isabel is, indeed, doubly immured, first by her husband, then by her author's description of her. Yet, unlike Pansy, Isabel is also compelled by her author to seek out what has happened to her, as Kahane suggests a Gothic heroine must. And it is Isabel Archer's intelligence that distinguishes her from her mock-Gothic step-daughter. In the course of wandering about her "prison-house"[18] of fiction, Isabel pushes at the limitations of self-consciousness. She not only wonders why she has been trapped in a gloomy, Gothic marriage, but she also attempts to see beyond the boundaries of her knowledge. By so doing, Isabel transforms herself, or to use a favored Jamesian description, "expands" herself. It is this expansion that makes her an original of conscious individuality.

Striving, then, to puzzle her way through her own memoir, Isabel sits by the fire, contemplating her life's story. James himself, and many critics such as Charles Feidelson, focus on the scene of chapter 42 as the central moment, the pivot of the novelistic "*tragedy* of consciousness" (CF, p. 749) that is the *Portrait.* However, Isabel begins her self-examination by groping her way around not her own dilemma, but around Pansy's. She asks herself: does her former suitor, Lord Warburton, seek Pansy's hand simply to be nearer the "rose"? If so, doesn't that make him rather base? "Isabel wandered among these ugly possibilities until she had completely lost her way ... Then she broke out of the labyrinth" (p. 355). This traipsing through the labyrinth of Pansy's Gothic entrapment leads Isabel to a disturbing discovery. She sees that her life is as encompassed by vague terrors as is poor Pansy's. Osmond's mind has "become her habitation" (p. 358), and it grows dark, soon "impenetrably black" (p. 356). At last her wandering leads to a memory that seems to hold an eerie secret. She recalls seeing "her husband and Madame Merle unconsciously and familiarly associated" (p. 364).

When Isabel finally opens the door to that dark association, what she discovers is not literally a secret room of death or a ghost. Yet she does find a secret that has been silenced by a death and haunted by a ghost who isn't, as Fiedler has written of Gothic spectres, *really* a ghost. This is the secret of Serena Merle's maternity. Madame Merle's motherhood has been covered up by the actions she and Osmond took to hide Pansy's birth—that is, the birth, being the result of infidelity, had to be hidden for the sake of propriety. Using the death of Gilbert Osmond's first wife as a cover, the Osmonds claim that Pansy's mother is dead. Yet, the secret of Pansy's origin is haunted by the ghost of a motherly solicitude Madame Merle maintains toward her denied child. And, most important for Isabel, it is Serena Merle's maternity that has caused Isabel's own ill-fated, death-like, Gothic incarceration of a marriage—for, as Isabel tells herself, Madame Merle, in desiring the Osmond marriage, had a "conception of gain" (p. 432) in mind, a gain that the Countess Gemini lays bare when she says to Isabel, "Osmond's marriage has given his daughter a great little lift. . . . And do you know what the mother thought? That you might take such a fancy to the child that you'd do something for her" (p. 454).

Isabel discovers, in fact, that a mother has, as Isabel herself puts it, "married her" (p. 430) and so is at the heart of her mysterious fate, just as Fiedler and Kahane have put the maternal, albeit differently emphasized, at the heart of Gothicism. Moreover, since the nineteenth-century America of James's upbringing "define[d] the true woman in predominantly biological terms, locating feminine identity within the straits of passive sexuality and selfless maternity,"[19] the traditional Gothic heroine is a particularly revealing figure for Isabel. That is, given that the prevailing construction of ideal femininity was the maternal, for a nineteenth-century heroine engaged in a search for self—as is Isabel Archer—the mother is the primary emblem of that selfhood. Upon opening the door to the cultural mandate of a selfless maternity, seeking a pattern for her own being, the Gothic heroine of nineteenth-century fiction quite often finds, as she does in Louisa May Alcott's "A Whisper in the Dark,"[20] that the secret of her own horror story is bound to the secret of her murdered, missing, or ghostly mother. Finally, while Fiedler's mother-ghost and Kahane's spectral mother may seem to be, in a certain sense, theoretical opposites, since Fiedler is on the trail of masculine authority and Kahane is tracking female selfhood, yet, in Isabel Archer's tragedy, as well as in Pansy's mock-Gothic mirror of that tragedy, it is precisely the intersection of these two ghost stories— the dialectic between a strict Freudian fantasy of proprietal possession of the mother and the post-Freudian fantasy of the pre-Oedipal mother's murder—that fuels the deepest horror in *The Portrait of a Lady*. In other words, what James maps out in this novel is the horror of a culturally mandated matricide.

II

Isabel, in tracing out the Gothic labyrinth of her life and supposedly expanding her "self" consciousness in the process, eventually finds what Kahane has described as the dead/undead mother: she discovers Serena Merle, who, as Pansy's mother, is both alive and yet has been represented to Isabel, in the guise of Osmond's first wife, as deceased. Isabel also finds out that this dead/undead mother is the ghost in the machine of her marriage. Serena Merle says of herself that she is "Everything!" (p. 430) to Isabel, just as a mother is at the center of a Freudian female identity. Of course, Madame Merle is not literally Isabel's mother, who is, as are most Gothic mothers, dead before the story begins. Yet James makes it clear that Merle's importance to Isabel is suggestive of a mother-daughter bond. When Madame Merle first appears at Gardencourt, she exerts an immediate, and inexplicable, pull on Isabel that grows as Isabel discovers a cluster of facts that draw her to this woman. She finds that her cousin Ralph, of whom she is inordinately fond, was once in love with Serena. He also tells Isabel that Serena Merle is the "cleverest woman I know, not excepting yourself" (p. 154). Ralph remarks, too, that his own mother "would like to be Madame Merle" (p. 155), while Ralph's father, Daniel Touchett, has noted that Isabel reminds him of his wife. Madame Merle is thus tied by association into the family and linked to Isabel by maternal reference.

In fact Serena and Isabel develop what amounts to an "eternal friendship" (p. 163). James tells us that, "The gates of the girl's confidence were opened wider than they had ever been; she said things to this amiable auditress that she had not yet said to any one" (p. 163)—surely a description of how a daughter, at least ideally, relates to her mother. For Isabel then, Madame Merle is both a role model and something a little more—as she says, "I should like awfully to be *so!*" This "so" refers to the "great lady" (pp. 165–66) Isabel sees in Madame Merle, who looks "as if she were a Bust, Isabel judged—a Juno or a Niobe" (p. 154). This Niobe has, in fact, said of herself that she "shall never be anything but abject with the young; they touch me and appeal to me too much" (p. 170). Her one fault might be that "she existed only in her relations, direct or indirect, with her fellow mortals" (p. 167), although Isabel is undecided as to whether this last is a fault or a virtue. All of these attributes indicate that Isabel finds in Serena Merle a classic mother-figure to adopt as her own pattern—for it is a mother who is supposed to be particularly "abject"[21] with the young, a mother who is known primarily by her relational status within the familial/social circle and, after all, both Juno and Niobe were goddess-mothers. Finally, Ralph has assured Isabel that Serena Merle would "be sure to spoil" (p. 155) a child, should she have one. So, when Madame Merle tells Isabel, "I give you *carte blanche* . . . I shall . . . horribly spoil you" (p. 170), the string of descriptive associations drawn between this symbolic mother and daughter becomes tighter.

Madame Merle is, in fact, a Kahanian ghost signifying the problematics of femininity for Isabel. Isabel's desire to be Serena Merle, "in a word a woman of strong impulses kept in admirable order" (p. 154), is a sign of her attempt "to recreate her symbiotic closeness with her mother."[22] Indeed, throughout what Feidelson has denominated the "social comedy" (CF, p. 747) part of this novel, that is, up until Isabel sees her husband and Madame Merle as closer than old friends need be, she is passionately and almost libidinally tied to Madame Merle. She has qualms, but they repeatedly resolve into a wish "to imitate her" (p. 338).

That connection retains its pull, if not its strength, up until the crisis of selecting Pansy's husband. It is then that Isabel begins to comprehend how a longing for the mother can be dangerous. After Isabel's interior journey of chapter 42, as the novel modulates into Feidelson's "comedy of triumphant consciousness" (CF, p. 748), Madame Merle's influence, specifically with regard to Pansy's marital prospects, becomes a suspect one. In psychic terms, the daughter (Isabel or Pansy), despite her connection to the mother (Serena), must also resist that tie if she is going to avoid engulfment. While Isabel desires to be like Serena, she also sees in that woman something to be resisted—something, indeed, Gothically horrific: "It was a worse horror than that [of insolence]. 'Who are you—what are you?' Isabel murmured. 'What have you to do with my husband?' " (p. 430). Madame Merle herself has earlier hinted at her own problematic status. She has said, "I've been shockingly chipped and cracked. . . . I've been cleverly mended . . . But when I've to come out and into a strong light—then, my dear, I'm a horror!" (p. 168). Finally, when the novel turns into Feidelson's "tale of an evil fate" (CF, p. 748) and flowers into the tragedy of Isabel's consciousness, what she uncovers is that the unnamed horror hanging over her is Madame Merle's illicit maternity. Once Isabel has pulled up the curtain over Madame Merle's hidden self and has seen the secret of birth, then "the truth of things, their mutual relations, their meaning, and for the most part their horror, rose before her with a kind of architectural vastness" (p. 465). Motherhood is the hidden biological fact that allows Isabel to see the house of fiction built upon her. Isabel's dawning consciousness, then, is founded upon the Gothic discovery of her "mother's" (and her own) sexuality, the reproductive power marking all women with the ability to be mothers.

However, it is not simply a daughter's psychodynamic fear of maternal engulfment that explains Isabel's reaction of chill despair toward Madame Merle. Rather, it is Isabel's realization that no matter what form of resistance she forges against Madame Merle, she will not forget her or separate from her entirely. It does not matter that Isabel's "eyes were absent from her companion's face" because "there were phases and gradations in her speech, not one of which was lost upon Isabel's ear" (p. 458). Serena Merle will remain mysterious and forever something of a painful loss—as Isabel laments, "The only thing to regret was that Madame Merle had been—well, so unimaginable" (p. 465). Isabel finds herself caught in the paradoxical fastness of a Western cultural (Gothic) fantasy wherein the daughter, having taken up the attractive image of the pre-Oedipal mother/self, is then coerced into a devaluation of that image in exchange for a legitimized place in her society. In Isabel's case, although she has loved Madame Merle, she must forget her in exchange for the social power of a limited but nevertheless legal wifehood. To leave Osmond would be to leave social legitimacy and become as outcast and as "unimaginable" as Madame Merle, a fate she has learned to fear. However, Isabel's turning away from Serena results not in adjustment, as strict Freudians might say, but in despair, or in what Kaja Silverman identifies, in *The Acoustic Mirror,* as the definitive melancholia of female subjectivity. According to Silverman, melancholia is fundamental to female subjectivity because the daughter, having first accepted a positive mother *imago,* is then coerced, in order to function in society, into despising "her."[23] Thus in a curiously evocative way, Feidelson's structural mapping of *The Portrait of a Lady* dovetails with Silverman's re-mapping of Oedipal dynamics, insofar as this novel is a "social" comedy that turns out to be, after all, a tragedy about female self-consciousness or, as Feidelson so eloquently suggests, the tale of an evil fate.

Indeed to look at *The Portrait of a Lady* from Serena Merle's point of view (as it were) is to see a strong relational web of mother-daughter bonding between Merle, Isabel Archer, and Pansy Osmond, a web whose importance Claire Kahane's analysis of Gothicism helps to illuminate. That is, since these relations have seldom been examined for their similarities rather than for their differences, much of the significance of *The Portrait*'s trajectory has gone unremarked, leaving critics grasping at straws in order to explain Isabel's fate. For instance, although it has been noted that Isabel and Pansy resemble one another, the resemblance is seen as triumphantly comparative: Pansy is Isabel's "little" foil, the empty vessel Isabel is not. More importantly, the connection between these women has not been well integrated into any discussion of the novel's ending; for, having uncovered Serena Merle's manipulation of her marriage and consequently the hollowness of that bond, having seen that Pansy will never disobey her father, why should Isabel return to Osmond? Pansy's part in Isabel's retreat to Osmond's horror show does not go unnoticed, but most critics speak of Pansy as a weak plot device.[24] Dorothy Van Ghent's summary is representative:

> The quaint figure of Pansy, always only on the edge of scenes, is of great structural importance in the latter half of the book; for she shows the full measure of the abuse Isabel resists, and it is to nourish in her (Pansy) whatever small germ of creative volition may remain—to salvage, really, a life—that Isabel returns to Rome and to Osmond's paralyzing ambiance. (P. 699)

Pansy is both a marginalized foil and the *raison d'être* for the novel's odd ending. Critics tend to claim that Isabel's choice to return to Osmond, like her choice to marry him, was made "freely" and done altruistically for Pansy's sake.[25] Furthermore, in various discussions that focus on Isabel's flight from Casper Goodwood (most often read as her flight from heterosexuality),[26] it is Isabel's supposedly heightened consciousness, purchased at the expense of sexual expression, that makes her so much more valuable than either poor Pansy or the "horror" of Serena Merle. Indeed, Isabel's consciousness, "deprived of every reference point except its own intrinsic freedom" (CF, pp. 750–51), as Feidelson argues, makes her the stunning original that she is to him and, I might add, to James himself.

Yet what remains unaccounted for is Isabel's clear knowledge that she cannot save Pansy. Nor is it for Pansy's sake that she will return to Osmond. She goes so far as to admit this to her friend, Henrietta Stackpole:

> "Well," said Miss Stackpole at last, "I've only one criticism to make. I don't see why you promised little Miss Osmond to go back."

"I'm not sure I myself see now," Isabel replied. "But I did then."

"If you've forgotten your reason perhaps you won't return."

Isabel waited a moment. "Perhaps I shall find another." (P. 469)

What also remains obscure is the fact that Isabel's creative volition is purchased at the rather violent expense of her connection to Madame Merle. James offers Isabel no choice: she must trade in her view of Serena as a powerful Juno, after whom she had patterned herself, for a view of Merle as one who lacks morality.

In fact, Isabel's tragedy, if viewed as a daughter's search for her self, is the tragedy of a female subjectivity in the process of the melancholic discovery that, in order to achieve a self, she must both become like her mother and learn, as well, to hate her (self). She must pattern herself on the Juno and yet aid in covering up the shameful secret of a culturally inscribed maternal diminishment. If, like Pansy, Isabel plays a daughter's role to Madame Merle's motherhood, then Pansy's veiled mock-Gothic operetta becomes a vividly congruent parallel to Isabel's opera. In this context, Pansy's last conversation with Isabel takes on a powerfully suggestive resonance: "I don't like Madame Merle!" she says. Isabel replies, "You must never say that—that you don't like Madame Merle" (p. 463), as if Isabel, in echoing and yet altering her step-daughter's statement, acknowledges both that Pansy has spoken for her and that, in order for a daughter to survive, she must help to hide the mother's (social and by extension moral) diminishment and her own (self-) hatred. This congruence leads me to question whether the expansion of Isabel's consciousness is a triumph at all—for does not Pansy's fate, and Isabel's acknowledgment of it, indicate a darker future for the heroine than most criticism allows? Isabel says herself, "She should never escape" (p. 466). How much creative volition does she have? And ultimately the darkness of these daughters' twin fates leads me to reexamine whose tragedy The Portrait describes, especially when Madame Merle herself claims that "the tragedy's for me!" (p. 436).

III

To treat The Portrait as a Gothic novel still begs the question: does a ghost of Oedipal paternal anxiety also haunt Roccanera? I have been at pains to outline how Isabel's consciousness is linked to her discovery of Madame Merle's maternity. Is paternity not implicated as well? If Pansy and Isabel share a Gothic heritage, and if they both bear a daughterly relation to Serena Merle, then they should also be related to Osmond as father. This relation is suggested in the dark association between Osmond and Merle, especially since Isabel's discovery of it bears an uncanny resemblance to Freud's narrative of how a child might unknowingly witness the parental sexual relation. More compelling, though, is the way James describes Osmond's desire for Isabel in terms congruent with Osmond's relation to Pansy. Pansy is Osmond's figurine, a part of his castle's decor. When Isabel is introduced to Osmond, she tells her Aunt Lydia that she is to go "and see his view, his pictures, his daughter" (p. 215), as if all three were in some fashion equal—and all at

Osmond's disposal. James then shows that Osmond believes Isabel should belong to him in the same way Pansy does. Finding that Isabel has rejected Lord Warburton's proposal, Osmond thinks she "had qualified herself to figure in his collection of choice objects by declining so noble a hand" (p. 258), and Isabel slowly finds that her mind was to be Osmond's, "attached to his own like a small garden-plot to a deer-park.... a pretty piece of property for a proprietor" (p. 362).

Of course, it is undeniable that Isabel, unlike Pansy, feels the full horror of becoming a (daughterly) piece of property. As James tells us, Isabel knows that Roccanera "was the house of darkness, the house of dumbness, the house of suffocation" (p. 360), and she learns that, to Osmond, "The real offence, as she ultimately perceived, was her having a mind of her own at all" (p. 362). Osmond, having made his daughter "a blank page, a pure white surface, successfully kept so" (p. 268) upon which he is at liberty to paint, also believes that Isabel will be "richly receptive. He had expected his wife to feel with him and for him, to enter into his opinions" (p. 362). But Isabel has ideas of her own. Osmond cannot paint over her because she is not a blank page. At least, not for Osmond.

However, she *is* a blank page to somebody else—her author.[27] In his Preface to *The Portrait of a Lady*, Henry James names Isabel his "unattached character" (p. 5), "the mere slim shade of an intelligent but presumptuous girl" (p. 8), descriptions that are seemingly better suited to Pansy than to Isabel. More telling, though, is the congruence between Osmond's paternal view of Pansy as his own "precious work of art" (p. 442) that he wishes to place in advantageous social niches and James's attitude toward Isabel, whom he sees as "an acquisition I had made ... after a fashion not here to be retraced. Enough that I was, as seemed to me, in complete possession of it" (p. 7), a property he wishes to place in the world as a masterpiece. The worth of such a possession is evident as James continues with a description of Isabel that could apply equally to Osmond's view of his daughter: "The 'value' I here speak of [is] the image of the young feminine nature that I had had for so considerable a time all curiously at my disposal" (p. 8). Like Osmond, James harbors "a pious desire but to place [his] treasure right" (p. 8). So, although Henry James distances himself from Osmond by expressing the darkness of Isabel's condition, still he echoes Osmond when he prefaces his novel with such proprietary descriptions.

Yet it is not simply the Preface that links James to Osmond. During Isabel's famed interior journey, a duality develops. Suddenly, Isabel is not by the fire alone. James's "I" intrudes—"When she saw this rigid system [of Osmond's mind] close about her, draped though it was in pictured tapestries, that sense of darkness and suffocation of which I have spoken took possession of her" (p. 361)—as if Isabel had a doubled consciousness, her own and this overseeing "I" who speaks for her, just as Osmond claims an unquestioned right to speak for his daughter. What Pansy desires "doesn't matter" (p. 315), says Osmond, because she is his "winged fairy in the pantomime" who only "soars by the aid of the dissimulated wire ... prettily ... directed and fashioned" (p. 267). James aligns himself with Osmond's paternal right to create a world for his "daughter" since he not only speaks for Isabel (as well as

allowing Osmond to claim "I'm talking for my wife as well as for myself" [p. 420]),
but he also makes of Isabel, if not a fairy, yet another winged creature—"the angel
of disdain" (p. 402). Indeed because Isabel is *The Portrait of a Lady,* when Theodora Bosanquet, James's last secretary, remarked that the author felt "paternally
responsible" (p. 494) for his literary progeny, her estimation is a shade more than
acute.

James's position toward Isabel thus can be seen as analogous to Osmond's
relation to Pansy as daughter, since both exhibit a possessive paternalism that
equates feminine nature with precious objects. Desire is then figured as a pious
wish to place the daughter/artwork well within the realm of the social, to put her
where she won't get, as Osmond says of Pansy, "knocked about too much" (p.
442). Or perhaps "knocked up" would be a better way to describe Osmond's
anxiety? Certainly it is the disposition of Pansy's sexuality that is at stake in the
heated contest over her marriage, and it is made clear from that contest that if
money and sexuality are bound together, they are linked as well to the father's
wealth. As Pansy candidly laments to Isabel, her father is not wealthy and "it costs
so much to marry!" (p. 268). Therefore, just as Isabel's relation to Madame Merle
is that of daughter to mother, so does Isabel's status as James's possession mirror
Pansy's relation to Osmond. The *jeune fille,* in fact, is the material upon which
creativity will be inscribed, and insofar as the pure Pansy is as virginal as that blank
page upon which Osmond "had already transferred ... the delicate, finely-tinted
disk" (p. 444) of an antique coin, insofar as Pansy and her *belle-mere* "are like two
sisters" (pp. 462–63), Pansy is a figure for the metaphorical prize Isabel becomes,
which the artist/father must possess in order to create. In this psychic economy, the
father who lacks a daughter is a failure. Without a masterpiece, there can be no
Master. Owning the daughter allows the father to own creative potential, or, as
Isabel notes, Osmond's genius is evident in the delicate organism of Pansy.

This paternal possession of the daughter is clearly sexual as well as proprietal.
The incestuous nature of a father-daughter relation is suggested symbolically by
Isabel, if she stands in a daughter's position as property toward Osmond, but Pansy
herself makes a bald reference to incest when she says, "I don't care for any
gentleman; I mean for any but him. If he were not my papa I should like to marry
him" (p. 268). Recently, several important analyses have shown how the Freudian
Oedipal crisis, while forbidding mother-son incest, encourages, even institutes
father-daughter incest as a constitutive part of a successful patriarchal economy.[28]
This incestuous economy has a particular resonance for the nineteenth century, as
Martha Banta and Carolyn Porter have pointed out in focusing on how the daughter
was used as a figure for value. Indeed, Banta, in *Imaging American Women,* uses
Isabel Archer as the prototype of how white, Protestant, bourgeois American
cultural iconography privileged the figure of the white American Girl as the "visual
emblem of the greatness of a nation which 'had nothing left to be desired.' "[29]
Porter traces out the implications of this national desire when she argues that James,
in attempting to rescue the cultural value accorded to feminine nature from the
commodification of an expanding marketplace economy, enacts "the behavior of a
patriarchal father who uses his authority both to protect and to control his daugh-

ter."[30] Paradoxically, protective paternalism is still based on the idea that female = money = commodity = value. James might attempt to rescue Isabel/daughter/value from a commodity status, but what he creates is yet another version of an exchangeable object, a "Portrait." Now the father is caught in a double-bind. In order to increase his status, he ought to marry off his daughter, but in order to claim creativity and avoid losing capital, he ought to retain her—just as Osmond retains Pansy by putting her in the convent while claiming this action will make her more marriageable. As Porter argues, like Claire of *The American*, "Isabel herself must return behind the stone walls of Osmond's dark prison, but her value remains enshrined in the portrait" so that James can retain "possession of . . . an 'original' which the preface serves to place in his own personal Louvre—the New York Edition."[31] The daughter, as precious as an antique gold coin, must be saved and yet, since she is wealth, she must be capitalized upon. Indeed, the successful patriarchal social contract is one that not only operates on a "traffic in women"[32] economy, but also, and with increasing pressure under capitalism, upon the conflicting incestuous demand that the father save his daughter for himself.

Further, for this economy to run smoothly, the capital in question, while emanating from the daughter, must never remain in her hands. And, in *The Portrait of a Lady*, capital does not remain in Isabel's control. Isabel only seems to be a source of value; in fact, she merely facilitates a transfer of one father's wealth into another father's house, keeping value under masculine direction. As James says, "At bottom her money had been a burden, had been on her mind, which was filled with the desire to transfer the weight of it . . . to some more prepared receptacle" (p. 358). Isabel is left as bankrupt of value as I believe she is bankrupt of that independent volition so often ascribed to her. All belongs to the "father"—no matter whether friend or fiend. To expand: it is known from the outset that Ralph Touchett's paternal legacy—a banker's legacy—is Isabel's treasure. This monetary capital forms Isabel's chief source of desirability for Osmond—or as Madame Merle says to Isabel, the Touchetts "imparted to you that extra lustre which was required to make you a brilliant match" (p. 464). Reading this lustre from a more sexualized angle, one should recall, as Kahane notes, that the erotic threat in the Gothic, being incestuous, can come from either a father or a brother. In Isabel's case, her father is on one level Osmond, on another level Uncle Daniel Touchett, and on a third, Henry James, but her brother is certainly Ralph Touchett, who has inadvertently threatened her by making of her an object of social as well as sexual desire. The erotic threat Isabel tries to flee is not only a combination of fatherly and brotherly love but also part of the constitutively incestuous nature of a nineteenth-century patriarchal masculinity. Just as a nineteenth-century idea of femininity wedded female to mother, masculinity was tied to paternity. All the men in the book want to own Isabel—as James says, "They all had Isabel for subject" (p. 271). This desire is frequently expressed through a paternal medium of precious objects and is considered benign—after all, the Touchetts do not mean Isabel harm. Isabel herself comes to name Daniel Touchett as "the beneficent author of her infinite woe" (p. 358). Isabel believes this benevolence is safer to her liberty than heterosexual desire. She refuses both Goodwood and Warburton because they are active men who have a social importance. Isabel fears Goodwood's sexualized activity will erase her; she fears Warburton's aristocratic wealth will make her a dependent. When Aunt Lydia says of Osmond, "There's nothing *of* him," Isabel replies, "Then he can't hurt me" (p. 282), implying her former lovers might. What she has not understood is that the aggressive Goodwood, the aristocratic Warburton, and the benign Osmond actually belong to the same paternal order.

In this sense, I would agree with those critics who feel that Isabel tries to flee sexuality—since the heterosexuality of a nineteenth-century psychic economy requires her to be a mirror for the father and a possession who, in learning to loathe her mother(self), must acquiesce in being made a ghost within a Western cultural patriarchy that binds men together by making her into that ghost. As Eve Kosofsky Sedgwick has argued in her essay on Henry James's "The Beast in the Jungle," in the nineteenth century "the normal condition of the male heterosexual entitlement"[33] was a panicky state of both homophobia and homosociality; for Sedgwick, evidence of this unstable entitlement is most evident in a nineteenth-century Gothicism that showed a marked "preference of atomized male individuality,"[34] or for what she describes as a sarcastic bachelor figure. Interestingly, both Ralph Touchett and Gilbert Osmond fit Sedgwick's "bachelor taxonomy."[35] Both have acute powers of sarcastic observation, and Isabel herself believes that Ralph and Osmond share the "appearance of thinking that life was a matter of connoisseurship" (p. 225). They are also said to hate each other. Isabel's *Portrait* seems, in fact, to have been painted first by Touchett's money and then by Osmond's use of that fortune, so that, despite their supposed hatred of one another, Touchett and Osmond are bound together by their concern with Isabel: she is "between" these "men."[36] Touchett is nearly Osmond's halo. To Isabel, he personifies the generosity her husband lacks; he is "a lamp in the darkness" (p. 363), whose brightness, however, only gains its most illuminating shine against Osmond's perfidy. In effect, Isabel separates and connects the two men. There is a wedge of hatred between Gilbert Osmond and Ralph Touchett, yet their opposition, projected onto Isabel, glues them together, Janus-faced. She is their common desire; they both want possession of her. Isabel's own desire seems to weigh very little in this contest. So too, although there is a difference between Henry James and Gilbert Osmond, that difference shrinks when seen in light of Ralph Touchett's bonded relation to Osmond. Bluntly, because James sympathizes with Ralph Touchett, the psychic economies of all three men—Osmond, Touchett, James—if viewed as interlocking parts of a paternal, homosocial entitlement, seem weirdly congruent. For aren't Osmond and Touchett two sides of the same psychic coin, that coin being the paternal consciousness of Henry James?

IV

This paternalistic scenario, as well as Isabel's relation to Madame Merle, leaves Isabel standing primarily in a daughter's position. So, if in the father's Freudian/

Gothic fantasy the mother is the locus of paternal desire, what is the daughter doing here? But if, according to the paternal economy I've just sketched out, the daughter represents value, does the father need the mother? And, after all these familial positions have been shuffled around the psychic chessboard, where *does* Isabel stand?

First, Isabel's discovery of Madame Merle's maternity puts Serena Merle into a maternal role toward both Pansy and Isabel. Then, if one follows out the meta-phorics in the fatherly plot of possession, again, symbolically, Madame Merle plays mother to Isabel. But in the course of the novel, Isabel takes over maternity, changing from Pansy's sister into Pansy's stepmother—in effect a daughter who is, as well, a mother. Alternately, by examining the way the bonds of homosocial entitlement operate, a drift-line of "fatherhood" can be detected that leads irrevo-cably back, through Osmond as proprietor, Ralph Touchett as procurer, Daniel Touchett as patron, to Henry James as painter. Here, Isabel is a daughter who represents the virginal value of "a quick fanciful mind which saved one repetitions and reflected one's thought on a polished, elegant surface" (p. 296), and she plays the role of value-*cum*-daughter.

Given these two daughterly roles, what becomes clear is that Isabel stands at a crossroads: she is both virginal property and potentially sexual mother. Still, Isabel is not maternal in the way that her "mother" is—she will never be wholly tainted with a threatening reproductivity. Her physical maternity is missing—her child dies and her pregnancy is unrepresented. And, as the Lady is inscribed upon the blank *jeune fille* in the *Portrait,* both are recoded as masculine conceptions. The maternal (Serena) from which both maiden and Lady (Pansy and Isabel) came, at least in part, is diminished and disposed of (exiled to America), leaving the father (Osmond) in possession of the field. The daughter-role is a blind to the fact that the father, in order to ensure his position in this economy, must show potency and yet obliterate any reproductive creativity besides his own. He must demonstrate "fatherhood" without revealing his dependency on the maternal. The daughter is a perfect blind for this, insofar as she, being ideally virginal and also ideally the father's creation or possession alone, is safe from the taint of an alien reproductivity. Here, Isabel's power as a character comes from the fact that she appears to remain virginal while stepping blindly into Serena Merle's dispossessed maternity. She occupies the moth-er's place while remaining daughterly. For doesn't Isabel replace Serena Merle as Pansy Osmond's mother, and is it not precisely Serena Merle's personal style that Isabel comes to adopt? And yet, as Isabel's affect grows to resemble the serenity invoked by Serena's name, Isabel becomes a static work of daughterly art, without an independent erotic desire. She becomes in fact, as James calls her, an exquisite Madonna (p. 392), Western culture's most developed icon of maternal daughter-hood.

In this light, motherless Pansy is the figure who most sharply reveals Henry James's relation not only to Isabel, but more broadly to the *Portrait* as an art object of the highest valuation upon which James, retrospectively in his 1907 New York edition, founded a family of American literature. That is, what Pansy's—and

Isabel's—daughterly Gothic fate reveals is that the Jamesian "house of fiction" (p. 7) is both dependent on, but also ruthlessly compelled to deface, or at least diminish, a conceptual energy defined or represented as maternal, a position that Serena Merle inhabits and Isabel inherits from her. In other words, as Isabel, the pure and valued creation expands, Serena Merle, the alien mother, contracts and is swept, at last, out of the picture. She leaves behind a daughter who has acquired her attributes but who is marked as a male-generated possession, a representation of the father's art.

Still, in coming to be as serene as Serena, what happens to Isabel is that, as the logic of Kahane's Gothic suggests, in discovering the dead/undead mother she has actually begun to discover what will become of her "self." Which brings me to Isabel's consciousness, her valuable, original selfhood. By figuratively transferring a conceptual power designated as an implicitly sexual, biological maternity from the mother Serena Merle to the patriarchally created, sexually inert daughter Isabel, by essentially transferring the notion of "conception" from mother to daughter and then incarcerating the daughter in a perpetual patriarchal daughterhood, James can, through the ownership of Isabel's virginal (daughterly) consciousness, appropriate the power of "conception" and, I would argue, self-conception, entirely to himself or to the (supposedly) invisible artist's eye. The (male) artist with a (female) consciousness can then gestate and bring to term a perfect *Portrait,* without risking either a threatening involvement with the taboo mother or a homosexually tainted brush with the feminized—without himself risking the gender confusion that marks all the artistic male characters in the novel. For who owns the consciousness that is Isabel's sensitivity? What *The Portrait of a Lady* reveals is that aesthetic value is derived from the acquisition and regendering of the power to *conceive,* a power defined as maternal.

However, the extrusion of the mother upon which mastery rests is a painful process that leaves traces of agony. In *The Portrait,* when Isabel hears Countess Gemini's account of how Serena Merle lost her daughter, she weeps. Nor is it surprising to find Madame Merle described as a Niobe—in weeping for the children, in weeping for each other, these women are weeping for themselves. Another painful trace of erasure remains in James's notebooks and, like a Gothic ghost, haunts the hallways of the *Portrait*'s architecture: it is a scene that James describes as "the great scene," but which he did not include in the final versions of the novel. It appears in his notebooks as follows:

> Isabel resents Madame Merle's interference, demands of her what she has to do with Pansy. Whereupon Madame Merle, in whose breast the suppressed feeling of maternity has long been rankling, and who is passionately jealous of Isabel's influence over Pansy, breaks out with the cry, she alone has the right—that Pansy is her daughter.[37]

I'd like to suggest that James found himself more or less forced to leave this scene out in the cold because it revealed too sharply and too painfully what *The Portrait of a Lady* enacts. That is, this novel sets out to establish who has the cultural right to both create and endow a girl with value, that "who" being the painter of *The Portrait of a Lady,* the Master left standing in the most prominent paternal position toward her—for it certainly cannot be, as Isabel's sadness, fear, and ultimate incarceration reveal, the girl—or the mother—herself.

NOTES

[1] *The Portrait of a Lady,* ed. Robert D. Bamberg (New York: Norton, 1975), p. 442, emphasis added. All further references to this novel appear in the text.

[2] James refers to Isabel as slight or frail in his Preface to the 1907 edition of *The Portrait of a Lady* and in his notebooks; see *The Complete Notebooks,* ed. Leon Edel and Lyall H. Powers (Oxford: Oxford Univ. Press, 1987), p. 13.

[3] Various critics have termed Isabel's story "tragic"; see esp. Charles Feidelson, "The Moment of *The Portrait of a Lady,"* in *The Portrait of a Lady,* ed. Robert D. Bamberg (New York: Norton, 1975), p. 749. Further references to this essay are cited parenthetically as CF.

[4] *Love and Death in the American Novel,* rev. ed. (New York: Dell, 1966), p. 131.

[5] Fiedler, p. 131.

[6] Fiedler, p. 127.

[7] Fiedler, pp. 132–33.

[8] Fiedler, p. 129.

[9] Fiedler, p. 132.

[10] Fiedler, p. 129.

[11] "The Gothic Mirror," in *The (M)Other Tongue: Essays in Feminist Psychoanalytic Interpretation* (Ithaca: Cornell Univ. Press, 1985), pp. 334–51.

[12] Kahane, p. 334.

[13] See *The Reproduction of Mothering* (Berkeley: Univ. of California Press, 1978), pp. 111–29.

[14] Kahane, p. 336.

[15] *Bearing the Word* (Chicago: Univ. of Chicago Press, 1986), p. 12. Homans revises Oedipal dynamics dually, using Chodorow to reexamine both Freud and Jacques Lacan's use of the Oedipus Complex with regard to language.

[16] Homans, pp. 7–13.

[17] For this argument, I am most concerned with the nineteenth-century Gothic. See Kahane, Fiedler, and Eve Kosofsky Sedgwick, "The Beast in the Closet: James and the Writing of Homosocial Panic," in *Papers for the English Institute* (Baltimore: Johns Hopkins Univ. Press, 1987) and Sedgwick, *Between Men: English Literature and Homosocial Desire* (New York: Columbia Univ. Press, 1985), pp. 83–96.

[18] See Fredric Jameson, *The Prison-House of Language* (Princeton: Princeton Univ. Press, 1972). Isabel Archer's story aptly illustrates Jameson's headquote from Nietzsche.

[19] Kahane, p. 350.

[20] "A Whisper in the Dark," in *Frank Leslie's Illustrated Newspaper* (June 1863), rpt. in *The Hidden Louisa May Alcott,* ed. Madeline Stern (New York: Avenel Books, 1984), pp. 537–589.

[21] See Julia Kristeva, "Stabat Mater," in *The Kristeva Reader,* ed. Toril Moi (New York: Columbia Univ. Press, 1986), pp. 160–87, and *The Powers of Horror* (New York: Columbia Univ. Press, 1982).

[22] Homans, p. 25.

[23] *The Acoustic Mirror: The Female Voice in Psychoanalysis and Cinema* (Bloomington: Indiana Univ. Press, 1988), pp. 152–59.

[24] See Dorothy Van Ghent, "On *The Portrait of a Lady,"* in *The Portrait of a Lady,* ed. Robert D. Bamberg (New York: Norton, 1975), pp. 689–704. Also William Veeder, *Henry James: The Lessons of the Master* (Chicago: Univ. of Chicago Press, 1975).

[25] On Isabel's limited consciousness as her freedom, see also Feidelson, Veeder, and Dorothea Krook, *The Ordeal of Consciousness in Henry James* (New York: Cambridge Univ. Press, 1962). James himself saw Isabel as primarily a consciousness in the process of becoming unique.

[26] Cf. with particular reference to Veeder, pp. 86, and Alfred Habegger, *Gender, Fantasy, and Realism in American Literature* (New York: Columbia Univ. Press, 1982), p. 76.

[27] For a discussion of the woman as art object, see Susan Gubar, " 'The Blank Page' and the Issues of Female Creativity," in *Writing and Sexual Difference,* ed. Elizabeth Abel (Chicago: Univ. of Chicago Press, 1982), pp. 73–95.

[28] See Judith Herman, *Father-Daughter Incest* (Cambridge: Harvard Univ. Press, 1981).

[29] *Imaging American Women: Idea and Ideals in Cultural History* (New York: Columbia Univ. Press, 1987), p. xxvii.

[30] "Gender and Value in *The American*," in *New Essays on* The American (New York: Cambridge Univ. Press, 1987), p. 126.

[31] Porter, p. 126.

[32] See Lynda E. Boose, "The Father's House and the Daughter in It: The Structures of Western Culture's Daughter-Father Relationships," in *Daughters and Fathers*, ed. Lynda E. Boose and Betty S. Flowers (Baltimore: Johns Hopkins Univ. Press, 1989), pp. 25–32.

[33] Sedgwick, "The Beast in the Closet," p. 151.

[34] Sedgwick, "The Beast in the Closet," p. 152.

[35] Sedgwick, "The Beast in the Closet," p. 155.

[36] Sedgwick, *Between Men*.

[37] *The Complete Notebooks*, p. 14. I am deeply indebted to Carolyn Porter for her incisive commentary and unfailing support. I would also thank Elizabeth Abel and Susan Schweik for their time and patience.

William Veeder

THE FEMININE ORPHAN
AND
THE EMERGENT MASTER

> It was of course an impression then obscurely gathered, but into which one was later to read strange passages . . . and indeed [I] have a strong impression that I didn't at any moment quite know what I was writing about: I am sure I couldn't otherwise have written so much.
>
> —*A Small Boy and Others*

There is a coherence to Henry James that enables us to bring together basic questions of biography, literary form, and genre. Keeping in mind recent critical admonitions against totalization, I believe I can demonstrate that central to the structure of James's personality was a self-representation that appeared in his childhood, helped shape his adulthood and his fiction from *The Portrait of a Lady* to *The Golden Bowl,* and found express articulation in his autobiography.

Henry James, like us all, spent his days (and nights) attempting to realize himself, to make exigent who he was and could be. Essential to this process was the creation of a self-representation composed of two figures: one drawn from fantasy, the other from American culture. The fantasy figure is an orphan positioned in a bizarre version of Freud's family romance. This figure James combines with a phenomenon of his culture, the American girl. The compulsive repetition of the feminine orphan throughout James's life and art allows us some purchase on basic questions of biography (where did the self-representation come from and what psychological work did it do?), of literary form (how does the self-representation help shape *The Portrait* and subsequent novels and tales through the major phase?), and genre (how does autobiography relate to biography? how can we take as "fact" what is posited five decades later in a time of stress and in a mode intensely rhetorical?). Embedded in all these questions is the issue of gender. If self-realization is envisioned by Henry James in terms of "becom[ing] a (sufficiently) great man" (Edel II, 105), why does this process require accommodation with, and indeed

From *Henry James Review* 12, No. 1 (Winter 1991): 20–38.

assumption of, the role of woman in a culture puritanical and capitalist? Why, in other words, does James need *two* figures to facilitate self-realization, the orphan of family romance *and* the heroine of the Gilded Age?

I. Figures of Fantasy: Defense and Compensation

With his "imagination of disaster" Henry James felt threatened from his earliest years to his final days, threatened by an intimation of absence, a sense of lack at the center of human existence, a fear of castration and extermination. Danger emanated both from within his family and from the culture outside. Against each danger James defended himself by developing a compensatory fantasy.

At home young Henry felt threatened, as Edel and others have shown, by the lethal weakness of Henry Sr., by the smothering strength of Mary Walsh James, and by the frenetic intrusiveness of his brothers. How does Henry defend himself? He fantasizes a bizarre version of family romance.[1] James says of himself as a child, "I seemed to have been constantly eager to exchange my lot for that of somebody else" (*SB* 175). Normally when a child imagines himself somebody else, he imagines somebody grand, some crown prince whose real parents are the King and Queen. Though young Henry James occasionally engages in such fantasies, his core family romance is more bizarre.[2]

In describing a cousin, Henry exults that "this genial girl, like her brother, was in the grand situation of having no home" (*SB* 188). The homeless orphan: here is the ideal. In James's negative version of the family romance, parents are replaced not by monarchs but by corpses. Or rather, by absences. "I think my first childish conception of the enviable lot, formed amid these associations, was to be little fathered or mothered" (*SB* 14). James clarifies what is idyllic about orphanhood when he explains why "cousin Albert, still another of the blest orphans" (*SB* 120), surpasses even the genial girl: she was encumbered by a sibling—"If it was my habit, as I have hinted, to attribute to orphans *as* orphans a circumstantial charm, a setting necessarily more delightful than our father'd and mother'd one, so there spread about this appointed comrade [Albert], the perfection of the type, in as much as he alone was neither brother'd nor sister'd, an air of possibilities that were none the less vivid for being quite indefinite" (*SB* 120–21). There is a possibility for life only if family is impossible. James thus idealizes a negated role, a position of lack (fa-ther*less*, mother*less*, home*less*) so that he can defend against, can in fact negate, the negating forces of experience.[3] Among these forces are both parents.

Henry Sr.'s "rash failure," his "precipitate and general charity" (*SB* 300), and his "almost pathetic incoherence" (*SB* 302) are part of a childhood universe where James cousins and uncles die in legion. What father in his right mind would submit his five children to the fatal transitions of this world of flux, where the very ships that plied the Atlantic went down like stones? "Since the wretched Arctic had gone down in mortal woe . . . her other companion, the Pacific, leaving England a few months later and under the interested eyes of our family group, then temporarily settled in London, was never heard from more" (*SB* 278). Young Henry's core fantasy of negation is thus an attempt to beat reality at its own game. It is also a page from his father's book. Henry Sr. told Ralph Waldo Emerson that "he wished sometimes the lightning would strike his wife and children out of existence, and he should have to suffer no more from loving them." Henry Jr.'s core fantasy of the orphan enacts this project. He exterminates his father before Henry Sr. can get him.[4]

Since the most tangled of young Henry's emotional relationships is with his mother, in young adulthood he defends against the additional difficulties by elaborating the exclusionary fantasy of his childhood. When Mary writes to him in London that "your life must need this [my own] succulent, fattening element more than you know yourself" (Edel I, 47), Henry knows himself well enough to forego his cake and eat it too. So he gains *dozens* of pounds in London, then informs Mary that "I am as broad as I am long, as fat as a butter-tub and as red as a British *materfamilias*" (Edel II, 343). The once skinny son has thus incorporated maternal nurturance while escaping mother. London as "a good married matron" fosters "British stoutness" (Edel II, 295, 419). Surrounding himself with a barrier of fat—"my flesh hangs over my waistband in huge bags" (Edel II, 343)—Henry keeps the world at a distance. Obesity constitutes the physical equivalent of his family romance of exclusion.

Such a physical articulation of fantasy is something that Henry had sought since childhood play with neighborhood children: "Our general medium of life in the situation I speak of was such as to make a large defensive veranda, which seems to have very stoutly and completely surrounded us, play more or less the part of a raft of rescue in too high a tide.... it must really have played for us, so far as its narrowness and exposure permitted, the part of a buffer-state against the wilderness immediately near, that of the empty, the unlovely, and mean" (*SB* 37). Again protection is imagined "stoutly," as a "buffer-state." In childhood, alas, architectural buffers failed to prove stout enough, as T. S. Perry testified: "Those unhappy [James] children fight like cats and dogs.... [Henry] was trying to obtain solitude in the library, with the rest of the family pounding at the door, and rushing in all the time. He so far forgot himself at one time as to try to put and lock me out of the house. It was a terrible sight, and I can assure you I pitied poor Harry, and asked him to come and stay with me" (Edel I, 43). Only in adulthood does the expatriate James find an adequate geographic buffer: the Atlantic Ocean provides a supplementary moat to his wall of fat.

A second source of threat was cultural, the negating force of American capitalist society. "Disconnected from business we [Jameses] could only be connected with the negation of it" (*NSB* 71). Familial negation inevitably marks the small boy. "I never dreamed of competing—a business having in it at the best, for my temper, if not for my total failure of temper, a displeasing ferocity" (*SB* 176). The word "business" here does not mean commerce specifically, but its appearance in James's sentence underscores his lack of competitive ferocity. William James's famous taunt, "*I* play with boys who curse and swear," is followed by lines less often quoted but eloquent of Henry's sense of self-negation. "I had sadly to recognize that I didn't, that I couldn't pretend to have come to that yet.... It wasn't that I mightn't have been drawn to the boys in question, but that I simply wasn't qualified" (*SB* 259, 260).

Negation is especially threatening because the small boy's chief buffer against the commercial environment, his father, seemed to him egregiously negated. "That the head of our family was *not* in business" was "tasteless and even humiliating" (*NSB* 71); that his father espoused no organized religion meant that "our pewless state ... involved, to my imagination, much the same discredit that a houseless or a cookless would have done" (*SB* 234); that Henry Sr. "cared only for virtue that was more or less ashamed of itself" (*SB* 216) meant that he was compromised even as a moralist. Besides the obvious physical sign of lack, the amputated right leg, Henry James Sr., with his "almost eccentrically home-loving habit," seemed to his son "afraid to recognize certain anxieties, fairly declining to dabble in the harshness of practical precautions or imposition" (*SB* 72, 200).

Especially in light of a father whom Henry Jr. sees as effeminated as well as lethal, and in the context of a culture where negation is traditionally gendered, the small boy quite inevitably sees himself not only as an orphan but also as a woman. Let me begin with a gender opposition that James himself sometimes made and Edel has succinctly formulated. "Downtown was the world of the money-makers that he [James] didn't know and couldn't write about. Uptown represented leisure, largely feminine (since the males were Downtown making the money), and this world was useable in his books" (I 103). I want to complicate considerably this gender opposition, but first I need to foreground what is useful in it, the association of Henry James and the feminine. Virtually everything about young Henry seemed to him to bespeak woman.[5] Take, for example, "my long fair curls," which are described early in *A Small Boy* (*SB* 12). On the same page James presents an aunt featuring "long light 'front' ringlets, the fashion of the time and the capital sign of all our paternal aunts." One such aunt is Catherine James, "whose fair hair framed her pointed smile in full and far-drooping 'front' curls" (*SB* 40). In addition to other ladies, like a Mrs. Rogers with her "long black glossy ringlets" and a Miss Emily Mestayer "coifed in a tangle of small, fine, damp-looking short curls" (*SB* 17, 156), there are the artistic women, various female authors "glossily ringleted" and an actress with "very tight black curls" (*SB* 59, 108). When the small boy who grows up with the women Uptown chooses a literary vocation far removed from Downtown business, the last thing he wants is to hear his prose called effeminate. William thus finds a nerve when he says of Henry's early travel sketches, "the style ran a little more to *curliness* than suited the average mind" (Edel II, 71).

Since James's adult vocation carries on his childhood associations with femininity, why does the Downtown-Uptown opposition need to be complicated? Because gender cannot be equated, finally, with either genital endowment or professional status. Indicative of James's prescience about gender is his recognition

that scarce aught but disaster *could,* in that so unformed and unseasoned society, overtake young men who were in the least exposed. Not to have been immediately launched in business of a rigorous sort was to *be exposed*—in the absence I mean of some fairly abnormal predisposition to virtue; since it was a world so simply constituted that whatever wasn't business, or exactly an office or a 'store,' places in which people sat close and made money, was just simply pleasure, sought, and sought only, in places in which people got tipsy. (*SB* 48–49)

The basic distinction here is less between man and woman than between business and pleasure. To explain why *this* distinction complicates, to the point of subversion, the Downtown-Uptown gender opposition, I cannot claim that James resists the implicit association here of pleasure and women. Indeed he insists upon the association. After establishing "the wondrous fact that ladies might live for pleasure, pleasure always, pleasure alone," Henry focuses upon aunt Catherine, who "was distinguished for nothing whatever so much as for an insatiable love of the dance; that passion in which I think of the 'good,' the best, New York society of the time as having capered and champagned itself away" (*SB* 40). Woman is as evanescent as champagne bubbles, as transitory as waltz music. Aunt Catherine proved it by dying young.

Rather than resisting the association of the feminine with pleasure and death, James emphasizes it by implicating himself. He has opted, like woman, for pleasure over business, so he must face the music when his two principal sources of pleasure, art and Europe, prove fatal all around him. Cousin Bob "seemed exposed, for his pleasure—if pleasure it was!—and my wonder, to every assault of experience.... it was all in the right key that, a few years later, he should, after 'showing some talent for sculpture,' have gone the way of most of the Albany youth ... and died prematurely and pointlessly" (*SB* 188). "Exposed" next is "another slim shade, one of the younger and I believe quite the most hapless of those I have called the outstanding ones ... succumbing to monstrous early trouble after having 'shown some talent' for music" (*SB* 189). The danger inherent in an inclination to the arts is compounded by an attraction to Europe. Death is again the reward of pleasure as James catalogues the family fatalities: first, "a young collateral ancestor who died on the European tour" (*SB* 123); then cousin Albert, "a small New York Orestes ridden by the furies" whose "early Wanderjahre" ended as soon as he "disembarked in England.... He just landed and died" (*SB* 133, 142, 143), and finally cousin J. J., who makes it back to New York, "but he had verily performed his scant office on earth.... [being one of] those to whom it was given but to toy so briefly with the flowers" (*SB* 192–93).

Why must the Downtown-Uptown gender opposition be complicated? Because Bob, Albert, J. J., the musical cousin, and the collateral ancestor are all male. Pleasure is fatal to men as well as to women. And not merely to a few artists and European travelers like the Jameses. Henry James understood what recent feminist scholars have insisted upon, that gender is socially produced. When his society equates business with men-life-presence and pleasure with women-death-absence, James recognizes that a puritanical capitalism is presenting as a "natural," "essential" opposition what is in fact a defense against anxiety, a reaction formation. Paramount for me in the prescient passage I have quoted on the preceding page (*SB* 48–49) is not the manifest opposition of the sexes but the barely latent anxiety underlying that opposition. "Exposed . . . exposed" intimates the menace of castration that awaits anyone who fails to "sit tight." "Exposed" was the term used with artistic cousin Bob, yet here it appears twice with his supposed antitheses, the young men of business. No less doomed than aunt Catherine James was her youthful bride-groom who survived her by less than two years. "It is at all events to the sound of fiddles and the popping of corks that I see even young brides, as well as young grooms . . . vanish untimely" (*SB* 42). By turning the wedding waltz into a *danse macabre,* James is saying not so much that women die of pleasure but that anyone, everyone does.

Henry James does not resist the equation of women with pleasure and death because he sees that incontestably women do enjoy and do perish. But he insists that men also enjoy and also perish. "Business" is no more than a defense against a vulnerability endemic to human existence. "Woman" as a gender construct is a social fate available to persons of either sex. *Everyone* is "feminine" because anyone can be effeminated by the negating force of mortality. The only valid opposition is between those who admit their vulnerability and those who do not. James thus subverts that basic opposition of the sexes upon which patriarchal hegemony is based, for he insists upon lack, "castration," at the very heart of capitalist America. That archtypical American entrepreneur Caspar Goodwood becomes "quite as sick, in a different way, as Mr. Touchett" (*PL* 492) once he ceases to sit tight and travels to Europe.

Henry James thus provides a compelling variation upon the insight of Claridge and Langland that "maleness exists in relation to patriarchy as a third term of gender discourse, whose terms are woman, man, and patriarchy."[6] In James's variation, a three-term structure counterpoints patriarchy against both those women (and men) who are capable of pleasure and are therefore seen as "feminine" (effemi-nated, fatal), and those men (and women) who are commited to the puritanical repressiveness characteristic of business and are therefore safely "masculine" so long as they sit tight and expose nothing. To establish that the latter group is no more restricted to men than the former is to women, to establish in other words that the crucial factor is one's attitude toward pleasure rather than one's genitals or profession, Henry James reveals in two early heroines the anxiety that pleasure can generate. Mary Garland puritanically fears the allure of Europe and ventures across the sea only to try to rescue the expatriated Roderick Hudson. She then experi-ences what American business is configured to defend against: "I used to think . . . that if any trouble came to me I should bear it like a stoic. But that was at home, where things don't speak to us of enjoyment as they do here. . . . This place has destroyed every scrap of consistency that I ever possessed" (*RH* 456–57). Isabel Archer is much more cosmopolitan than Mary, but she, too, is a daughter of the Puritans (as Osmond points out contemptuously), and she, too, fears pleasure. "There was a terror in beginning to spend. If she touched it, it would all come out"

(*PL* 18).[7] Isabel is explicitly referring to her inheritance here, but, as Carren Kaston points out, James is deploying unmistakably a "figure for orgasm" (45). Kaston goes on to show how this "old and tired figure" is "revitalized by being made to echo the overall concerns of the book." Another type of revitalization is operative as well. What is old and tired about the figure of spending is that it appears everywhere in the nineteenth century, but it is everywhere applied to men.[8] Capitalist culture feared that spending too much semen in nighttime pleasures would deny men the energy necessary to succeed in the daytime, paramount world of business. That Henry James can apply an ejaculatory image to a woman indicates that anyone, everyone in bourgeois culture is threatened with "castration," effeminization. Not the sex, but the attitude toward pleasure is what matters.

This distinction is, I feel, what Joyce W. Warren is overlooking when she attacks psychological explanations of James's empathy with women. "One problem with these explanations is that James did not identify only with his female characters. To conclude that he saw himself as a woman is no more valid than to say that he saw himself as an impoverished London bookbinder" (243). But James *did* see himself in Hyacinth Robinson, and for the same reason that he saw himself in Isabel Archer. Hyacinth, too, is culturally "feminine." Though he does "work" for a living, Hyacinth's craft of bookbinding indicates his inclination to literature and the arts rather than to commerce, and it prepares us for his ravishment by beauty in Venice. After such pleasures, death is inevitable for this surrogate James who was provided "exactly with an office or a 'store,' places in which people sat close and made money," but who could not sit still.

More than this needs to be said, however. Henry James was far more alive to experience (more affirmative in his responses, more resilient before setbacks, more daring as an artist) than I have indicated so far. Despite the menace of death inherent in exposure to pleasure, James was committed to life (to travel, to art, above all to the play of consciousness) with a quiet ferocity that resisted the anxieties of capitalist patriarchy. Even as a small boy he believed deep down, deeper than anyone at the time could guess, that *he* was marked by presence, that he had a productive genius. James's defenses were thus compensations as well, facilitations. The fantasy of the orphan freed him from domestic menace so that he could be free for significant achievement. The orphan role could not produce such achievement, however. It was too thoroughly negative, negated. For James to become "a (sufficiently) great man," he had to find a second role that would make practicable the freedom garnered by the fantasy of orphanhood. Fortunately he did not have far to look.

In America the figure of Woman had positive as well as negative aspects. Freedom and daring of mind, and even of action, characterized the American girl long before she debuted in James's fiction. In the society around him, in other words, young Henry saw not only active male figures who could never express his self but also active female figures who could.[9] Woman's capacity to resist anxiety and embrace pleasure is dramatized by Mary Garland, who goes beyond her puritan fear of "enjoyment" in Europe and exclaims "but even if I must myself say something sinful I love it!" (457). Henry James particularly needed a compensatory affiliation with the figure of woman as heroine because he had to defend against one additional threat—from the "feminine" nature of his own sexuality.

Henry's erotic inclinations toward William have been suggested by various biographers.[10] If the younger brother was "in love with" the older, what are the causes and the effects of this emotion? Causation in Henry's case seems virtually paradigmatic of one type of homosexual object choice defined by Freud: a son prevented by paternal ineffectuality and maternal oversolicitude from accomplishing the oedipal transfer from mother to father seeks men for two reasons. On the one hand, his failure to bond with the father means that the boy remains joined to mother and thus "feminine" sexually. He desires what she desires: men. The most dominating male presence in Henry's immediate view was the dynamic William. On the other hand, the son who has failed to affiliate with the father lacks a role model and thus seeks to incorporate a male ego ideal to solidify his sense of himself as masculine. Again William stands forth inescapably. What complicates the paradigm, of course, is that the male chosen by Henry abides *within the family*. To one taboo, homosexuality, is thus added another, incest. A young man whose orphan fantasy shows him already wary of all relationships will of course repress such desires, but he must deal with the narcissism involved in loving someone who is both of his sex and in his family. If solipsism is obviously the danger of Henry's family romance of negation, obliterating everyone but himself, things are only made worse by the addition of a narcissistic object choice.

How long Henry could have gone on managing these conflicting forces becomes suddenly moot in 1878. William James, at the age of thirty-seven, announces his decision to wed Alice Gibbens. In the same year, 1878, Henry James begins to write novels about heroines instead of about heroes.[11] If passive Henry, already "feminine" in his self-perceived negation, functions as "the girl" in his unconscious homosexual bond with active William, he becomes the girl rejected, the woman scorned, when William weds. Henry compensates by projecting his female self outwards: he enacts through his fiction what no longer works as private fantasy. Moreover, the change in Henry's narrative pattern coincides with the other major change of 1878. His enormous gain in weight occurs precisely at this time, the fall and winter of 1878–79. Henry is using body as well as art to buffer himself against the shock of William's rejection. Body can never compensate enough, however. James must tell himself a story. Over and over.

Woman is thus indispensable to James's art because she is indispensable to his psyche. The relationship between James's professionalism and his "use" of women has recently been addressed by John Carlos Rowe:

> What makes James's identification with women so successful . . . is his tendency
> to transform the social psychology of women into the formal esthetics as well
> as the psychohistory of the author. Even as this identification marks James as
> singularly sympathetic to the larger social issues of feminism, it is based on
> James's own inevitable defense: that process by which Henry James, the

Master, *uses* feminism, uses the "other sex" as part of his own literary power for the sake of engendering his own identity as Author. (91)

Rowe effectively demonstrates how James uses the feminine to defend against professional dangers such as the influence of strong predecessors and the challenge of popular women writers. What I want to explore are dangers more exclusively psychological and more resolutely archaic, dangers that threaten Henry James's very existence as a human being. Woman he uses here, too, as defense and compensation.[12] How fiction-as-fantasy deploys the feminine orphan we can see in James's first major masterpiece.

II. The Portrait of a Lad(d)y

When Henry James was eight years old, he endured in the studio of Matthew Brady a portrait session described, like so much in *A Small Boy,* in terms of negation. "Sharp again is my sense of not being so adequately dressed as I should have taken thought for had I foreseen my exposure" (87). Again the threat of "exposure," emphasized this time by the photography pun. Henry James never exposed himself in fiction so vulnerably as he did in Brady's headbrace.

The Portrait of a Lady contains much autobiographical data, but it also contains traps for unwary equators of life and art.[13] In discussing Minny Temple's tuberculosis, Edel maintains that "she became, nine years after her death, the heroine of *The Portrait of a Lady"* (I, 331). There is indeed a death from tuberculosis in the novel, but the victim is Ralph Touchett. Isabel Archer evinces traits of Minny Temple, as she does of Henry James, but Isabel is *not* Minny, any more than she (or Ralph) *is* Henry. The small boy who grew up too wary of exposure to entrust himself to any one personal relationship became a novelist whose distaste for "the terrible *fluidity* of self-revelation" (*AC* 372) precluded one-to-one correspondence with any character. Studying *The Portrait of a Lady* as autobiography is useful precisely because it requires us to see how diverse James's self-representation is, how many characters reflect him. His "problem [of how] to live in England, and yet not be of it" (*PL* 35) is confronted by Daniel Touchett; his awareness that parents attempt to atone through their children for their own lives having "failed so dreadfully" (*PL* 503) is dramatized with Madame Merle and Pansy; the "selfishness" inherent in "the preference for a single life" (*PL* 282) marks Gilbert Osmond; and the Jamesian fear of "exposure" is expressed through three women. Isabel feels "the fear of exposing—not her ignorance; for that she cared comparatively little— but her possible grossness of perception" (*PL* 243); Lydia Touchett parodies James's fussiness about his health when she affirms "her wisdom in not exposing herself to the English climate" (*PL* 35); and Pansy's sense of the inadequacy of her dress recalls James's anxiety at Matthew Brady's studio as she asks Merle, "why should I expose it beside your beautiful things?" (*PL* 249).

James's self-portrayal in *The Portrait of a Lady* achieves coherence not because of any one-to-one correspondence with life, but because of the consistency with which he represents three of the things we saw in *A Small Boy:* the negating threat of mortal transience, the realization that men as well as women are marked by emasculation and lack, and the Jamesian defenses against and compensations for such a situation. Attention to these essential matters will, I hope, enable us both to gain new insight into a complicated novel and to confront the notoriously difficult end of *The Portrait of a Lady* in a way that will help account for its difficulties, though by no means explain them away, in terms of James's core fantasy of negation.

Transience marks mortals as negated from the opening of *The Portrait of a Lady.* Daniel Touchett "was not likely to displace himself" (*PL* 7), and Ralph "was not very firm on his legs" (*PL* 8). That James is representing not physical invalidism but ineluctable human vulnerability is established by the fact that robust Lord Warburton is sick too. "He is sick of life" (*PL* 10). Warburton's negation is political, for "he doesn't take himself seriously.... and he doesn't know what to believe in.... [he] can neither abolish himself as a nuisance nor maintain himself as an institution" (*PL* 66, 67). Warburton admits, "I don't approve of myself in the least" (*PL* 119). That political negation constitutes, in effect, the condition of "woman" is confirmed when Warburton goes on to equate himself, however ironically, with his powerless sister. "We neither of us have any position to speak of" (*PL* 120). Association with another powerless woman is anticipated in the first scene of the novel. Here Warburton wears "a hat which looked too big for him" (*PL* 7–8); later Pansy will wear a "hat [which] always seemed too big for her" (*PL* 326). That "she does not really fill out the part" (*PL* 340) is equally true of Warburton, as Isabel confirms. "I said she [Pansy] was limited. And so she is. And so is Lord Warburton" (*PL* 380).

Emasculate men inhabit the condition of the "feminine" at the opening of *The Portrait of a Lady,* since they are the tea drinkers. Roles seem to be reversed. Lydia and Isabel, who should be doing the honors at tea, are, the men assume, out in the great world while *they* dally on the domestic sward. If simple role reversal were, however, what James is dramatizing here, his vision of late-Victorian gender relations would be less dark than it actually is. In fact, unbeknownst to the men, the women are ensconced in Gardencourt at this moment. Thus neither sex has taken possession of the great world. The women are absent without being liberated. And as for the men, "they were not of the sex which is supposed to furnish the regular votaries of the ceremony" (*PL* 5). To be the negative of absence would give presence to men if life and art were mathematics, if in human relationships a double negative equaled a positive. In *The Portrait of a Lady,* however, doubling the negative exacerbates, rather than redeems, the condition of lack. "A woman, perhaps, can get on.... But the men ... what do they make of it over here? I don't envy them, trying to arrange themselves. Look at poor Ralph Touchett.... 'An American who lives in Europe.' That signifies absolutely nothing' " (*PL* 181–82). Negated like Ralph, who "does nothing" (*PL* 36), are his servant, who "is good for nothing; he is always looking out the window" (*PL* 524); Mr. Luce, who "was the most unoccupied man in Europe, for he not only had no duties, but he had no pleasures" (196); and Ned Rosier, who "can't go home and be a shopkeeper. . . . can't be a doctor. . . . can't be a clergyman. . . . can't be a lawyer" (*PL* 199–200).

To such negation a Gilded Age businessman might react, "what do you expect? Of course men who don't work become dysfunctional." But Henry James, as we have seen, resists this reaction formation. Everyone is negated. Goodwood and Warburton are men of the world, actively engaged in industry and politics. Yet we have seen that Caspar "is as sick . . . as Mr. Touchett," and Warburton is "sick" too. At stake is not what you do, but what doing means. As soon as you expose yourself to the vast life outside the defensive confines of any vocation, you enter the relays of mortality. Moreover, and finally more importantly, if business is not necessarily safer than leisure, leisure is not inherently superior morally. What James found distasteful about business, its competitive ferocity, its determination to appropriate, is equally true of leisure. Predation is coeval with living. Osmond confines Isabel as tightly as Warburton or Goodwood would. Her mistake is not in rejecting the ostensibly active men but in accepting the apparently passive one. Essential to the acquisitive I is the appropriating eye. To understand what *The Portrait of a Lady* is saying about negation, in other words, we must go beyond profession to perception itself.

"You look at things in a way that could make everything wrong" (*PL* 169). This sounds like a fair criticism of Gilbert Osmond, but the "you" here is Ralph Touchett.[14] It could be anyone in *The Portrait of a Lady*. Endemic to seeing is desiring. Reification, that paradigmatic motion by which capitalism reduces all value to exchange value, is the routine practice of James's leisured characters. Turning persons into objects is unmistakable with Osmond, who defines Isabel as "qualified . . . to figure in his collection of choice objects" (*PL* 279), but it also characterizes Ralph, who initially sees Isabel as "a Titian, by the post, to hang on my wall" (*PL* 59). Moreover, gender is no determinant here. Madame Merle's active role in the manipulation of Isabel is reflected in Osmond's question, "what do you want to do with her" (*PL* 222). When Ralph addresses the same question to his mother, "what do you mean to do with her. . . . what do you mean to do with her. . . . what do you mean to do with her. . . . what [do] you intend to do with her" (*PL* 39, 41), Lydia seems to respond with a moral propriety impossible to Merle. "Do with her? You talk as if she were a yard of calico" (*PL* 41). Buy Lydia is in fact already tarred with her own brush. "For a woman of my age there is no more becoming ornament than an attractive niece" (*PL* 40). That Isabel is an object for women as well as for men is evident when Ralph says

> 'I shall have the entertainment of seeing what a young lady does who won't marry Lord Warburton.'
> 'That is what your mother counts upon too,' said Isabel.
> 'Ah, there will be plenty of spectators!' (*PL* 138–39)

The "gaze" is not exclusively masculine in *The Portrait of a Lady*.[15] When Merle says to Isabel, "I want to see what life makes of you" (*PL* 174), she foresees direct entertainment for Osmond and indirect profit for herself. Both sexes are unable *not* to treat human beings as objects because both sexes sense their own essential reification. Without a positive sense of one's own subjectivity, one cannot value the other as subject, as sacredly *other*. Essential negation is what expatriation represents for both sexes in *The Portrait of a Lady*. "If we are not good Americans we are certainly poor Europeans; we have no natural place here" (*PL* 181).

Isabel attempts to maintain traditional sex divisions when she asserts that "I am not an adventurous spirit. Women are not like men" (*PL* 140). But in fact no one in the novel is "like men." Everyone is "woman" because no one is truly "adventurous."[16] No one can get beyond the "mere spectatorship" (*PL* 137) that marks Ralph and mars Osmond. Gilbert's litany, "I have neither fortune, nor fame, nor extrinsic advantages of any kind" (*PL* 287), is echoed by Merle. "What have I got? Neither husband, nor child, nor fortune, nor position, nor the traces of a beauty which I never had" (*PL* 184). Distinctions of sex vanish in a wash of negatives as relentless in *The Portrait of a Lady* as in *A Small Boy*.

> 'I never do anything,' said this young lady (*PL* 124). . . . 'I don't come up to the mark' (*PL* 136). . . . 'No; the best part is gone, and gone for nothing' (*PL* 184). . . . 'What have my talents brought me? Nothing but the need of using them still' (*PL* 185). . . . Nothing tender, nothing sympathetic . . . no wind-sown blossom, no familiar moss (*PL* 204). . . . 'I teach nothing' (*PL* 212). . . . He seemed to intimate that nothing was of much consequence (*PL* 236). . . . 'there is nothing, nothing, nothing' (*PL* 251). . . . 'I have nothing on earth to do' (*PL* 266). . . . 'He does nothing. But he doesn't like me' (*PL* 450). . . . 'Do you mean that without my *bibelots* I am nothing?' (*PL* 486). . . . 'It has not been a successful life' (*PL* 525).

The spirit that prompted James's family romance of negation prompts Ralph Touchett to say "I think I am glad to leave people" (*PL* 530).

Having as a small boy defended against the threat of extirpation by engaging in the fantasy of orphanhood, James enacts this fantasy as an adult by filling *The Portrait of a Lady* with orphans. In addition to Warburton, who "had lost both parents" (*PL* 64), and Henrietta, who is "without parents and without property" (*PL* 49), there is Ned, whose mother is never mentioned and whose "father was dead and his *bonne* was dismissed" (*PL* 198), Merle, who never refers to her mother and praises her father in the past tense (*PL* 162), and Osmond and Gemini, whose "mother had died three years after the Countess's marriage, the father having died long before" (*PL* 258–59).[17] It is left to Isabel to articulate that attractive potential of orphanhood that James fantasized about in his family romance. She functions as James's chief autobiographical resource in *The Portrait of a Lady* because she is *attracted to* negation, whereas the other characters, even Ralph Touchett, are simply constituted as negated. Isabel says, "I belong quite to the independent class. I have neither father nor mother" (*PL* 149).

The freedom of orphanhood is associated in *The Portrait of a Lady* with another obsession of *A Small Boy*, as Isabel goes on to say "I am poor." She experiences the Jamesian opposition between business, which necessitates restrictions, and pleasure, which promises liberation. This opposition originates in her life where it did in Henry's own. Her father too exhibited "occasional incoherency of conduct" (*PL* 32). On the one hand, Isabel represents that isolation from the world of money that marked the children of Henry James, Sr. Since business is "everything" in America, Isabel, like Henry James, Jr., is inevitably characterized by "nothing." "Isabel of course knew nothing about bills.... 'I don't know anything about money'.... 'She has nothing but the crumbs of that feast [her father's spending of his capital] to live on, and she doesn't really know how meagre they are'" (*PL* 22, 171).

Economic naïveté is only one aspect of Isabel's psychic economy, however, because she functions in the novel as more than a replication of Henry James. She is also a wish fulfillment that assures him compensation. Isabel is thus endowed with a childhood free of the anxiety over paternal incoherence and financial uncertainty that scarred Henry's own youth. "If he [Mr. Archer] had been troubled about money matters, nothing ever disturbed their [his children's] irreflective consciousness of many possessions" (*PL* 32). The wish-fulfilling bliss of such ignorance persists into adulthood. Since Isabel avoids the financial anxieties that James knew in his twenties and early thirties, *The Portrait of a Lady* might be seen as a fairy tale solution to such anxieties. First a good witch whisks Isabel away to Henry's cherished refuge, England; then an ideal father-surrogate absolves her of financial worry for life. Isabel has achieved material independence without having to grub for it in business.

What makes the ending of *The Portrait of a Lady* so difficult is that wish fulfillment proves finally incompatible with fairy tale. If James were writing a storybook romance, the now-rich princess would marry her prince charming and live happily ever after. Isabel marries disastrously. To understand how such an anti-fairy tale can function compensatorily as a wish fulfillment, we must understand why James's protagonist chooses a prince uncharming. "I am marrying a nonentity.... a person who has none of Lord Warburton's great advantages—no property, no title, no honours, no houses, nor lands, nor position, nor reputation, nor brilliant belongings of any sort. It is the total absence of all these things that pleases me" (*PL* 305, 321). Part of the attraction here is Isabel's power to launch Gilbert's boat, the "maternal" power to *make* him, which many critics have noticed. But the words "nonentity" and "absence" and all the negatives indicate that more is involved. Or rather, less.

Osmond is for Isabel the quintessence of absence, the essential nullity. And why would that attract her? "Of all liberties, the one she herself found sweetest was the liberty to forget" (*PL* 208). Here is where the freedom of the orphan leads ultimately: not to action but to nada. James knows well the limitations of his family romance of extirpation. It is at best a local, provisional solution because the ultimate threat is not external, not familial or even social, but internal, inherent. What is mortal about us is our own mortality; we will die even if no one kills us. Thus for a person obsessed with vulnerability, the only way to deal with the fear of being killed is to kill it—which means to kill the self. In the animal world, the dog bites the wounded paw that is wounding him; in the human world, thanatophobia leads often to suicide (Rank 71). Isabel Archer expresses Henry James's desire to escape from suffering altogether. Her Osmond constitutes his ultimate nada. Osmond has expressly defined his life to Isabel as a negative surrender. "Not to worry—not to strive nor struggle. To resign myself" (*PL* 245). That these words do not in fact characterize competitive, emulous Gilbert is irrelevant to Isabel's charmed reception of them. What Gilbert offers her is what she wants, negation. And she is willing to pay a high price for it. "It was *not* that, however, his objecting to her opinions; that was *nothing*. She had *no* opinions—*none* that she would *not* have been eager to sacrifice in the satisfaction of feeling herself loved" (*PL* 395, my emphasis).

Thus, when we see Isabel mastered by negativity after her marriage—"there was nothing to gape at, nothing to criticize, nothing even to admire" (*PL* 362)—we must not jump to the melodramatic conclusion that Ned reaches and that Isabel tries to persuade herself of: that this is all Osmond's doing. Of course he has sought a certain type of "nothing" in his wife. But Isabel has sought "nothing" too. The tragedy, almost the comedy, is that they have not meant the same thing by nothing. Negatives saturate the portrait of Isabel after her marriage:

> she appeared now to think there was nothing worth people's either differing about or agreeing upon (*PL* 363). . . . she was resolved to assume nothing. . . . she would recognize nothing (*PL* 387). . . . she answered nothing. . . . She answered nothing (*PL* 389). . . . Nothing was a pleasure to her now (*PL* 400). . . . 'I have heard nothing of it'. . . . Isabel could say nothing more; she understood nothing (*PL* 489). . . . 'I have guessed nothing'. . . . 'I don't know what you mean' (*PL* 499). . . . 'I don't know why you say such things! I don't know what you know' (*PL* 515). . . . Nothing seemed of use to her to-day (*PL* 516). . . . 'She asked nothing' (*PL* 517).

We would succumb to the temptation to blame Gilbert for Isabel's negation if we were to ignore that the desolating negatives that proliferate after her marriage derive not simply from that marriage but from the years of her life before it. Isabel has always been afraid—of knowing.

> 'I don't know—I can't judge' (*PL* 18). . . . 'I don't know what you are trying to fasten upon me, for I am not in the least an adventurous spirit' (*PL* 140). . . . 'She doesn't know what to think about the matter at all' (*PL* 193). . . . 'I don't want to know anything more—I know too much already' (*PL* 237). . . . 'I would rather hear nothing that Pansy may not!' (*PL* 329).

Fear of knowledge involves what Henry James fears most: exposure. "A large fortune means freedom, and I am afraid of that. . . . I am not sure that it's not a greater happiness to be powerless" (*PL* 206). In expressing her specific fear about inherited wealth, Isabel is giving voice to the larger fear and the larger issue of freedom itself, the orphan's legacy. It necessitates exposure. It flaunts that very vulnerability to which James was pathologically sensitive. Gilbert Osmond as negation is the ultimate defense against and compensation for the negating forces of experience.

He is also more. He is compensation for the terrible year of 1878. To indulge, through *The Portrait of a Lady,* his homoerotic love for William, Henry must do more than switch from male to female protagonists and invest Isabel with aspects of himself. He must also project aspects of William onto Gilbert. This is easy enough. In his last big novel, *The American* (1877), Henry had already portrayed unflattering aspects of his older brother, both in the coldness of the elder Belle-garde, and, as William himself recognized, in the hypercritical morbidity of the little American tourist, Reverend Babcock.[18] What is startling about the portrait of Gilbert Osmond is not that these features recur, but how much more obviously and extensively William is present by 1881: "He was a man of forty, with a well-shaped head, upon which the hair, still dense but prematurely grizzled, had been cropped close. He had a thin, delicate, sharply cut face, of which the only fault was that it looked too pointed; an appearance of which the shape of his beard contributed not a little" (*PL* 211). Born in 1842, William James is on the threshold of "forty" in 1881. Although his hair would not grizzle until later, the other features of Isabel/Henry's portrait of Gilbert are accurate enough; all are suggested in the two illustrations I have included, the photograph from 1865 and the self-portrait (sans beard) from 1867. In body type, William shares Gilbert's "light smooth slenderness of structure" (*PL* 242). The intellectual acuity of each man is signaled in "his luminous intelligent eye" (*PL* 211). And temperamentally, William as well as Gilbert "was certainly fastidious and critical" (*PL* 242). Isabel adds to her portrait that "he was *probably* irritable" (*PL* 242, my emphasis) because she does not know yet what her creator had already suffered from for years, how punishingly irritable William's fastidiously critical sensibility could be. What the younger brother said about the elder while he was composing *The Portrait of a Lady,* "he takes himself and his nerves and his physical condition too seriously" (Edel II, 419), is said about Osmond in the novel. "He takes himself so seriously" (*PL* 319).

Probably most aggressive is Henry's implication of William in one other trait conferred upon Osmond. "In itself your little picture is very good. . . . But as the only thing you do it's so little" (*PL* 224). Both William and Gilbert are amateur painters of some talent. By denying to Gilbert all true creative genius, Henry can take revenge upon the artistic and scholastic superiority that William flaunted through-out their school years. The genius evident in producing *The Portrait of a Lady* allows Henry to take the high ground here. And high ground is essential for wish fulfillment. As the woman scorned by William, Henry expresses through Isabel a double triumph. Her marriage with Osmond is the realization of Henry's courtship of William, while the public revelation of Osmond's marital failure constitutes Henry's revenge upon the one who had failed him by marrying another.

More than such nastiness is involved, however. The year 1878 confirmed Henry James in renunciation: there would be no more intimate relationships. For *The Portrait of a Lady* to function as truly compensatory wish fulfillment, James must handle not only Isabel's marriage to and rupture with Osmond but also her life afterwards. She must walk the narrow line between two types of negation presented in the novel. She must avoid the deadening lovelessness of Gilbert, Merle, and Lydia, who end up cut off from life, yet she must not succumb to the deadening self-effacement inherent in unions like Warburton's with "Lady Flora, or Lady Felicia—something of that sort" (*PL* 526). How Isabel walks this line caused immediate controversy in 1881 and has remained controversial ever since. To walk my own fine line through the critical controversy and through James's text, I must proceed carefully.

Readers who find the ending of *The Portrait of a Lady* satisfying tend to stress Isabel's renewed commitment to life. They are supported by important textual moments, particularly Ralph's immense words, "Dear Isabel, life is better; for in life there is love. Death is good—but there is no love" (*PL* 530). At one level of the consciousness Henry James believed this sincerely. He practiced a commitment to people throughout his long life, proving himself a devoted son and a generous sibling and a good friend again and again. Since most readers share with Ralph, Isabel, and Henry James the belief that life is better than death, how can the ending of the novel have generated substantial reader dissatisfaction?

There is, I believe, something else going on, in Henry James and in *The Portrait of a Lady*, something subversive to a commitment to life. And it is this something that many readers are responding to when they find Isabel's return to Rome unsatisfying. What makes critical analysis particularly complicated here is that these readers have tended, I believe, to misexplain their dissatisfaction. They are in touch with something real, but they misdefine it. They tend to explain their dissatisfaction with Isabel's return to Rome by saying that what she should do is run off with Caspar. They find Isabel problematic, in other words, because they see her fleeing the first truly erotic experience of her life. Though these readers have for textual support the famous kiss (and the still more lurid "white lightning" image of the New York Edition), the kiss scene as a whole cannot, I believe, be enlisted to prove that Henry James espouses Isabel's elopement with Caspar. Before I attempt to define what I feel *is* subversive about the final pages of the novel, let me rule out adultery as the subversive element.

For all his phallic puissance, Caspar, too, is marked by lack. " 'There *is* nothing left for Mr. Goodwood'.... The future had nothing for him.... He was hopeless, he was helpless, he was superfluous.... 'I have nothing else to do'....'I can't understand, I can't penetrate you" (*PL* 464, 467, 468, 471). Caspar, "quite as sick ... as Mr. Touchett" and Lord Warburton, has not learned James's lesson about negation. He holds to patriarchal stereotypes that credit the male with presence and reduce the woman to absence. Having said early on that "an unmarried woman—a girl of your age—is not independent. There are all sorts of things she cannot do" (*PL* 149), Caspar continues at the end to give the negative constructions to Isabel, and now he bestows the positive on himself. "You don't know where to turn. Now it is that I want you to think of me.... You don't know where to turn; turn to me!" (*PL* 542, 543). What Caspar offers Isabel is a future not of sexual liberation but of perpetuated inequality. Freedom is not the watchword here because the absence of any truly egalitarian viewpoint characterizes Caspar's empty rhetoric. He emphasizes his paternalism by incorporating Isabel into that exchange of women that Lévi-Strauss defines as the origin of patriarchy: "he [Ralph] left you to my care" (PL 541). For his sins Caspar then becomes the butt of something close to outright sarcasm from the Jamesian narrator: " '. . . my care,' said Goodwood, as if he were making a great point" (PL 541).

If James does not present adultery with Caspar as a serious alternative to Isabel's commitment to Rome, and yet if, as I believe, reader dissatisfaction with Isabel is a response to something truly unsettling about the end of the novel, where does the subversion lie? One answer is suggested by a narrative fact, a decision made by James, that has never to my knowledge been noticed by critics. What is Isabel's *final* situation? The answer seems obvious: "she has gone back to her husband." How easily James could have arranged things this way. But in fact *The Portrait of a Lady* ends not with Isabel having gone back to her husband, but with her *going* back. "She came here yesterday, and spent the night. But this morning she has started for Rome" (PL 545). How easily James could have had Henrietta say: "she came here yesterday, and took the afternoon train that brought her to Rome this morning." Why does James end the novel with Isabel in transit between London and Rome? If he wants to end with an unqualified espousal of commitment, he need only position Isabel in Rome already reengaged with Osmond and Pansy. He could even have Henrietta say: ". . . to Rome this morning. She was going directly to Pansy's convent." Why does James leave Isabel suspended between London and Rome?

For the same reason that he has her flee from Caspar in the first place. Freedom abides finally for James the artist where it did for the orphan Henry: not in relationships, but in isolation. James leaves Isabel suspended between departure and arrival, poised between separation and commitment. Isabel is neither with the pair who represent the bondage of advocated adultery, Caspar and Henrietta, nor with the pair who represent the bondage of conventional domesticity, Gilbert and Pansy. Isabel is alone, yet not solipsistic, neither exposed nor dead. Her train ride is a timeless suspension. Like the figures on Keats's Grecian Urn, Isabel is preserved in mid-motion: ". . . do not grieve;/She cannot fade. . . . for ever young;/All breathing human passion far above" (18–19, 27–28).

> To cease utterly, to give it all up and not know anything more—this idea was as sweet as the vision of a cool bath in a marble tank, in a darkened chamber, in a hot land. She had moments, indeed, in her journey from Rome, which were almost as good as being dead. She sat in her corner, so motionless, so passive, simply with the sense of being carried, so detached from hope and regret, that if her spirit was haunted with sudden pictures, it might have been the spirit disembarrassed of the flesh. There was nothing to regret now—that was all over. (PL 516)

Immediately a fact must be faced: this passage presents Isabel's emotions on the ride *to*—not *from*—England. If withdrawal represents James's ultimate ideal, why is there no rearticulation of Isabel's emotion on the ultimate ride, the one *back to Italy?*[19] "Life is better." Granted the power of Ralph's words, the issue is not whether he speaks for Henry James here, but whether he says all that is on James's mind. Unlike the readers whose satisfaction with the ending of *The Portrait of a Lady* derives from a sense that Ralph does indeed speak for an unambiguous James, a James who finally sides unilaterally with life and allows Ralph's words to redeem Isabel from the death-in-life represented by the tank image, I experience a more conflicted ending. I believe that James wants to have things both ways. Commitment and isolation.

Which is to say that James cannot affirm commitment unilaterally. The orphan fantasy, the need for freedom through isolation, is too strong. At war in James are the life and death drives as Freud defined them.[20] The tank image represents the death drive, the organism's determination to return to the condition of nonexistence. Suicide cannot be countenanced as the resolution of either James's novel or his family romance, however. He shares too determinedly Ralph's belief in life. What is the fantasy of the feminine orphan, after all, but a way to stay alive? Thus James's lifelong dilemma confronts him now: how to remain committed to love, and yet maintain enough distance to escape the exposure inevitable with intimacy; how to remain in life, but not of it? The ending of *The Portrait of a Lady* must answer this question by doing double duty: it must foster both relationships and isolation, must espouse both the socially responsible commitment to life that James shares with his Victorian readers, and the private fantasy of subversive separation that defends him from the menaces of human bonds. How can the ending effect this?

What James cannot do is simply repeat the tank image as Isabel rides back to Rome. Her mood is altered substantially. Caspar's kiss, or rather her reaction against it as she flees back to the house, has ended the ambivalence, the attraction to both orthodox relationships *and* nada, that marked her trip from Rome, even as it has marked Henry James's whole life. Now, returning to Rome, Isabel no longer shares James's need for isolation. Her role as a character in her own right has, in other words, come into conflict with her role as James's wish fulfillment figure. The heroine no longer feels the attraction to the cool tank of water that still impels her author. His solution? Rather than give up his fantasy of isolation, James in his genius manages to discover a formal equivalent *at the level of the plot* to the image of the tank. By allowing Isabel to return to marriage and yet by suspending her between England and Rome, James can both make a commitment to commitment, a pledge to life, and yet avoid having to honor it. Isabel need never reach Italy—life—*in this narrative.* James thus allows himself both the comfort of his good intentions and the pleasure of fantasized isolation. His artistry assures both that Isabel's train will never arrive and that her acts of commitment will suffice as a rejection of suicide.

James's attempt to have his cake and eat it too is what has caused, I believe, much of the century-old controversy over the ending of *The Portrait of a Lady*. Great works of art often feature the war between life and death, but these works, *Hamlet* say, are not often required to satisfy a private authorial fantasy that is at war with the public commitment shared with his audience. In *The Portrait of a Lady*, a manifest commitment to life is subverted by a latent espousal of orphanhood. Remember: the same character who said that life is better than death also says *in the same speech* that he is glad to leave people. Ralph articulates both of Henry James's contradictory desires. That these two desires cannot both be satisfied by the ending of the novel is what has left many readers dissatisfied. James's need, however, his determination to use fiction as a fantasy to satisfy what life cannot provide, is so strong that he insists upon self-satisfaction regardless of the risk to his artifact. Isabel is thus allowed to hang suspended in her train car, enwombed, floating as free of humans as the blessed, the fantasized orphan is. Like Ralph, she can do without the people, yet unlike Ralph she is saved from the death feared by Henry James and us all.

NOTES

To the friends who attended patiently upon and contributed imaginatively to the protracted development of this essay, I am most sincerely grateful: Beth Sharon Ash, Sarah Daugherty, Paul John Eakin, Susan M. Griffin, Alfred Habegger, Carol Holly, Marcia Jacobson, and Lyall Powers.

[1] For studies of family romance more recent than Freud's see: R. C. Bak, Helen K. Gediman, Phyllis Greenacre, Linda Joan Kaplan, and Christine van Boheemen-Saaf.

[2] Young Henry James comes closest to this classic version of the fantasy when he describes with empathy and even envy the Prince Imperial, the baby son of Napoleon III, "borne forth for his airing or his progress to Saint-Cloud in the splendid coach that gave a glimpse of appointed and costumed nursing breasts and laps, and beside which the *cent-gardes,* all light-blue and silver and intensely erect quick jolt, rattled with pistols raised and cocked" (*SB* 332). The nursing breasts and the cocked pistols represent well the Imperial Parents of fantasy.

[3] Again and again the fantasy recurs: the "rare radiance of privation" experienced by orphaned cousin Gus, "the undomesticated character at its highest" enjoyed by orphaned cousin Bob (*SB* 173, 188; see also 15, 129, 189, 402). Wilkie reflects Henry's obsession with orphanhood when he expresses the classic family romance fantasy. "I became quite convinced by the time I was twelve years old that I was a foundling" (Maher 12; also quoted by Edel I, 60).

[4] The full quotation from Emerson appears in Perry (3). An indication of how young Henry felt menaced by parental aggression is indicated by another version of the family romance of childhood that was also articulated by James in old age. In 1907 James recalls his boyhood fascination with the fairy tale "Hop o' My Thumb," "my small romance of yearning predilection" (*HJL* 446–47). He emphasizes "the parents plotting to mislay their brood," and "the small boy, smaller than one's self, who had in that crisis gained immortality" (447). This small boy flees the lethal parents, in effect orphaning himself before he is destroyed by them. For calling my attention to "Hop o' My Thumb," and for much else, I am indebted to Professor Susan M. Griffin. Feinstein recognizes astutely Henry Sr.'s "death wish" for his children (255–56). Strouse focuses on the lethal side of Henry Sr. when she discusses his dealing with Alice's suicidal inclinations (188). That Alice may have harbored some of the homicidal aspect of Henry's desire to *be* an orphan is also suggested by Strouse (139).

[5] James tends to make the man-versus-woman split especially sharp in *The American Scene,* where his intention is quite different from that of *A Small Boy.* Depicting American society at the beginning of the twentieth century, James is showing what has happened to the country in the more than fifty years since the time of *A Small Boy.* In the autobiographical volume he is presenting both a family situation and a more leisured society, where men and women were not as relentlessly divided as they had become by the turn of the century.

[6] Laura Claridge and Elizabeth Langland, personal correspondence with William Veeder.

[7] That this quotation comes from the New York Edition of *The Portrait of a Lady* indicates that James was more self-conscious about the non-gendered nature of "spending" after the turn of the century than he was in 1881.

[8] For a detailed discussion of "spending," see Barker-Benfield's chapter on "The Spermatic Economy and Proto-Sublimation."

[9] Edel and Strouse give proper stress to the enormous contribution that the anima made to James's psyche. In "The American Girl of the Period," I discuss this figure prior to James's presentations of her. Taylor speaks for many critics when she observes that "in the fiction of Henry James, the female characters often seem much more 'masculine' than the males. In all his fiction it is the women who dare to act, who move about . . . who simply *live*" (157). Though Taylor also stresses a second link between James and women, what she calls "physical vulnerability," I am finally making a different argument when I maintain that *no one* in James is in fact "masculine," that everyone is effeminated by culture and mortality.

[10] James's homosexual inclinations were first given serious treatment by Edel in connection with the novelist's relationship with the Scandinavian sculptor Henrik Anderson in the 1890s (IV, 306–316). In 1979, Hall traced these inclinations back to the 1870s in connection with Henry's relations with his brother William. In addition to Feinstein's subsequent work on identification and twinship, see Horwitz's unfairly neglected study of the forces which produced James's homosexual inclinations. In a recent essay, Hall quotes a letter from Edel: " 'your entire line of evidence is certainly convincing to me' " ("Henry James" 84–85). Edel added that "once we agree on Henry's love fixation on William, that explains a lot of things" (86). As early as 1962, Maxwell Geismar discusses "The Pupil" in terms of male bonds and implicates William James (115–16).

[11] Edel first noticed this fact about James's protagonists; Hall then took it up. Warren correctly notes that "of course, *Daisy Miller* was written before the marriage" (306 n. 26). Her additional criticisms of the Edel-Hall position seem weaker, however. "Christina Light was created four years earlier. Furthermore, some of his best male protagonists—Lambert Strether, Hyacinth Robinson—came long afterward. To draw such conclusions on the basis of the tenuous evidence available (most of which relies upon a personal interpretation of the fiction, e.g., the novel *Confidence*) overlooks other forces active in James's life at the time, including his reading and his European experience" (306 n. 26). Christina Light is not the *protagonist* of *Roderick Hudson*. Moreover, Edel and Hall are not of course pretending that after 1878 Henry James never again presented male protagonists. Their focus is upon Henry's *immediate* response to abandonment by William. Finally, Hall and Edel would surely agree that only by combining a psychoanalytic perspective with others (which would include not only James's reading and European experience but also his prescient recognition of gender as a social construct) can we understand so overdetermined a phenomenon as his personality and creativity.

[12] Taylor summarizes various explanations, especially those of Virginia Woolf and Simone de Beauvoir, for the use of female masks by male writers (1–4) and relates James's empathy with women to his sense of physical vulnerability.

[13] James himself connects Isabel's childhood to his own (*SB* 9). Edel notes several important autobiographical aspects of *The Portrait of a Lady* (I, 51, 61, 85, 86, 237, 332–33), though some connections between art and life seem forced. In addition to the claim that Minny Temple *became* the heroine of the novel, there is the argument that Frank Boott is the model for Gilbert Osmond, despite Edel's admission that Gilbert's principal trait, his cruelty, is utterly lacking in the kindly Boott (I, 254).

[14] Although Kaston has recently reaffirmed the view that Ralph is indeed authoring a different scenario from that of Osmond, and though I would certainly accept Isabel's distinction between the two men ("Ralph was generous and her husband was not" [*PL* 400]), I agree with many readers who see little to choose between the two men early in the novel. Ralph is terribly proprietary. His Osmond-like view of Isabel as "an entertainment of high order" (*PL* 58) is contested first by Daniel: "you speak as if it [changing the will] were for your entertainment" (*PL* 171); then by Henrietta: "Is that why your father did it—for your amusement" (*PL* 205); and finally by Isabel herself: "You say you amused yourself in planning out my future. . . . Don't amuse yourself too much, or I shall think you are doing it at my expense" (*PL* 318).

[15] For a lucid discussion of Freud's making the gaze a phallic activity in "The Uncanny" and French feminism's response to such gendering, see Moi, 134–35, 180 n. 8.

[16] Two exceptions might seem to be Henrietta and Caspar. Both, however, are unable to sustain their adventurousness. Isabel's disappointment at Henrietta's succumbing to marriage is supported by the name James gives to Henrietta's fiancé. "Bantling" means "baby." Caspar is active in the factory and would have been valiant on the battlefield, but Caspar was, emblematically, born too late to fight in the Civil War.

[17] No mention is made of Caspar's mother; his father is referred to in ways that make it unclear whether the factory proprietor is still alive (107).

[18] For William's recognition of himself in Babcock, see Perry I, 371. Edel's discussion of the link between William and *The American* (I, 299) is criticized by DeLoach, who goes beyond noting the often

mechanical quality of Edel's insistence upon the Esau-Jacob motif in James's life and fiction and insists unconvincingly that Henry borrows from William some of the positive aspects of Christopher Newman.
[19] For his help with this question, which dogged early drafts of my essay, I am indebted to Professor Lyall Powers.
[20] See especially section IV of *The Ego and the Id*.

KEY TO WORKS BY HENRY JAMES

AM—The Ambassadors. 2 vols. New York: Scribner's, 1909.

AC—The Art of Criticism. Ed. William Veeder and Susan M. Griffin. Chicago: U of Chicago P, 1986.

NB—The Complete Notebooks of Henry James. Ed. Leon Edel and Lyall H. Powers. New York: Oxford U P, 1987.

GB—The Golden Bowl. 2 vols. New York: Scribner's, 1909.

HJL—Henry James Letters. Vol. 4. Ed. Leon Edel. Cambridge: Harvard U P, 1984.

NSB—Notes of a Son and Brother. New York: Scribner's, 1914.

PL—The Portrait of a Lady. New York: Signet, 1963 (1881 text).

RH—Roderick Hudson. New York: Scribner's, 1907.

SB—A Small Boy and Others. New York: Scribner's, 1913.

SP—The Spoils of Poynton. New York: Scribner's, 1908.

WD—The Wings of the Dove. 2 vols. New York: Scribner's, 1909.

OTHER WORKS CITED

Bak, R. C. "Discussion of Greenacre's 'Family Romance of Artist.'" *Psychoanalytic Study of Children* 13 (1958): 42–43.

Barker-Benfield, G. J. *Horrors of the Half-Known Life*. New York: Harper & Row, 1976.

Cargill, Oscar. *The Novels of Henry James*. New York: Macmillian, 1961.

DeLoach, Charles. "The Influence of William James on the Composition of *The American*." *Interpretations* 7 (1975): 38–43.

Eakin, Paul John. *Fictions in Autobiography*. Princeton: Princeton U P, 1985, 56–125.

———. "Henry James's 'Obscure Hurt': Can Autobiography Serve Biography?" *New Literary History* 19 (1987–88): 675–92.

Edel, Leon. *Henry James*. 5 vols. Philadelphia: J. B. Lippincott, 1953–72.

Feinstein, Howard M. *Becoming William James*. Ithaca: Cornell U P, 1984.

Fowler, Virginia C. *Henry James's American Girl: The Embroidery on the Canvas*. Madison: U of Wisconsin P, 1984.

Freud, Sigmund. *The Ego and the Id. The Standard Edition of the Complete Psychological Works of Sigmund Freud*. Ed. James Strachey. 24 vols. London: The Hogarth Press, 1961. Vol. 19, sect. 4, 40–47.

———. "Family Romances." In *Collected Papers*. Ed. James Strachey. 5 vols. New York: Basic Books, 1959. Vol. 5, 74–78.

Gediman, Helen K. "Narcissistic Trauma, Object Loss, and the Family Romance." *Psychoanalytic Review* 61 (1974): 203–215.

Geismar, Maxwell. *Henry James and the Jacobites*. Boston: Houghton Mifflin, 1963.

Greenacre, Phyllis. "Family Romance of Artist." *Psychoanalytic Study of Children* 13 (1958): 9–36.

Hall, Richard. "Henry James: Interpreting an Obsessive Memory." In *Literary Visions of Homosexuality*. Ed. Stuart Kellogg. New York: Haworth, 1983, 83–97.

———. "An Obscure Hurt." *The New Republic* (April 28 and May 5, 1979): 25–31, 25–29.

Hirsch, David H. "Henry James and the Seal of Love." *Modern Language Studies* 13 (1985): 39–60.

Holly, Carol. " 'Absolutely Acclaimed': The Cure for Depression in James's Final Phase." *The Henry James Review* 8 (1987): 126–38.

———. "Review of Paul John Eakin, *Fictions in Autobiography*." *The Henry James Review* 9 (1988): 148–51.

Horwitz, B. D. "The Sense of Desolation in Henry James." *Psychocultural Review* 1 (1977): 466–92.

Kaplan, Linda Joan. "The Concept of the Family Romance." *Psychoanalytic Review* 61 (1974): 169–202.

Kaston, Carren. *Imagination and Desire in the Fiction of Henry James*. New Brunswick: Rutgers U P, 1984.

Maher, Jane. *Biography of Broken Fortunes: Wilkie and Bob, Brothers of William, Henry, and Alice James*. Hamden, CT: Archon, 1986.

Moi, Toril. *Sexual/Textual Politics*. London: Methuen, 1985.

Perry, Ralph Barton. *The Thought and Character of William James*. Vol. 1. Boston: Little, Brown, 1935.

Rank, Otto. *The Double*. Trans. and ed. Harry Tucker, Jr. Chapel Hill: U of North Carolina P, 1971.

Rowe, John Carlos. *The Theoretical Dimensions of Henry James*. Madison: U of Wisconsin P, 1984.

Taylor, Anne Robinson. *Male Novelists and Their Female Voices: Literary Masquerades*. Troy: Whitson, 1981.

van Boheemen-Saaf, Christine. " 'The Universe Makes an Indifferent Parent': *Bleak House* and the Victorian Family Romance." In *Interpreting Lacan*, ed. Joseph H. Smith and William Kerrigan, *Psychiatry and the Humanities* 6 New Haven: Yale U P, 1983: 225–57, reprinted in modified form in van Boheemen-Saaf's *The Novel as Family Romance*. Ithaca: Cornell U P, 1987: 101–131.

Veeder, William. "The American Girl of the Period." Elizabeth K. Helsinger, Robin Lauterbach Sheets, and William Veeder. In *The Woman Question: Society and Literature in Britain and America, 1837–1883*. 3 vols. New York: Garland, 1983. Vol. 3, 171–192.

Warren, Joyce W. *The American Narcissus*. New Brunswick: Rutgers U P, 1984.

CONTRIBUTORS

HAROLD BLOOM is Sterling Professor of the Humanities at Yale University and Henry W. and Albert A. Berg Professor of English at the New York University Graduate School. He is a 1985 MacArthur Foundation Award recipient, served as the Charles Eliot Norton Professor of Poetry at Harvard University (1987–88), and is the author of nineteen books, the most recent being *The Book of J* (1990). Currently he is editing the Chelsea House series Modern Critical Views and The Critical Cosmos, and other Chelsea House series in literary criticism.

TONY TANNER is Director of English Studies at King's College, Cambridge. His works include *The Reign of Wonder: Naivety and Reality in American Literature* (1965), *Henry James: The Writer and His Work* (1985), and *Scenes of Nature, Signs of Men* (1987). He is also the editor of *Henry James: Modern Judgments* (1968).

ANNETTE NIEMTZOW has taught in English departments at Queen's College, CUNY, and Bryn Mawr. She has written on the slave narrative, Frederick Douglass, and Virginia Woolf, and is presently manager of Central Park's School of Tennis.

NINA BAYM is Professor of English at the University of Illinois at Urbana. She is the author of *The Shape of Hawthorne's Career* (1976), *Novels, Readers, and Reviewers: Responses to Fiction in Antebellum America* (1984), and has written on Cooper, Melville, James, and women's fiction.

ZEPHYRA PORAT teaches at Tel-Aviv University.

JONATHAN FREEDMAN is Associate Professor of English at Yale University and is the author of *Professions of Taste: Henry James, British Aestheticism, and Commodity Culture* (1990).

STEPHANIE A. SMITH is Assistant Professor of English at the University of Florida. She is the author of two novels, *Snow Eyes* (1985) and *The Boy Who Was Thrown Away* (1987), and is presently working on a book on American literature.

WILLIAM VEEDER is Professor of English at the University of Chicago. Among his works are *Henry James: The Lessons of the Master: Popular Fiction and Personal Style in the Nineteenth Century* (1975) and *Mary Shelley & Frankenstein: The Fate of Androgyny* (1986). He also co-edited, with Susan M. Griffin, *The Art of Criticism: Henry James on the Theory and the Practice of Fiction* (1986) and, with Gordon Hirsch, Dr. Jekyll and Mr. Hyde *After One Hundred Years* (1988).

BIBLIOGRAPHY

Allen, Elizabeth. "*The Portrait of a Lady.*" In *A Woman's Place in the Novels of Henry James.* New York: St. Martin's Press, 1984, pp. 58–82.

Anderson, Charles R. "Introduction" to *The Portrait of a Lady.* New York: Collier Books, 1962, pp. 5–11.

————. "Person, Place, and Thing in James's *The Portrait of a Lady.*" In *Essays on American Literature in Honor of Jay B. Hubbell,* edited by Clarence Gohdes. Durham, NC: Duke University Press, 1967, pp. 164–82.

Anesko, Michael. "Stuff as Dreams Are Made On: Henry James and His Audience." In *"Friction with the Market": Henry James and the Profession of Authorship.* New York: Oxford University Press, 1986, pp. 11–60.

Auchard, John. "Dialectical Marriage in *The Portrait of a Lady* and *The Spoils of Poynton.*" In *Silence in Henry James: The Heritage of Symbolism and Decadence.* University Park: Pennsylvania State University Press, 1986, pp. 55–84.

Auchincloss, Louis. "The International Situation: *The Portrait of a Lady.*" In *Reading Henry James.* Minneapolis: University of Minnesota Press, 1975, pp. 56–70.

Bellringer, Alan W. "American Girls—'Daisy Miller,' 'The Pension Beaurepas,' *Washington Square, The Portrait of a Lady.*" In *Modern Novelists: Henry James.* New York: St. Martin's Press, 1968, pp. 48–68.

Berkson, Dorothy. "Why Does She Marry Osmond? The Education of Isabel Archer." *American Transcendental Quarterly* No. 60 (June 1986): 53–71.

Berland, Alwyn. "The Sacred Quest: *The Portrait of a Lady.*" In *Culture and Conduct in the Novels of Henry James.* Cambridge: Cambridge University Press, 1981, pp. 90–135.

Blackmur, R. P. "In the Country of the Blue." *Kenyon Review* 5 (1943): 595–617.

————. "Introduction" to *The Portrait of a Lady.* New York: Dell, 1961, pp. 5–12.

Blodgett, Harriet. "Verbal Clues in *The Portrait of a Lady:* A Note in Defense of Isabel Archer." In *Studies in American Fiction* 7 (1979): 27–36.

Bloom, Harold, ed. *Henry James's* The Portrait of a Lady. New York: Chelsea House, 1987.

Bobbitt, Joan. "Aggressive Innocence in *The Portrait of a Lady.*" *Massachusetts Studies in English* 4, No. 1 (Spring 1973): 31–37.

Boren, Lynda S. "Undoing the Mona Lisa, Henry James's Quarrel with da Vinci and Pater." *Mosaic* 20, No. 3 (Summer 1987): 95–111.

Bowden, Ernest T. "The Mighty Individual." In *The Dungeon of the Heart: Human Isolation and the American Novel.* New York: Macmillan, 1961, pp. 89–102.

————. "The Theme of Moral Decision." In *The Themes of Henry James: A System of Observation through the Visual Arts.* New Haven: Yale University Press, 1956, pp. 53–66.

Broderick, John C. " 'Henry James and Gestation': A Reply." *College English* 21 (1959): 499.

Brooks, Peter. "The Melodramatic Imagination." *Partisan Review* 39 (1972): 195–212.

Brownell, W. C. "James's *Portrait of a Lady.*" *The Nation,* February 2, 1882, pp. 102–3.

Buitenhuis, Peter, ed. *Twentieth Century Interpretations of* The Portrait of a Lady: *A Collection of Critical Essays.* Englewood Cliffs, NJ: Prentice-Hall, 1968.

Burrell, John Angus. *The Dial,* September 27, 1917, pp. 260–62.

Cameron, Sharon. "The Preface, Revision, and Ideas of Consciousness." In *Thinking in Henry James.* Chicago: University of Chicago Press, 1989, pp. 32–82.

Canby, Henry Seidel. "Henry's Imagination Turns Home." In *Turn West, Turn East: Mark Twain and Henry James.* Boston: Houghton Mifflin, 1951, pp. 151–60.

Cargill, Oscar. "*The Portrait of a Lady:* A Critical Reappraisal." *Modern Fiction Studies* 3 (1957): 11–32.

Collins, Martha. "The Narrator, the Satellites, and Isabel Archer: Point of View in *The Portrait of a Lady.*" *Studies in the Novel* 8 (1976): 142–57.

Crews, Frederick C. "Society and the Hero." In *The Tragedy of Manners: Moral Drama in the Later Novels of Henry James.* New Haven: Yale University Press, 1957, pp. 13–19.

Daiches, David. "Sensibility and Technique (Preface to a Critique)." *Kenyon Review* 5 (1943): 573–77.

Djwa, Sandra. "Ut Pictura Poesis: *The Making of a Lady.*" *Henry James Review* 7 (1986): 72–85.

Donoghue, Denis. "Plot, Fact and Value." In *The Ordinary Universe: Soundings in Modern Literature.* New York: Macmillan, 1968, pp. 51–77.

Dove, John Roland. "Tragic Consciousness in Isabel Archer." *Studies in American Literature* 8 (1960): 78–94.

Drew, Elizabeth. "The Game of Art: *The Portrait of a Lady.*" In *The Novel: A Modern Guide to Fifteen English Masterpieces.* New York: W. W. Norton, 1963, pp. 224–44.

Dryden, Edgar A. "The Image in the Mirror: The Double Economy of James's *Portrait.*" In *Money Talks: Language and Lucre in American Fiction,* edited by Roy R. Male. Norman: University of Oklahoma Press, 1981, pp. 31–49.

Eakin, Paul John. "The Tragedy of Self-Culture: *The Portrait of a Lady.*" In *The New England Girl: Cultural Ideals in Hawthorne, Stowe, Howells, and James.* Athens: University of Georgia Press, 1976, pp. 168–94.

Edwards, Lee R. " 'Weddings Be Funerals': Sexuality, Maternity, and Selfhood in *Jude the Obscure, The Awakening* and *The Portrait of a Lady.*" In *Psyche as Hero: Female Heroism and Fictional Form.* Middletown, CT: Wesleyan University Press, 1984, pp. 104–40.

Fogel, Daniel Mark, ed. "New Essays on *The Portrait of a Lady.*" *Henry James Review* 7, Nos. 2–3 (Winter–Spring 1986): 1–6.

Garrett, Peter K. "Henry James: The Creations of Consciousness." In *Scene and Symbol from George Eliot to James Joyce: Studies in Changing Fictional Mode.* New Haven: Yale University Press, 1969, pp. 76–159.

Geismar, Maxwell. "The Seventies: The Nostalgic Poison." In *Henry James and the Jacobites.* Boston: Houghton Mifflin, 1963, pp. 40–45.

Gervais, David. *Flaubert and Henry James: A Study in Contrasts.* New York: Barnes & Noble, 1978.

Gribble, Jennifer. "Introduction" to *The Lady of Shalott in the Victorian Novel.* London: Macmillan, 1983, pp. 26–35.

Habegger, Alfred. "The Fatherless Heroine and the Filial Son: Deep Background for *The Portrait of a Lady.*" In *Henry James and the "Woman Business."* New York: Cambridge University Press, 1989, pp. 151–81.

Halperin, John. "Trollope, James, and the International Theme." In *Jane Austen's Lovers and Other Studies in Fiction and History from Austen to le Carré.* New York: St. Martin's Press, 1988, pp. 108–17.

Hirsch, David H. "Henry James and the Seal of Love." *Modern Language Studies* 13, No. 4 (Fall 1985): 39–60.

Horne, Philip. "Perspectives in *The Portrait of a Lady.*" In *Henry James and Revision: The New York Edition.* Oxford: Clarendon Press, 1990, pp. 184–227.

Howells, W. D. "Henry James, Jr." *Century* 26 (1882): 25–29.

Hutchinson, Stuart. "Beyond the Victorians: *The Portrait of a Lady.*" In *Reading the Victorian Novel: Detail into Form,* edited by Ian Gregor. New York: Barnes & Noble, 1980, pp. 274–87.

Johnson, Courtney. "Adam and Eve and Isabel Archer." *Renascence* 21 (1969): 134–44, 167.

Kaul, A. N. "*The Portrait of a Lady:* Henry James and the Avoidance of Comedy." In *The Action of English Comedy: Studies in the Encounter of Abstraction and Experience from Shakespeare to Shaw.* New Haven: Yale University Press, 1970, pp. 250–83.

Kenney, Blair Gates. "The Two Isabels: A Study in Distortion." *Victorian Newsletter* No. 25 (Spring 1964): 15–17.

King, Jeannette. "*The Portrait of a Lady.*" In *Tragedy in the Victorian Novel: Theory and Practice in the Novels of George Eliot, Thomas Hardy and Henry James.* Cambridge: Cambridge University Press, 1978, pp. 139–49.

Kleinberg, Seymour. "Ambiguity and Ambivalence: The Psychology of Sexuality in Henry James's *The Portrait of a Lady.*" *Markham Review* 1 (1969): 2–7.

Knights, L. C. "Henry James and Human Liberty." *Sewanee Review* 83 (1975): 10–13.

Krause, Sydney J. "James's Revisions of the Style of *The Portrait of a Lady.*" *American Literature* 30 (1958): 67–88.

Krier, William J. "The 'Latent Extravagance' of *The Portrait of a Lady.*" *Mosaic* 9, No. 3 (Spring 1976): 57–65.

Leavis, F. R. "George Eliot: *Daniel Deronda* and *The Portrait of a Lady.*" *Scrutiny* 14 (1946): 102–31.

———. "Henry James: To *The Portrait of a Lady.*" In *The Great Tradition: George Eliot, Henry James, Joseph Conrad.* London: Chatto & Windus, 1948, pp. 126–53.

Leavis, Q. D. "A Note on Literary Indebtedness: Dickens, George Eliot, Henry James." *Hudson Review* 8 (1955): 423–28.

Lebowitz, Naomi. *The Imagination of Loving: Henry James's Legacy to the Novel.* Detroit: Wayne State University Press, 1965.

LeClair, Robert C. "Henry James and Minny Temple." *American Literature* 21 (1949): 35–48.

———. "Point of View in *The Portrait of a Lady.*" *English Studies* 52 (1971): 136–47.

Levine, George. "Isabel, Gwendolen, and Dorothea." *ELH* 30 (1963): 244–57.

Liebman, Sheldon W. "The Light and the Dark: Character and Design in *The Portrait of a Lady.*" *Papers on Language and Literature* 6 (1970): 163–79.

Long, Robert. "*The Portrait of a Lady:* The Great Dramatic Chiaroscuro." In *The Great Succession: Henry James and the Legacy of Hawthorne.* Pittsburgh: University of Pittsburgh Press, 1979, pp. 98–116.

Mackenzie, Manfred. "Ironic Melodrama in *The Portrait of a Lady.*" *Modern Fiction Studies* 12 (1966): 7–23.

———. "The Pandora Situation." In *Communities of Honor and Love in Henry James.* Cambridge: Harvard University Press, 1976, pp. 152–60.

McMaster, Juliet. "The Portrait of Isabel Archer." *American Literature* 15 (1973): 50–66.

Matthiessen, F. O. "The Painter's Sponge and Varnish Bottle." In *Henry James: The Major Phase.* New York: Oxford University Press, 1944, pp. 152–86.

Miller, Elise. "The Marriages of Henry James and Henrietta Stackpole." *Henry James Review* 10 (1989): 15–31.

Montgomery, Marion. "The Flaw in the Portrait." *University of Kansas City Review* 16 (1960): 215–20.

Nettels, Elsa. "Romance I." In *James & Conrad*. Athens: University of Georgia Press, 1977, pp. 100–107.

Newton, J. M. "Isabel Archer's Disease and Henry James's." *Cambridge Quarterly* 2 (1966–67): 3–22.

O'Conner, Dennis L. "Intimacy and Spectatorship in *The Portrait of a Lady*." *Henry James Review* 11, No. 1 (Fall 1980): 25–35.

Perloff, Marjorie. "Cinderella Becomes the Wicked Stepmother: *The Portrait of a Lady* as Ironic Fairy Tale." *Nineteenth-Century Fiction* 23 (1969): 413–33.

Peterson, Carla L. "Dialogue and Characterization in *The Portrait of a Lady*." In *Studies in English Fiction* 8 (1980): 13–22.

Porte, Joel, ed. *New Essays on* The Portrait of a Lady. New York: Cambridge University Press, 1990.

Rahv, Philip. "The Heiress of All the Ages." In *Image and Idea: Fourteen Essays on Literary Themes*. Norfolk, CT: New Directions, 1949, pp. 42–62.

Reid, Stephen. "Moral Passion in *The Portrait of a Lady* and *The Spoils of Poynton*." *Modern Fiction Studies* 12 (1966): 24–43.

Robinson, Donita. "Henry James' Preface to *The Portrait of a Lady*." *Bluegrass Literary Review* 2, No. 2 (Spring–Summer 1981): 31–36.

Roman, Christine M. "Henry James and the Surrogate Mother." *American Transcendental Quarterly* 38 (Spring 1978): 193–205.

Routh, Michael. "Isabel Archer's Double Exposure: A Respectful Scene in *The Portrait of a Lady*." *Henry James Review* 1 (1980): 262–63.

———. "Isabel Archer's 'Inconsequence': A Motif Analysis of *The Portrait of a Lady*." *Journal of Narrative Technique* 7 (1977): 128–41.

Rowe, John Carlos. "What the Thunder Said: James's *Hawthorne* and the American Anxiety of Influence: A Centennial Essay." *Henry James Review* 4 (1983): 81–119.

Sabiston, Elizabeth. "The Prison of Womenhood." *Comparative Literature* 25 (1973): 336–51.

Sangari, Kumkum. "Of Ladies, Gentlemen, and 'The Short-Cut.'" *New Literary History* 19 (1988): 713–37.

Schirmeister, Pamela. "James: The Scene of Response." In *The Consolations of Space: The Place of Romance in Hawthorne, Melville, and James*. Stanford: Stanford University Press, 1990, pp. 137–66.

Schneider, Sister Lucy, C. S. J. "Osculation and Integration: Isabel Archer in the One-Kiss Novel." *CLA Journal* 10 (1966): 149–61.

Schriber, Mary Suzanne. "Henry James: The Summit of the Male Imagination." In *Gender and the Writer's Imagination: From Cooper to Wharton*. Lexington: University Press of Kentucky, 1987, pp. 117–56.

Sicker, Philip. "The Requirements of Imagination: *The Portrait of a Lady* and *The Princess Casamassima*." In *Love and Quest for Identity in the Fiction of Henry James*. Princeton: Princeton University Press, 1980, pp. 53–72.

Springer, Mary Doyle. *A Rhetoric of Literary Character: Some Women of Henry James*. Chicago: University of Chicago Press, 1978.

Stein, Allen F. "Henry James: The Novels." In *After the Vows Were Spoken: Marriage in American Literary Realism*. Columbus: Ohio State University Press, 1984, pp. 175–61.

Stein, William Bysshe. "*The Portrait of a Lady: Vis Inertiae*." *Western Humanities Review* 13 (1959): 177–90.

Stelzig, Eugene L. "Henry James and the Immensities of Perception: Actors and Victims in *The*

Portrait of a Lady and *The Wings of the Dove.*" *Southern Humanities Review* 11 (1977): 253–65.

Strandberg, Victor H. "Isabel Archer's Identity Crisis." "*University Review* 34 (1968): 283–90.

Taylor, Gordon O. "The Friction of Existence: Henry James." In *The Passages of Thought: Psychological Representation in the American Novel 1870–1900.* New York: Oxford University Press, 1969, pp. 42–84.

Templeton, Wayne. "*The Portrait of a Lady:* A Question of Freedom." *English Studies in Canada* 7 (1981): 312–28.

Tintner, Adeline R. "English Popular Literature." In *The Pop World of Henry James: From Fairy Tales to Science Fiction.* Ann Arbor: UMI Research Press, 1989, pp. 145–202.

Van Ghent, Dorothy. "On *The Portrait of a Lady.*" In *The English Novel: Form and Function.* New York: Holt, Rinehart & Winston, 1953, pp. 211–15.

Ventura, Mary K. "*The Portrait of a Lady:* The Romance/Novel." *American Literary Realism* 22, No. 3 (Spring 1990): 36–49.

Wagenknecht, Edward. "Destiny 'Affronted': Isabel Archer." In *Eve and Henry James: Portraits of His Women and Girls in His Fiction.* Norman: University of Oklahoma Press, 1978, pp. 35–53.

Wallace, Jack E. "Isabel and the Ironies." *College English* 21 (1959): 173–75.

Wallace, Ronald. "The Jamesian Character." In *Henry James and the Comic Form.* Ann Arbor: University of Michigan Press, 1975, pp. 15–52.

Ward, J. A. "The Portraits of Henry James." *Henry James Review* 10 (1989): 1–14.

Warner, John M. "Renunciation as Enunciation in James's *The Portrait of a Lady.*" *Renascence* 39 (1987): 354–64.

Weisenfarth, Joseph. "*The Portrait of a Lady:* Gothic Manners in Europe." In *Gothic Manners and the Classic English Novel.* Madison: University of Wisconsin Press, 1988, pp. 120–40.

Westervelt, Linda A. "'The Growing Complexity of Things': Narrative Technique in *The Portrait of a Lady.*" *Journal of Narrative Technique* 13 (1983): 74–83.

Wiseman, Adele. "What Price the Heroine?" *International Journal of Women's Studies* 4 (1981): 459–71.

ACKNOWLEDGMENTS

"Books in General" by Edward Sackville West from *New Statesman and Nation*, April 17, 1943, © 1943 by *New Statesman and Nation*. Reprinted by permission of The Observer, Ltd.

"Introduction" by Graham Greene from *The Portrait of a Lady* by Henry James, © 1947 by Oxford University Press. Reprinted by permission of the Estate of Graham Greene.

"The Portrait of a Lady Reprinted" by F. R. Leavis from *Scrutiny* 15, No. 3 (Summer 1948), © 1948 by Cambridge University Press. Reprinted by permission of Cambridge University Press.

"The Lesson of the Master: *The Portrait of a Lady"* by Richard Chase from *The American Novel and Its Tradition* by Richard Chase, © 1957 by Richard Chase. Reprinted by permission of Doubleday, a division of Bantam Doubleday Dell Publishing Group, Inc.

"The High Brutality of Good Intentions" by William H. Gass from *Fiction and the Figures of Life* by William H. Gass, © 1958, 1970 by William H. Gass. Reprinted by permission of International Creative Management, Inc.

"The Portrait of a Lady" by Richard Poirier from *The Comic Sense of Henry James: A Study of the Early Novels* by Richard Poirier, © 1960 by Richard Poirier. Reprinted by permission of the author.

"A Band of Egotists" by Leon Edel from *Henry James 1870–1881: The Conquest of London* by Leon Edel, © 1962 by Leon Edel. Reprinted by permission.

"The Portrait of a Lady" by Dorothea Krook from *The Ordeal of Consciousness in Henry James* by Dorothea Krook, © 1962 by Cambridge University Press. Reprinted by permission of Cambridge University Press.

"Communities of Knowledge: Secret Society in Henry James" by Manfred Mackenzie from *ELH* 39, No. 1 (March 1972), © 1972 by The Johns Hopkins Press. Reprinted by permission of The Johns Hopkins University Press.

"Henry James: Femininity and the Moral Sensibility" by Lisa Appignanesi from *Femininity and the Creative Imagination: A Study of Henry James, Robert Musil and Marcel Proust* by Lisa Appignanesi, © 1973 by Vision Press. Reprinted by permission.

"The Jamesian Character" by Ronald Wallace from *Henry James and the Comic Form* by Ronald Wallace, © 1975 by The University of Michigan. Reprinted by permission of The University of Michigan Press.

"Pragmatism and *The Portrait of a Lady"* by Peter Jones from *Philosophy and Literature* 5, No. 1 (Spring 1981), © 1981 by Peter Jones. Reprinted by permission of the author and The Johns Hopkins University Press.

"The Fearful Self" (originally titled "The Fearful Self: Henry James's *The Portrait of a Lady"*) by Tony Tanner from *Critical Quarterly* 7, No. 3 (Autumn 1965), © 1965 by *Critical Quarterly*. Reprinted by permission of the author.

INDEX

Acoustic Mirror, The (Silverman), 170
Adam Bede (Eliot), 17
Adams, Henry, 108
Aggie (*The Awkward Age*), 37
Albany, 50, 52, 78, 99, 185
Albert, cousin, 182, 185
Alceste (*Le Misanthrope*), 78
Alcott, Louisa May, 168
Alden, Bessie ("An International Episode"), 34
"Altar of the Dead, The," 165
Ambassadors, The, 18, 28–29, 37, 66, 102
America, 25–26, 29, 35, 47, 53, 57, 62, 65–66, 96, 103, 129n.1, 168, 177, 186–87, 193
American, The, 11, 21, 28, 41, 52, 112, 116, 175, 195, 201n.18
"American Girl of the Period, The" (Veeder), 200n.9
American Scene, The, 199n.5
"American Scholar, The" (Emerson), 132
Amerigo, Prince (*The Golden Bowl*), 113
Andersen, Hans Christian, 9
Anderson, Henrik, 200n.10
Anderson, Quentin, 91, 117, 126
Andrews, Stephen Pearl, 104–5, 117n.9
Anna Karenina (Tolstoy), 87–88
Antonio (*The Merchant of Venice*), 17
Antony, Mark (*Antony and Cleopatra*), 17
Archer, Isabel: as American figure, 3, 34–35, 58, 98; her attitude toward marriage, 106–7, 109–10, 126, 128; character of, 10–14, 24, 26, 37, 60–61, 81–88, 91, 93, 96, 98, 102–3, 120–23, 130n.3, 141–43; her choice of husband, 1–2, 38, 43, 57, 99, 126, 176; egotism of, 53, 85; as Gothic heroine, 165, 167–68; and Henrietta, 53, 59, 66, 78, 85, 93, 109–10, 123–25, 129, 135–37, 171; idealism of, 1, 37–38, 40, 58, 73–74, 78, 94, 97, 129, 139–40, 143–47; identity of, 65, 67, 71; inheritance of, 44, 63, 83–84, 127; and Madame Merle,

39–40, 48, 67–68, 70, 73–74, 83, 96, 137–40, 169–70; and Osmond, 2–3, 5, 38–40, 49, 55, 59, 61–62, 69–70, 74, 85–88, 93–96, 100, 110, 154–55, 159–61, 193–94; and Pansy, 63, 139, 164–65, 167, 171–74, 177; perceptiveness of, 75, 85, 94, 97, 154–55, 159–60; as a portrait, 131, 153–54, 175–76, 191; and Ralph, 44, 80, 85, 87, 101–2, 123, 134, 136, 142–43, 154–55; her rejection of Goodwood, 3, 14, 53, 66, 84–85, 93, 102, 108–11, 126, 148–49; her rejection of Warburton, 34–35, 38, 53, 66, 84, 93, 126, 144, 167; sexuality of, 53, 75–76, 102, 108–11, 122, 171, 176–77; as tragicomic heroine, 76–80, 88
Archer, Mr., 193
Aristedes the Just, 135
Arnolphe (*L'Ecole des femmes*), 78–79
Art of Fiction, The, 43
Assingham, Mrs. (*The Golden Bowl*), 31
Atlantic Monthly, 8, 104, 106, 116, 117n.9, 125, 129n.1
Austen, Jane, 1, 77, 116, 125
"Author of Beltraffio, The," 156
Awkward Age, The, 37, 45

Babcock, Reverend (*The American*), 195, 201n.18
Balzac, Honoré de, 22–23, 27
Banta, Martha, 174
Bantling, 123, 129, 135, 145, 200n.16
Bartleby ("Bartleby the Scrivener"), 98
Bassanio (*The Merchant of Venice*), 17
Bearing the Word (Homans), 166
"Beast in the Jungle, The," 176
Beauvoir, Simone de, 200n.12
Beecher, Henry Ward, 117n.9
Beecher-Tilton scandal, the, 105, 117n.9
Being and Nothingness (Sartre), 97
Bellegarde, Marquis de (*The American*), 195
"Bench of Desolation, The," 102
Bernanos, Georges, 31
Blackmur, R. P., 130n.3, 152

Blithedale Romance, The (Hawthorne), 41
Bob, cousin, 185–86
Boott, Francis, 54, 200n.13
Boott, Lizzie, 54
Bosanquet, Theodora, 174
Boston, 2, 135
Bostonians, The, 46, 115, 126, 133
Brady, Matthew, 189
Brand, Ethan ("Ethan Brand"), 39
Brook Farm, 132
Brooke, Dorothea (*Middlemarch*), 1, 51, 77–78
Brookenham, Nanda (*The Awkward Age*), 37
Browning, Robert, 131, 162
Brydon, Spencer ("The Jolly Corner"), 29
Buddha, 146
"Bunner Sisters" (Wharton), 24

Cargill, Oscar, 76–77, 130n.3
Casaubon, Edward (*Middlemarch*), 77–78
Cassirer, Ernst, 92
Castle of Otranto, The (Walpole), 167
Century Magazine, 56
Character and Opinion in the United States (Santayana), 51
Chase, Richard, 111, 130n.3
Chillingworth, Dr. (*The Scarlet Letter*), 39
Chodorow, Nancy, 166
Chopin, Frédéric, 112
Cimabue, Giovanni, 135
Cinderella (*Cinderella*), 72–73
Cintré, Claire de (*The American*), 175
Civil War, the, 200n.16
Claridge, Laura, 186
Cleopatra (*Antony and Cleopatra*), 17
Complete Notebooks of Henry James, The, 70
Conduct of Life, The (Emerson), 145
Confidence, 200n.11
Corneille, Pierre, 26
Correggio (Antonio Allegri), 135, 155
Coyne, Aurora (*The Sense of the Past*), 20
"Crapy Cornelia," 102
Crews, Frederick, 76
Croy, Kate (*The Wings of the Dove*), 30–31
"Curé de village, Le" (Balzac), 27

Daisy Miller, 165, 200n.11
Daniel Deronda (Eliot), 13, 17, 19–20, 32
DeLoach, Charles, 201n.18
Densher, Merton (*The Wings of the Dove*), 29–31
Deronda, Daniel (*Daniel Deronda*), 21
Diana, 75–76
Dickens, Charles, 17
Disraeli, Benjamin, 25
Don Juan (*Don Juan*), 78
Dr. Breen's Practice (Howells), 125
Du Maurier, George, 159

Edel, Leon, 72, 76, 130n.3, 182, 184, 189, 200nn.9–11, 13, 201n.18
Egoist, The (Meredith), 32
Eliot, George, 1, 8, 17–21, 33, 36, 51, 77–78
Elizabeth I (Queen of England), 10
Emerson, Ralph Waldo, 1–2, 49–50, 98, 131–40, 143–45, 147, 149, 183, 199n.4
"Emerson," 132–33, 151n.56
"Emperor's New Clothes, The" (Andersen), 9
England, 7, 11, 25, 34, 46, 71, 129n.1, 185, 189, 193, 197–98
Esau, 201n.18
Europe, 11, 43, 46, 52, 54, 57, 65, 67, 70, 92, 121, 143, 185–87, 190
Europeans, The, 28, 34, 37
"Experience" (Emerson), 144

Falstaff, Sir John, 135
Faulkner, William, 50
Feinstein, Howard M., 199n.4, 200n.10
Fiedelson, Charles, 167, 169–71
Fiedler, Leslie, 165–68
Finn, Huck (*Adventures of Huckleberry Finn*), 98
Flaubert, Gustave, 27
Florence, 12, 25, 50, 54, 69–70
French Poets and Novelists, 131, 133
Freud, Sigmund, 165–66, 172, 181, 188, 198
"Friendship" (Emerson), 145
Frye, Northrop, 77
Fuller, Margaret, 132

Gardencourt, 7, 22, 46, 67, 69, 71, 97, 99, 101–3, 112, 131, 169, 190
Gareth, Mrs. (*The Spoils of Poynton*), 41

Garland, Mary (*Roderick Hudson*), 73, 186–87
Gass, William H., 130n.3
Geismar, Maxwell, 200n.10
Gemini, Countess (Amy), 7, 64, 84; character of, 37, 134–35, 138, 192; and Isabel, 87, 138–39, 142; her revelation to Isabel, 6–7, 37, 71, 93, 108, 110, 157, 168, 178
"George Sand," 141
Gibbens, Alice, 188
Gilmore, Michael, 161–62, 163n.9
Goethe, Johann Wolfgang von, 103, 132
Goffman, Erving, 97
Golden Bowl, The, 29, 31, 75, 113, 115, 133, 158, 181
Goodwood, Caspar: as American figure, 2, 35, 66, 103, 186; character of, 1, 11, 20, 25, 27, 53, 91, 121, 126, 186, 191, 197, 200nn.16–17; and Henrietta, 22, 124; and Isabel, 2–3, 7–9, 14, 23, 25–26, 30, 35, 38, 43, 49, 53, 56, 63, 66–68, 75–77, 80, 84–88, 93–94, 102–3, 108–11, 115, 126, 128, 148–49, 154, 171, 175–76, 196, 198; and Osmond, 70, 84, 88, 127, 143; rejection of, by Isabel, 2–3, 14, 53, 66, 84–85, 93, 102, 108–11, 126, 148–49; sexuality of, 3, 53, 56, 76, 102, 109, 176
Gossman, Lionel, 78
"Gothic Mirror, The" (Kahane), 166
Grandcourt, Henleigh (*Daniel Deronda*), 20–21, 32
Grandet, Eugénie (*Eugénie Grandet*), 21
Grandoni, Madame (*The Princess Casamassima*), 73
Graslin, Mme. ("Le Curé de village"), 27
Great Tradition, The (Leavis), 91
Greeley, Horace, 104–5
Guy Domville, 116

Hall, Richard, 200nn.10–11
Hamlet (Shakespeare), 198
Harleth, Gwendolen (*Daniel Deronda*), 13, 17, 19–21, 32–34
Harlowe, Clarissa (*Clarissa*), 1
Harpagon (*L'Avare*), 78
Hawthorne, Nathaniel, 1–2, 39, 41–42, 50, 115, 131–32, 145

Hazlitt, William, 27
Henry James: The Lessons of the Master (Veeder), 130n.7
Henry James: The Major Phase (Matthiessen), 33
Hilda (*The Marble Faun*), 1
Homans, Margaret, 166
"Honoré de Balzac," 137
Hope, Miranda ("A Bundle of Letters"), 21
Horowitz, B. D., 200n.10
Howells, William Dean, 8, 116, 125
Hudson, Roderick (*Roderick Hudson*), 31, 46, 53, 156, 186

Iago (*Othello*), 44
Imaging American Women (Banta), 174
"International Episode, An," 34
"Is Marriage Holy?" (James, Sr.), 104–5, 117n.9
Isabel (*Pierre*), 167
Isabella of Vicenza (*The Castle of Otranto*), 167
Italy, 7, 27, 103, 198

J. J., cousin, 185
Jacob, 201n.18
James, Alice, 199n.4
James, Catherine , 184–86
James, Henry: artistic methods of, 9–10, 12, 22–24, 26–27, 30, 42, 47, 56, 72, 108, 115–17, 156; his attitudes toward gender, 185–90; his attitudes toward society, 64, 98–99, 103, 112–17, 126; childhood of, 52, 182–84; and Eliot, 1, 20–21, 33, 51, 77–78; and Emerson, 1, 49–50, 132–33, 151n.56; and his father, 106, 182–84; and William James, 133, 188, 195; and his mother, 182–83; and the novel, 115–17; his portrayal of Isabel, 1, 8, 16, 19–22, 46, 52, 76, 107–8, 117, 120–22, 127, 129, 134, 163, 167, 173, 175, 178; his revision of *The Portrait of a Lady,* 119–25; self-representation of, in his characters, 52, 54–57, 60, 156, 173–74, 176, 187, 189, 193; sexuality of, 188, 200n.10; on writing *The Portrait of a Lady,* 5–7, 15–16, 22, 72, 115–17
James, Henry, Sr., 92, 104–5, 107,

James, Henry, Sr. (*continued*)
  111–12, 117n.9, 128, 182–84,
  193, 199n.4
James, Mary Walsh, 182–83
James, William, 51, 57, 80–82, 106,
  133, 140, 183–84, 188, 195,
  200nn.10–11, 201n.18
"Jolly Corner, The," 29, 65, 165
Jourdain, M. (*Le Bourgeois Gentil-
  homme*), 133
Journal (Fuller), 132
Joyce, James, 117
Juliet (*Romeo and Juliet*), 17
Jung, Carl, 141, 150n.40
Juno, 135, 169, 172

Kahane, Claire, 166–68, 171, 175, 178
Kant, Immanuel, 41, 50, 92, 96
Kaston, Carren, 187, 200n.14
Keats, John, 197
Kermode, Frank, 116
Knightley, George (*Emma*), 77
Krook, Dorothea, 130n.3

La Bruyère, Jean de, 26
La Rochefoucauld, Francois de Marsillac,
  duc de, 26–27
Ladislaw, Will (*Middlemarch*), 20–21, 77
Lambeth, Lord ("An International Epi-
  sode"), 34
Langland, Elizabeth, 186
Lawrence, D. H., 37
Leavis, F. R., 91
Leonard, John, 114
Lévi-Strauss, Claude, 197
Levin, Konstantine (*Anna Karenina*), 88
Light, Christina (*Roderick Hudson*), 73,
  200n.11
Lockleigh, 99
London, 7, 129, 183, 197
Longdon, Mr. (*The Awkward Age*), 45
*Love, Marriage, and Divorce, and the
  Sovereignty of the Individual* (An-
  drews, Greeley, and James, Sr.),
  117n.9
Luce, Mr., 190
"Lys dans la vallée, Le" (Balzac), 27

Machiavelli, Niccolò, 94
Macmillan's Magazine, 129n.1
"Madonna of the Future, The," 136
Mallet, Rowland (*Roderick Hudson*),
  22, 46, 156

"Manners" (Emerson), 131
Marble Faun, The (Hawthorne), 1
March, Augie (*The Adventures of
  Augie March*), 98
Matthiessen, F. O., 33, 45, 76, 107, 124
Maule's Curse (Winters), 32
Mauriac, François, 31
Mauves, Madame de ("Mme. de
  Mauves"), 21, 70
Mellifont, Lord ("The Private Life"), 98
Melville, Herman, 50, 167
Meredith, George, 25, 32
Merle, Madame (Serena): 5–7, 84, 87,
  135, 141, 143, 154, 160, 163, 175;
  as American figure, 31, 57, 67,
  146; her betrayal of Isabel, 30, 33,
  70–71, 191; character of, 27, 36,
  43, 47, 68–69, 85–86, 97, 120,
  123, 127, 134, 137, 139, 196;
  identity of, 26, 37, 56, 168–69;
  her influence on Isabel, 22, 24–25,
  39, 40, 45, 48, 50, 54, 67, 73–74,
  79, 83, 98, 139–40, 142, 169–72,
  174, 176–78; and Osmond, 57,
  60, 94–96, 103, 106, 108, 113,
  139–40, 157–59, 162, 167–68;
  and Pansy, 68, 75, 96, 138, 140,
  168, 170–72, 177–78, 189; regret
  of, 75, 96, 137, 139–40, 192
Mestayer, Miss Emily, 184
Middlemarch (Eliot), 1–2, 17, 20, 51,
  78, 81
Mill on the Floss, The (Eliot), 17
Miller, Daisy (*Daisy Miller*), 19, 34
Molière (Jean-Baptiste Poquelin), 78–80
"Mora Montravers," 102
Morocco, Prince of (*The Merchant of
  Venice*), 17
Morse, James Herbert, 56–57
Mortsauf, Mme. de ("Le Lys dans la
  vallée"), 27
Munster, Eugenia (*The Europeans*),
  21
"My Last Duchess" (Browning), 162

Napoleon III (Emperor of France),
  199n.2
Nathaniel Hawthorne, 131, 133,
  144–45
New England, 25, 35, 51, 99
New York, 29, 51, 117n.9, 185
New York Tribune, The, 104, 128
Newman, Christopher (*The American*),

20–22, 31, 51–52, 57, 76, 78, 80, 112–13, 116, 201n.18
Nietzsche, Friedrich, 2
Niobe, 169, 178
Norton, Grace, 52, 64
Notes of a Son and Brother, 29

Opposing Self, The (Trilling), 98
Orestes, 185
Orgon (*Tartuffe*), 78
Osmond, Gilbert: his attitude toward Pansy, 39, 62, 70–71, 95, 113, 164–65, 168, 172–75; character of, 2, 12–13, 20–21, 25, 27, 29, 31, 36, 40, 47, 50, 54–57, 59–60, 62, 68–71, 73, 77, 85–87, 94–95, 99–100, 113–14, 135, 142–43, 152, 156, 162–63, 173, 195, 200n.13; compared to Ralph, 1, 43–44, 101, 111, 114, 137, 142, 152–53, 176, 192, 200n.14; and Isabel, 3, 26, 33, 38, 40, 48–49, 55, 58–63, 69–70, 74–75, 79–80, 84–88, 93–97, 100, 103, 110, 122, 127–28, 139, 143, 148, 155, 159–61, 163, 170–71, 173–74, 177, 193–94; and Madame Merle, 33, 37, 56–57, 95–96, 98, 106, 108, 120, 123, 141, 143, 157–59, 162, 168, 172, 191; and Warburton, 1, 38, 68–69
Osmond, Pansy, 5–7, 80, 100, 110, 114, 134–35, 138, 141, 148, 160, 170, 194, 197; character of, 20–21, 54, 61, 164–65, 171; identity of, 26, 37, 56, 168; and Isabel, 41, 45, 63–64, 74, 85–87, 139, 142, 162, 163n.9, 165, 167, 171–74, 177–78; and Madame Merle, 68, 157, 169, 177–78, 189; molding of, by Osmond, 39, 62, 71, 95, 175; and Rosier, 164; and Warburton, 69–71, 167, 190

Palazzo Roccanera, 73, 161, 167, 172–73
Pater, Walter, 160
Paul, Saint, 59
Pernelle, Madame (*Tartuffe*), 78
Perry, Ralph Barton, 199n.4, 201n.18
Perry, T. S., 183
Philistia Defiant (Du Maurier), 159
Pierre (Melville), 167

Plato, 41
"Plato" (Emerson), 147
Pluralistic Universe, A (James), 133
Poirier, Richard, 1, 115–16, 130n.3
Porter, Carolyn, 174–75
Portia (*The Merchant of Venice*), 17
Portrait of a Lady, The: conclusion of, 9, 14–15, 26, 30, 71, 101–3, 115, 149, 162–63, 171, 196–99; compared to *Daniel Deronda,* 13, 20, 32; compared to *Middlemarch,* 51, 78, 81; preface to, 15–19, 58, 119–20, 124, 134, 161, 167, 173, 175; revision of, 2, 119–25, 129, 129nn.1–2; structure of, 5–8, 23–25, 28, 33, 37, 42–43, 69, 72, 81, 115, 119, 128, 156–57, 162–63, 178, 198; themes in, 25, 28, 31, 33–37, 41–43, 45–46, 51, 55, 59, 63–65, 81, 88–89, 91–92, 97, 103–4, 108, 111, 114, 119, 122, 125–29, 131, 149, 155, 165, 168, 172, 174–75, 177–79, 190–92, 198
Poussin, Nicolas, 29
Pragmatism (James), 80, 133
Presentation of Self in Everyday Life, The (Goffman), 97
Prince Imperial, the (son of Napoleon III), 199n.2
Princess Casamassima, The, 24, 48
Principino, the (*The Golden Bowl*), 113
Principles of Psychology (James), 133
"Private Life, The," 98
Prospero (*The Tempest*), 136, 143
Prynne, Hester (*The Scarlet Letter*), 1–2, 108, 115
Punch, 159
"Pupil, The," 200n.10
Puritans, the, 111, 186
Putt, S. Gorley, 130n.3

Rahv, Philip, 72
Renaissance, The (Pater), 154, 160
Reverberator, The, 145
Richardson, Samuel, 1
Robinson, Hyacinth (*The Princess Casamassima*), 24, 48, 103, 114, 187, 200n.11
Roderick Hudson, 28, 34, 46, 51, 65, 133, 156, 200n.11
Rogers, Mrs., 184
Rome, 2, 5, 7, 22, 50–51, 69, 86–87,

Rome (continued)
    100–103, 106, 121, 124, 131, 135,
    155, 161–62, 171, 196–98
Romeo and Juliet (Shakespeare), 17
"Rose-Agathe," 112
Rosier, Edward (Ned), 5–7, 61, 114,
    156, 164, 191–92, 194
Rossetti, Dante Gabriel, 163
Rousseau, Jean-Jacques, 92, 96
Rowe, John Carlos, 188–89

Sabran, Madame de, 133–34
Sacred Fount, The, 42, 103
St. Mawr (Lawrence), 37
Saint Peter's Church, 121, 154
"Sainte-Beuve," 137
Sainte-Beuve, Charles Augustin, 141–42
Samuels, Charles, 130n.3
Sand, George, 132
Santayana, George, 51
Sartre, Jean-Paul, 97
Scarlet Letter, The (Hawthorne), 1–2,
    131
Scott, Sir Walter, 17
Sedgwick, Eve Kosofsky, 176
"Self-Reliance" (Emerson), 98, 145
Sganarelle (L'Ecole des maris), 78–79
Shakespeare, William, 17, 19, 96
Sharp, Becky (Vanity Fair), 48
Shaw, George Bernard, 112
Shylock (The Merchant of Venice), 17
Silverman, Kaja, 170–71
Sloper, Austin (Washington Square), 54
Sloper, Catherine (Washington Square),
    21–22, 54, 74
Small Boy and Others, A, 181, 184,
    189–90, 192, 199n.5
Sorrel, Hetty (Adam Bede), 17, 77
Stackpole, Henrietta, 7, 10, 21, 27, 36,
    59, 64, 82, 84, 86, 107, 114, 126–
    27, 134, 136, 143, 145, 154, 197,
    200n.14; character of, 35, 37, 46,
    53, 109, 123–25, 128–29, 135,
    137, 192, 200n.16; and Good-
    wood, 14, 30, 66, 109; and Isabel,
    22–23, 47–48, 53, 66–67, 78, 85,
    93, 109–10, 125, 137, 171,
    200n.16
Stallman, R. W., 130n.3
Stant, Charlotte (The Golden Bowl), 31
Stein, William Bysshe, 108, 130n.3
Stein, Gertrude, 117
Stevenson, Robert Louis, 17

Stone, Donald D., 115, 130n.7
Strether, Lambert (The Ambassadors),
    66, 103, 200n.11
Striker, Barnaby (Roderick Hudson), 46
Svengali (Trilby), 42

Tanner, Tony, 130n.3
Taylor, Anne Robinson, 200n.9, 12
Temple, Mary (Minny), 29–30, 52, 77,
    189, 200n.13
Thackeray, William Makepeace, 8
Theale, Milly (The Wings of the Dove),
    29–31, 45, 51, 120
Thoreau, Henry David, 48, 98
Tilton, Elizabeth Richards, 117n.9
Titian, 153, 191
Touchett, Mr. (Daniel), 43–44, 62, 64,
    169, 175, 177, 189, 190, 200n.14
Touchett, Mrs. (Lydia), 7, 10, 27, 67,
    114, 135, 154, 157, 172, 176,
    189–90; character of, 36–37, 81,
    121, 128, 134, 191, 196; and Isa-
    bel, 35–36, 47, 49–50, 61, 72,
    86–87, 94, 142; and Ralph, 147
Touchett, Ralph, 7, 20–21, 28, 35, 49,
    66–67, 69, 71, 77, 93–94, 106–7,
    109, 124, 131, 186, 191, 197; as
    artist figure, 36, 43–44, 101, 136,
    156, 198; his bequest to Isabel,
    32–33, 44, 46, 83, 127, 136, 175;
    character of, 36, 43, 53, 81, 84,
    133, 169, 190, 199; compared to
    Osmond, 1, 43–44, 95, 101, 111,
    114, 137, 152–53, 176, 192,
    200n.14; death of, 26–27, 31, 86–
    88, 123, 147, 189, 196; and Isabel,
    2, 11–12, 14, 23, 25, 27, 38–39,
    44–45, 47, 53, 55–56, 60, 64, 80,
    82–83, 85, 101–2, 123, 127, 133–
    36, 142–48, 153–55, 175, 177;
    and Madame Merle, 169; as spec-
    tator, 22, 192
Touchetts, the, 43, 63–64, 133, 138, 175
Townsend, Morris (Washington
    Square), 59
Traffle ("Mora Montravers"), 102
Tragic Muse, The, 126, 133
"Transcendentalist, The" (Emerson), 143
"Transitional American Woman, The"
    (Wells), 125
Trilling, Lionel, 98
Tulliver, Maggie (The Mill on the Floss),
    17

Turgenev, Ivan, 18, 21
Turn of the Screw, The, 28, 165

Van Ghent, Dorothy, 130n.3, 171
Veeder, William, 130n.7
Venice, 187
Venus de Medici, 135
Verver, Adam (*The Golden Bowl*), 31,
    133
Verver, Maggie (*The Golden Bowl*), 31,
    75, 113
Vincy, Rosamond (*Middlemarch*), 17,
    77
Vionnet, Madame de (*The Ambassa-
    dors*), 37

Walpole, Horace, 167
Warburton, Lord, 5–6, 27, 64, 67, 75,
    77, 87, 91, 94, 106, 109, 121, 127,
    145–46, 154–55; character of, 34,
    38, 45, 53, 126, 190–92; and Isa-
    bel, 11, 25, 34, 40, 43, 46, 48, 66,
    68, 78, 84, 167, 196; nobility of,
    34, 38, 48, 53, 61, 80, 114, 173,

176; and Osmond, 49, 68–70,
    114, 193; and Pansy, 69–71, 167,
    190; rejection of, by Isabel, 1–2, 8,
    34–35, 38–39, 53, 56, 66, 80, 84,
    93, 99, 126, 144, 167, 175–76
Warren, Joyce M., 187, 200n.11
Washington Square, 21–23, 28, 52, 54,
    59, 126
Watch and Ward, 31, 53
Wegelin, Christoff, 130n.7
Weinstein, Philip, 130n.3
Wells, Kate Gannett, 125
Wharton, Edith, 24
What Maisie Knew, 113
"Whisper in the Dark, A" (Alcott), 168
Whitman, Walt, 98
"William Dean Howells" (Trilling), 98
Wings of the Dove, The, 26, 28–29,
    45
Winters, Yvor, 32
Woodhouse, Emma (*Emma*), 77–78
Woodhull & Claflin's Weekly, 117n.9
Woolf, Virginia, 200n.12
Wordsworth, William, 132